The United States' Defend Forward Cyber Strategy

The United States' Defend Forward Cyber Strategy

A Comprehensive Legal Assessment

Edited by

JACK GOLDSMITH

OXFORD
UNIVERSITY PRESS

OXFORD
UNIVERSITY PRESS

Oxford University Press is a department of the University of Oxford. It furthers
the University's objective of excellence in research, scholarship, and education
by publishing worldwide. Oxford is a registered trade mark of Oxford University
Press in the UK and certain other countries.

Published in the United States of America by Oxford University Press
198 Madison Avenue, New York, NY 10016, United States of America.

© Oxford University Press 2022

CIP data is on file at the Library of Congress
ISBN 978-0-19-760180-8 (pbk.)
ISBN 978-0-19-760179-2 (hbk.)

DOI: 10.1093/oso/9780197601792.001.0001

1 3 5 7 9 8 6 4 2

Paperback printed by LSC Communications, United States of America
Hardback printed by Bridgeport National Bindery, Inc., United States of America

Contents

PART IV: COMPARATIVE PERSPECTIVES

Acknowledgments

I thank the Hoover Institution at Stanford University, and its Jean Perkins Foundation Working Group, for sponsoring the workshops from which many of the papers in this book emerged. Hoover also published an earlier version of many of these papers. In particular, I thank Gary Corn for his indispensable help at every step of this process; Denise Elson and Jacquelyn Bowen Johnstone for their help on the workshops; Barbara Arellano for her terrific editing; the many commentators at the Hoover workshops for their insights; Casey Corcoran and Matt Morris for their great editorial assistance; and Delany Sisiruca, Logan Brown, Ellen Kim, and Lorenzo d'Aubert for their research and related help.

Jack Goldsmith
October 2021

Contributors

James Baker, a Deputy General Counsel at Twitter and formerly the General Counsel of the Federal Bureau of Invesitgation. The views expressed are his own and do not necessarily reflect those of his current or former employees.

Elena Chachko, Rappaport Fellow, Harvard Law School and Academic Fellow, Berkeley Law Miller Center for Global Challenges

Robert M. Chesney, James A. Baker III Chair in the Rule of Law and World Affairs, University of Texas

Gary P. Corn, Director, Technology Law & Security Program, and Adjunct Professor of Law, American University Washington College of Law

Ashley Deeks, Professor, University of Virginia School of Law

Kristen E. Eichensehr, Martha Lubin Karsh and Bruce A. Karsh Bicentennial Professor of Law, University of Virginia School of Law

Emily Goldman, Cyber Strategist, Directorate of Operations, US Cyber Command

Jack Goldsmith, Learned Hand Professor of Law, Harvard Law School

Eric Talbot Jensen, Robert W. Barker Professor of Law, Brigham Young University Law School

Alex Loomis, Associate at Quinn Emanuel Urquhart & Sullivan, LLP (affiliation provided for idenifitcation purposes only)

Matt Morris, Harvard Law School, J.D. 2021

Peter Renals, Principal Researcher at Palo Alto Networks

Michael Warner, US Cyber Command Historian

Sean Watts, Professor of Law, United States Military Academy at West Point

Matthew C. Waxman, Liviu Librescu Professor of Law, Columbia Law School

List of Abbreviations

AUMFs	Authorizations for Use of Military Force
CCA	Center for Cyber Assessment
CERT	Cyber Emergency Response Team
CESG	Communications-Electronics Security Group
CI	critical infrastructure
CIA	Central Intelligence Agency
CIKR	Critical Infrastructure and Key Resources
CISA	Cybersecurity and Infrastructure Security Agency
CISA 2015	Cybersecurity Information Sharing Act of 2015
CISAA 2018	Cybersecurity and Infrastructure Security Agency Act of 2018
CiSP	Cyber Security Information Sharing Partnership
CMF	Cyber Mission Force
CMMC	Cybersecurity Maturity Model Certification
CNI	critical national infrastructure
CNMF	Cyber National Mission Force
COMSEC	communications security
CPNI	Centre for the Protection of National Infrastructure
CSSPs	cybersecurity service providers
DARS	2001 Draft Articles on Responsibility of States for Internationally Wrongful Acts
DDoS	Distributed Denial of Service
DHS	Department of Homeland Security
DIB	Defense Industrial Base
DIRNSA	Director of NSA
DISA	Defense Information Systems Agency
DMI	Directorate of Military Intelligence
DNC	Democratic National Committee
DOD	Department of Defense
EI	equipment interference
FBI	Federal Bureau of Investigation
FCEB	Federal Civilian Executive Branch
FISA	Foreign Intelligence Surveillance Act
FISMA	Federal Information Security Management Act
GCHQ	Government Communications Headquarters
GDPR	European Union's Global Data Protection Regulation

GGE	Group of Governmental Experts on Developments in the Field of Information and Telecommunications in the Context of International Security
GIG	DoD's Global Information Grid
GRU	Russian military intelligence agency
ICJ	International Court of Justice
ICT	information and communication technologies
IDF	Israel Defense Forces
ILA	International Law Association
ILC	International Law Commission's
IOCs	indicators-of-compromise
IoT	Internet of Things
IPA	Investigatory Powers Act
IRA	Internet Research Agency
ISA	Israeli Security Agency
ISACs	Information Sharing and Analysis Centers
ISIS	Islamic State in Iraq and Syria
ISPs	internet service providers
JFCC-NW	Joint Functional Component Command–Network Warfare
JTF-CND	Joint Task Force–Computer Network Defense
JTF-GNO	Joint Task Force–Global Network Operations
JFHQ-DoDIN	Joint Force Headquarters–DoD Information Networks
MoD	Ministry of Defence
NATO	North Atlantic Treaty Organization
NCF	National Cyber Force
NCSC	National Cybersecurity Centre
NDAA	National Defense Authorization Act
NISCC	National Infrastructure Security Co-ordination Centre
NIST	National Institute of Standards and Technology
NMCI	Navy Marine Corps Intranet
NOCP	National Offensive Cyber Programme
NPPD	National Protection and Programs Directorate
NSA	National Security Agency
NSS	national security systems
OCSIA	Office of Cyber Security and Information Assurance
OEWG	Open-Ended Working Group
OGS	Operation Glowing Symphony
OLC	Office of Legal Counsel
OMB	Office of Management and Budget
PDD-63	Presidential Decision Directive 63
RSG	Russia Small Group
SCA	Stored Communications Act
SIGINT	signals intelligence

SMCO	sensitive military cyber operations
TVPA	Trafficking Victims Protection Act
USCYBERCOM	US Cyber Command
USEUCOM	US European Command
USNORTHCOM	US Northern Command
USSTRATCOM	US Strategic Command
VEP	vulnerability equities process
WPR	War Powers Resolution

Introduction

Jack Goldsmith

During the second decade of the twentieth century, US adversaries conducted a number of hostile cyber operations against the United States, including the Office of Personnel Management breach, the Sony attack, distributed denial of service attacks on US banks, China's pervasive intellectual property theft, and the Russian operations to interfere in and influence the 2016 presidential election. The success of these and many other such operations were surprising to many. As President Obama bragged in the midst of the Russian operation, in September of 2016, the US government has more "[cyber] capacity than anybody[,] both offensively and defensively."[1] Why, then, couldn't the United States blunt or deter these operations?

There were many reasons, but two stand out. One was a perceived escalation problem. The United States is among the world's most digitally dependent nations. Its networks are vast and difficult to defend. As a result, US leaders often hesitate to respond to cyberattacks out of fear that adversaries will escalate in response and leave the United States in a worse position. The concern that Russia could achieve "escalation dominance" is one reason President Obama hesitated to respond to its electoral interference in the summer and fall of 2016. It is also why the United States did not respond forcefully to Iranian denial-of-service attacks on US banks in 2012. Then-Director of National Intelligence James Clapper later said that the United States had "teed up a bunch of options for [a] cyberattack against" those responsible for the attacks, but then aborted the plans after Treasury Secretary Tim Geithner argued that US banks might not be able to withstand the anticipated counterretaliation.[2]

A second reason the United States did not respond more robustly concerned perceived legal constraints. The cyber operations against the United States did not rise to the level of "uses of force" or "armed attacks" under international law. They were, in the parlance, "below the threshold." International law places limits—uncertain and contested limits, but limits nonetheless—on how states can respond to such "below the threshold" incidents, and these limits cabined the United States' response options. According to Clapper, when the United States discussed cyber tools to use against North Korea in response to its 2014 hack of Sony Pictures, the plan required going "through some other country's infrastructure"— perhaps China's.[3] "The lawyers went nuts, so we didn't do anything on the cyber front," Clapper says. "We ended up sanctioning a bunch of North Korean generals."[4]

Hostile operations "below the threshold" also raise a number of difficult questions about the executive branch's *domestic* legal authorities to respond. The questions include: Do Defend Forward operations trigger the president's Article II powers, military or otherwise, and if not, what statutory authorities can the president possess, with what constraints? If carried out by the military, would the cyber operation potentially run afoul of statutory proscriptions such as the Computer Fraud and Abuse Act, or be subject to process and transparency burdens such as those imposed in the covert action regime? And how could domestic institutions like the FBI assist the operation by providing domestic intelligence consistent with the Fourth Amendment, the Foreign Intelligence Surveillance Act, and other legal limitations? Uncertainty about the answers to these questions, and gaps in legal authorities, discouraged US leaders from fully responding to cyber operations against the nation.

As a result of these and related factors, the United States appeared at the end of the Obama administration to have no effective strategy for dealing with the "below the threshold" problem in cyberspace. For several years it had tried a "name and shame" approach that deployed its prodigious intelligence capabilities to identify the responsible individuals, publish their names, threaten legal action, and thereby hopefully deter them. But by the end of the Obama administration, it was clear that this approach was inadequate. "[T]he idea that somehow public shaming is going to be effective I think doesn't read the thought process in Russia very well," Obama said in December of 2016 while discussing Russian electoral interference.[5] Clapper was even more discouraging a few weeks later when, near the end of his six-year stint monitoring these cyber operations as Director of National Intelligence, he testified to Congress that "[w]e currently cannot put a lot of stock, at least in my mind, in cyber deterrence. . . . It is . . . very hard to create the substance and psychology of deterrence."[6]

In 2018, the United States dramatically shifted its approach to confronting digital national security threats. The shift had several elements. The first element involved a pivot at United States Cyber Command, a military unit established in 2010 within the Defense Department to defend the Department's information networks, support US Combatant Commanders, and defend the nation in cyberspace. In March 2018, Cyber Command issued a "Command Vision" that reconceptualized its operational approach: "We must stop attacks before they penetrate our cyber defenses or impair our military forces; and through persistent, integrated operations, we can influence adversary behavior and introduce uncertainty into their calculations."[7] Two months later, General Paul Nakasone became the dual-hatted leader of Cyber Command and the National Security Agency. In his first publication as commander, he declared that "USCYBERCOM will operate forward and at scale where our adversaries are. This is the primary mission of cyber forces, which gives rise to Cyber Command's concept of defend forward."[8] Nakasone added that Cyber Command must "maneuver seamlessly across the interconnected battlespace, globally, as close as possible to adversaries and their operations, and continuously shape the battlespace to create operational advantage for us while denying the same to our adversaries."[9]

The same day that General Nakasone was promoted, the secretary of defense elevated Cyber Command to an independent unified combatant command within the Defense Department. This elevation "gave cyber issues a more powerful voice within the Department of Defense" and resulted in "[i]ncreased authorities and funding," as Nakasone later wrote.[10] In August 2018, President Trump revised Obama-era rules and delegated more decision authority to the secretary of defense for offensive cyberspace operations. The change effectively gave Cyber Command more latitude to operate outside Department of Defense (DoD) networks.

Later that fall, the Defense Department issued a "Cyber Strategy" that announced a new strategic concept: "We will *defend forward* to disrupt or halt malicious cyber activity at its source, including activity that falls below the level of armed conflict" and "persistently contest malicious cyber activity in day-to-day competition."[11] It added: "Our primary role in this homeland defense mission is to defend forward by leveraging our focus outward to stop threats before they reach their targets."[12] And in August 2018, Congress authorized Cyber Command to "take appropriate and proportional action in foreign cyberspace" in order "to disrupt, defeat, and deter" ongoing adversarial activity in the cyber domain in the event of "an active, systematic, and ongoing campaign of attacks against the Government or people of the United States in cyberspace" by any of four nations: Russia, China, North Korea, or Iran.[13]

Defend Forward is a defensive strategy, but it involves activity in adversary networks. As Nakasone explained, Defend Forward seeks "to achieve and maintain the initiative in cyberspace over an adversary by continuously contesting them *where they operate*, particularly below the level of armed conflict."[14] He has also remarked that the new strategy is about "confronting our adversaries from where they launch cyber attacks."[15] Defend Forward thus appears to include *US government cyber operations against cyber infrastructure in the physical territories of other nations to halt or disrupt planned malicious cyber activity.*

Defend Forward is implemented by an operational approach called "persistent engagement." "The idea behind persistent engagement," Nakasone explained, "is that so much of the corrosive effects of cyber attacks against the United States occur below the threshold of traditional armed conflict."[16] It reflects the need to engage with adversaries on a continuing basis, to include with "hunt forward" operations, so that Cyber Command can "disrupt and degrade the capabilities our adversaries use to conduct attacks."[17] One aim of persistent engagement is to identify and stop cyber threats abroad before they reach US networks.

The United States' new Defend Forward Strategy constitutes a major change in how the nation with the world's most powerful cyber arsenal views when and how this arsenal should be employed. It is a large step in the direction of more assertive action in cyberspace. The United States has not attempted to hide this new and more proactive cyber posture. To the contrary, it has telegraphed the change. But the telegraphing has taken place at a highly abstract level. Little is known about the specific operations associated with Defend Forward and Persistent Engagement, with the exception of those against Russian influence and interference in the 2018 US midterm elections. And while the US government has asserted that Defend Forward is consistent with domestic and international law, it has not explained how that is so in any detail.

This volume aims to fill these gaps and to bring Defend Forward out of the shadows, so to speak. To do so it has gathered legal academic and policy experts, three of whom serve in the US government and most of whom have significant prior US government experience. The volume is not an official or even an unofficial statement of the United States' legal views on these issues. The authors of the legal articles in the volume do not as a group agree on all (or even most) issues under study, do not take the same approach to the issues, and definitely do not speak on behalf of the US government. Most of the articles offer descriptive accounts of how legal constraints currently operate, but many also make normative arguments about how these restraints should operate or be interpreted. The articles are not, and do not purport to be, a "defense" of Defend Forward—either individually or in the aggregate. But these articles together do provide the first comprehensive account of what Defend Forward is and what legal issues it implicates. And they offer expert, informed, and sometimes pointed legal analysis of Defend Forward. The volume thus aims to be a comprehensive and definitive introduction to the historically important yet academically understudied DoD Cyber Strategy and its operational construct of Defend Forward.

Part I presents the background to the legal analysis in Parts II–IV. Chapter 1, "Defend Forward and Persistent Engagement," is by Gary P. Corn (American University Washington College of Law, R Street Institute, and formerly Staff Judge Advocate to US Cyber Command) and Emily Goldman (Cyber Strategist, Directorate of Operations, US Cyber Command). It explains the history and theory of Defend Forward. Chapter 2, "Scenarios for Defend Forward," contains detailed hypothetical "Scenarios" of the various types of operations that Defend Forward might include. It is written by Gary P. Corn and Peter Renals, a principal researcher at Palo Alto Networks. These hypotheticals, though not exhaustive, form the basis for the legal analyses that follow. The scenarios are very useful in giving one a picture of what types of cyber operations might be in play with Defend Forward. Chapter 3, "US Cyber Command's First Decade," is written by Michael Warner, the US CYBERCOM historian.

Part II focuses on domestic legal issues. In Chapter 4, Bobby Chesney (University of Texas School of Law) canvasses the extensive but underappreciated extent to which Congress has expressly authorized Defend Forward operations. As Chesney argues, in an era in which Congress is supposedly disengaged from war issues, it has over several years developed a comprehensive legal regime that authorizes Defend Forward and related operations that is akin to the Covert Action Statute. In Chapter 5, Matthew Waxman (Columbia Law School, formerly National Security Council, Department of Defense, and Department of State) examines the constitutional issues implicated by Defend Forward. The main thrust of his chapter is that "war powers" is the wrong lens through which to understand Defend Forward. In Chapter 6, James Baker (Deputy General Counsel at Twitter, formerly FBI General Counsel) and Matt Morris (a 2021 Harvard Law School graduate) examine domestic legal restraints on the information collection that is often vital to the US government's ability to discover, trace, and respond to cyber incidents. This chapter examines the slew of complicated, interlocking, and frequently ambiguous legal regimes restricting the United States' freedom to act (and act quickly), and proposes reforms.

Part III examines international law issues. In Chapter 7, Jack Goldsmith (Harvard Law School, formerly assistant attorney general, Office of Legal Counsel) and Alex Loomis (an attorney at Quinn Emanuel Urquhart & Sullivan, LLP) address the issue of "sovereignty" as an international law constraint. They argue, contrary to claims in the Tallinn Manual 2.0 (a leading study on international law in cyberspace), that sovereignty should not be viewed as an independent constraint on Defend Forward operations. In Chapter 8, Ashley Deeks (University of Virginia School of Law, formerly Deputy Legal Advisor to the National Security Council) examines the extent to which Defend Forward operations can be justified as "countermeasures" under international law. In Chapter 9, Corn analyzes whether and when foreign influence operations implicate (or should implicate) the international law rule of prohibited intervention—an analysis that informs when the aperture of Defend Forward operations might be widened to include countermeasures to stop or prevent such operations.

In Chapter 10, Eric Jensen (Brigham Young University Law School, formerly a Judge Advocate in the US Army) and Sean Watts (West Point, and also a former Judge Advocate in the US Army) write about Defend Forward and due diligence—the notion that international law includes a duty to cease and remedy damage originating from a State's territory. They argue that extensive US diplomatic practice and practical considerations counsel the United States to complement its commitment to defending forward with a clear articulation of the legal duties and doctrinal limits associated with due diligence, which they outline. In Chapter 11, Kristen Eichensehr (University of Virginia School of Law, formerly Department of State) examines when international law requires attribution—and what the standards for attribution are—for countering "below the threshold" cyber operations.

Part IV analyzes comparative law issues in the two countries with known legal authorities and capacities to engage in actions akin to Defend Forward: Israel and the United Kingdom. In Chapter 12, Elena Chachko (a Fellow at Harvard Law School and Berkeley Law School), and formerly in Israel's Foreign Ministry) critically examines the Israeli legal architecture for Defend Forward–like operations. Chesney does something similar for the United Kingdom in Chapter 13, by putting Defend Forward and its U.K. equivalents in historical and comparative context.

The cyber threats the United States faces are growing and fast-changing, and surely the Defend Forward strategy will evolve as well. These chapters seek to capture the practice, and the law, as they stand in October 2021.

Notes

1. President Barack Obama, Press Conference after G20 Summit (Sept. 5, 2016).
2. Shaun Waterman, *Clapper: U.S. Shelved 'Hack Backs' Due to Counterattack Fears*, CYBERSCOOP (Oct. 2, 2017), https://www.cyberscoop.com/hack-back-james-clapper-iran-north-korea.
3. *Id.*
4. *Id.*
5. President Barack Obama, Press Conference by the President (Dec. 16, 2016).
6. *Foreign Cyber Threats to the United States: Hearing Before the S. Comm. on Armed Servs.*, 115th Cong. (2017) (statement of James Clapper, Director of National Intelligence).
7. U.S. CYBER COMMAND, ACHIEVE AND MAINTAIN CYBERSPACE SUPERIORITY: COMMAND VISION FOR US CYBER COMMAND 2 (2018).
8. Paul M. Nakasone, *A Cyber Force for Persistent Operations*, JOINT FORCE Q., 1st Quarter 2019, at 13.
9. *Id.*
10. Paul M. Nakasone & Michael Sulmeyer, *How to Compete in Cyberspace: Cyber Command's New Approach*, FOREIGN AFFAIRS (Aug. 25, 2020), https://www.foreignaffairs.com/articles/united-states/2020-08-25/cybersecurity.
11. U.S. DEP'T OF DEF., SUMMARY: DEPARTMENT OF DEFENSE CYBER STRATEGY 1–4 (2018)(emphasis in original).
12. *Id.* at 2.
13. 10 U.S.C. § 394 note (2018) (Active Defense Against the Russian Federation, People's Republic of China, Democratic People's Republic of Korea, and Islamic Republic of Iran Attacks in Cyberspace).
14. *Hearing to Consider Pending Nominations Before the S. Comm. on Armed Servs.*, 115th Cong. 15 (2018) (written statement of Lieutenant General Paul Nakasone, Nominee for Commander, U.S. Cyber Command and Director, National Security Agency and Chief, Central Security Service in response to advance policy questions).
15. *Hearing to Review Testimony on United States Special Operations Command and United States Cyber Command in Review of the Defense Authorization Request for Fiscal Year 2020 and the Future Years Defense Program Before the S. Comm. on Armed Servs.*, 116th Cong. 4 (2019) (statement of General Paul M. Nakasone, Commander, U.S. Cyber Command).
16. Nakasone & Sulmeyer, *supra* note 10.
17. *Id.*

PART I

BACKGROUND

1

Defend Forward and
Persistent Engagement

*Gary P. Corn and Emily Goldman**

The year 2018 marked a dramatic shift in the United States' approach to confronting national security threats emanating from cyberspace and to utilizing cyber as an instrument of national power. The preceding decade saw a substantial rise in the number, level of sophistication, and destructive nature of state-sponsored cyber operations. Events like the breach in the Office of Personnel Management, the hack of Sony Pictures International, and the WannaCry, Petya, and NotPetya ransomware attacks, to name a few, led strategists and policymakers alike to the realization that the United States' existing cybersecurity posture, with its emphasis on restraint, was failing. The lack of effective obstacles to or meaningful consequences for malicious behavior emboldened adversary states, and these states steadily increased the scope and scale of their hostile cyber operations.

In response, the Department of Defense (DoD) published a new cyber strategy in the fall of 2018. The strategy drew on lessons learned from US Cyber Command's successful operations beginning in 2016 against the Islamic State in Iraq and Syria (ISIS). It built on the 2017 National Security Strategy of the United States with its emphasis on the return to great power competition and a commitment to deterring and disrupting malicious cyber actors before they are able to impact US interests. Taking account of the persistent, hostile cyber campaigns of the United States' strategic competitors, the new strategy is anchored in the recognized need to "take *action in cyberspace during day-to-day competition* to preserve U.S. military advantages and to defend U.S. interests."[1] Key to this shift in strategic posture is the introduction of the concept of defending forward in cyberspace "to disrupt or halt malicious cyber activity at its source, including activity that falls below the level of armed conflict."[2]

The significance of the Defend Forward concept and the broader shift in US cyber strategy cannot be understated. Like any strategy, to be effective it requires resources, implementing policies, and supporting legal structures. The chapters that follow in this book address a number of the legal and policy implications of the United States' evolving strategic approach to cyber, and by extension, information threats, with a particular emphasis on Defend Forward operations. This introductory chapter provides a general overview of the DoD's strategy shift and the Defend Forward concept.

Protecting the 2018 Midterm Elections

The Defend Forward concept was immediately put to the test as part of the US government's broader efforts to protect the 2018 midterm elections from continued Russian interference. In June 2018, the newly appointed Commander of US Cyber Command (USCYBERCOM) and Director of the National Security Agency (NSA), General Paul Nakasone, undertook an initiative called the Russia Small Group (RSG). The RSG was part of a whole-of-government effort to defend the integrity of the 2018 midterm elections from foreign interference and influence. It involved a range of groundbreaking operations in support of wider US government actions, including discrete offensive cyber operations to disrupt Russia's active use of cyber capabilities to spread disinformation and undermine the 2018 elections.

In testimony before the Senate Armed Services Committee in 2019, General Nakasone described how the RSG effort supported US European Command (USEUCOM), US Northern Command (USNORTHCOM), the Department of Homeland Security (DHS), the Federal Bureau of Investigation (FBI), and others by "bringing together intelligence, cyber capabilities, interagency partnerships, and a willingness to act."[3] Senators from both political parties praised the effort. Senator Mike Rounds (R-SD) suggested it was "not a coincidence that [the 2018] election went off without a hitch" and affirmed that "the types of cyber activity that Russia, through multiple agencies and third parties [was conducting], was most certainly impacted during this process."[4] Senator Richard Blumenthal (D-CT) stated that the operation prevented "what would have been some very serious cyber incursions."[5]

Proactive, Defend Forward cyber operations formed a centerpiece of the RSG-led efforts to protect the 2018 midterm elections. These operations would not have been possible without several major developments that enabled DoD, and USCYBERCOM in particular, to successfully act to disrupt Russia's interference efforts. Among the most consequential were the new DoD Cyber Strategy with its Defend Forward concept and USCYBERCOM's operational approach of Persistent Engagement; cyber-specific statutory provisions in the FY19 National Defense Authorization Act that, among other things, clarified the status of military cyber operations as traditional military activities exempt from the approval and oversight procedures applicable to covert actions; and a new presidential policy delegating more authorities to DoD for cyberspace operations.

DoD's Strategy Shift

The activities and operations associated with Defend Forward and Persistent Engagement represent a significant shift in DoD's approach to strategic competition and cyber threats. The operational cyber elements within DoD broadened their focus from traditional wartime planning and execution to also confronting the reality of constant, widespread hostile cyberspace campaigns deliberately calibrated by US adversaries to remain below the use-of-force threshold, yet which cumulatively over time result in strategic gains for these adversaries. It is important to understand how DoD came to realize the need for new thinking and then developed concepts to meet that requirement.

Until 2018, the United States had applied a deterrence strategy in cyberspace. For example, the 2011 International Strategy for Cyberspace called for "credible response options" to dissuade and deter—passive approaches based on threats of prospective action and episodic response after a declared threshold had been crossed.[6] An unclassified fact sheet released by the White House in January 2013 on Presidential Policy Directive 20, which was signed in October 2012, declared, "It is our policy that we shall undertake the least action necessary to mitigate threats and that we will prioritize network defense and law enforcement as preferred courses of action."[7] The 2015 DoD Cyber Strategy reaffirmed this approach, stating that "[a]s a matter of principle, the United States will seek to exhaust all network defense and law enforcement options to mitigate any potential cyber risk to the U.S. homeland or U.S. interests before conducting a cyberspace operation," thus committing the United States to "always conduct cyber operations under a doctrine of restraint."[8] The 2015 strategy called for a "comprehensive cyber deterrence strategy to deter key state and non-state actors from conducting cyberattacks against U.S. interests."[9]

Under this approach, deterrence was essentially treated as a synonym for security and had come to mean all things to all people. Rather than ask how to increase security in cyberspace, policymakers asked how to deter in cyberspace. This approach was doubly flawed, as it (1) failed to distinguish between deterring the malicious use of cyber capabilities against the United States and the United States using cyber as a tool to deter non-cyber threats, and (2) rested on the incorrect assumption that deterrence concepts developed to address nuclear and other traditional threats apply equally in the context of cyberspace. The question presumed the answer. Deterrence was going to stop strategic cyber war, stop ISIS in cyber, stop intellectual property theft, and prevent attacks against the government's systems. Everything was called deterrence and framed in deterrence language (i.e., impose costs and deny benefits). Fearing that cyber operations were escalatory, policy guidance limited DoD to conducting cyber operations within the confines of its own networks, with the exception of allowing circumscribed operations within designated areas of hostilities to support combat operations and the theoretical authority to respond to "cyberattacks of significant consequence."[10]

Unfortunately, experience and a thorough accounting of the distinctive attributes of cyberspace have demonstrated the inapt, limited utility of deterrence models for addressing strategic, cyber-based national security threats. Cyberspace offers novel ways to gain strategic advantage and erode national sources of power without resort to territorial aggression, invasion, or armed conflict. These characteristics include global interconnectedness; a condition of constant (vice imminent or potential) contact; difficulty of attribution; constantly contested terrain; informal boundaries between acceptable and unacceptable behavior that are routinely ignored and altered; and no sanctuary or operational pause. Leveraging these characteristics, adversaries act persistently in cyberspace in campaigns deliberately calibrated to avoid direct and open armed conflict by remaining opaque and below the use-of-force threshold, thereby generating uncertainty, decision delay, and inaction. Most significantly, the gains they amass are cumulative. Each intrusion, hack, or technical action may not be strategically consequential on its own, but the total cumulative gains are tantamount to what in generations past required armed hostilities.

At present, the central strategic challenge for the United States is the emergence of long-term strategic competition with China and Russia, who are both engaged in sustained and systemic cyber campaigns intended to alter the relative distribution of power internationally to the disadvantage of the United States, Western democracies, and the rules-based international order. Owing to the unique characteristics of the domain, China and Russia have aggressively leveraged cyberspace to their competitive advantage.

The core concepts of Defend Forward and Persistent Engagement were developed to respond to these strategic realities based on a deep analysis of the strategic and operational environments.

DoD's pivot hinged on several insights, which flowed from this analysis and which gained momentum from Operation Glowing Symphony (OGS), USCYBERCOM's first global-scale operation to persistently disrupt and degrade ISIS infrastructure and operations worldwide. It is important to emphasize that this and other operations gave the Command (and the DoD) not only confidence in its tactics, organization, and capabilities but also a feeling for how campaigns can be won in cyberspace by seizing and retaining the operational initiative.

The first insight was that US policies of restraint and reaction had allowed most adversary activity to go unchallenged. Rather than stopping or preventing attacks, this approach ceded the initiative to, and emboldened, adversaries. With relatively free rein to exploit US vulnerabilities for strategic gain, they were setting de facto norms by default.

Second, the structural imperative and strategic incentives in cyberspace drive states to be active continuously below the use-of-force threshold, where they can make strategic gains cumulatively with actions that individually never rise to the threshold that elicits a deterrent response.[11] In other words, in cyberspace, restraint is punished while persistence and action are rewarded.

Third, deterrence is a strategy based on operational restraint and the threat of force and, thus, is misaligned with the strategic and operational realities of cyberspace. Relying on threats to impose consequences after the fact cedes initiative and erodes strategic advantage. As General Nakasone has explained, "[I]n this domain, the advantage favors those who have initiative. If we want to have an advantage in cyberspace, we have to actively work to either improve our defenses, create new accesses, or upgrade our capabilities."[12] He added that "superiority in cyberspace is temporary; we may achieve it for a period of time, but it's ephemeral. That's why we must operate continuously to seize and maintain the initiative in the face of persistent threats." As a result, security in cyberspace cannot be found in strategies that strive to deter actors from being active.[13]

Finally, cyberspace gains are cumulative; thus, it is insufficient to concentrate on potential individual significant incidents or catastrophic attacks because ongoing campaigns comprising activities whose effects never rise to the level of a significant incident—and therefore rarely elicit a timely response—cumulatively produce strategic gains.

For all these reasons, DoD and USCYBERCOM concluded by late 2016 that a strategy of deterrence (operational restraint and the threat of prospective action) failed to address the preponderance of cyberspace aggression, which is persistent and occurs below the armed attack use-of-force threshold. Measures to deter significant cyber incidents (i.e., cyber "armed-attack" equivalent operations) must be pursued in tandem with steady, sustained activities that persistently contest and frustrate adversary cyberspace campaigns below the use-of-force threshold. To regain the initiative in strategic cyber competition, DoD needs to partner with other government agencies, the private sector, and allies to increase cyber resilience of government and critical infrastructure networks, defend forward beyond the perimeter of DoD networks, and proactively contest, disrupt, and degrade cyber aggression before it reaches US, allied, and partner networks.

Thus, the 2018 DoD Cyber Strategy directs cyber forces to *"[p]ersistently contest malicious cyber activity in day-to-day competition*: The Department will counter cyber campaigns threatening U.S. military advantage by defending forward to intercept and halt cyber threats."[14] Implementing Defend Forward begins with "continuously engaging and contesting adversaries"[15]—which DoD refers to as "Persistent Engagement." The 2018 DoD Cyber Strategy still calls for deterrence but only for "cyber activities that constitute a use of force against the United States, our allies, or our partners";[16] this is often referred to in shorthand as "significant cyber incidents" or "cyberattacks of significant consequence." Importantly, as with any threat of this weight, the United States should, and does, reserve the right to use all means of national power in response—not just cyber capabilities.

Genesis of Defend Forward and Persistent Engagement Concepts

"Defend Forward" and "Persistent Engagement" were new terms officially introduced into the DoD lexicon in early 2018. Defend Forward first appears in the US Cyber Command Vision released in March 2018 by then-Commander Admiral Michael S. Rogers.[17] USCYBERCOM coined the term "Defend Forward" as one of three aspects of the command's approach to sustaining strategic advantage in cyberspace: increasing resiliency, defending forward, and contesting adversaries. Defend Forward appears next in the DoD Cyber Strategy released in September 2018, which identifies five lines of effort: increase lethality; compete and deter; partner; reform the department; and cultivate talent. Defending forward falls under the "compete" portion of the "compete and deter" line of effort. The Department never billed the operational elements of its cyber strategy as Defend Forward, but it has evolved to this position. Indeed, Defend Forward was the most innovative concept in the 2018 strategy and has engendered the greatest amount of interest and analysis.

The origin of the term "Persistent Engagement" also resides in the US Cyber Command Vision, which asserts "[s]uperiority through persistence seizes and maintains the initiative in cyberspace by continuously engaging and contesting adversaries and causing them uncertainty wherever they maneuver."[18] The vision refers to persistence, persistent action, and persistent operations. It was Admiral Mike Rogers's successor, General Paul Nakasone, who coined the term "Persistent Engagement." In his 2019 interview for *Joint Forces Quarterly*, Nakasone explains, "*Persistent engagement* is the concept that states we are in constant contact with our adversaries in cyberspace, and success is determined by how we *enable* and *act*. In persistent engagement, we *enable* other interagency partners. Whether it's the FBI or DHS, we enable them with information or intelligence to share with elements of the CIKR [critical infrastructure and key resources] or with select private-sector companies."[19] Persistent Engagement also "rests with our ability to act—that is, how we act against our adversaries in cyberspace. Acting includes defending forward. How do we warn, how do we influence our adversaries, how do we position ourselves in case we have to achieve outcomes in the future? Acting is the concept of operating outside our borders, being outside our networks, to ensure that we understand what our adversaries are doing. If we find ourselves defending inside our own networks, we have lost the initiative and the advantage."[20]

The DoD Cyber Strategy adopted the term "Defend Forward" rather than "Persistent Engagement" but the conceptual frameworks align perfectly. USCYBERCOM and DoD now both refer to Defend Forward as a core part of DoD's strategy and Persistent Engagement as USCYBERCOM's approach to implementing that strategy.

Defend Forward and Persistent Engagement in Practice

General Nakasone testified in 2019 that ensuring a safe and secure election in 2018 was his number one priority and drove him to establish a joint US Cyber Command/National Security Agency effort called the Russia Small Group that "tested our new operational approach."[21] The RSG demonstrated USCYBERCOM's pivot from a "response force" to a "persistence force."[22] In the words of its commander, "USCYBERCOM has learned that successful engagement against adversaries in cyberspace requires that we continuously seek tactical, operational, and strategic initiative. Such persistence requires that we remain ahead of [our adversaries] both in knowledge and in action. It also demands that we leverage our strengths across intelligence and operations to achieve this end."[23]

USCYBERCOM and NSA joined forces to identify and counter threats as they emerged, thereby enabling the interagency to act with remarkable coordination and cooperation. The RSG engaged with allies and the private sector to build resiliency. For the first time, defensive cyber teams were sent abroad (with host country permission) to hunt for adversary activity on foreign networks. By going where adversaries were currently operating, cyber teams discovered new activity, alerted foreign partners and helped secure their networks, and shared information directly with industry so they could develop countermeasures. By leveraging insights to contest cyber aggression, the RSG was reportedly able to take the Internet Research Agency, a Kremlin-linked troll farm known to have waged an influence campaign in 2016, offline ahead of the November midterms.

General Nakasone touted the RSG as a success. It had tested and "demonstrated persistent engagement in practice."[24] The 2018 DoD Cyber Strategy identified the need to Defend Forward during day-to-day competition with adversaries. USCYBERCOM demonstrated how it would implement the DoD strategy through its new approach of Persistent Engagement. General Nakasone testified that Persistent Engagement impacted adversaries while allowing the United States to sustain key competitive advantages and increase cyber capabilities. Lessons learned from 2018 were applied to build on success and further instate the new strategy, and they also informed efforts to successfully secure the 2020 elections.

Cautions and Mischaracterizations

It is not surprising for new concepts to engender increased scrutiny and debate; even more so since the pivot from a response force to a persistence force represents a paradigm shift in how the United States approaches cyberspace.[25] Further, people view new constructs through traditional lenses.[26] "People use analogies, metaphors, and parables, both explicitly and implicitly, to link what is new to what is already known, as a bridge between the familiar and the new."[27] Finally, intellectual shifts do not occur overnight; for a time they co-exist side by side with previous constructs.[28] Hence, it is not surprising that the impulse to equate deterrence with security and thus to prescribe deterrence for everything remains very powerful.[29] That being said, it is important to dispel several misconceptions about the concepts of Defend Forward and Persistent Engagement and their implementation.

First, Defend Forward is often equated incorrectly with "forward defense" or "forward positioning" (presence as a deterrent) as practiced by the United States and NATO during the Cold War. Defend Forward is not about messaging through force posture and disposition. It is about actively operating and engaging. What matters in cyber strategic competition short of armed conflict is not that the United States has assets forward but that its assets are engaging and seizing the initiative. Messaging regarding Defend Forward operations may have incidental deterrence benefits, but the primary purpose is to actively counter adversaries' ability to operate against US interests.

Second, some critique Defend Forward and Persistent Engagement as exercises of preemptive self-defense, raising inapt objections to the lack of severity and imminency of adversary threats necessary to justify proactive, counter-cyber operations. Couching Defend Forward in the framework of the *jus ad bellum* and concepts of national self-defense misconstrues the strategic environment they are designed to address, the nature of Defend Forward operations and activities, and the international law framework applicable to them. Defend Forward and Persistent Engagement are concepts developed precisely to address continuous competition and persistent hostile cyber actions occurring outside of armed conflict and deliberately calibrated not to cross the use-of-force threshold.

They do not involve uses of force and therefore need not be legally predicated on an assessment of actual or threatened armed attack, imminent or otherwise. Defend Forward operations are non-use of force actions designed to counter ongoing hostile cyber operations taking place during day-to-day strategic competition.

In addition, confusion about the nature and meaning of these strategic concepts is often driven by misplaced reference to evolving doctrinal terms meant only to describe tactical or operational missions or actions; terms such as computer network exploitation, operational preparation of the environment, computer network attack, defensive cyberspace operations, and cyber effects operations. Defend Forward operations might involve any one or a mix of these tactical actions—from basic target reconnaissance actions, to access generation, to data extraction and analysis, and ultimately actions to degrade, disrupt, or manipulate the targeted system or data it contains. The legal and policy implications of each of these discrete actions will vary, but that is a discussion separate from the strategic purposes of the Defend Forward concept and the premises on which it is grounded—principally the need for proactive and persistent action to counter and disrupt cyber threats.

The DoD Cyber Strategy and the nascent implementation of Defend Forward and Persistent Engagement have not and cannot alone eliminate the ongoing threat or impact of hostile cyber operations; however, they are a key component to resetting the strategic environment and reducing the effectiveness of adversary cyber campaigns. The significant SolarWinds and Microsoft Exchange breaches discovered at the end of 2020 and in early 2021—widely attributed to Russia and China, respectively—have led some to question this proposition and even place blame on the Defend Forward construct. Their criticisms are premature and rest on flawed understandings too numerous to expound on here. Such critics presume without evidence that the DoD was provisioned with the authorities and resources necessary to fully execute Defend Forward operations at scale, and they ignore the uncomfortable fact that the Russian government, by operating on US domestic infrastructure, exploited a legally imposed blind spot in the intelligence picture. The lesson to be drawn from these compromises is not that Defend Forward failed but that more needs to be done.

The DoD Cyber Strategy and the operational approach of Persistent Engagement encompass an array of activities beyond defending forward, many of which raise little if any legal and policy issues. Driving persistence in innovation to maintain strategic advantage and overmatch is simply a sound strategic imperative, as is persistence in building partnerships across the public and private sectors and internationally. As noted above, the real fulcrum of the shift in cyber strategy is the embrace of the need, under certain circumstances, to conduct out-of-network cyber operations and campaigns to disrupt cyber threats at or as close as practicable to their source. Neither Defend Forward nor Persistent Engagement is inherently aggressive or offensive as some have claimed. Both may involve traditional reconnaissance and intelligence collection to generate actionable insights. They may employ predominantly defensive measures or be conducted with the consent of the system or device owner or the state in whose territory cyber infrastructure resides. Such was the case with the "hunt forward" operations conducted as part of the RSG effort in 2018.[30]

There is no question, however, that non-consensual cyber-effects operations are a core element of the Defend Forward concept and it is unlikely that we will see a reversal of this strategy shift any time soon. Initial indications are that the Defend Forward concept has borne fruit, and it has been endorsed, in essence, by the Cyberspace Solarium Commission and tacitly by Congress through enabling legislation and statements of support. It is to this core element of Defend Forward that the following chapters turn to assess the legal and policy implications and boundaries of employing cyber capabilities outside of DoD networks to actively disrupt emerging and ongoing cyber and information conflict threats.

Notes

* The opinions expressed herein are those of the authors and do not necessarily reflect the views of the US government or any other organization or entity with which the authors are affiliated.

1. U.S. DEP'T OF DEFENSE, SUMMARY: DEPARTMENT OF DEFENSE CYBER STRATEGY 2018, at 1 (2018) (emphasis in original).

2. *Id.*

3. *United States Special Operations Command and United States Cyber Command in Review of the Defense Authorization Request for Fiscal Year 2020 and the Future Years Defense Program: Hearing Before the S. Subcomm. on Pers. of the S. Comm. on Armed Servs.*, 116th Cong. 21 (2019) [hereinafter *Nakasone Transcript*] (stenographic transcript of testimony of Gen. Paul M. Nakasone, Commander, U.S. Cyber Command and Director, National Security Agency and Chief, Central Security Service); *United States Special Operations Command and United States Cyber Command in Review of the Defense Authorization Request for Fiscal Year 2020 and the Future Years Defense*

Program: Hearing Before the S. Comm. On Armed Servs., 116th Cong. 4 (2019) [hereinafter *Nakasone Testimony*] (statement of Gen. Paul M. Nakasone, Commander, U.S. Cyber Command).

4. Ellen Nakashima, *U.S. Cyber Force Credited with Helping Stop Russia from Undermining Midterms*, WASH. POST (Feb. 14, 2019).

5. *Id.*

6. OFFICE OF THE PRESIDENT OF THE UNITED STATES, INTERNATIONAL STRATEGY FOR CYBERSPACE 12 (2011).

7. OFFICE OF THE WHITE HOUSE PRESS SEC'Y, FACT SHEET ON PRESIDENTIAL POLICY DIRECTIVE 20 (2013).

8. U.S. DEP'T OF DEFENSE, THE DOD CYBER STRATEGY 5, 6 (2015).

9. *Id.* at 10.

10. *See id.* at 5.

11. Fischerkeller and Harknett explain, "A structural imperative is a theoretically derived absolute, but it does not mean that states can't make bad decisions and suffer the consequences. A strategic incentive is a set of cost/benefit calculations that creates a rationale for a certain set of choices." Michael P. Fischerkeller & Richard J. Harknett, *Cyber Persistence Theory, Intelligence Contests, and Strategic Competition*, TEX NAT'L SECURITY REV. (Sept. 17, 2020). The structure of cyberspace is interconnectedness, which creates a condition of constant contact. This combination induces an imperative for persistent action to maximize cumulative gains and minimize cumulative losses. *See* Richard J. Harknett, *Progress Is the Promise in National Cybersecurity Strategy*, LAWFARE (Mar. 23, 2020, 3:20 PM). (A corollary to this is that strategies of coercion, which focus on changing the decision calculus of the opponent by imposing costs and denying benefits, are misaligned with the realities of cyberspace, which reward action.) This structural imperative is reinforced by two strategic incentives for persistent action below the threshold of armed conflict: first, that experimentation has shown that strategic gains accrue from cyber campaigns short of armed conflict; and second, that violation of an armed attack threshold legitimates cross-domain, conventional, kinetic responses in self-defense, "thereby introducing a very different, and likely less predictable, set of risks, costs, and challenges." Fischerkeller & Harknett, *supra* note 11.

12. Joint Force Q, *An Interview with Paul M. Nakasone*, 92 JOINT FORCE Q. 4, 4 (2019).

13. *Id.*

14. U.S. DEP'T OF DEFENSE, *supra* note 1, at 4 (emphasis in original).

15. U.S. CYBER COMMAND, ACHIEVE AND MAINTAIN CYBERSPACE SUPERIORITY: COMMAND VISION FOR US CYBER COMMAND 6 (2018).

16. U.S. DEP'T OF DEFENSE, *supra* note 1, at 4.

17. *See* U.S. CYBER COMMAND, *supra* note 15, at 4.

18. *Id.* at 6.

19. Joint Force Q, *supra* note 12, at 6 (emphasis in original).

20. *Id.* at 6–7.

21. *Nakasone Transcript, supra* note 3, at 21. .

22. Joint Force Q, *supra* note 12, at 5.

23. *Id.* at 12.

24. *Nakasone Testimony, supra* note 3, at 4.

25. Emily O. Goldman, *The Cyber Paradigm Shift, in* 45 NEWPORT PAPERS, TEN YEARS IN: IMPLEMENTING STRATEGIC APPROACHES TO CYBERSPACE 31 (Jacqueline G. Schneider, Emily O. Goldman & Michael Warner eds., 2020).

26. For example, the Cyberspace Solarium Commission presented its own definition of Defend Forward as an element of a deterrence strategy. *See* U.S. CYBER SOLARIUM COMMISSION, FINAL REPORT 2 (2020).

27. Emily Goldman & John Arquilla, Introduction, *in* NAVAL POSTGRADUATE SCHOOL, NPS-DA-14-001, CYBER ANALOGIES 5 (Emily Goldman & John Arquilla eds. 2014).

28. Competing paradigms can co-exist, much as the nuclear and conventional paradigms co-existed for much of the Cold War. *See* Richard J. Harknett, State Preferences, Systemic Constraints, and the Absolute Weapon, *in* THE ABSOLUTE WEAPONS REVISITED: NUCLEAR ARMS AND THE EMERGING INTERNATIONAL ORDER 47, 47–49 (T. V. Paul, Richard J. Harknett & James J. Wirtz eds., Univ. of Mich. Press 1998).

29. The clearest example of this is the Cyberspace Solarium Commission report that lumps everything—resilience, network defense, STEM training, Defend Forward, and deterrence of major cyber war—under one overbroad construct of layered deterrence. *See* U.S. CYBER SOLARIUM COMMISSION, *supra* note 27.

30. With the consent of Ukraine, the Former Yugoslav Republic of Macedonia, and Montenegro, U.S. Cyber Command deployed teams to each of those states to conduct coordinated hunt operations within defined networks, operations that identified indicators of compromise and malware that were made available to the partners and publicly to the cyber security industry.

2

Scenarios for Defend Forward

Gary P. Corn and Peter Renals[*]

In October 2020, media reports emerged that US Cyber Command conducted operations to disrupt a malicious botnet known as TrickBot as part of its ongoing efforts to protect the 2020 presidential elections from Russian interference. At the time, Trickbot was one of the most extensive and persistent botnets on the internet, having infected over a million computing devices globally. A modular, multi-purpose platform widely attributed to Russian actors, Trickbot provided substantial reconnaissance and access capabilities and was frequently used as a ransomware delivery capability. Although the Russian botnet was frequently used for criminal purposes, there were reportedly concerns that it could be leveraged to attack voting systems and processes. For similar reasons, Microsoft took simultaneous actions to disrupt Trickbot. The combined effect was a disruption, at least temporarily, of the botnet's command and control servers. According to reporting, code uploaded to the servers was sent out as an update to the Trickbot nodes on infected computers effectively severing their communications with the control servers.

If true, this was not the first out-of-network US Cyber Command operation conducted against Russian cyber infrastructure to protect US elections. It was widely reported that two years earlier, as part of the Russia Small Group effort to protect the 2018 midterm elections, the command conducted a series of disruptive operations against the Internet Research Agency (IRA) and other Russian cyber entities which, among other impacts, severed the IRA's access to the internet during a crucial period and thereby disrupted its online campaign of disinformation and interference.

The technical details of these operations are understandably not available. By all accounts and indications, consistent with official statements about the Defend Forward and Persistent Engagement components of the Department of Defense's 2018 Cyber Strategy, they involved some level of out-of-network operations below the level of a use-of-force to degrade or disrupt Russia's malicious cyber operational capabilities. Beyond this surface level reporting and understanding, the extent to which US Cyber Command is actively conducting defend-forward operations remains unclear. Given the imperative for operational security in the domain, it is unlikely that details will be available in the near term, and thus true context for evaluating the legal and policy issues surrounding these operations is thin. Following is a series of illustrative, hypothetical cyber operations that reflect a sampling of the types of activities that might be conducted under the umbrella of Defend Forward. They are not derived from nor do they represent any actual operations. They are fictional scenarios offered solely as a backdrop to aid in contextualizing the legal and policy discussion in the ensuing chapters.

Background

Country A is a large democratic nation with a globally dominant economy. Over the past decade it has risen to prominence on the world stage and is often considered a key player in helping to resolve global conflicts. The country has thrived due to its early adoption and investment in internet technologies. This digital revolution within the country has propelled its economy to new heights but has also created a dependency on technology among its population. To protect their way of life, Country A recently approved the establishment of a new military cyber organization and granted it the authority to take proactive defensive measures to Defend Forward against ongoing cyber threats.

In contrast, Country B is a small totalitarian state with a very weak economy. In recent years the ruling regime has initiated several conflicts with various countries around the globe. More often than not, these conflicts have been met with coordinated international sanctions which impose significant economic pressure on an already weak economy. However, over the last five years, the regime has turned to the internet as a means to circumvent these traditional sanctions. Leveraging the power of the internet, Country B has pursued a series of unpredictable and detrimental activities including, but not limited to, stealing cryptocurrency, distributing ransomware, destroying civilian digital infrastructure, and launching malign influence campaigns that interfere with democratic election processes. While enabling the country to improve its financial and military situation, these activities have undoubtedly challenged international norms.

Country A has detected a number of malicious cyber activities it attributes to Country B. It is considering the following options as part of its strategy to Defend Forward against these threats.

Scenario 1: Botnet

Country A recently identified a suspicious internet signal originating from a civilian address within its borders and connecting to a known government research facility in Country B. Network traffic research revealed that the signal originated from a specific type of small Internet of Things (IoT) device. The device was produced by a global tech giant and has grown immensely popular over the past year as citizens can use it to buy things, make grocery lists, and play music within their homes. According to its manufacturer, the device was designed for usability, and as a result, it has no security and allows anyone in the world to connect to it. Based on available intelligence and further forensic analysis, Country A determined that Country B was actively exploiting this vulnerability and gaining access to 5,000 new devices per week globally in an attempt to build a giant botnet. In addition to the threat that a botnet this large poses to global internet infrastructure, Country A assesses that Country B's purpose for building the botnet is to hold Country A's critical infrastructure at risk. Country A is therefore considering the following options to counter the threat from the botnet:

- Software Patch Deployment—Country A has studied the software code associated with the IoT device and has developed a software patch that would uninstall the botnet malware and install security features that would eliminate the vulnerability exploited by Country B. Because the IoT device is not tethered to a security-update infrastructure, requesting the manufacturer to deploy the patch is not an option. To successfully deploy this patch, Country A's cyber operators would need to connect to and gain unauthorized access to each civilian device using the same technique that Country B has employed to build its botnet. One option would be to deploy the patch in essentially the same way that companies perform routine updates to operating systems and programs. Like those updates, there would be little to no impact on the patched devices, but the success rate of this technique would be limited. The operators are prepared to deploy a more robust patching tool. However, through testing, programmers have warned that the installation process would take fifteen minutes and during that time, citizens would be unable to use their devices. Furthermore, the installation overwrites the existing software on the device and as such, any lists/music/preferences would be erased and reset to factory settings.

- Immunization—For routine intelligence collection purposes, Country A monitors internet activity associated with the research facility in Country B. Over the past year, Country A has gained unauthorized clandestine access to several devices within the facility. One of those devices is the control server that is connected to the thousands of vulnerable IoT devices. Having access to this server, and therefore the botnet control software, Country A's programmers are confident that they can successfully use this server to send a disconnect message to all of the compromised IoT devices globally. In doing so, they would leverage the existing connection between the server in Country B and the compromised devices to send a message that is opaque to the IoT device owners and would not impact the server's functionality. However, this action will undoubtedly be noticed by system administrators in Country B, which will allow them to reconstitute the botnet and the command and control connections within some period of time. Therefore, to prevent reconstitution, the operators also propose to encrypt the entire hard drive of the control server to cover their tracks and to render the server unusable.

- Interrupt Communication—For routine intelligence collection purposes, Country A monitors internet activity associated with the research facility in Country B. To do so, Country A maintains clandestine access to a core Internet Service Provider (ISP) router that connects the facility to the greater internet. The ISP and the physical router are both located in a third-party nation just outside the border of Country B. With this access, Country A has the ability to change a configuration setting on the router that would block all internet access to the entire facility and therefore block all connections between the facility and the compromised IoT devices globally. In exploring this option, Country A's programmers have warned of several potential risks to the operation and of unintended collateral effects. First, once the configuration setting is changed, it is likely that the facility IT staff and ISP technicians will at some undetermined point identify and remediate the changed configuration. Thus, there is no guarantee that Country A's programmers will maintain access long enough for the operation to achieve maximum effect, or to reverse the configuration change in the event necessary to mitigate any unintended collateral effects. Second, if successful, this option will block all internet access to the entire facility and as such benign services and functions will be impacted. Finally, there is no guarantee that this router serves as the only source of internet for the facility. Should Country B reroute traffic, analysts are unable to assess how a shift to a redundant internet source would impact other Internet Service Providers and the flow of network traffic through neighboring nations.

Scenario 2: Foreign Malign Influence

Country B's regime recently established a covert organization with the mission of conducting global influence operations. More specifically, these operations are intended to target democratic elections in several nations around the world in order to sow internal division and promote candidates that would be most favorable to Country B. Aware of this activity, Country A began monitoring the covert organization and discovered it relied on a large virtual server that was hosted in a third-party country. This server was leveraged as the primary connection point between the covert organization and the thousands of Facebook, Twitter, LinkedIn, and other accounts it had established to push propaganda and culturally divisive news topics. To counter this activity, Country A is considering these actions:

- Hack and Watermark—Country A recently acquired credentials for the virtual server through an ongoing intelligence operation. These credentials enable Country A to gain clandestine unauthorized access to and unrestricted control of the virtual server located in the neutral nation. Leveraging this access, Country A plans to upload a small program to the server that would enable its programmers to embed watermarks in all current and future files on the server. More specifically, the program would run continuously in the background and append the phrase "CountryB_InfluenceOp" to the code associated with every DOC, PPT, XLS, GIF, JPG, PDF file on the system. Of note, this means that all content on the server will be modified with Country A's watermark to include content that Country B chooses to use against other nations. This modification will be opaque to Country B operators and the program would have minimal impact on the performance of the server.

Once operational, Country A then plans to notify and request that social media companies take action to remove any content containing this watermark.

- Hack and Notify—Country A recently identified a vulnerability associated with the virtual server hosted in the third-party nation. The vulnerability can be exploited to grant clandestine unauthorized access to the server, but will only afford read access with no ability to create, delete, or modify any files. To launch this exploit, a programmer from Country A needs to establish a connection to the server and transfer a unique sequence of data to a specific program on the server. Doing so risks causing the program on the server to become unstable. In testing, this technique has been successful in granting read access to system files without any system impact 80% of the time. However, the remaining 20% of tests resulted in the system crashing completely, but that can be remedied with a system reboot. Country A's programmers are recommending that this technique be leveraged to gain access for the purpose of identifying the thousands of social media accounts associated with this server. Once collected, the list can be shared with social media companies who in turn can begin dismantling the malign influence campaign.
- Hack and Corrupt—Country B just chose to install a new free program on the virtual server to facilitate easier remote management. However, this free program is known in hacking communities to contain several vulnerabilities that can easily be exploited. Country A is aware of these vulnerabilities and has high confidence that it can use one of these vulnerabilities to gain unrestricted control over the virtual server. In developing the concept, the programmers from Country A have proposed using one of the exploits to upload a small malicious tool that will delete all data in the virtual server and could go one step further to encrypt the specific physical hard drive allocated to State B's use to prevent any recovery efforts. Analysts assess that this option will permanently disable Country B's influence campaign, but it will come at a cost of causing physical damage to equipment owned by a hosting provider in the third-party nation.

Scenario 3: Malware

Country A recently identified a new malware campaign launched by Country B. The malware was distributed globally, targeting banking institutions and cryptocurrency exchanges. Delivered through a phishing campaign, the malware infects laptop, desktop, and point-of-sale systems. Once infected, the malware steals credentials and credit card information, which it then transfers unencrypted to a control server located at a government-affiliated public university in Country B. In seeking to defend against this campaign, Country A is considering the following:

- Fake Victim Data—An analysis of the malware shows that victim data are transferred to a control server at the public university using a simple web request that looks like:

  www.university.com/a=[username]b=[password]c=[creditcard]

Given the simplicity of the data transfer mechanism, programmers in Country A have proposed using an automated tool to generate thousands of web requests that would send fake usernames, passwords, and credentials to the control server. Doing so is not expected to impede the normal or intended functions of the control server or university network, but it would directly impede country B's ability to discern legitimate from fake stolen credentials. Unfortunately, in attempting to assess second-order impacts, analysts are unable to quantify what, if any, impacts there would be on global financial institutions should Country B attempt to connect to their services using these thousands of fake credentials.

- Distributed Denial of Service—Country A has recently developed a Distributed Denial of Service (DDoS) capability that can send over 100 Gbps of network traffic to an intended target. The public university in Country B is known to have a network capacity of only 10 Gbps, and therefore Country A's new capability will undoubtedly be able to block global malware connections to the university. Additionally, analysis shows that if the malware is unable to connect to its control server for a period of six hours, it automatically takes action to delete itself. Thus, Country A plans to use the capability for a period of only six hours. However, at the same time, analysts have identified potential collateral impacts with employing the new tool. Specifically, given the distance between Country A and Country B, there is no guarantee concerning the path that the network traffic will follow through third-party countries. It's possible that a DDoS of this magnitude may impact and possibly overwhelm network connections elsewhere in the world.

Additionally, within Country B, there is no guarantee that the effects of the DDoS will be limited to only the university. It's possible that the DDoS may impact connectivity for other users, such as surrounding hospitals, emergency services, and public infrastructure. Finally, as it applies to the university itself, once launched, the DDoS will impact all university functions and personnel equally, to include foreign students and faculty.

Scenario 4: Disrupt Exfiltration

Country B has compromised a government network belonging to Country A and is actively exfiltrating sensitive data at a steady rate. Country A recently became aware of the intrusion and is determining the best course of action. While it believes that removing infected systems from the network will remedy the current compromise, this action will fall short of recovering and protecting data already stolen. In examining the compromise itself, analysts have found a steady connection and flow of sensitive data from their file server to a compromised hop point/staging server in a third-party country. It appears that this staging server is owned by a medical facility and as such, connecting through it allowed Country B to obscure its activities. Additionally, while the connection between Country A's file server and the staging server is steady, the connection between the staging server and Country B is intermittent. This leads analysts to believe that Country B is connecting once a week to the hop point to download all of the stolen data. Given the extent of the compromise and sensitivity of the data, Country A is considering the following:

- Encrypt Stolen Data—Given the steady stream of data between Country A's compromised file server and the staging server, analysts are confident that any tools and programs added to their file server will be transmitted back to the staging server, and eventually to Country B. As such, programmers have recommended creating a custom variant of ransomware designed to encrypt hard drives without actually asking for a ransom. To increase the effectiveness of this plan, programmers have further recommended adding a worm component to the ransomware that would allow it to spread automatically to nearby connected systems. This technique will allow the ransomware to automatically infect the staging server, as well as all systems in Country B associated with the compromise, thereby encrypting all data that have already been stolen. However, while this approach will be effective at securing all compromised data, analysts have also identified a risk that the ransomware could spread to non-targeted networks and devices.

Note

* The opinions expressed herein are those of the authors and do not necessarily reflect the views of the US government or any other organization or entity with which the authors are affiliated.

3

US Cyber Command's First Decade

Michael Warner

United States Cyber Command (USCYBERCOM) turned ten years old in 2020. It is a unique institution—a military command that operates globally in real time against determined and capable adversaries and yet never fires a shot or launches a missile. The Command comprises an amalgam of military, intelligence, and information technology capabilities that came together into its present shape more by design than by fortuitous chance. That design, however, was itself a work in progress.

The Command's first decade built upon the notion that states must operate in cyberspace at scale and in real time. "Operating" means that key national systems and data have to be "fought" like a weapons platform; in other words, they enable and execute critical sovereign functions and thus cannot be switched off or managed as discrete and individual devices.[1] Indeed, each system and device affects the whole, and that whole is now immense. Only operational processes can harness the military's and the government's limited talent and resources in ways that can accomplish such global tasks on behalf of the nation, and only military components have the training, expertise, equipment, and resources to fulfill key elements of that requirement full-time and without interruption.

That vision dawned on military and civilian leaders years before the establishment of USCYBERCOM. The Command then refined the vision through actual operations. USCYBERCOM was by no means a passive medium on which other government and industry actors imposed their visions. On the contrary, the Command's leaders, experts, and experiences influenced the course of discussions and resulting decisions. The evolution began two decades back, as key decisions were made that framed the institutional context for USCYBERCOM. This history is interesting not only for what it says about military innovation and bureaucratic change in the US government but also for the insight it offers on the development of other military cyber components among America's allies, partners, and adversaries.

Antecedents

The Joint Chiefs of Staff in 2004 labeled cyberspace a "domain" of military operations, meaning that the systems that processed, stored, and moved data in digital forms had collectively become a venue where states could use force to coerce other states. Thus that year's National Military Strategy declared that

> [the nation's armed forces] must have the ability to operate across the air, land, sea, space and cyberspace domains of the battlespace. Armed Forces must employ military capabilities to ensure access to these domains to pro-tect the Nation, forces in the field and US global interests.[2]

This recognition of cyberspace as an arena for inter-state conflict and coer-cion might appear from the perspective of 2021 to be rather premature. Yet in 2004 it culminated almost two decades of public and private debates over the characteristics and prospects of cyberspace for national security.

Cyber capabilities began growing in America's intelligence agencies, armed services, and computer and telecommunications industries in the 1970s. For reasons beyond the scope of this chapter, no single government actor possessed the situational awareness and authority to demand that users connecting to digital networks around the nation employ best practices (like patching, passwords, encryption, and enterprise management) that were well known—if haphazardly applied—in the computer security community.[3] Governmental and private capabilities through the 1980s evolved on rela-tively closed networks based on a variety of digital protocols. Technological and strategic events in the 1990s, however, created the modern security problem. Now-familiar debates over cybersecurity began in earnest with the global adoption of TCP/IP packet switching to link thousands of "intra-nets," as well as with the nearly simultaneous opening of dictatorial regimes to the internet in the mid-1990s.[4]

American experts soon understood that other nations too could now em-ploy what the RAND Corporation called "strategic information warfare" against the United States. A tabletop exercise at RAND in 1995 showed that America, with its "complex, interconnected network control systems for such necessities as oil and gas pipelines, electric grids, etc.," had become vul-nerable even to states with much inferior militaries that were nonetheless willing to utilize cyber techniques to leapfrog US forces and hit America's critical infrastructure.[5] "In sum," RAND's report concluded, "the US home-land may no longer provide a sanctuary from outside attack."[6]

Even the Department of Defense (DoD) rapidly came to depend on globally networked digital infrastructure to run its routine business oper-ations. Such networks could be largely hardware agnostic as long as they ran operating systems that could send emails and display pages on the new World Wide Web; thus the Department suddenly needed fewer costly and personnel-intensive DoD-tailored communications systems.[7] Yet linking military systems on digital infrastructures that were not only outside of DoD control but also used by millions of foreign (and essentially anony-mous) actors also created an unprecedented "tunnel of vulnerability" for the nation, as the DoD Defense Science Board warned in 1996.[8] Congressional auditors that same year recorded their concern with these developments, noting that "major disruptions to military operations and readiness could threaten national security if attackers successfully corrupted sensitive infor--mation and systems or denied service from vital communications backbones or power systems."[9] Such concerns heightened in 1998, when DoD network administrators spotted a set of intrusions into US government systems that American observers soon dubbed "Moonlight Maze."[10] Michael Vatis of the Federal Bureau of Investigation (FBI) put these developments in context for Congress in 1999:

> In the past few years we have seen a series of intrusions into numerous Department of Defense computer networks as well as networks of other federal agencies, universities, and private sector entities. Intruders have successfully accessed US Government networks and took large amounts of unclassified but sensitive information. . . . It is important that the Congress and the American public understand the very real threat that we are facing in the cyber realm, not just in the future, but now.[11]

The Information Revolution thereafter accelerated, locking in technolog-ical consequences almost before policymakers realized their significance. Military doctrine struggled to keep pace. Even though the Department of Defense had secretly foretold the rise of "information warfare" as early as 1992, the Joint Chiefs of Staff in 1996 decided that offensive and defensive cyber operations should be treated doctrinally as facets of "information op-erations."[12] This temporarily grouped the rapidly evolving and highly spe-cialized skill sets for defending and attacking digital data and networks with a set of tangentially related missions such as psychological warfare, electronic warfare, and operations security.[13]

The Department of Defense soon developed an operational approach to securing its information systems. It created an organization in 1998 to guide such efforts—the Joint Task Force–Computer Network Defense (JTF-CND)—and tapped experts at the National Security Agency (NSA) to help identify threats to its networks. The Clinton administration's subsequent national cybersecurity strategy hinted that the Agency's contribution stemmed in part from its intelligence capabilities: "The NSA is uniquely qualified to serve its customers/partners because of its ability to perform in-depth technical analysis of serious intrusions and because it is the only organization positioned to link intrusion data to foreign signals intelligence."[14] JTF-CND helped invent and apply the concept of "NetOps" for sustaining the capabilities of DoD's Global Information Grid (GIG), which itself had become indispensable for the US military's operations. US Strategic Command (USSTRATCOM) would inherit JTF-CND's successor in 2002 and then refine and summarize NetOps as its operational construct for operating and defending the GIG:

> The goal of NetOps is to provide assured and timely net-centric services across strategic, operational and tactical boundaries in support of DOD's full spectrum of war fighting, intelligence and business missions. The desired effects of NetOps are: assured system and network availability, assured information protection and assured information delivery.[15]

In the early 2000s, a rough consensus developed in the Department of Defense that the United States must employ its military to operate in cyberspace at scale and in real time. Secretary of Defense Donald Rumsfeld explained this in his Information Operations Roadmap, published in classified form in October 2003 and released with redactions three years later. The DoD systems, and foreign threats to them, were growing so fast that they required a robust "defense in depth" based on the premise that "the Department will 'fight the net' as it would a weapons system."[16] Like ships at sea, DoD's networks had to sustain unbroken operations on a global scale despite the constant threat of degradation from adversarial action. Commanders therefore must be confident that system defenses would "ensure the graceful degradation of the network rather than its collapse."[17] The conclusion that Secretary Rumsfeld and the Department drew was that only operational processes could harness limited talent and resources in ways that could cope with such a global, real-time task, and only military components had the training, expertise, equipment, and resources to meet that DoD requirement.

That consensus resulted in Secretary Rumsfeld's creation of two joint military cyber components. The Clinton administration in 2000 had merged JTF-CND with the military's relative handful of computer-network-attack planners in a joint task force (the Joint Task Force—Computer Network Operations) under US Space Command. Secretary Rumsfeld two years later shifted that unit into the reorganized USSTRATCOM. In 2004 he split the unit into defensive and offensive components, respectively the Joint Task Force–Global Network Operations (JTF-GNO), and the Joint Functional Component Command–Network Warfare (JFCC-NW). The point of this institutional shuffle was to keep both elements under a functional combatant commander in USSTRATCOM while allowing them to grow to perform the tasks that confronted them. Both components would now be headed by three-star general officers, both of whom were "dual-hatted" as heads of combat support agencies (the Director of NSA [DIRNSA] for JFCC-NW, and the Director of the Defense Information Systems Agency [DISA] for JTF-GNO).

Modest operational successes for each joint task force helped convince Secretary of Defense Robert Gates in 2008 that they could and should be linked under a single commander. Hence, in June 2009, Secretary Gates directed USSTRATCOM "to establish a subordinate unified command designated as U.S. Cyber Command (USCYBERCOM)." JFCC-NW and JTF-GNO personnel would be reassigned to USCYBERCOM, which Gates "preferred" to see based at Fort Meade with NSA.[18]

The armed services at the same time began reorganizing their cyber capabilities, creating headquarters units (in addition to those already assigned to USSTRATCOM) to function alongside the emerging USCYBERCOM. These components (in 2010) were the Army Cyber Command, Marine Forces Cyber Command, Fleet Cyber Command/US Tenth Fleet, and Air Force Cyber Command/24th Air Force. USSTRATCOM delegated operational control of various service cyber units (and their headquarters) to USCYBERCOM in late 2010.[19]

Creation and Early Steps

USCYBERCOM thus began operations in 2010 with the merger of JTF-GNO and JFCC-NW under the command of the officer who also directed NSA.[20] The Command has since performed three main missions: (1) defending the DoD information systems, (2) supporting joint force commanders with cyberspace operations, and (3) defending the nation from significant cyberattacks. The Command has worked at home and abroad to employ military capabilities at scale against adversaries in and through cyberspace, conducting most of its missions in collaboration with various partners, including the other combatant commands, federal agencies, intelligence services, allied forces, and industry experts.

The Command has worked under three commanders. Each officer gained his fourth star upon appointment to the post. Each also came to the job with significant professional experience in intelligence, and all three likewise served as the "dual-hatted" director of NSA. General Keith B. Alexander (US Army) advocated the Command's creation and served as its first head from 2010 to 2014. Admiral Michael S. Rogers (US Navy) succeeded him and led USCYBERCOM as it grew from 2014 to 2018. General Paul M. Nakasone (US Army), the current commander, took over on May 4, 2018, the day USCYBERCOM was elevated to full unified combatant command status.

Several issues faced the new command at its inception. An internal analysis summarized them as "building capability and capacity in Service cyber forces, and gaining the requisite authorities and fully resourcing the Command."[21] Each of these issues in turn presented an interlocking series of complications. USCYBERCOM had to determine how it would exercise command and control over the service cyber components that were assigned to it, and also had to plan how it would integrate its operations with those of the geographic combatant commands. The Command also started out with fewer people than it needed. Its combined JFCC-NW and JTF-GNO numbers totaled just over five hundred FY10 billets, versus the nine hundred–plus its headquarters had been projected to have in FY12 to perform its expanded missions.[22] In addition, in its haste to begin operations, USCYBERCOM sacrificed proficiency for speed. Admiral Rogers told Congress in 2015 that he had arrived at USCYBERCOM a year earlier and found it had been (for understandable reasons) sub-optimally constructed:

> The organizations had been well scoped and granted the authorities necessary to do our work. The bad news was that USCYBERCOM was built from the ground up by cutting manning to the bone, initially sacrificing vital support functions and institutional infrastructure to build mission capabilities as fast as possible.[23]

The Cyber Mission Force

As USCYBERCOM grew, leaders in the White House, Congress, and the Department of Defense responded to its requirements for additional resources and clarified authorities. The Command created the Cyber Mission Force (CMF) in 2013 to orient the armed services in their task of manning, training, and equipping the nation's military cyberspace forces. The CMF was designed to overcome the problem of force presentation that plagued cyberspace operations from the outset.[24] The issues involved in this project were two. The first and most critical was a talent gap in the US military and across the nation. General Alexander explained this to Congress in early 2012:

> At present we are critically short of the skills and the skilled people we as a Command and a nation require to manage our networks and protect US interests in cyberspace. Our prosperity and our security now depend on a very skilled technical workforce, which is in high demand both in government and industry. We in DoD need to build a cyber workforce that can take action quickly across the full range of our mission sets as necessary. This will require us to adopt a single standard across the Department and the Services, so that we can truly operate as a single, joint force.[25]

Second, the available talent was not yet well allocated and organized, even with roughly eleven thousand people in the "force mix" across USCYBERCOM and its service components. Each service organized, trained, and equipped its "cyber" forces in various ways.[26] This made it difficult for anyone to understand just how much "combat power" DoD could dedicate to particular operations or concerns. "We need to foster a common approach to force development and force presentation—up to and including the Service component and joint headquarters—given the intrinsically joint nature of this domain," explained General Alexander to Congress in 2013.[27]

The Cyber Mission Force, Alexander assured Congress, would become a "high-quality, certified, and standardized force." It would increase predictability and decrease risk for joint force commanders receiving these increments of cyber power:

> We will be able to present cyber forces with known capability sets to our Combatant Commanders—forces they can train with, plan for, plan on, and

employ like forces and units [in] any other military domain. This gets at the essence of normalizing cyber capabilities for the Department of Defense.[28]

Deputy Secretary of Defense Ashton Carter in late 2012 approved the creation of the CMF, setting the dimensions of the force at 133 teams and 6,187 billets—a manpower cost that one key congressman publicly told General Alexander was "enormous."[29] Yet the Department and General Alexander held to the plan, telling Congress in 2014: "I am convinced we have found a force model that will give useful service as we continue to learn and improvise for years to come."[30]

CMF teams came in three types, each intended to represent a standard increment of combat power for cyberspace operations, as General Alexander explained to Congress in 2014:

> This force has three main aspects: (1) Cyber National Mission Teams to help defend the nation against a strategic cyberattack on our critical infrastructure and key resources; (2) Cyber Combat Mission Teams under the direction of the regional and functional Combatant Commanders to support their objectives; and (3) Cyber Protection Teams to help defend [the] DoD information environment and our key military cyber terrain.[31]

The 133 CMF teams would be built and presented by the armed services, with each service assigned a set number of teams to build and forty-two work roles to fill.[32] Secretary of Defense Chuck Hagel reported to Congress that the types of teams were distributed as follows:

- 13 National Mission Teams (NMTs) with 8 National Support Teams (NSTs)
- 27 Combat Mission Teams (CMTs) with 17 Combat Support Teams (CSTs)
- 18 National Cyber Protection Teams (CPTs)
- 24 Service CPTs
- 26 Combatant Command and DoD Information Network CPTs[33]

The teams were not fully created until 2016, and all were built to full operational capability only in mid-2018.

Standardization of team training and capability, as well as of organization, was a primary USCYBERCOM goal in building the CMF. Joint force commanders employing these teams, as well as other agencies and forces operating alongside them, needed to know that they could not only perform their missions but could do so with minimal risk to friendly operations. General Alexander explained to Congress how this goal would be reached:

> The training for this force is happening now on two levels. At the team level, each cyber mission team must be trained to adhere to strict joint operating standards. This rigorous and deliberate training process is essential; it ensures the teams can be on-line without jeopardizing vital military, diplomatic, or intelligence interests. Such standards are also crucial to assuring intelligence oversight and to securing the trust of the American public that military operations in cyberspace do not infringe on the privacy and civil liberties of US persons. Our training system is in the midst of certifying thousands of our people to high and joint military-wide standards.
>
> At the individual level, we are using every element of capacity in our Service schools and in NSA to instruct members of the Cyber Mission Force teams.[34]

While building the CMF teams, USCYBERCOM added two operating components to employ its own NMTs and CPTs for specialized missions. The first of these, the Cyber National Mission Force (CNMF), came into being under the Commander of USCYBERCOM in early 2014; General Alexander called this "the US military's first joint tactical command with a dedicated mission focused on cyberspace operations."[35] The Joint Force Headquarters–DoD Information Networks (JFHQ-DoDIN) stood up a year later under the control of the second Commander of USCYBERCOM, Admiral Michael S. Rogers, who explained the new component to Congress in 2015:

> JFHQ-DoDIN's mission is to oversee the day-to-day operation of DoD's networks and mount an active defense of them, securing their key cyber terrain and being prepared to neutralize any adversary who manages to bypass their perimeter defenses. Placing the just-established JFHQ-DoDIN under USCYBERCOM gives us a direct lever for operating DoD's information systems in ways that make them easier to defend, and tougher for an adversary to affect. It also gets us closer to being able to manage risk on a system-wide basis across DoD, balancing warfighter needs for access to data and capabilities while maintaining the overall security of the enterprise.[36]

JFHQ-DoDIN brought operational perspectives and intelligence to bear on problems confronting local systems administrators and cybersecurity service providers (CSSPs), and was co-located with the Defense Information Systems Agency (DISA), whose three-star director also served as JFHQ-DoDIN's commander.

Shifting Strategic and Policy Contexts

Significant developments in cyberspace operational authorities and doctrine occurred in 2012. Late that year, President Obama approved Presidential Policy Directive 20 (PPD-20) to govern cyberspace operations outside of US networks. The directive—which remains classified but was publicly summarized by the White House—established "principles and processes for the use of cyber operations so that cyber tools are integrated with the full array of national security tools." Its goal was "a whole-of-government approach consistent with the values that we promote domestically and internationally," and it sought that goal through "exercising restraint in dealing with the threats we face." PPD-20 sought to ensure that the US government took "the least action necessary to mitigate threats" and gave priority to "defense and law enforcement as preferred courses of action."[37]

The Obama administration that same year complained that adversaries who might be deterred from attacking the United States in cyberspace manifestly were not being deterred from trying to infiltrate US military, government, and critical infrastructure systems. Secretary of Defense Leon Panetta described their threatening behavior, with a warning:

> We know that foreign cyber actors are probing America's critical infrastructure networks. They are targeting the computer control systems that operate chemical, electricity [sic] and water plants and those that guide transportation throughout this country. We know of specific instances where intruders have successfully gained access to these control systems. We also know that they are seeking to create advanced tools to attack these systems and cause panic and destruction and even the loss of life.[38]

A coordinated series of such attacks, warned Secretary Panetta, "could be a cyber Pearl Harbor" that worked to "paralyze and shock the nation."[39]

General Alexander recognized this peril, though he seemed optimistic that USCYBERCOM had attained a degree of offensive power that would enable the United States to retaliate for cyberattacks that caused physical destruction or loss of life. This deterrence-enhancing capability of the Command was rarely discussed in public, a fact that makes two such instances all the more noteworthy. Asked about the Command's combat power at a 2012 hearing, General Alexander explained:

> The co-location of Cyber Command with the National Security Agency provides our Command with "unique strengths and capabilities" for cyberspace operations planning and execution. I can assure you that, in appropriate circumstances and on order from the National Command Authority, we can back up the Department's assertion that any actor contemplating a crippling cyberattack against the United States would be taking a grave risk.[40]

At another hearing a year later, General Alexander added:

> We believe our offense is the best in the world. Cyber offense requires a deep, persistent and pervasive presence on adversary networks in order to precisely deliver effects. We maintain that access, gain deep understanding of the adversary, and develop offensive capabilities through the advanced skills and tradecraft of our analysts, operators and developers. When authorized to deliver offensive cyber effects, our technological and operational superiority delivers unparalleled effects against our adversaries['] systems.[41]

While General Alexander professed his "confidence in our ability to deter major state-on-state attacks in cyberspace," he also worried that hostile reconnaissance such as that described by Secretary Panetta seemed to have no remedy. In short, USCYBERCOM had attained an ability to react, but it had not yet learned how to anticipate or prevent cyberattacks. As General Alexander publicly lamented in 2013, "[W]e are not deterring the seemingly low-level harassment of private and public sites, property, and data."[42]

By Admiral Rogers's second year as commander, he and other leaders had concluded that adversaries held the ability to strike America's critical infrastructure in ways that neither the Command nor the nation could yet prevent. Admiral Rogers publicly explained this situation to Congress in September 2015:

> Digital tools in cyberspace give adversaries cheap and ready means of doing something that until recently only one or two states could afford to do: that is, to reach beyond the battle-field capabilities of the US military. They have demonstrated the capacity to hold "at risk" our military and even civilian infrastructure. . . . We have recently seen Russian- and Chinese-sponsored intrusions in United States information systems—penetrations that were designed to (and in some cases did) gain persistent presence in the targeted networks.[43]

Senate Armed Services Committee chair John McCain (R-AZ) at that same hearing complained that adversary actions in cyberspace ventured well beyond harassment. He blamed the Obama administration for this state of affairs, expressing his unhappiness about its approach to cyber operations policy and strategy:

> Make no mistake, we are not winning the fight in cyberspace. Our adversaries view our response to malicious cyberactivity as timid and ineffectual. Put simply, the problem is a lack of deterrence. As Admiral Rogers has previously testified, the administration has not demonstrated to our adversaries that the consequences of continued cyberattacks against us outweigh the benefit. Until this happens, the attacks will continue, and our national security interests will suffer. . . . Establishing of cyberdeterrence also requires robust capabilities, both offensive and defensive, that can pose a credible threat to our adversaries.[44]

Senator McCain was no outlier in his call for better deterrence. Admiral Rogers hinted in spring 2016 that change was needed because cyber actors could now affect security conditions at a national level; that is, they could cause strategic effects: "Some of these threat actors are seeking to shape us, narrowing our options in international affairs to limit our choices in the event of a crisis."[45] Although a deterrence posture had not stopped such effects and seemed unable to mitigate them, Senator McCain and Admiral Rogers nonetheless saw the solution in more and better deterrence. Indeed, deterrence had been the strategic frame for DoD since the Cold War. The Joint Chiefs of Staff had almost by default classed cyberspace operations in that frame, as can be seen in this passage from the 2004 edition of the *National Military Strategy*:

> The non-linear nature of the current security environment requires multi-layered active and passive measures to counter numerous diverse conventional and asymmetric threats. These include . . . threats in cyberspace aimed at networks and data critical to US information-enabled systems. *Such threats require a comprehensive concept of deterrence encompassing traditional adversaries, terrorist networks and rogue states able to employ any range of capabilities.*[46]

Despite the dominance of deterrence thinking, however, Admiral Rogers also hinted to Congress in 2016 that a reconsideration of that paradigm had begun. He explained:

> We at USCYBERCOM are thinking more strategically about shifting our response planning from fighting a war to also providing decision makers with options to deter and forestall a conflict before it begins. These new options would be in addition to capabilities that help our combatant commanders succeed in their missions if and when conflict erupts and the joint forces receive an "execute order" to commence kinetic as well as cyberspace operations.[47]

As this rethinking progressed, the Obama administration launched a related debate over the wisdom of elevating USCYBERCOM from a sub-unified to a full unified combatant command. Discussions had commenced in 2012 but became public knowledge in early 2016, with Admiral Rogers feeling confident enough in its likelihood to advocate elevation while testifying before the sympathetic Chairman McCain. At the same time, however, sentiment arose in the administration in favor of splitting the "dual-hat" command relationship between USCYBERCOM and NSA. Admiral Rogers felt USCYBERCOM was unready for such a split, even if it came with elevation to unified command status.[48] Senator McCain agreed and publicly scolded the administration that September after hearing rumors that the "dual-hat" would end soon:

I'm troubled by recent reports that the Obama administration may be trying to prematurely break the dual-hat before . . . President Obama leaves office. [Four days earlier] it was reported that Secretary of Defense Ash Carter and Director of National Intelligence James Clapper have backed a plan to separate Cyber Command and the NSA. . . . I do not believe rushing to separate the dual-hat in the final months of an administration is appropriate, given the very serious challenges we face in cyberspace and the failure of this administration to develop an effective deterrence policy.[49]

Subsequent reporting suggested that Senator McCain's concern was not misplaced. The *Washington Post* noted anonymous tips indicating that Secretary Carter and Director of National Intelligence James Clapper had "recommended to President Obama that the director of the National Security Agency, Adm. Michael S. Rogers, be removed."[50] The firing had not occurred, alleged the *Post*'s Ellen Nakashima, because it was "tied to another controversial recommendation: to create separate chains of command at the NSA and the military's cyberwarfare unit, a recommendation by Clapper and Carter that has been stalled because of other issues."[51] President Obama declined to act on their recommendation in his final weeks in office. Asked about the rumor while attending a conference in Peru, the president publicly called Admiral Rogers "a terrific patriot [who] has served this country well in a number of positions."[52] Yet President Obama insisted that a split of the dual-hat was indicated:

After directing a comprehensive review of this issue earlier this year, and consistent with the views of the Secretary of Defense and the Director of National Intelligence, I strongly support elevating CYBERCOM to a unified combatant command and ending the dual-hat arrangement for NSA and CYBERCOM. . . . The two organizations should have separate leaders who are able to devote themselves to each organization's respective mission and responsibilities, but should continue to leverage the shared capabilities and synergies developed under the dual-hat arrangement.[53]

Operating in Cyberspace

Incoming president Donald Trump retained Admiral Rogers for over a year and asked the new secretary of defense, James Mattis, to make recommendations regarding elevation and the dual-hat issue. Congress influenced the Secretary's deliberations, having added (in the same National Defense Authorization Act for FY17) a provision in 10 USC. § 167b directing the executive branch to create "a unified combatant command for cyber operations forces."[54] Secretary Mattis thus decided to elevate the Command under Rogers's successor, who ultimately proved to be the US Army's Paul M. Nakasone. The succession occurred on May 4, 2018, the same day that US Cyber Command became a unified combatant command (when Nakasone, now general, pinned on his fourth star). Secretary Mattis made no decision on the dual hat, and thus General Nakasone served as both commander, USCYBERCOM, and director, NSA.

USCYBERCOM during this time engaged adversaries in a variety of offensive and defensive operations. For a sense of how its engagement evolved, it helps to glance at General Alexander's valedictory congressional testimony in 2014, in which he summarized developments and offered members a glimpse of the future shortly before retiring. His remarks were important as much for what he implied as for what he mentioned. Looking back over the previous decade, General Alexander noted:

> The level and variety of challenges to our nation's security in cyberspace differs somewhat from what we saw and expected when I arrived at Fort Meade [as Director, NSA] in 2005. At that time many people, in my opinion, regarded cyber operations as the virtual equivalents of either nuclear exchanges or commando raids. What we did not wholly envision were the sort of cyber campaigns we have seen in recent years. Intruders today seek persistent presences on military, government, and private networks (for the purposes of exploitation and disruption). These intruders have to be located, blocked, and extracted over days, weeks, or even months. Our notion of cyber forces in 2005 did not expect this continuous, persistent engagement, and we have since learned the extent of the resources required to wage such campaigns, the planning and intelligence that are essential to their success, and the degree of collaboration and synchronization required across the government and with our allies and international partners.[55]

There is a lot to unpack in this statement. Essentially it showed USCYBERCOM in 2014 pondering its need to operate at different strategic, operational, and tactical levels in the United States and abroad, and with varying degrees of freedom to maneuver in each.

Within Department of Defense systems in the United States and abroad, USCYBERCOM operated to defend the US military in cyberspace—a mission at least as important as its offensive mission. USCYBERCOM performed its defensive missions until 2018 under USSTRATCOM's Operation Gladiator Phoenix, which Secretary Gates had endorsed in early 2011.[56] While defenses improved, the "attack surface" provided by DoD's millions of network devices proved a tempting target that was too large to defend at all points. In 2013, for instance, cyber actors found a breach in the Navy Marine Corps Intranet (NMCI), a huge system that congressional staffers called "an unclassified but important and pervasive internal communications network."[57] Senator McCain asked then vice admiral Rogers at his confirmation hearing about the intrusion, which Rogers agreed was indeed a significant penetration:

> As a result, I directed a rather comprehensive operational response to that. That response was much broader than just be able to come back and say they're not there anymore. I wanted to use this as an opportunity to try to drive change. So we put a much more comprehensive, much longer term effort in place.[58]

Vice Admiral Rogers implied that traditional distinctions between operational and "business" systems had grown obsolete.[59] All systems had to be defended, because a penetration of even an unclassified network could cause significant disruption for the US military. Rogers's successor at Tenth Fleet (and the first woman to command a numbered fleet), Vice Admiral Jan Tighe, sketched the new dynamic in 2014:

> To some extent, the new cyber norm is a big challenge—every day we're under some type of threat. Fighting our networks every day and making sure we're providing for and operating networks that are secure is job one. That's looking at both the threats that are coming after us and the vulnerabilities that are inherent and always going to be there—and what we do to lower that risk calculus for the entire Navy, and share that knowledge and information with our other services and components to ensure the whole DoD is better.[60]

The Navy and (by implication) the larger military was undergoing a "cultural shift" toward recognizing this challenge, Vice Admiral Tighe explained, but while Navy leaders grasped the problem, not everyone shared this awareness. Indeed, "as you get lower down the food chain, it gets a lot more spotty—there are pockets of understanding, there are pockets of non-understanding."[61]

USCYBERCOM's offensive operations initially concentrated on terrorist targets—making them like the "commando raids" that General Alexander alluded to above. These missions increased in complexity and tempo as a result of Secretary of Defense Ashton Carter's decision to employ them in support of the overall coalition campaign (Operation Inherent Resolve) against the Islamic State in Iraq and Syria (ISIS). Admiral Rogers created a dedicated element for this fight in mid-2016, establishing Joint Task Force ARES under Army Cyber Command. As these efforts developed, senior officials grew less reticent in describing them to the public; Deputy Secretary of Defense Robert Work told reporters in April 2016 the US military was dropping "cyber bombs" on ISIS.[62]

The cyberspace campaign against ISIS received mixed reviews. Secretary of Defense Ashton Carter discounted it: "I was largely disappointed in Cyber Command's effectiveness against ISIS. It never really produced any effective cyber weapons or techniques."[63] This was not wholly the fault of USCYBERCOM, Carter added. When the Command did produce "something useful, the intelligence community tended to delay or try to prevent its use, claiming cyber operations would hinder intelligence collection"; thus "none of our agencies showed very well in the cyber fight." Secretary Carter's criticism may reflect his temporal vantage point; he left office in January 2017, just as the ground offensive against ISIS accelerated and supporting cyber effects increased. General Joseph L. Votel, commander of US Central Command, praised the conduct of cyberspace operations in support of his forces:

> At the tactical level, we have integrated [cyberspace operations] and fielded cyberspace capabilities to support Special Forces and, more recently, conventional ground forces. These tactical cyberspace and [electronic warfare] capabilities are synchronized with the ground scheme of maneuver providing an additional level of force protection to the warfighter by disrupting the adversaries' ability to command and control their forces in the battlespace.[64]

Then lieutenant general Stephen Townsend, who commanded Operation Inherent Resolve (2016–17), publicly noted a synergy between conventional and cyber missions for more than force protection. A reporter summarized one of General Townsend's examples of cyberspace operations enabling kinetic strikes:

> The coalition identified primary command posts ISIS was operating from but didn't know where alternate command posts were located. Rather than hitting the sites with missiles and having the militants be unknown for a while, Townsend said, they used "multidomain operations capabilities" from space and cyber to deny the enemy's primary command posts, forcing them to move and unveil alternate command posts. Once identified, the coalition struck the alternate command posts, working its way back to the primary sites. . . . While the operation overall was a success, Townsend said it took weeks to plan with only about a week of payoff.[65]

Both Secretary Carter and General Votel also hinted at cyberspace successes against ISIS propaganda and media outlets. One bright spot for cyberspace operations, Carter noted, was the "international effort to combat ISIS's hateful online presence with countermessaging, an effort that did achieve significant reach and had a real impact."[66] General Votel added that "our first success at true multidomain operations through synchronized lethal and nonlethal effects was against ISIS's critical media operatives; we denied key infrastructure and degraded their ability to execute external operations through social media."[67] Newly declassified documents offer some details on this campaign.

The most prominent and consequential operation against ISIS media efforts was code-named Operation Glowing Symphony (OGS) and began in late 2016. Occasional "commando raid" missions against ISIS had been episodic and lacked impact, noted National Public Radio reporter Dina Temple-Raston (in an article for which she was allowed to interview USCYBERCOM leaders and OGS participants):

> U.S. Cyber Command had been mounting computer network attacks against the group, but almost as soon as a server would go down, communications hubs would reappear. The ISIS target was always moving and the group had good operational security. Just physically taking down the ISIS servers wasn't going to be enough. There needed to be a psychological component to any operation against the group as well.[68]

Only a tightly synchronized campaign against ISIS media operations would work, but fortunately USCYBERCOM learned the group ran its media empire through a handful of accounts and servers. This was careless; ISIS network administrators had taken "a shortcut and kept going back to the same accounts to manage the whole ISIS media network. They bought things online through those nodes; they uploaded ISIS media; they made financial transactions. They even had file sharing through them."[69]

The complication for USCYBERCOM emerged from the globally distributed nature of those ISIS media nodes. The Command had authorization to support Operation Inherent Resolve where US forces were directly engaged in Iraq and Syria, but striking targets outside of this "area of responsibility" required extensive interagency coordination and White House approval. "The amount of informal meetings, briefings, and overall information sharing that occurred was extremely in-depth and time consuming for both USCYBERCOM and JTF ARES staffs," complained a USCYBERCOM after-action review.[70] Indeed, noted a briefing prepared in USCYBERCOM a couple weeks into OGS, interagency coordination was so cumbersome because "deconfliction processes were too immature to execute operational deconfliction."[71] One reporter summarized documents recently released by the Command under Freedom of Information Act requests as follows, quoting internal USCYBERCOM complaints:

> "Interagency policies and processes are not established to meet the demand for speed, scale, and scope required for effective cyberspace operations," the documents say. . . . In one case, deliberations in the National Security Council Principals Committee . . . took so long that they delayed some Glowing Symphony missions, possibly to the detriment of the operation's goals. "The time required to elevate and negotiate the Interagency non-concurs prevented USCYBERCOM from [redacted] as originally designed," one briefing document says.[72]

Nevertheless, OGS eventually won approval in the interagency review process and launched synchronized strikes against the key ISIS media nodes on a single night in November 2016, according to Temple-Raston's account for NPR:

> Once they had taken control of the 10 nodes, and had locked key people out of their accounts, ARES operators just kept chewing their way through the

target list. "We spent the next five or six hours just shooting fish in a barrel," [a USCYBERCOM operator] said. "We'd been waiting a long time to do that and we had seen a lot of bad things happen and we were happy to see them go away."[73]

General Nakasone, who commanded JTF-ARES that night, told Temple-Raston that the early results from OGS were impressive:

> Within the first 60 minutes of go, I knew we were having success. . . . We would see the targets start to come down. It's hard to describe but you can just sense it from being in the atmosphere, that the operators, they know they're doing really well. They're not saying that, but you're there and you know it.[74]

Over the next several months, OGS operators (with help from coalition partners) harassed the ISIS media outlets.[75] ISIS's online presence never vanished, of course, but such an unrealistic goal was never proposed as an objective of Glowing Symphony. OGS should be appraised for its contribution to Operation Inherent Resolve's overall goal of eradicating ISIS's territorial base and hampering its global reach. General Nakasone told Congress in early 2020 that ISIS had lost the initiative online:

> ISIS is now mostly confined to publishing text-only products, instead of their previous, gruesome multi-media products. These products used to be disseminated in multiple languages through mass-market platforms. Now, ISIS struggles to publish in non-Arabic languages and is confined to less-traditional messaging applications. Of course, the collapse of the physical caliphate made it harder for ISIS to operate online. But Cyber Command's efforts through JTF-ARES remain important to contesting ISIS's attempts at establishing a virtual caliphate as well.[76]

A USCYBERCOM after-action review called Glowing Symphony "the most complex offensive cyberspace operation that USCYBERCOM has undertaken to date."[77] The reviewers hinted that the operation would have lasting effects on the conduct of offensive cyberspace operations: "The scale and complexity of OGS has also allowed us to learn a number of lessons that will benefit the community as we move forward."[78] General Votel seemed to agree on the utility of lessons gained from the overall campaign in cyberspace: "These operations against ISIS have informed efforts across CENTCOM as well as other Combatant Commands."[79]

A New Operational Paradigm

Executive and legislative guidance in 2018 expanded the scope of military cyberspace activities in operations short of armed conflict. Congress affirmed that August via the National Defense Authorization Act for Fiscal Year 2019 that clandestine military operations against adversary activities in cyberspace could proceed as "traditional military activity" under the exceptions provided for in the covert action statute.[80] The same act encouraged "active defense" in cyberspace against Russia, China, North Korea, and Iran. This provision offered the president the authority to order US Cyber Command "to disrupt, defeat, and deter cyberattacks" by nations that conduct an "active, systematic, and ongoing campaign of attacks against the Government or people of the United States in cyberspace, including attempting to influence American elections and democratic political processes."[81] President Trump implemented these provisions in part through National Security Presidential Memorandum 13 (NSPM-13), the still-classified guidance that rescinded the procedures mandated by PPD-20.[82]

Cyber operations undertaken below the level of armed conflict would now be guided by the concept of "Persistent Engagement." USCYBERCOM proposed this in a public white paper that Admiral Rogers approved in March 2018. This Vision Statement, as it soon became known, summarized the rationale and thrust of the concept as follows:

> Defending forward as close as possible to the origin of adversary activity extends our reach to expose adversaries' weaknesses, learn their intentions and capabilities, and counter attacks close to their origins. Continuous engagement imposes tactical friction and strategic costs on our adversaries, compelling them to shift resources to defense and reduce attacks. We will pursue attackers across networks and systems to render most malicious cyber and cyber-enabled activity inconsequential while achieving greater freedom of maneuver to counter and contest dangerous adversary activity before it impairs our national power.[83]

Rogers's successor, General Nakasone, endorsed Persistent Engagement soon after taking command.[84] The Department of Defense in turn adopted and adapted it in the new DoD Cyber Strategy in September 2018, which applied the term "Defend Forward" to describe the overall strategy, within which Persistent Engagement would now be considered the operational approach. The secretary's principal cyber advisor, Kenneth Rapuano, explained this to Congress in early 2020:

> The Department defends forward by conducting operations that range from collecting information about hostile cyber actors, to exposing malicious cyber activities and associated infrastructure publicly, to directly disrupting malicious cyber actors. In order to be successful, we must be in malicious cyber actors' networks and systems and continually refresh our accesses, capabilities, and intelligence. Defending forward simultaneously puts "sand in the gears" of the offensive operations of malicious cyber actors, and generates the insights that enable our interagency, industry, and international partners to strengthen their resilience, address vulnerabilities, and defend critical networks and systems.[85]

By the time Assistant Secretary Rapuano testified, the department and USCYBERCOM could cite a recent application of the Defend Forward strategy. The 2016 US presidential race had been famously targeted by Russian cyber actors, who worked to sow division in the American electorate.[86] Their efforts corresponded with leaks of emails exfiltrated by Russian intelligence from the headquarters of the Democratic Party and released to the news media to embarrass Hillary Clinton's campaign.[87] To avoid a repeat of foreign interference with American democratic processes, the Trump administration two years later ordered the Department of Defense to assist the Department of Homeland Security (DHS) and the FBI in defending the upcoming midterm elections. National Security Advisor John Bolton revealed a week before the elections that the United States was conducting "offensive cyber operations" for this purpose; he had earlier explained, "Our hands are not tied as they were in the Obama administration."[88]

In this context, General Nakasone organized a "Russia Small Group" (RSG) to coordinate actions by USCYBERCOM and NSA in defense of the 2018 balloting. Together with interagency partners in DHS and the FBI, as he explained to Congress afterward, the RSG's effort "helped disrupt plans to undermine our elections." According to Nakasone:

> [USCYBERCOM in particular] executed offensive cyber and information operations. Each featured thorough planning and risk assessments of escalation and other equities. Each was coordinated across the interagency. And each was skillfully executed by our professional forces. Collectively, they imposed costs by disrupting those planning to undermine the integrity of the 2018 midterm elections.[89]

Gauging the success of the RSG is difficult without access to Russian records, but American observers regarded the lack of significant foreign interference in the midterms as a positive sign. "US officials believe the [American] disruption effort," observed columnist David Ignatius in the *Washington Post*, "has frazzled some of the Russian targets and may have deterred some interference during the midterms."[90] After hearing classified briefs on the operation, Senator Mike Rounds (R-SD) in early 2019 publicly asked General Nakasone if it would be fair to say that it was "not a coincidence that this election went off without a hitch." The general replied simply that "the security of the midterm election was the number one priority" at USCYBERCOM and NSA. Senator Richard Blumenthal (D-CT) rhetorically pressed this point, wishing that such operations could be more widely discussed: "Without going into any of the details, there are some successes that the American people should know happen[ed]."[91]

One particular RSG innovation, the "hunt forward" mission, continued after 2018. General Nakasone explained to Congress in early 2020 that USCYBERCOM's RSG element had deployed experts to search for intrusions on foreign governments' information systems:

> During multiple hunt forward missions, Cyber Command personnel were invited by other nations to look for adversary malware and other indicators of compromise on their networks. Our personnel not only used that information to generate insights about the tradecraft of our adversaries, but also to enable the defenses of both our foreign and domestic partners. And by disclosing that information publicly to private-sector cybersecurity providers, they took proactive defensive action that degraded the effectiveness of adversary malware.[92]

Assistant Secretary Rapuano added in the same hearing that CNMF's subsequent hunt-forward missions and malware releases (on the VirusTotal cybersecurity website) had allowed "organizations and individuals around the world to mitigate identified vulnerabilities, thereby degrading the efficacy of malicious tools and campaigns."[93] General Nakasone summarized the value of this effort later in 2020: "The net effect of the many hunt-forward missions that Cyber Command has conducted in recent years has been the mass inoculation of millions of systems, which has reduced the future effectiveness of the exposed malware and our adversaries."[94]

USCYBERCOM's faster operational tempo after 2016 produced a spiraling set of lessons regarding the intelligence, capabilities, personnel, and partners required for success in both defensive and offensive cyber operations. General Nakasone told NPR's Dina Temple-Raston that the experience gained by JTF-ARES in operating against ISIS influenced the direction of the Russia Small Group: "It provided us with a very, very good road map of what they might do in the future."[95] Lessons learned by the RSG, in turn, influenced the composition and tasking of a successor task force at USCYBERCOM and NSA, the Election Security Group (ESG), as General Nakasone explained to Congress in March 2020. "Last year," he noted, "we institutionalized our efforts from the Russia Small Group before the 2018 elections into an enduring Election Security Group for 2020 and beyond."[96] Partnerships and "persistent engagement with our adversaries," he predicted, would facilitate the ESG's work, "ensuring that exquisite intelligence drives tailored operations, which in turn generate more insight and opportunities to harden defenses and impose costs if necessary."[97] On Election Day 2020, General Nakasone gave a brief interview at which he spoke of a measure of success in the fact that the balloting saw no significant foreign disruption. He said he was "very confident in the actions that have been taken against adversaries over the last several weeks and several months to ensure they are not going to interfere in our elections."[98]

General Nakasone had suggested to Temple-Raston a few months earlier that USCYBERCOM had fulfilled its promise by attaining proficiency and permanence: "I think it's important for the American public to understand that as with any domain—air, land, sea, or space—cyberspace is the same way; our nation has a force."[99] The incoming Biden administration acknowledged the value of that force, with Secretary of Defense Lloyd Austin In his written confirmation testimony recognizing the "agility and seamless coordination" fostered by having a single commander over both USCYBERCOM and NSA, and pledging to mitigate "risk to both organizations" however they were to develop In the future.[100]

Conclusion

When Cyber Command was established in 2010, the operative assumption was that its focus should be on trying to prevent the military's networks from being infiltrated or disabled. But a reactive and defensive posture proved inadequate to manage evolving threats. Even as the military learned to better protect its networks, adversaries' attacks became more frequent, sophisticated, and severe. We learned that we cannot afford to wait for cyberattacks to affect our military networks. We learned that defending our military networks requires executing operations outside our military networks. The threat evolved, and we evolved to meet it.[101]

US Cyber Command has instantiated an idea that emerged and developed over four successive presidential administrations and roughly ten congresses. Simply put, that notion holds that advanced states must operate in cyberspace at scale and in real time—which means they must use military entities to fill key national requirements. Various threats envisioned when USCYBERCOM began operations in 2010 have since come to pass: command elements now work every day against determined and capable cyber actors seeking to penetrate Department of Defense information systems and disrupt key military and national functions.

USCYBERCOM's course was not inevitable, however, and the nation could have found other solutions to the dilemma of operating in cyberspace. The Command at the time of this writing has a budget of $596 million (for FY20) and 1,778 military and civilian personnel (plus contractors). At the start of 2020, the Command rostered 5,094 active-duty service members and civilians in its Cyber Mission Force.[102] Such resources might have come together in very different ways; indeed, USCYBERCOM might not have existed all. If it had not been created, the US government could, and probably would, have improvised various work-arounds for defensive and offensive functions. But at what cost in time, losses, and risk?

In this context, it is disconcerting even to imagine how much less secure the United States would be without USCYBERCOM's defensive efforts. There is no reason to believe that the highly capable adversaries that confront America and its democratic partners today would have abandoned or even slackened their respective quests to develop dangerous cyberspace capabilities if the United States had unilaterally forsaken (or even substantially slowed) its building of military cyberspace elements after the middle of the 2000s. Indeed, had the United States done so, its strategic situation in 2020 would be grave. Even with current challenges, however, the federal government still retains control of its information systems, and US commanders around the world can still control their forces. These capabilities can no longer be taken for granted. They owe their safety in no small part to the functioning of USCYBERCOM.

USCYBERCOM's offensive achievements, on the other hand, appear more modest. Here one can point to, as evidence of success, the strategic (if not yet permanent) defeat of ISIS and the seeming determination of adversaries to keep cyber conflict under the threshold of armed conflict. The idea that the Command has offensive power, moreover, probably has had some deterrent effect, supplementing the massive strength of America's nuclear and conventional forces. Finally, the Command's genesis and growth probably have also persuaded other actors to build their own military cyber forces. With that probability acknowledged, it seems safe to say that USCYBERCOM has kept the nation safer.

The Command's Cyber Mission Force played a key role in both its offensive and defensive achievements. It created teams that offered predictable increments of power in cyberspace and mandated readiness and capabilities to bring the teams to a higher plane, making them more responsive and agile in their missions. Whether USCYBERCOM has influenced allies, partners, and adversaries to imitate it is a question that must be left for later scholars, but there has been no lack of foreign interest in the CMF model.

What does the future hold? USCYBERCOM will continue; there are no realistically foreseeable circumstances in which the US government decides it does not need to defend its military networks in a joint manner or to supplement DoD's combat operations with missions in cyberspace. On the contrary, USCYBERCOM could receive significant augmentations of resources and authorities, perhaps even midwifing the creation of a new military service, a "Cyberspace Force." Assuming these alternatives define the limits of the possible for USCYBERCOM, then it seems probable the

Command will continue more or less on its present course for the next several years.

Notes

1. The definition of "operating" is broad and imprecise. As the Joint Chiefs of Staff explain:

   > [The operational art is] a thought process to mitigate the ambiguity and uncertainty of a complex [operational environment] and develop insight into the problems at hand. Operational art also promotes unified action by enabling [joint force commanders] and staffs to consider the capabilities, actions, goals, priorities, and operating processes of interagency partners and other interorganizational participants, when they determine objectives, establish priorities, and assign tasks to subordinate forces. It facilitates the coordination, synchronization, and, where appropriate, the integration of military operations with activities of other participants, thereby promoting unity of effort.

   Joint Chiefs of Staff, Joint Pub. 3-0, Joint Operations II-3 (2018).

2. JOINT CHIEFS OF STAFF, THE NATIONAL MILITARY STRATEGY OF THE UNITED STATES OF AMERICA: A STRATEGY FOR TODAY; A VISION FOR TOMORROW 18 (2004).
3. I summarized these in Michael Warner, *Notes on the Evolution of Computer Security Policy in the US Government, 1965–2003*, 37 IEEE ANNALS HIST. COMPUTING 8 (2015). For an example of the sophistication that could be applied in the 1970s, see STAFF OF S. COMM. ON GOV'T OPERATIONS, 95TH CONG., COMPUTER SECURITY IN FEDERAL PROGRAMS 135–38 (1977).
4. Anthony Rutkowski, *Marking the 30th Anniversary of the Internet and Cybersecurity Treaty*, CIRCLEID (June 22, 2020).
5. The exercise, based on a hypothetical clash with Iran, was described in ROGER C. MOLANDER, ANDREW S. RIDDILE, AND PETER A. WILSON, RAND, STRATEGIC INFORMATION WARFARE: A NEW FACE OF WAR xii, xvii (1996).
6. *Id.*
7. ALBERT J. EDMONDS, C4I ISSUES, PRESENTATION TO THE PROGRAM ON INFORMATION RESOURCES POLICY, CENTER FOR INFORMATION POLICY RESEARCH, HARVARD UNIVERSITY, IN GUEST PRESENTATIONS, at 181–92 (1994); *see also* ALBERT J. EDMONDS, INFORMATION SYSTEMS SUPPORT TO DOD AND BEYOND, PRESENTATION TO THE PROGRAM ON INFORMATION RESOURCES POLICY, CENTER FOR INFORMATION POLICY RESEARCH, HARVARD UNIVERSITY, IN GUEST PRESENTATIONS, at 194 (1996).
8. OFFICE OF THE UNDERSEC'Y OF DEF. FOR ACQUISITION & TECH., REPORT OF THE DEFENSE SCIENCE BOARD TASK FORCE ON INFORMATION WARFARE-DEFENSE, EXEC. SUMMARY (1996); *see also* JOINT CHIEFS OF STAFF, JOINT PUB. 3-13.1, JOINT DOCTRINE FOR COMMAND AND CONTROL WARFARE I-4 (1996); Rebecca Slayton, *What Is a Cyber Warrior? The Emergence of US Military Cyber Expertise, 1967–2018*, 4 TEX. NAT'L SECURITY R. 62, 79–80 (Winter 2020–2021).

9. GEN. ACCT. OFF., INFORMATION SECURITY: COMPUTER ATTACKS AT DEPARTMENT OF DEFENSE POSE INCREASING RISKS 4 (1996); *see also* Dan Verton, *IT Lessons Emerge from Kosovo*, FCW (Aug. 31, 1999).

10. James Adams, *Virtual Defense*, 80 FOREIGN AFF. 98 (2001).

11. *Critical Information Infrastructure Protection: The Threat Is Real: Hearing before the S. Comm. on the Judiciary, Subcomm. on Tech. and Terrorism*, 106th Cong. 14 (1999) (statement of Michael A. Vatis, Fed. Bureau of Investigation).

12. US DEP'T OF DEF., DoD DIRECTIVE NO. TS 3600.1: INFORMATION WARFARE (1992); US DEP'T OF DEF., DoD DIRECTIVE NO. S-3600.1: INFORMATION OPERATIONS (1996); *see also* JOINT CHIEFS OF STAFF, JOINT PUB. 3-13.1, JOINT DOCTRINE FOR COMMAND AND CONTROL WARFARE (1996).

13. *See* JOINT CHIEFS OF STAFF, JOINT PUB. 3-12, CYBERSPACE OPERATIONS (2018) (freeing offensive and defensive cyberspace missions from the doctrinal category of "information operations"). I discuss the evolution of relevant doctrine in Michael Warner, *Notes on Military Doctrine for Cyberspace Operations in the United States, 1992–2014*, CYBER DEF. REV. (Aug. 27, 2015).

14. OFFICE OF THE PRESIDENT, DEFENDING AMERICA'S CYBERSPACE: NATIONAL PLAN FOR INFORMATION SYSTEMS PROTECTION 41, 49 (2000).

15. US STRATEGIC COMMAND, JOINT CONCEPT OF OPERATIONS FOR GLOBAL INFORMATION GRID NETOPS, III (2005); *see also* Bradley K. Ashley and Gary Jackson, *Information Assurance through Defense in Depth*, 3 IA NEWSLETTER 3 (1999).

16. US DEP'T OF DEF., INFORMATION OPERATIONS ROADMAP 44–49 (2003).

17. *Id.*

18. Memorandum from Robert M. Gates, Sec'y of Def., to Dep't of Def. Leadership, Establishment of a Subordinate Unified U.S. Cyber Command under U.S. Strategic Command for Military Cyberspace Operations (June 23, 2009).

19. Michael Warner, *US Cyber Command's Road to Full Operational Capability, in* STAND UP AND FIGHT! THE CREATION OF US SECURITY ORGANIZATIONS, 1942–2005, at 131 (Ty Seidule and Jacqueline E. Whitt eds., 2015).

20. *Id.*

21. *Id.*

22. Keith B. Alexander, *Building a New Command in Cyberspace*, 5 STRATEGIC STUD. Q. 3, 4, 10 (2011).

23. *Department of Defense Authorization for Appropriations for Fiscal Year 2016 and the Future Years Defense Program: Hearing on S. 1376 before the S. Comm. on Armed Servs., Subcomm. on Intelligence, Emerging Threats and Capabilities*, 114th Cong. 415 (2015) [hereinafter 2015 Senate Hearings] (statement of Admiral Michael S. Rogers, Commander, US Cyber Command).

24. In the American military system, the armed services raise, train, and equip forces, which they then "present" to the combatant commands that employ them in actual operations.

25. *Department of Defense Authorization for Appropriations for Fiscal Year 2013 and the Future Years Defense Program: Hearing on S. 3254 before the S. Comm. on Armed*

Servs., 112th Cong. 971 (2012) [hereinafter 2012 Senate Hearings] (statement of Gen. Keith B. Alexander, Commander, US Cyber Command).

26. *Information Technology and Cyber Operations: Modernization and Policy Issues to Support the Future Force: Hearing before the H. Comm. on Armed Servs., Subcomm. on Intelligence, Emerging Threats and Capabilities*, 113th Cong. 63 (2013) [hereinafter 2013 House Hearings] (statement of Gen. Keith B. Alexander, Commander, US Cyber Command).

27. *Id.* at 70.

28. *Id.* at 71.

29. *Department of Defense Authorization for Appropriations for Fiscal Year 2014 and the Future Years Defense Program: Hearing on S. 1197 before the S. Comm. on Armed Servs.*, 113th Cong. 199–200 (2013) (statement of Gen. Keith B. Alexander, Commander, US Cyber Command); *see also* OFFICE OF INSPECTOR GEN., US DEP'T OF DEF., US CYBER COMMAND AND MILITARY SERVICES NEED TO REASSESS PROCESSES FOR FIELDING CYBER MISSION FORCE TEAMS 2, 12–13 (2015). Rep. Jim Langevin commented: "I understand that Cyber Command [CYBERCOM] is beginning to organize itself into mission teams, which is an exciting step. But the manpower cost is enormous and the education and training requirement significant. This is going to take, obviously, a lot of work to get right." 2013 House Hearings, *supra* note 26, at 2.

30. *Information Technology and Cyber Operations: Modernization and Policy Issues in a Changing National Security Environment: Hearing before the H. Comm. on Armed Servs., Subcomm. on Intelligence, Emerging Threats and Capabilities*, 113th Cong. 3 (2014) [hereinafter 2014 House Hearings] (written statement of Gen. Keith B. Alexander, Commander, US Cyber Command).

31. *Id.* at 43–44.

32. *See* 2013 House Hearings, *supra* note 26, at 85.

33. US DEP'T OF DEF., QUADRENNIAL DEFENSE REVIEW 2014, at 41 (2014).

34. 2014 House Hearings, *supra* note 30, at 5 (written statement of Gen. Alexander).

35. *Id.*

36. 2015 Senate Hearings, *supra* note 23, at 416 (statement of Admiral Rogers).

37. OFFICE OF THE PRESIDENT, FACT SHEET ON PRESIDENTIAL POLICY DIRECTIVE 20 (2013); *see also* David Alexander, *Hagel, Ahead of China Trip, Urges Military Restraint in Cyberspace*, REUTERS (Mar. 28, 2014).

38. Secretary of Defense Leon Panetta, Remarks on Cybersecurity to the Business Executives for National Security (Oct. 11, 2012).

39. *Id.*

40. 2012 Senate Hearings, *supra* note 25, at 8 (statement of Gen. Alexander).

41. *See* 2013 House Hearings, *supra* note 26, at 87.

42. *Id.* at 65.

43. *United States Cybersecurity Policy and Threats: Hearing before the S. Comm. on Armed Servs.*, 114th Cong. 24–25 (2015) (statement of Admiral Michael S. Rogers, Commander, US Cyber Command).

44. *Id.* at 2 (statement of Sen. John McCain).

45. *Department of Defense Authorization for Appropriations for Fiscal Year 2017 and the Future Years Defense Program: Hearing on S. 2943 before the S. Comm. on Armed Servs.*, 114th Cong. 462 (2016) [hereinafter 2016 Senate Hearings] (statement of Admiral Michael S. Rogers, Commander, US Cyber Command).

46. JOINT CHIEFS OF STAFF, *supra* note 2, at 18 (emphasis added).

47. 2016 Senate Hearings, *supra* note 45, at 5 (statement of Admiral Rogers).

48. Jordana Mishory, *Rogers: CYBERCOM Should Be a Fully Unified Command, but Stay Dual-Hatted with NSA*, INSIDE DEFENSE (Apr. 5, 2016); *see also* Jordana Mishory, *Lawmakers Want to Elevate CYBERCOM, Review Relationship with NSA*, INSIDE DEFENSE (Apr. 25, 2016).

49. *Cybersecurity, Encryption and United States National Security Matters: Hearing before the S. Comm. on Armed Servs.*, 114th Cong. 45 (2016) (statement of Sen. John McCain).

50. Ellen Nakashima, *Pentagon and Intelligence Community Chiefs Have Urged Obama to Remove the Head of the NSA*, WASH. POST (Nov. 19, 2016).

51. *Id.*

52. Press Release, White House, Office of the Press Sec'y, Press Conference by President Obama in Lima, Peru (Nov. 20, 2016).

53. Press Release, White House, Office of the Press Sec'y, Statement by the President on Signing the National Defense Authorization Act for Fiscal Year 2017 (Dec. 23, 2016).

54. National Defense Authorization Act for Fiscal Year 2017, Pub. L. No. 114-328, Div. A, Title IX, § 923(a), 130 Stat. 2000, 2357 (2016).

55. 2014 House Hearings, *supra* note 30, at 3 (written statement of Gen. Alexander).

56. Warner, *supra* note 19, at 131.

57. Warner, *supra* note 3, at 16.

58. *Hearing to Consider Pending Nominations of Gen. Paul J. Selva & Vice Admiral Michael S. Rogers: Hearing before the S. Comm. on Armed Servs.*, 113th Cong. 15 (2014) (statement of Gen. Paul J. Selva, US Air Force).

59. Warner, *supra* note 3, at 16.

60. Amber Corrin, *Fighting to the New Norm at Fleet Cyber Command*, C4ISR & Networks (May 8, 2014).

61. Sean Lyngaas, *Sending Cyber Sense Down the Navy Chain of Command*, FCW (May 6, 2014).

62. *U.S. Military Says Using Cyber Capabilities against Islamic State*, REUTERS (Apr. 12, 2016) (describing Deputy Secretary Work as stating that "U.S. and coalition forces were putting pressure on Islamic State from all directions, using every possible military capability, including cyber attacks, to defeat the group").

63. ASH CARTER, BELFER CENTER, A LASTING DEFEAT: THE CAMPAIGN TO DESTROY ISIS 33 (2017).

64. Joseph L. Votel, David J. Julazadeh, and Weilun Lin, *Operationalizing the Information Environment: Lessons Learned from Cyber Integration in the USCENTCOM AOR*, 3 CYBER DEF. REV. 18 (2018).

65. Gen. Townsend was then commander of Army Training and Doctrine Command, and he spoke to the Association of the US Army. *See* Mark Pomerleau, *Army Leaders Need More Payoff from Cyber*, FIFTH DOMAIN (May 24, 2018).

66. CARTER, *supra* note 63, at 33.

67. Votel et al., *supra* note 64, at 18.

68. Dina Temple-Raston, *How the U.S. Hacked ISIS*, NPR (Sept. 26, 2019).

69. *Id.*

70. US CYBERCOM, USCYBERCOM 120-DAY ASSESSMENT OF OPERATION GLOWING SYMPHONY 3 (2017).

71. The same document states that a new process was in place by November 22. US CYBERCOM, OPERATION GLOWING SYMPHONY: J3 AAR OBSERVATIONS (2016).

72. Shannon Vavra, *Top Secret Documents Show Cyber Command's Growing Pains in its Mission Against ISIS*, CYBERSCOOP (Jan. 21, 2020).

73. Temple-Raston, *supra* note 68.

74. *Id.*

75. Stephanie Borys, *Licence to Hack: Using a Keyboard to Fight Islamic State*, ABC [Australian Broadcasting Corporation] (Dec. 17, 2019).

76. *The Fiscal Year 2021 Budget Request for US Cyber Command and Operations in Cyberspace: Hearing before the H. Comm. on Armed Servs., Subcomm. on Intelligence, Emerging Threats and Capabilities*, 116th Cong. 47 (2020) [hereinafter 2020 House Hearings] (statement of Gen. Paul M. Nakasone, Commander, US Cyber Command).

77. US CYBERCOM, USCYBERCOM 30-DAY ASSESSMENT OF OPERATION GLOWING SYMPHONY (2016).

78. *Id.*

79. Votel et al., *supra* note 64, at 18.

80. John S. McCain National Defense Authorization Act for Fiscal Year 2019, Pub. L. No. 115-232, § 1632, 132 Stat. 1636, 2123–24 (2019) (stating that a "clandestine military activity or operation in cyberspace shall be considered a traditional military activity for the purposes of section 503(e)(2) of the National Security Act of 1947 (50 USC. § 3093(e)(2))").

81. *See id.* § 1642.

82. Dustin Volz, *White House Confirms It Has Relaxed Rules on U.S. Use of Cyberweapons*, WALL STREET J. (Sept. 20, 2018).

83. US CYBER COMMAND, ACHIEVE AND MAINTAIN CYBERSPACE SUPERIORITY: COMMAND VISION FOR US CYBER COMMAND 6 (2018).

84. William T. Eliason, *An Interview with Paul M. Nakasone*, 92 JOINT FORCE Q. 5 (2019).

85. 2020 House Hearings, *supra* note 76, at 28 (statement of Kenneth Rapuano, Assistant Sec. of Def. for Homeland Def. and Global Sec. and Principal Cyber Advisor).

86. Indictment, *United States of America v. Internet Research Agency LLC*, No. 1:18-c00032-DLF (D.D.C. filed Feb. 16, 2018); *see also* Scott Shane, *These Are the Ads Russia Bought on Facebook in 2016*, N.Y. TIMES (Nov. 1, 2017).

87. Deputy Att'y Gen. Rod Rosenstein, Remarks Announcing the Indictment of Twelve Russian Intelligence Officers for Conspiring to Interfere in the 2016 Presidential Election through Computer Hacking and Related Offenses (July 13, 2018).

88. Ellen Nakashima and Paul Sonne, *Bolton Says US Is Conducting 'Offensive Cyber' Action to Thwart Would-Be Election Disrupters*, WASH. POST (Oct. 31, 2018); *see also* Ellen Nakashima, *White House Authorizes 'Offensive Cyber Operations' to Deter Foreign Adversaries*, WASH. POST (Sept. 20, 2018).

89. 2020 House Hearings, *supra* note 76, at 46 (statement of Gen. Nakasone).

90. David Ignatius, *The US Military Is Quietly Launching Efforts to Deter Russian Meddling*, WASH. POST (Feb. 7, 2019).

91. *Hearing to Review Testimony on United States Special Operations Command and United States Cyber Command in Review of the Defense Authorization Request for Fiscal Year 2020 and the Future Years Defense Program: Hearing before the S. Comm. on Armed Servs.*, 116th Cong. 19, 20 (2019) (statement of Sen. Richard Blumenthal).

92. 2020 House Hearings, *supra* note 76, at 46 (statement of Gen. Nakasone).

93. *Id.* at 34 (statement of Assistant Sec'y of Def. Rapuano).

94. Paul M. Nakasone and Michael Sulmeyer, *How to Compete in Cyberspace: Cyber Command's New Approach*, FOREIGN AFF. (Aug. 25, 2020).

95. Temple-Raston, *supra* note 68.

96. 2020 House Hearings, *supra* note 76, at 45 (statement of Gen. Nakasone).

97. *Id.* at 46.

98. David Sanger and Julian Barnes, *U.S. Tried a More Aggressive Cyberstrategy, and the Feared Attacks Never Came*, N.Y. TIMES (Nov. 9, 2020).

99. Temple-Raston, *supra* note 68.

100. *Hearing to Consider Pending Nominations Before the S. Comm. on Armed Servs.*, 117th Cong. 61 (2021 (written statement of General Lloyd Austin, Nominee for Secretary of Defense, U.S. Department of Defense in response to advance policy questions).

101. Nakasone and Sulmeyer, *supra* note 94.

102. 2020 House Hearings, *supra* note 76, at 43 (statement of Gen. Nakasone).

PART II
DOMESTIC FRAMEWORK

4

The Domestic Legal Framework for US Military Cyber Operations

Robert M. Chesney

Conventional wisdom holds that Congress has abandoned its duty regarding the government's war powers. It is not hard to understand why. Between the agelessness and flexibility of the 2001 and 2002 Authorizations for Use of Military Force[1] (AUMFs) and periodic unilateral uses of military force in Libya, Syria, and Iraq, the executive branch appears to act largely at its own discretion when it comes to conventional military operations. But matters are different in the cyber domain. With little fanfare and less public notice, Congress and the executive branch have cooperated effectively over the past decade to build a legal architecture for military cyber operations. This framework reflects recurring and constructive congressional engagement. The resulting structure is far less familiar to most observers than its cousins—those architectures associated with conventional military operations and intelligence activities—but is no less important. This is particularly true in light of the Pentagon's commitment to the "Defend Forward" operational model.

Context: Defending Forward

Amid the fallout from the coronavirus pandemic, a group of senators from both major political parties dispatched a remarkable letter in April 2020 to General Paul Nakasone, commander of US Cyber Command (USCYBERCOM). The senators expressed "profound concerns" about "sophisticated hacking operations" targeting pandemic-related health services and research programs. In particular, they cited activity attributed to Russia, China, Iran, and North Korea. The letter concluded by asking Nakasone to "evaluate further necessary action to *defend forward* in order to detect and deter" such activity.[2]

What did they mean by "Defend Forward"? For anyone who had been following the evolution of the policy and legal frameworks associated with USCYBERCOM in recent years, the phrase was a familiar and significant one.

In the spring of 2018, Nakasone released a "command vision" document calling for USCYBERCOM to sustain an operational tempo of continuous—or persistent—engagement with adversaries in the cyber domain. Of course, those adversaries were already persistently engaging the United States through intrusions into US networks. The real novelty in Nakasone's vision was his insistence that USCYBERCOM need not remain in a defensive crouch, defending largely or even solely from within its own networks. Instead, it could and should focus on "defending forward as close as possible to the origin of adversary activity [in order to extend] our reach to expose adversaries' weaknesses, learn their intentions and capabilities, and counter attacks close to their origins." By defending forward, Persistent Engagement could be made to impose "tactical friction and strategic costs on our adversaries" rather than vice versa.[3] The 2018 Defense Department Cyber Strategy, released later that year, affirmed the concept, "direct[ing] the Department to defend forward."[4]

Introduction of the Defend Forward strategy sparked a great deal of debate.[5] For some, the phrase appeared euphemistic, masking what might better be described as offensive operations. A Chinese scholar (and former People's Liberation Army colonel) insisted that the new posture would be destabilizing.[6] But for others, defending forward was a welcome development that was, if anything, long overdue given the growing array of hostile cyber activities directed against US interests.[7]

In the two years since the release of General Nakasone's command vision, we have had several glimpses of Defend Forward in action. Some examples—such as USCYBERCOM's forward deployment to help countries like Macedonia, Ukraine, and Montenegro defend their networks—have been innocuous (though still important) in that they did not necessarily involve operational activity in "red space"—that is, in an adversary's systems.[8] But the broader potential of the concept also has been on display. At the time of the 2018 midterm elections, for example, USCYBERCOM disrupted the networks of the "Internet Research Agency," the infamous Russian troll farm known for its efforts to spread propaganda in the United States during the 2016 election, and directly messaged individual Russian hackers to make clear that the United States was aware of their roles and identities.[9]

Against this backdrop, it is not hard to understand the real meaning of the senators' request that Nakasone explore opportunities to "Defend Forward" in the face of Russian, Chinese, Iranian, and North Korean hacking directed at pandemic-related medical and research entities in the United States. Simply put, the senators wanted USCYBERCOM operating inside the networks of those adversaries, at the very least to identify such activities but if necessary to go further and shut them down at their source.[10]

Whether or not USCYBERCOM conducts such high-stakes operations, the prospect draws attention to a critical question that lurks in the background of out-of-network operations in general but especially those targeting the systems of foreign governments: What is the domestic legal framework that governs them?

The question matters in circumstances beyond the prospect of responding to pandemic-related espionage, of course. USCYBERCOM conducted dozens of operations in foreign networks to counteract efforts by adversaries to impact the 2020 election, for example, including "eleven hunt forward operations in nine different countries."[11] We also should not lose sight of the fact that USCYBERCOM's capacity for out-of-network operations is not limited to the defend-forward scenario. As illustrated by the summer 2019 crisis in which USCYBERCOM carried out disruption operations against Iranian assets after Iran shot down a US Navy surveillance drone (providing what proved to be a de-escalatory response at a time when the White House reportedly was considering missile strikes), there are times when such operations are intended to achieve effects unrelated to detecting, deterring, or disrupting an adversary's operations.[12]

In short, the desire to conduct such operations will arise in a wide array of settings, and in many of them the stakes will be quite high. This places considerable pressure on the domestic legal framework that governs such operations.

In the pages that follow, I describe that framework in detail, emphasizing how Congress and the executive branch have collaborated in recent years to create a system that facilitates—but also monitors—precisely the sort of operations described above. I do so by breaking the framework down into four constituent elements:

- Authorization rules (which allocate decision-making authority between Congress and the executive branch);

- Process rules (which impact the decision-making process within the executive branch);
- Transparency rules (which compel the executive branch to share information with Congress); and
- Substantive rules (which prohibit certain actions).

Authorization Rules

Military cyber operations, like military operations in general, raise complex separation of powers questions. In what circumstances has Congress authorized such actions by statute, thus rendering constitutional issues moot? To what extent can the executive branch act in the absence of statutory authorization, relying instead on authority from Article II of the Constitution? And what about Congress's major effort to curb executive branch military unilateralism, the War Powers Resolution?

Existing Statutory Authority

At the time of this writing in the spring of 2021, three statutes provide some degree of authorization for military cyber operations. Two are generally applicable military authorizations while the third is specifically focused on USCYBERCOM.

Let's start with the two generally applicable military authorizations. First and most famously, the 2001 AUMF[13] remains on the books. It authorizes the president to use "all necessary and appropriate force" against groups and individuals whom the chief executive determines to have come within the AUMF's scope. Second, the 2002 AUMF,[14] relating to Iraq, also remains active. Together, they eventually became the basis for the full spectrum of military operations directed against the Islamic State in Syria and Iraq. These operations came to include an array of cyber activities conducted by Joint Task Force-Ares.[15] In contexts properly associated with either or both of these AUMFs, therefore, the simplest answer to the war powers question is that Congress has authorized the use of military force generally, and this encompasses operations that happen to be carried out in the cyber domain.

However broad the two AUMFs may be, though, they are not limitless. And so it matters whether there is any separate statute authorizing military cyber operations in other settings.

The answer is yes: Section 1642 of the John McCain National Defense Authorization Act (NDAA) for fiscal year 2019[16] eliminates any doubt about the authority of the executive branch to conduct cyber activities in response to certain provocations. Specifically, Section 1642 authorizes USCYBERCOM to "take appropriate and proportional action in foreign cyberspace" in order "to disrupt, defeat, and deter" ongoing adversarial activity in the cyber domain, though only where the National Command Authority—the president and secretary of defense or their deputized alternates—determines that two conditions have been met:

(1) there is "an active, systematic, and ongoing campaign of attacks against the Government or people of the United States in cyberspace, including attempt[s] to influence American elections and democratic political processes" and

(2) the entity deemed responsible for the campaign is Russia, China, North Korea, or Iran.

The importance of Section 1642 for the defend-forward concept should be apparent. Section 1642's triggering conditions read like a road map to the most strategically significant areas in which the defend-forward concept might be employed: those involving systematic adversarial activity conducted by any of the four countries usually considered primary threats to the United States in the cyber domain. This is not an accident. The act's legislative history makes clear that Congress intended for it to prune away any lingering concerns about whether USCYBERCOM has the authority to conduct cyber operations in these circumstances.

Note, however, that the relative specificity of Section 1642 raises a further question: Do its narrowing conditions imply that all *other* USCYBERCOM operations of the defend-forward or offensive varieties are illegal, absent fresh legislation or a colorable AUMF argument? No. The best understanding of Section 1642 is that it functions as a belt-and-suspenders provision, mooting separation-of-powers objections that might otherwise arise. It does not, however, concede that those objections would have been well-taken without Section 1642. (Certainly nothing in the text or legislative history suggests such an understanding by Congress or the president.) From that point of view, the question that arises for any operation that falls outside the scope of the AUMFs and Section 1642 is the same question that existed prior to Section 1642's passage: Does a given operation even require congressional authorization in the first place, or does Article II of the Constitution confer adequate authority for the executive branch to conduct the operation?

Authority to Conduct Cyber Operations Without Statutory Authorization

The Office of Legal Counsel (OLC) has in recent decades, under administrations of both major political parties, employed a consistent framework to determine when a military operation requires separation-of-powers analysis. That framework is described in both an Obama-era analysis of the legality of using force against the Qaddafi regime in Libya in 2011 and again in a Trump-era analysis involving force against the Assad regime in Syria in 2018. In each one, the OLC takes the position that the separation-of-powers issue arises only when the military activity in question reaches the level of "war." In this instance, *war* is a constitutional term of art turning on a variety of factors, including whether service members' lives are at risk on a sustained basis.[17] As the Syria opinion puts it: "Consistent with that early recognition, we have repeatedly distinguished between limited hostilities and prolonged and substantial military engagements, typically involving exposure of U.S. military personnel to significant risk over a substantial period."[18] Under that analysis, the OLC concluded that a substantial (though localized) kinetic strike on a Syrian military airfield did not rise to the level of war, nor did the much more substantial and sustained campaign of airstrikes that ultimately played a key role in toppling the Qaddafi regime.

So long as *that* is the framework for determining when congressional authorization might be required, military operations conducted in the cyber domain, standing alone, will not likely qualify as war, barring the most extreme fact patterns. (For example, it is conceivable that an operation that would deprive a large population of electricity for a long period would entail enough anticipated harm to compel a different conclusion despite the absence of boots on the ground, though even that is unclear under the OLC's exceedingly narrow approach.) Put simply, most if not all cyber operations, when analyzed standing alone, will fall short of this standard and thus not require a constitutional war powers analysis.

What About the War Powers Resolution?

What of the War Powers Resolution of 1973?[19] The WPR is best understood as an attempt by Congress both to reinforce a particular vision of the Constitution's distribution of war powers and to generate a set of new transparency rules increasing congressional awareness of the executive branch's more significant decisions relating to the use of the military. I will review those rules in the appropriately labeled section below. For now, I will focus on how the attempt to reinforce Congress's conception of the distribution of war powers relates to USCYBERCOM's out-of-network operations.

The WPR addresses the distribution of war powers in two ways. First, it provides a statement of Congress's views on the doctrinal boundaries between the respective roles of Congress and the president in this area. Second, it attempts to put teeth into this vision by establishing a deadline for the withdrawal of US armed forces from certain situations absent sufficient congressional authorization.

Let's turn first to the WPR's claims about the Constitution. As a mere statute, of course, the WPR cannot actually alter the Constitution's allocation of military authority between Congress and the president. But since the details of the Constitution's allocation are themselves contested (as noted earlier), this part of the WPR might bear weight in interpretive calculations with some audiences, and thus it warrants brief consideration here.

The WPR opens with an assertion of Congress's view of when the president has the authority "to introduce United States Armed Forces into hostilities, or into situations where imminent involvement in hostilities is clearly indicated by the circumstances." Specifically, it claims that there are three such circumstances: "(1) a declaration of war, (2) specific statutory authorization, or (3) a national emergency created by attack upon the United States, its territories or possessions, or its armed forces."[20] First, note that this list seems incomplete insofar as it omits, for example, the use of the armed forces to protect citizens abroad. That said, the provision hinges entirely on the meaning of *hostilities*. This is a statutory term of art, and if it is interpreted to be coextensive with the OLC's understanding of the constitutional term of art *war*, then much if not all of the potential tension between this language and the OLC's constitutional analysis described above simply drops out.

Perhaps not surprisingly, the executive branch has interpreted *hostilities* that way. The best illustration, including a summation of past executive interpretations, may be the testimony in 2011 before the Senate Foreign Relations Committee of Harold Koh, at the time the State Department legal advisor. He explained the Obama administration's interpretation of *hostilities* for the purpose of analyzing the WPR's implications in the United States' continuing role in the Libya conflict.[21] Citing the course of practice since 1973 along with a consistent interpretive practice by the executive branch, Koh identified a set of factors that compelled the conclusion that America's actions did not constitute the introduction of our armed forces into hostilities—notwithstanding the existence of armed conflict and direct participation by the United States in the form of airstrikes. Specifically, the mission had a very limited purpose; the risk of US casualties was almost non-existent since our role did not include boots on the ground; the risk of unintended escalation also was almost non-existent for the same reason; and the military means employed were quite limited (and certainly far short of a "full military engagement"). Koh cautioned, however, that the answer might be different were any of these factors not present.

As with the interpretation of *war* for purposes of constitutional analysis, the executive branch's restrictive interpretation of *hostilities* is contested. But insofar as the executive interpretation continues to prevail in practice, as it did in Libya, it is clear that military activities in the cyber domain, analyzed as a stand-alone proposition, would not constitute the introduction of US forces into hostilities. The executive branch's decision to prioritize in the analysis the physical exposure of US service members foreordains this outcome.

In light of this analysis, the second feature of the WPR's attempt to regulate the distribution of war powers—that is, its attempt to establish an automatic deadline for the withdrawal of US forces in the form of a sixty-day "clock"—has little practical relevance for military operations in the cyber domain, at least when one analyzes such operations on a stand-alone basis. If cyber operations do not constitute the introduction of armed forces into "hostilities" (or into situations where hostilities are imminent) in the first place, the sixty-day clock never starts running.

A note of caution before moving on from these authorization rules: It should be obvious that the executive branch's restrictive approach to both "war" and "hostilities" depends upon an increasingly dated understanding of the manner and means through which the United States projects military power. Disruptive technological changes with respect to the array of capabilities for delivering kinetic attacks without placing service members in range of hostile fire, not to mention the emergence of the cyber domain in its entirety, are producing an ever-larger set of circumstances in which the United States can exercise coercion without putting troops in harm's way. To be sure, this dynamic should not change the "war" and "hostilities" analyses if in both cases the ultimate determining factor is indeed whether service members' lives are in immediate danger. But if instead considerations of escalation risk drive these analyses, their logical foundations are eroding. All of which is another reason to continue to pay attention to the potential applicability of the AUMFs and Section 1642 of the NDAA when analyzing particular operational proposals, since those authorities obviate the "war" and "hostilities" questions where they apply.

Process Rules

Proceeding on the assumption that the executive branch as a whole has the authority to conduct a particular military operation in the cyber domain (whether based on Section 1642, one of the AUMFs, or Article II), the next question is whether the domestic legal architecture requires compliance with certain decision-making procedures. More specifically, does the law require the approval of a particular person before the operation can take place?

The idea that certain operations cannot occur without the approval of particular persons is hardly foreign to military operations. From the commander in chief on down, it is common to use this approach to ensure that matters of particular sensitivity are decided only at higher levels in the chain. It is a matter of policy preference, expressed in the form of rules of engagement, execute orders, orders from the combatant commander, and so forth. What we are not accustomed to seeing in the military context is *legislation* that effectively does the same thing, mandating that certain military decisions be made only with the approval of, say, the commander in chief.

Contrast that with the legal framework governing covert action—which, as we shall see, has special relevance for the cyber domain. Famously, Congress in 1974 broke new ground (in the so-called Hughes-Ryan Amendment)[22] by leveraging the power of the purse to insist upon a documentable presidential role in authorizing covert action. Specifically, Congress forbade the expenditure of funds by or on behalf of the Central Intelligence Agency (CIA) for overseas operations intended for purposes other than intelligence collection, absent what would come to be known as a presidential "finding." This was a quaintly coy way of describing covert action (i.e., operations intended to cause overseas effects where the sponsoring role of the US government is not meant to be apparent or acknowledged) and mandating that the president take personal, written responsibility for approving such operations.[23]

Why did Congress do this? The *effect* was to eliminate presidential "deniability"—that is, the situation in which a president might plausibly claim to have not known of a program. But the *reason* for doing it? The normative justification for mandating a presidential finding—the public policy gain from doing so—is that the certainty of presidential accountability naturally tends to harness the self-interest of an administration, increasing incentives for it to screen out bad or unduly risky ideas ex ante. Indeed, over time this has resulted in the executive branch's adoption of vetting procedures through which proposed covert action programs are filtered within the larger National Security Council system.[24] Those procedures, notably, have a substantial interagency element to them, giving rise to the possibility that agencies with different equities, such as the State Department, will have a chance to weigh in on the wisdom and desirability of a proposed operation. The end result is a system that is less quick and efficient than what existed before and one that might even defeat some good-but-risky ideas. Yet on the whole it strikes a reasonable balance in a situation that can entail unusually serious risks in the event of a miscalculation, risks ranging from diplomatic friction to war.

If Congress had defined the scope of the covert action framework in institutional terms, applying it solely to deniable operations conducted by the Central Intelligence Agency, then we would now move on to ask whether Congress has adopted (or should adopt) something comparable for military operations in the cyber domain. But Congress did not so limit the covert-action framework. Rather, it created a two-step definition of covert action that left ample room for debate over its scope. At step one, the definition is inclusive of all parts of the US government: "covert action" as a default matter applies to *any* part of the US government that implements an operation intended to have an overseas effect with the sponsoring role of the United States neither apparent nor acknowledged. But at step two, the statute excludes various situations, including "activities the primary purpose of which is to acquire intelligence" as well as "traditional . . . military activities" (often referred to as TMA).[25]

Note the relevance of the intelligence-collection exemption for military activities in the cyber domain. There are many circumstances in which penetration of (and persistence within) someone else's network can fairly be described as activities whose "primary purpose" is intelligence collection, even though it is foreseeable that the very same access at some point might be used to generate an effect. If and when a decision is made to seek such an effect, of course, some other exception—most likely TMA—must apply or else the covert-action default rules will snap into place. But prior to that point, and for so long as it can be said fairly that the operation is primarily about acquiring information, the intelligence exception resolves the issue and obviates the need to wrestle with the question of just what counts as TMA in the cyber domain. Then again, as I will explain in more detail, characterizing an operation in this way rather than TMA potentially implicates the transparency rules that require keeping the two congressional Intelligence Committees fully apprised of significant intelligence activities. This fact alone might provide a significant incentive (from the military's perspective) for applying the TMA label instead.

All that being the case, what actually counts as TMA in the cyber domain? Had Congress simply used the shorter phrase "military activities" in crafting this exception, it would not be a difficult question. But that is not what Congress did. The *T* in *TMA* stands for *traditional*, and this term has invited debate over the scope of the exception. That debate in turn has cast a shadow over the decision-making process for some military activities in the cyber domain.[26]

The TMA-scope issue is not just a cyber-domain matter. It first became a significant issue in the post-9/11 period thanks to non-cyber, special-operations activities taking place away from combat zones. It has since become an issue with respect to military operations in the cyber domain as well.

In the two settings, the stakes are the same: If an operation is "in scope" for the TMA exception, it can be approved without a written presidential "finding" (and without the need for reporting to the House and Senate Intelligence Committees, in accordance with the transparency rules discussed in the next section). But if it does *not* qualify for the TMA exception, the opposite is true.

Complicating matters further, if the TMA exception does not apply to a proposed operation, an issue also might arise under Executive Order

12333's default rule providing that the CIA shall have responsibility for conducting "covert action" outside of contexts covered by a declaration of war or at least a notification under the War Powers Resolution.[27] The president, of course, can choose to direct the military to conduct the covert activity instead but in that case would need to make a specific determination on that point—thus ensuring elevation of the issue to the White House level in any event.

In recent years, such issues have proved to be a significant source of friction in the approval of military operations in the cyber domain. Such operations by their nature require concealment, at least at the stage of establishing and maintaining access to a system (though concealment may or may not remain necessary at the point of seeking an operational effect via that access), and at times they involve maintaining a presence on systems or networks in contexts in which it would be preferable not to acknowledge American responsibility in the event the presence is detected.

The fact that confusion would arise about TMA's applicability in this circumstance is not surprising. First, there has long been disagreement between those who focus on the word *traditional* in TMA (and thus attempt to resolve the scope question by pondering whether cyber operations are sufficiently analogous to operations historically conducted by the military and those who, instead, focus on the specific definitional compromise that Congress and the administration of President George H. W. Bush worked out on this point at the time of the relevant statutory enactment (in which case TMA applies to any operation that is [a] both commanded and implemented entirely by service members and [b] conducted in a context in which hostilities are ongoing or in which operational planning for hostilities has been approved by the National Command Authority). Second, even if everyone accepted and tried to apply the latter approach, hard questions might (and presumably did) arise with respect to whether a particular proposed operation relates sufficiently to a situation for which operational planning has been approved. Particularly in the context of gray zone engagements in the cyber domain, it is not hard to imagine circumstances for which that connection might be tricky to establish.

The first public sign of congressional concern about this issue emerged in 2011. The National Defense Authorization Act for fiscal year 2012, enacted in December 2011, was supported by a conference committee report that offered the following observation:

The conferees recognize that because of the evolving nature of cyber warfare, there is a lack of historical precedent for what constitutes traditional
military activities in relation to cyber operations and that it is necessary
to affirm that such operations may be conducted pursuant to the same
policy, principles, and legal regimes that pertain to kinetic capabilities. The
conferees also recognize that in certain instances, the most effective way to
deal with threats and protect U.S. and coalition forces is to undertake offensive military cyber activities, including where the role of the United States
Government is not apparent or to be acknowledged.[28]

Those words seemed cryptic to those who were unaware of the ongoing
disputes over the scope and relevance of the TMA exception. But understood
in that context, the passage was reasonably clear: The conferees wanted to establish that the TMA exception does indeed apply to deniable military cyber
operations. Unfortunately, the corresponding language in the statute itself
fell short of the mark. Rather than state the TMA point with clarity, Section
954 of the NDAA fiscal year 2012 states that military "offensive operations
in cyberspace" are "subject to . . . the policy principles and *legal regimes* that
the Department follows for kinetic capabilities, including the law of armed
conflict."[29] Read in context with the legislative history, the reference to "legal
regimes" could be understood as a veiled attempt to settle the TMA question
in favor of its applicability. But without that context, this is anything but obvious. The issue accordingly persisted.

The language of Section 954 also gave rise to two other issues. First, even
if Section 954 had been clear enough to settle the TMA issue related to military "offensive operations in cyberspace," a question of scope would nevertheless arise with respect to which cyber operations count as offensive.
The current-day language associated with "defending forward" underscores
the point: Not all out-of-network activities are necessarily offensive in nature. Second, Section 954 had the potential to give rise to further uncertainty because it also contains language confirming the general authority of
the Defense Department to conduct such operations "upon direction by the
President." That formulation might have been read to require presidential authorization on an operation-by-operation basis, in which case Section 954
would have been somewhat akin to the covert-action process rules associated
with presidential "findings" (but without the statutory requirement that the
authorization be in writing and without the transparency-rule requirement

of sharing the finding with Congress). The language was ambiguous on this point, however, and could just as well be read to mean that presidential authorization was required as a more general matter.

At any rate, Congress remained concerned about the TMA/covert-action issue, and in 2018 it returned to the subject with a far more specific and effective statutory intervention.

The conference report for the NDAA for fiscal year 2019 makes clear that Congress once again felt that TMA-scope issues were generating unjustified friction for military cyber operations. The conferees lamented that

> [t]he Department of Defense faces difficulties within the interagency in obtaining mission approval. One of the challenges routinely confronted by the Department is the perceived ambiguity as to whether clandestine military activities and operations, even those short of cyber attacks, qualify as traditional military activities as distinct from covert actions requiring a Presidential Finding. As a result, with respect to actions that produce effects on information systems outside of areas of active hostilities, the Department of Defense has been limited to proposing actions that could be conducted overtly on attributable infrastructure without deniability—an operational space that is far too narrow to defend national interests. The conferees see no logical, legal, or practical reason for allowing extensive clandestine traditional military activities in all other operational domains (air, sea, ground, and space) but not in cyberspace. It is unfortunate that the executive branch has squandered years in interagency deliberations that failed to recognize this basic fact and that this legislative action has proven necessary.[30]

In a bid to resolve this problem conclusively, Section 1632 of the NDAA for fiscal year 2019 first specifies that any activity constituting a "clandestine military activity or operation in cyberspace" necessarily qualifies as TMA.[31] This clarification alone was not enough to settle the question, however. Choosing to use the word *clandestine* as a way to describe the type of operations at issue added an unnecessary layer of difficulty. The word *clandestine*, after all, does not normally connote deniability, but simply secrecy. The two concepts are distinct. *Secrecy* means that an operation is meant to be undetected. *Deniability* implies that the US government's sponsoring role is not meant to be apparent or acknowledged. Without further clarification, therefore, the label "clandestine military activity" would not necessarily encompass the very set of actions (i.e., deniable cyber operations) that gave rise to the TMA/ covert-action dispute in the first place.

Some further definitional language, accordingly, was needed in order for the "clandestine" test to have the intended effect despite the term's usual meaning. And Section 1632 duly provided it. The phrase "clandestine military activity or operation in cyberspace" was specially defined there as referring to military operations in cyberspace that not only are clandestine in the traditional sense—that is, intended to go undetected—but also in the distinct sense of deniability. More specifically, the statute provided that the phrase must be understood to cover activities "marked by, held in, or conducted with secrecy, where the intent is that the activity or operation will not be apparent *or acknowledged publicly.*"[32]

Having thus swept all instances of deniable military cyber operations into the TMA exception (without respect to whether the operation would better be understood as offensive or defensive in nature), Congress might have stopped. But having just ensured that no presidential findings would be required (and, by extension, that no reporting to the Intelligence Committees would be necessary), Congress then imposed a substitute rule of process.

Specifically, the same section (1632) also imposed a requirement that *either* the president or the secretary of defense authorize the operation in question.[33] To be sure, this is not as demanding as a stipulation that the president alone make the necessary determination, nor does it require that the authorization be reduced to writing. And given that the authorization can be made at the secretary of defense level, it follows that this provision does not necessarily harness the self-interest of the White House in a way that might ineluctably lead to increased vetting, including voices from outside the military. Nonetheless, it is not meaningless to insist upon such high-level authorizations.

A final note: Section 1632 contains one final condition, and it is one that proves to be a bit of a mystery. In the relevant part, Section 1632 provides that the operation in question be carried out

(i) as part of a military operation plan approved by the President or the Secretary in anticipation of hostilities *or as directed by the President or the Secretary;*

(ii) to deter, safeguard, or defend against attacks or malicious cyber activities against the United States or Department of Defense information, networks, systems, installations, facilities, or other assets; or

(iii) in support of information related capabilities.[34]

At first blush, the existence of that final three-pronged condition—the trio of scenarios in which a secret and deniable military cyber operation might qualify for automatic inclusion in the TMA category—implied that the same old debate could continue to rage as to *other* scenarios. And perhaps the range of "other" scenarios might be broad. But on closer inspection, it seems quite the contrary. Focus on the first of the three eligible scenarios, with an emphasis on the language italicized above. The phrasing "or" sets it off from the first part of the sentence, making it an additional, fourth, eligible scenario. And it is a broad one indeed, covering any situation in which the president or secretary of defense has directed that an operation take place. Given that another part of Section 1632 already requires the approval of either of those two individuals, it appears that this part might have no practical impact.

Transparency Rules

This brings us to a topic already mentioned a few times above: transparency rules.

Transparency rules oblige executive branch actors to provide certain information to Congress (or to subparts of Congress), if not also to the public. In theory, they serve the important purpose of making it more feasible for Congress to conduct oversight of secret, highly sensitive activities and thus to be in a reasonable position to legislate or take other actions as needed. They also have the salutary effect of ensuring that the executive branch actors understand that someone from outside their immediate sphere will to some extent be aware of what they do (thus incentivizing greater care). Indeed, in extreme cases, transparency rules might allow these actors to intervene and stop undesirable activity. And while it may be that transparency rules at times also constitute a vector through which others are able to stop truly desirable activities without good enough reasons, that trade-off provides an essential element of legitimacy in a situation in which we want to have both rule of law in a democratic society and also the secrecy needed for national-security activities to be carried out effectively.

As noted above, we long ago struck such a balance in regard to covert action. In particular, for decades we have required that presidential findings for covert action be shared with the Intelligence Committees and so too with important updates to existing findings. We have parallel transparency rules for important intelligence-collection activities, moreover, and in the course of actual practice a great deal more oversight takes place through interactions at the staff level.

With the TMA issue seemingly settled in favor of *not* treating military cyber operations as covert action, the covert-action and intelligence-collection transparency rules fall by the wayside. Congress has not left matters there, however. Instead, it has gradually constructed a series of alternative transparency rules, geared toward the military and running to the Senate and House Armed Services Committees.

As was the case with the TMA debate, attention to this issue originated not with cyber-domain activities but, rather, with special operations activities conducted in physical space. In particular, it originated with a desire to craft replacement transparency rules concerning the killing or capturing of individuals that might take place outside of certain recognized areas of hostilities. In a series of NDAA provisions enacted over a period of years, Congress designated such scenarios "sensitive military operations" and mandated periodic reporting about them to both Armed Services Committees.[35]

We now have something analogous for the cyber-domain activities described above in the preceding section. In 2017, Congress borrowed from the "sensitive military operation" transparency rule to create a nearly identical rule for "sensitive military *cyber* operations" (SMCO).[36] Under the SMCO rule, the secretary of defense must submit a written notification to the Armed Services Committees within forty-eight hours of any military cyber operation that meets the SMCO definition.

That definition is complex, alas, and Congress has changed in repeatedly since 2017. As amended most recently, a military cyber operation is a reportable SMCO when two sets of conditions are met.[37]

First, the operation must be intended to have an effect on a foreign terrorist organization or a foreign government (including the armed forces and any proxy forces thereof), but only insofar as the armed forces of the United States are *not* currently involved in hostilities with that targeted organization or government. Thus, an operation targeting the Islamic State or al Qaeda would not be capable of qualifying for SMCO status. This is true, notably, even if a particular operation was intended to cause disruptive effects on a server located in a neutral or even an allied country (a significant departure from the version of this statute that existed prior to 2021). Further, the statute contains an intriguing (and perhaps disturbing) additional clause, extending that same rule to the curious (and perhaps hypothetical) situation in which the United States does not *publicly* acknowledge that its armed forces are involved in hostilities, even though they are.

For those military cyber operations that *do* satisfy the first SMCO criterion, the analysis then proceeds to a second set of considerations before SMCO status attaches: the operation must also entail one of five special-risk scenarios. Specifically, the operation in question must involve a medium (or higher) collateral effects estimate, intelligence gain/loss, risk of political retaliation, probability of detection (assuming concealment is intended), or actual collateral effects.[38] In this way, the SMCO transparency rule functions to ensure that Congress is notified about relatively risky operations (though not, as noted above, when the targeted adversary is one with which the United States is engaged in hostilities), while sparing the Defense Department from reporting burdens where risks are low (or in any event where hostilities are under way). This requirement is the most nuanced of the military cyber transparency rules. But it is not the only one.

First, back in 2013, Congress instituted an obligation for the secretary of defense to provide "quarterly briefings on all offensive and significant military operations in cyberspace carried out by the Department of Defense during the immediately preceding quarter."[39] The briefings must be broken down with reference to each geographic and functional command's separate experience during the reporting period and must include an "overview of authorities and legal issues applicable to the operations, including any relevant legal limitations."[40] They also must address "any hostile cyber activity directed at the command"[41] in question and "any interagency activities and initiatives relating to" the command's cyber operations.[42]

Second, in 2017, Congress imposed a separate transparency rule requiring the secretary of defense to notify the Armed Services Committees on a quarterly basis regarding the application of the Pentagon's "weapons review" process to cyber capabilities—that is, the process of ex ante review of the legality of novel weapons as required by Department of Defense Directive 5000.01. "Weapon" in this context is a term of art defined to encompass only those cyber capabilities where the effect is intended to injure or kill personnel or cause physical damage.[43] As for those capabilities, Congress requires forty-eight hours' notification of their actual use as a weapon, regardless of whether the SMCO rule would apply.[44]

Third, in late 2019 Congress enacted a different sort of transparency rule. As noted above, one of the most important authorization rules is Section

1642 of the NDAA enacted in late 2018, which eliminates any doubt that USCYBERCOM can conduct out-of-network operations in response to systematic hostile cyber activity conducted by Russia, China, Iran, or North Korea. Critically, that provision contains an embedded process rule in that it expressly lodges the authority to decide to act under color of that provision solely at the level of the National Command Authority. Then, in the NDAA for fiscal year 2020, Congress enacted a related transparency rule. Henceforth, the secretary of defense must give notice within fifteen days if the president delegates to the secretary any authority related to military operations in cyberspace that would otherwise be lodged at the National Command Authority level. That includes a description of the authority so delegated. Further, the same provision requires the secretary to notify the Armed Services Committees of any "concepts of operation" that the secretary may then approve under that delegated authority, again within fifteen days. Notably, this operational notification must include an array of particulars, including any actual activities that are conducted or planned to be conducted, the objectives to be achieved, the countries where the activities may occur, and details regarding any associated orders the secretary may have issued.[45]

Further research (in particular, interviews with persons involved in operationalizing these transparency rules over time) is needed to assess how well this complex array of overlapping rules is functioning, both in absolute terms and in comparison to the analogous rules for oversight of covert action and collection. For now, it is enough to observe that Congress rapidly built a parallel transparency rule architecture at much the same time it was endeavoring to shield military cyber operations from the covert action and intelligence legal frameworks, thus addressing in advance what otherwise might have been a significant objection to the latter project.

A final note, regarding the WPR, is in order. In addition to the distribution-of-powers rules discussed above, the WPR is known for its transparency rules. Specifically, it requires consultation and notification to Congress regarding the introduction of US armed forces into hostilities or situations in which hostilities are imminent. And though some administrations have questioned the constitutionality of that statutory obligation, all have chosen to comply with, or at least act "consistent with," that obligation. But due to the narrow reading of "hostilities" emphasized above, the use of cyber capabilities standing alone—especially without boots on the ground—would not trigger this obligation.

Substantive Rules

The legal frameworks that regulate national-security-related activities include not just rules of authorization, process, and transparency but also "substantive" rules, which simply prohibit certain actions or outcomes. Sometimes those rules are sourced in our domestic law, and sometimes they flow from international law. Sometimes it is both. With detainee treatment, for example, there are important domestic-law substantive rules (such as the Torture Act and the War Crimes Act) and also important international-law rules (the Geneva Conventions, for example).

Critically, the United States simply has not adopted *cyber-specific* domestic laws of this kind. There is no statute or executive order, for example, that flat-out forbids the implanting of malware in industrial control systems associated with the electrical grid in a foreign country. Nor have there been any significant proposals for statutes of that kind. Any applicable substantive rules, as a result, are those that apply more generally rather than being cyber specific. And there are no obvious examples of general domestic laws likely to significantly constrain USCYBERCOM operations of the sort described earlier, such as operations meant to disrupt Russian election interference or respond to Iranian military actions in and around the Persian Gulf.

What of international law as a source of substantive constraints? This is a topic that several other authors in this book will address. Here, I will make two observations.

First, we do not as yet have any *cyber*-specific international laws constituting substantive constraints. There is, to be sure, much talk of cyber *norms*—that is, a hoped-for convergence of international opinion regarding the moral or policy propriety of this or that action. But that should not be confused with the formation of customary international law, let alone a treaty. What we *do* have, instead, are general-purpose international law concepts that can be applied to cyber-domain operations as much as any other type of operation (though precisely how those general rules apply to cyber operations is, in some respects, hotly contested).

Second, there is a subtle but potentially important connection between those international law rules and the domestic legal frameworks described earlier in this chapter. A federal statute provides that activities formally qualifying as "covert action" must comport with the Constitution of the United States and federal statutes, while conspicuously omitting a similar obligation to comport with international law.[46] A cyber activity that constitutes TMA by definition does not come within the scope of that arrangement, however, and the Defense Department in any event takes the position that all of its operations must comply with international law (at least as a default matter). As a result, some might argue that USCYBERCOM's Defend Forward operations cannot violate a rule of international law unless one of two things happens. First, to overcome such an argument, USCYBERCOM personnel could be assigned temporarily to act under color of CIA covert-action ("Title 50") authority, much as occurred with SEAL Team Six in the operation that killed Osama bin Laden. This would drape USCYBERCOM with the legal architecture of covert action, for that operation. Second, the president could issue a directive expressly authorizing USCYBERCOM to conduct a particular operation as covert action as such, without CIA involvement, as outlined in Executive Order 12,333.[47]

Does anything turn on this potential difference between covert action and TMA status? Such considerations are merely academic insofar as USCYBERCOM's Defend Forward operations are compatible with international law, after all. And it does seem likely that most such operations are indeed compatible with well-settled rules of international law such as the UN Charter's prohibition on the "use of force" in international affairs and the customary international law prohibition on coercive intervention, given the narrow scope of those rules.

Serious problems would arise, however, insofar as the government might at some point decide to accept the existence of a broad rule of "sovereignty" sweeping far beyond the protections of the coercive intervention and use-of-force categories. Several chapters in this book address this issue. Notably, both the Goldsmith/Loomis chapter and my own chapter on the United Kingdom conclude that the United States does not recognize such a broad rule of sovereignty, at least not yet. So long as that is the case, then the potential interplay between America's domestic legal architecture and international law should not constitute an obstacle to most USCYBERCOM Defend Forward operations. Were the US position on the international law question to change, however, the domestic legal implications for such operations might prove to be significant. Depending on how broad a conception of a rule of sovereignty one embraces, the range of Defend Forward operations implicated might be wide—perhaps even wide enough to bring Congress once more onto the field, resulting in some future NDAA provision extending the covert-action model of international law compliance in a way that would apply expressly to at least some cyber TMA.

Conclusion

The domestic legal framework for military cyber operations is surprisingly robust, considering its recent vintage. Far more quickly than it did for earlier institutional innovations such as the emergence of the CIA's covert action capability, Congress has responded to the maturation of USCYBERCOM by adopting relatively detailed rules of authorization, process, and transparency. The resulting framework has gone far toward eliminating otherwise-debilitating obstacles to the ability of USCYBERCOM to carry out its mission through out-of-network operations, though issues remain. At the same time, it imposes increasingly detailed oversight mechanisms that one hopes will induce desirable care and caution in making use of this greater freedom of action. Time will tell if the interaction of these rules results in a stable and effective equilibrium.

Notes

1. Pub. L. No. 107-40, 115 Stat. 224 (2001); Pub. L. No. 107-243, 116 Stat. 1498 (2002).
2. Letter from Sen. Richard Blumenthal et al. to Christopher Krebs, Director, Cybersecurity and Infrastructure Security Agency, Department of Homeland Security, and Gen. Paul M. Nakasone, Commander, US Cyber Command (April 20, 2020) (emphasis added).
3. US Cyber Command, Achieve and Maintain Cyberspace Superiority 6 (2018).
4. US Dept. of Defense, Summary: Department of Defense Cyber Strategy 2018, at 7 (2018) (emphasis removed).
5. See, e.g., Monica Kaminska, Strauss Center, "Workshop Report: A Transatlantic Dialogue on Military Cyber Operations," August 13, 2019 (summarizing discussions from a two-day workshop in Amsterdam involving experts from military, civilian, and academic institutions from seven countries); Jacquelyn G. Schneider, "Persistent Engagement: Foundation, Evolution and Evaluation of a Strategy," LAWFARE (May 10, 2019).
6. Lyu Jinghua, *A Chinese Perspective on the Pentagon's Cyber Strategy: From 'Active Cyber Defense' to 'Defending Forward,'* LAWFARE (Oct. 19, 2018). For my response to that scholar, see Robert M. Chesney, *An American Perspective on a Chinese Perspective on the Defense Department's Cyber Strategy and 'Defending Forward,'* LAWFARE (Oct. 23, 2018).
7. See H.R. Rep. 115-874, at 1049 (2018) (Conf. Rep.).
8. See, e.g., Mark Pomerleau, *Here's How Cyber Command Is Using 'Defend Forward,'* FIFTH DOMAIN (Nov. 12, 2019).

9. See Ellen Nakashima, *U.S. Cyber Command Operation Disrupted Internet Access of Russian Troll Factory on Day of 2018 Midterms*, WASH. POST (Feb. 26, 2019); Julian E. Barnes, *U.S. Begins First Cyberoperation Against Russia Aimed at Protecting Elections*, N.Y. TIMES (Oct. 23, 2018).

10. This echoes the recent announcement that the Australian Signals Directorate (roughly equivalent to the American NSA) has been conducting disruption operations targeting criminal hacking crews that are exploiting the pandemic with ransomware attacks targeting Australians. See Senator the Hon. Linda Reynolds CSC, "On the Offensive Against COVID-19 Cyber Criminals," press release, April 7, 2020. Doing the same to state-sponsored attackers, of course, involves greater risks.

11. *Hearing on U.S. Special Operations and Cyber Commands in Review of the Defense Authorization Request for Fiscal Year 2022 and the Future Years Defense Program Before the S. Comm. on Armed Servs.*, 117th Cong. (2021) (statement of Gen. Paul Nakasone, Commander, U.S. Cyber Command and Director, National Security Agency and Chief, Central Security Service); *see e.g.*, Ellen Nakashima, *U.S. Undertook Cyber Operation Against Iran as Part of Effort to Secure the 2020 Election*, WASH. POST (Nov. 3, 2020).

12. Robert M. Chesney, *The Legal Context for CYBERCOM's Reported Operations Against Iran*, LAWFARE (Jun. 24, 2019).

13. Pub. L. No. 107-40, 115 Stat. 224 (2001).

14. Pub. L. No. 107-243, 116 Stat. 1498 (2002).

15. For a collection of declassified documents concerning JTF-Ares, see "Joint Task Force ARES and Operation GLOWING SYMPHONY: Cyber Command's Internet War Against ISIL," National Security Archive, August 13, 2018.

16. Pub. L. No. 115-232, 132 Stat. 1636, 2132 (2018).

17. See, e.g., Memorandum Opinion from Caroline D. Krass, Principal Deputy Assistant Attorney General, Office of Legal Counsel, to the Attorney General, "Authority to Use Military Force in Libya," April 1, 2011; Memorandum Opinion from Steven A. Engel, Office of Legal Counsel, to the Counsel to the President, "April 2018 Airstrikes Against Syrian Chemical-Weapons Facilities," May 31, 2018.

18. Engel, *supra* note 17 (internal citations and quotation marks omitted).

19. 50 U.S.C. §§ 1541–48 (2018).

20. 50 U.S.C. §§ 1541(c).

21. For the full text of his statement, and the colloquy at the hearing, see Libya and War Powers: Hearing Before the S. Comm. on Foreign Relations, 112th Cong. 89 (2011) (statement of Harold Koh, Legal Advisor, US Department of State). For a summary of his testimony, see Robert M. Chesney, *An Overview of Harold Koh's Testimony on the WPR at Today's SFRC Hearing*, LAWFARE (Jun. 28, 2011).

22. Section 32 of the Foreign Assistance Act of 1974, Pub. L. No. 93-559, 88 Stat. 1804, amended the Foreign Assistance Act of 1961, Pub. L. No. 87-195, 75 Stat. 424 (codified as amended in scattered sections of 22 U.S.C.), adding a new section 662 as described in the text above.

23. The provision is now found in 50 U.S.C. § 3093.

24. See, e.g., National Security Decision Directive 159, Covert Action Policy Approval and Coordination Procedures, January 18, 1985.

25. 50 U.S.C. § 3093(e)(1)–(2).

26. For an in-depth exploration of this debate and its practical relevance, see Robert M. Chesney, *Military-Intelligence Convergence and the Law of the Title 10/Title 50 Debate*, 5 J. OF NAT. SECURITY L. & POL'Y, 539 (Jan. 24, 2012).

27. Executive Order No. 12,333, 46 Fed. Reg. 59,941, at § 1.7(a)(4) (Dec. 4, 1981) ("No agency except the Central Intelligence Agency [or the Armed Forces of the United States in time of war declared by the Congress or during any period covered by a report from the President to the Congress consistent with the War Powers Resolution, Public Law Number 93-148] may conduct any covert action activity unless the President determines that another agency is more likely to achieve a particular objective.").

28. H.R. Rep. 112-329, at 686 (2011) (Conf. Rep.) (commenting on Section 954).

29. National Defense Authorization Act for Fiscal Year 2012, Pub. L. No. 112-81, § 954(1), 125 Stat. 1298, 1551 (2011) (emphasis added).

30. H.R. Rep. 115-874, at 1049 (2018) (Conf. Rep.) (commenting on Section 1632).

31. 10 U.S.C. § 394(c) (2018).

32. 10 U.S.C. § 394(f)(1)(A) (emphasis added).

33. 10 U.S.C. § 394(f)(1).

34. 10 U.S.C. § 394(f)(1)(B) (emphasis added).

35. For an overview, see Robert M. Chesney, *Expanding Congressional Oversight of Kill/Capture Ops Conducted by the Military: Section 1036 of the NDAA*, LAWFARE (Dec. 8, 2016).

36. 10 U.S.C. § 395 (2018) (emphasis added).

37. The codified version of this rule is 10 U.S.C. 395, but the details of its current iteration are found in Section 1702 of the National Defense Authorization Act for Fiscal Year 2021. 10 U.S.C. §395 (2018), *amended by* National Defense Authorization Act for FY 2021, Pub. L. 116-283, § 1702 (2021).

38. 10 U.S.C. § 395(c)(1)(C)(i). Originally, Congress specified that such operations triggered reporting requirements only if they constituted either "offensive" operations or operations to respond to "ongoing or imminent" threats. In late 2019, Congress abandoned that effort, albeit in an awkward way. The statute now specifies that the operation in question must be either offensive or defensive in nature. That pairing covers the waterfront, meaning that the language no longer is doing any work. See Pub. L. No. 116-92, § 1632, 133 Stat. 1198, 1746 (2019) (codified as amended in 10 U.S.C. § 395) (replacing the "ongoing or imminent" threat language).

39. 10 U.S.C. § 484(a) (2018).

40. 10 U.S.C. § 484(b)(2).

41. 10 U.S.C. § 484(b)(1).

42. 10 U.S.C. § 484(b)(3).

43. *See* DEP'T OF ARMY, REG. 27-53, LEGAL REVIEW OF WEAPONS AND WEAPON SYSTEMS (Sep. 23, 2019) (defining "cyber weapon or cyber weapon system.").

44. 10 U.S.C. § 396 (2018).

45. Pub. L. No. 116-92, § 1642, 133 Stat. 1198, 1751–52 (2019) (This provision now appears in the notes accompanying 10 U.S.C. § 394).

46. 50 U.S.C. § 3093(a)(5) (2018).

47. As described *supra* in endnote 27, Executive Order 12,333 provides as a default matter that only the CIA may conduct covert action unless there is a declaration of war or a situation covered by a WPR-based notification to Congress, though it also invites departures from this rule upon a determination by the president that in a given instance "another agency is more likely to achieve a particular objective." *See* Executive Order No. 12,333, 46 Fed. Reg. 59,941, at § 1.7(a)(4) (Dec. 4, 1981).

5

Cyberattacks and Constitutional Powers

Matthew C. Waxman

The United States has one of the world's strongest and most sophisticated capabilities to launch cyberattacks against adversaries. How does the US Constitution allocate power to use that capability? And what does that allocation tell us about appropriate executive-legislative-branch arrangements for setting and implementing cyber strategy?

The term "cyberattack" is often used loosely. In this chapter, I define a cyberattack as action that involves the use of computer code to disrupt, degrade, destroy, or manipulate computer systems or networks or the information on them.[1] I am not including cyber operations that are purely for information gathering or to map foreign networks in preparation for future cyberattacks.

This definition of cyberattack still includes a wide array of operations. On one end are attacks on computer systems that have effects—including kinetic, sometimes violent ones—outside those systems. Examples include the Stuxnet attack that brought down some of Iran's nuclear centrifuges and the 2017 NotPetya attack, widely attributed to Russia, that targeted major Ukrainian companies and government agencies but spread widely and disabled computers—as well as commerce dependent on them—around the globe.[2] At the other end are the types of low-level and often discrete attacks that appear to be contemplated by the United States Defend Forward concept. Examples include infiltrating adversary networks and deleting or corrupting data, or US Cyber Command's operations that disrupted the networks of Russia's infamous Internet Research Agency troll farm in the run-up to the 2018 US midterm elections.[3] There are of course many possibilities in between.

This chapter offers a way to think about the constitutional distribution of powers between the president and Congress governing the use of US cyberattack capabilities. Some commentators and analysts view this problem almost reflexively as a "war powers" issue—a term I use throughout this chapter to refer to *the political branches' respective constitutional authority over the hostile use of military force.* That is especially true as one moves up the scale of expected damage.[4] A corollary to that constitutional issue is a statutory question: Namely, how should the 1973 War Powers Resolution, which was intended to restrict extensive military hostilities without congressional approval, be interpreted or amended to account for cyberattacks?[5] The imprecise rhetoric of "cyberwar," "cyber conflict," and "cyberattacks" probably contributes to this legal framing.

But many—and probably almost all—cyberattacks undertaken by the United States cannot plausibly be viewed as exercises of war powers. Indeed, the entire Defend Forward concept appears to involve low-level operations well below the "use of force" threshold under international law and far short of the types of operations that have typically triggered war powers analysis under domestic constitutional law.

This chapter argues that as a conceptual and doctrinal matter, cyberattacks alone are rarely exercises of war powers—and they might never be. They are often instead best understood as exercises of other, non-war military powers, foreign affairs powers, intelligence powers, and foreign commerce powers, among other constitutional powers not yet articulated. Although this more fine-grained and fact-specific constitutional conception of cyberattacks leaves room for broad executive leeway in some operational contexts, this discretion is often the result of congressional delegation or acquiescence as opposed to any inherent constitutional authority on the part of the president. At the same time, these alternative understandings of cyberattacks also contain a strong constitutional basis for Congress to pursue legislative regulation of the procedural and substantive parameters governing cyber operations.

Beyond those descriptive and conceptual claims, this chapter argues that a rush to treat cyberattacks constitutionally as one would a kinetic military attack misguides criticisms about the role Congress is or is not playing in regulating cyberattacks and cyber-conflict. This is because participants in war powers debates often bring intense and polar normative stances about the appropriate institutional arrangements governing the exercise of those powers. On one end are those who prize executive speed, agility, and secrecy—and therefore presidential freedom from congressional interference. On the other end are those who see formal congressional approval for military campaigns as being of paramount constitutional importance. The latter, who want to roll back presidential unilateralism, often see cyberattacks as yet another problematic means by which presidents can evade proper congressional checks on war. But in their focus on congressional approval for military intervention, and by extension for at least some high-intensity cyberattacks, those critics may overlook other institutional arrangements that are better tailored to US cyber strategy, especially to the sort of lower-intensity activities that make up Defend Forward. They also may overlook the many important ways in which Congress is already actively involved in shaping and facilitating that strategy.

Cyberattacks as Exercising War Powers?

Suppose the executive branch launches an operation that, through in-filtration of foreign computer networks and insertion of code, disables an adversary's air defense system, knocks offline parts of its banking system, or takes over control of its intelligence service's social media accounts. Or suppose that a US cyber operation ruins an adversary's ballistic missile test, temporarily shuts down some internal government communications, or disrupts a state-owned business's operations. These direct effects might be small and temporary, but in some cases they might be large and long term. Assuming that such operations do not take place in the context of an ongoing armed conflict (and putting aside for now any additional statutory authorities or prohibitions), what constitutional powers is the president exercising?

The answer depends a lot on the facts. Cyberattacks, as defined in this chapter, encompass a very broad set of possible activities. But a common answer is that this is at least partly a war powers question, and thus the legality of such operations depends on the president's power to use military force in a given instance.

The Constitution's drafters studiously placed the power to declare war in Congress. Throughout American history, a strong current of thought has interpreted this choice to imply that Congress has exclusive (or near-exclusive) power to decide whether or not the country goes to war or initiates armed hostilities beyond cases of, in Madison's words, "repel[ling] sudden attacks."[6]

Several overlapping normative justifications are associated with this view. One is that requiring formal and express congressional approval ensures thorough deliberation and thereby prevents rash military intervention. Another common justification is that no one person ought to be able to bring violent conflict, and hence threats to American blood and treasure, upon the nation absent the most extreme emergency requirement for self-defensive action. For these and other reasons, including concerns that mobilizing military power would threaten republicanism at home, there was strong consensus among the constitutional founders that only Congress—not the president alone—should be able to take the country from peace to war.[7] Some would argue that these reasons have grown stronger over time, as American military power and war's destructive potential have grown. Nevertheless and owing to a variety of factors, over time the president has asserted, sometimes with the acquiescence of Congress and the courts, vast power to use military force without congressional approval far beyond the circumstances imagined by Madison.[8]

Modern executive-branch legal precedent and practice generally hold that the president has broad authority to launch military strikes without specific congressional authorization to defend American interests.[9] Indeed, the executive branch's view of expansive presidential powers to use kinetic military force is so well entrenched that putting cyber operations in the same category may be an attractive analytic move for justifying unilateral action in that domain, too (as well as for justifying the president's authority to take kinetic military responses in self-defense against *incoming* cyberattacks).

In a 2020 address, the Defense Department general counsel explained that the legal analysis for the military, in particular, to conduct cyberattacks looks the same as that for kinetic military attacks:

> The domestic legal authority for the DoD to conduct cyber operations is included in the broader authorities of the President and the Secretary of Defense to conduct military operations in defense of the nation. We assess whether a proposed cyber operation has been properly authorized using the analysis we apply to all other operations, including those that constitute use of force.[10]

Importantly, and elaborated below, "military operations in defense of the nation" implicate a much broader set of constitutional categories than just hostile applications of force; most such operations would not be exercises of war powers, and those 2020 remarks should not be interpreted to suggest otherwise. That said, the Defense Department general counsel went on to lay out the executive branch's overall legal framework for the use of military force—including to engage in armed hostilities—and applied it directly to the department's cyber operations:

The President has authority under Article II of the U.S. Constitution to direct the use of the Armed Forces to serve important national interests, and it is the longstanding view of the Executive Branch that this authority may include the use of armed force when the anticipated nature, scope, and duration of the operations do not rise to the level of "war" under the Constitution, triggering Congress's power to declare war. Furthermore, the Supreme Court has long affirmed the President's power to use force in defense of the nation and federal persons, property, and instrumentalities.[11]

One upshot of this analysis, he concluded, is that "the President has constitutional authority to order military cyber operations even if they amount to use of force in defense of the United States."[12]

Viewing some cyberattacks as the exercise of war powers may seem sensible for several reasons. If they are carried out by US Cyber Command, the organization of the armed forces tasked with conducting offensive cyber operations, the agent is the same one that conducts kinetic attacks. If a cyberattack causes damage that might otherwise be achieved by kinetic violence, or if the target is an adversary's armed forces, the effect is similar. If cyberattacks could foreseeably provoke an armed response, the consequences seem comparable.

It is questionable, though, whether the vast majority of actual and plausible cyberattacks should be understood as exercises of war powers at all. In other words, it may be a category error to analyze many cyberattacks as one would the application of hostile military force abroad, either as to the scope of the president's inherent constitutional authority or as to any constitutional requirement for congressional approval. As mentioned above, this is an area of constitutional law originally conceived for particular concerns about *physically armed* violence—specifically by military forces—including the risks of American bloodshed and escalation.

If war powers are a special constitutional category demanding formal congressional approval because of the risks to American blood, most cyberattacks barely if at all implicate this concern, because the risks are so tiny and remote. In modern executive-branch practice, as in many criticisms of that practice, risk to American service members is usually considered an affirmative factor in determining whether a military intervention is of such intensity as to amount to "war" in a constitutional sense that might require congressional approval. Low risk to American troops, on the flip side, may help justify presidential unilateralism.[13] Personnel conducting cyberattacks are physically and temporally distant from actions that might seem conceptually analogous to "combat." Of course, it has long been the case that military violence can be carried out remotely, with limited direct risks to American service members. Drone strikes are an obvious modern-day example, but even well before then, advances in aviation and munitions technology made possible massive bombing campaigns with low risk to American pilots. Missiles, of course, can deliver huge payloads from great distances.

Cyberattacks take human remoteness to an extreme, though, by placing no American lives immediately at risk. Except in the most extraordinary circumstances, they rarely even place foreign lives at risk (at least not directly). That human remoteness alleviates some concerns underlying arguments for congressional approval requirements, but it exacerbates others because the relative invisibility of cyberattacks means that political checks function weakly. As Jack Goldsmith and I have argued about "light-footprint" tools, including cyber-operations and drone attacks,

> [l]ight-footprint warfare is still lethal and very consequential warfare, and the lightness of the tools make them relatively easy for a President to deploy extensively. Light-footprint warfare thus has large foreign policy, strategic, and reputational consequences for the United States, akin to much heavier deployments, yet much less public examination. The President's legal theories treat this as a feature of such warfare. But it is also a bug for U.S. democracy, since the stealthy features mean that public debate and political checks—which reduce error as well as excess, and promote legitimacy—function ineffectively.[14]

Another important reason that war powers may be special—and why many argue that requirements of formal congressional approval are needed—is the risk of violent escalation. A common argument is that congressional approval (following careful interbranch deliberation) is especially important for measures that are likely to provoke armed retaliation. In recent decades, executive-branch practice and legal justifications have acknowledged this factor, too, in assessing whether a military intervention rises to the level of "war" perhaps requiring congressional authorization. In its 2018 opinion justifying President Trump's air attacks against Syria, for example, the Justice Department's Office of Legal Counsel considered this variable, noting that steps taken to reduce the probability of military reprisals strengthened the argument that the strikes were within the president's authority.[15] Inversely, if cyberattacks are likely to provoke violent responses, then arguably they ought to require congressional sign-off.

Real-world experience is still limited, and the escalation dynamics of cyberattacks are not yet well understood. That said, some studies suggest that cyberattacks are on the whole less likely than are kinetic attacks to provoke violent responses.[16] Some experimental data from crisis simulations indicate that even when they have destructive effects similar to those of conventional attacks, cyberattacks might not have the same political and emotional impacts that create pressures for violent retaliation (or even retaliation in cyberspace).[17] Other empirical and survey data show that, unlike conventional military attacks, cyber operations are not so escalatory and that they also offer escalatory off-ramps by providing response options other than conventional military conflict.[18] At several tense moments in 2019, for example, the United States reportedly chose to hit Iran with cyberattacks on military systems and intelligence facilities, rather than with kinetic strikes, in response to Iranian attacks on Saudi oil refineries and other provocations (including downing an American drone). That reporting suggests that the United States chose cyberattacks over kinetic ones in part because the former were viewed as less likely to drive escalation.[19]

Of course, there may be exceptions, especially for devastating cyberattacks. Moreover, cyberattacks can have far-reaching unintended consequences that may magnify resultant international friction or the risk of escalation. For example, as mentioned in the introduction, malicious computer code (widely attributed to the United States) targeted at Iranian nuclear plant control systems accidentally spread around the world.[20] Russian malware targeting Ukraine in 2017 quickly spread, too, and with far greater damage, crippling computer systems across the globe.[21] Furthermore, cyber operations, whether intended to be offensive or defensive, will often be perceived as threatening by targeted states, contributing to instability.[22]

However, evidence does not to date indicate that the risks are high that cyberattacks will provoke conventional military responses. The risk is clearly not zero, and cyberattacks might also result in escalation of other hostile measures, including economic ones or retaliation in cyberspace. But the same is true of so many other instruments of state power—for example, economic sanctions or diplomatic recognition decisions could cause a target state to lash out—that we would never categorize as exercises of constitutional war powers.

Separate from the issues of direct costs and risks, another possible reason it might make sense to categorize at least *some* cyberattacks as exercises of war powers for constitutional purposes is that states increasingly regard them as hostile military force as a matter of international law. This point is probably applicable only to cyberattacks that directly cause significant and direct physical destruction (say, causing a nuclear meltdown or plane crash) or that produce widespread harm (say, temporarily disabling a major electrical grid). The United States government has repeatedly asserted its right as a matter of international law to respond to some cyberattacks with kinetic military force, on the theory that cyberattacks could qualify as uses of "force" or "armed attacks" under the UN Charter.[23] Many other powerful states agree with this view, and many academics—myself included—argue that some cyberattacks are appropriately analogized as an international legal matter to kinetic attacks.[24] Defend Forward generally involves US cyber operations well below these levels. Although treating some cyberattacks as uses of force or armed attacks for international law purposes may not be determinative, it at least lends logical support to the idea that very physically destructive cyberattacks (maybe a narrow category) should also qualify as uses of force for constitutional purposes and thus trigger war powers analyses.

The international law and constitutional law analyses need not match up this way, though. Formally, the relevant legal provisions differ: The Constitution obviously predates the UN Charter, for example, and contains an intersecting set of relevant powers that have never been interpreted to map one-for-one onto international law. Normatively, the UN Charter and international self-defense law are almost entirely grounded in preserving international peace and security, whereas constitutional war powers are grounded also in concerns about both accountability and domestic control of military power. And, methodologically, international law and constitutional law draw on different histories and argumentative strategies for filling in legal gaps and ambiguities.

In sum, kinetic military attacks are rarely the correct constitutional analogy for cyberattacks. Rather than a presumption that any cyberattack involves an exercise of war powers, the presumption ought to be the opposite: that it does not. Although this chapter is concerned with constitutional issues, note that according to this logic it is also doubtful that most cyberattacks alone would or should be considered "hostilities" triggering the statutory limitations of the War Powers Resolution.[25] War powers were carved out as a special constitutional category—one that originally required congressional approval for particular actions and that some argue still ought to—and there should be a strong reason to expand the category to cover new kinds of activities. It is not clear that most cyberattacks make the cut.

Defend Forward and Constitutional Powers

If cyberattacks rarely (if ever) are exercises of war powers, then what constitutional powers are cyberattacks exercises of? The short answer is, it depends.[26] It is a mistake to try to fit them all into any one constitutional category. Cyberattacks, as stated at the outset, make up a broad category of activities. They could range from taking down or even destroying critical infrastructure to spoofing internal communications, and many things in between, like temporarily knocking offline air defense systems. Depending on the facts, cyberattacks could be viewed as exercises of non-combat military powers, foreign affairs powers, intelligence powers, and commerce powers—as well as combinations of these and still other powers. This section uses the US Defend Forward concept to illustrate how those powers can apply, and it also applies them to other hypothetical or past cyberattacks that may even have significant and direct destructive effects.

Defend Forward involves proactively countering malicious adversary cyber campaigns through day-to-day competition. Defend Forward aims to disrupt adversary cyber operations, deter future campaigns, and reinforce favorable international norms through activity conducted beyond US networks—that is, activity inside adversary and third-party networks.[27] According to the 2018 Defense Department Cyber Strategy, "[The Department] will defend forward to disrupt or halt malicious cyber activity at its source, including activity that falls below the level of armed conflict."[28]

Most operations contemplated by the Defend Forward concept do not involve activities that would count as "cyberattacks." Such operations include establishing a presence in foreign networks, mapping those networks, gathering information, and preparing for future operations. Some Defend Forward activities are cyberattacks, though. These might include interrupting communications from an adversary military facility used to infiltrate US military command and control systems, inserting malware that deletes or encrypts data on servers engaged in malign foreign influence campaigns online, or denying service to networks used by adversary intelligence agencies to conduct industrial espionage. Such operations involve combinations of several constitutional powers.

As Military Activity

Assuming the operation is conducted by the military (presumptively, US Cyber Command), one possibility is to treat it as an exercise of presidential power to engage in military activities but not, for constitutional purposes, the hostile application of armed force. The president, as commander in chief of the armed forces, can take many steps using military forces—forces provided by Congress—that impose costs on adversaries or involve risks of retaliation or escalation, including moving combat forces into foreign theaters or engaging in military exercises.[29] US Attorney General Robert Jackson offered a classic formulation of this view in a 1941 opinion concluding that the president had constitutional authority to order the instruction of British pilots by American military service members at US training facilities. As commander in chief of the armed forces, Jackson noted, the president "has supreme command over the land and naval forces of the country and may order them to perform such military duties as, in his opinion, are necessary or appropriate for the defense of the United States. These powers exist in time of peace as well as in time of war."[30]

Cyberattacks carried out by the US military inside foreign networks to, for example, prevent or deter adversary efforts to infiltrate US information systems could be understood much like the training of British pilots aimed at undermining German air superiority; without physical destruction, they deny or degrade an adversary's cyber capability. For that matter, looking beyond Defend Forward, cyberattacks to degrade an adversary's offensive or defensive military capability might also be treated as analogous. Such cyberattacks include the reported 2019 US cyber operation that wiped out information systems used by Iranian forces to target ships.[31] Yes, these examples may involve electronic transgression of territorial borders—and that may have international law implications—but any argument drawing constitutional conclusions from this fact just begs the question whether and how digital intrusion is constitutionally significant.

Importantly, although the president has wide latitude as commander in chief to engage in military activities other than force absent statutory restrictions, Congress restricts such types of military activities all the time.

For example, Congress regulates the US military's training and equipping of foreign armed forces with substantive, procedural, and fiscal restrictions,[32] and Congress has historically imposed various types of restrictions on peacetime deployments of troops abroad.[33] Congress could likewise do more to limit military cyber activities but has so far chosen not to.

As Foreign Relations

If a cyberattack is intended more for its communicative impact than its military impact, it might better be thought of as modern-day "gunboat diplomacy." This framing draws heavily on both the president's general powers as chief executive to conduct foreign relations, including communicating threats, and his commander-in-chief powers to control military forces.[34] Temporarily taking offline an enemy's digital infrastructure might be analogized to overflying its territory, for example, as a show of capability that demonstrates adversary vulnerability.

One might object that comparing cyberattacks that destroy or degrade adversary systems to coercive diplomacy is inapt because the latter activities lack any direct contact with the adversary and its assets. After all, most uses of military force that would unquestionably implicate war powers—for example, punitive air strikes—are also intended more for their communicative impact than their direct damage. But drawing constitutional conclusions from this distinction again begs the question of what type of "contact" with the adversary moves an action into the constitutional category of war powers.

As Intelligence Activities

Many cyberattacks of the sort envisioned by Defend Forward also involve exercises of constitutional intelligence powers.[35] This is a blurry area of constitutional law because secrecy precludes the sort of public articulation of government legal analysis that often accompanies military intervention. The executive branch has argued that the president possesses broad authority, implicitly derived from the president's power to conduct foreign relations as well as his commander-in-chief powers, to engage in clandestine intelligence activities to undermine enemy political, economic, and military systems. Another view is that much of this power comes from statutory delegations from Congress, both express and implied.[36] Cyber operations designed only to collect information would clearly fit within the category of intelligence powers, but this chapter is concerned with those intended to have disruptive or damaging effects.

The executive branch has at times taken the view that the president's power to engage in intelligence activities includes directing some quasi-military activities, such as paramilitary support to proxy groups or physical sabotage operations, as well as propaganda campaigns and other political manipulation when conducted covertly (that is, so that the hidden hand of the United States is plausibly deniable).[37] Whether some of those intelligence activities, particularly those involving physical violence, are really just a subset of war powers or a different constitutional category altogether—and one that did not become important until the Cold War—is unclear. Congress, for its part, has regulated covert intelligence activities by enacting procedural and reporting requirements, such as the covert action statute's requirements of presidential sign-off and notification to congressional intelligence committees.[38] Oversight statutes of this nature can be understood either as recognizing and limiting the president's broad inherent intelligence powers or as implicitly authorizing the president to engage in covert intelligence activities in the first place. Either way, the resulting institutional model is one in which the president has not been required to seek formal congressional approval for specific operations, but is required to meet other congressionally imposed requirements.[39]

Cyberattacks conducted as part of Defend Forward will often involve the exercise of intelligence powers, or perhaps can well be analogized to them. For starters, the means of cyberattacks—surreptitiously entering and mapping foreign information networks for vulnerabilities—is mostly an intelligence activity;[40] the difference between "defensive" intrusions and mapping of enemy networks and "offensive" disruptions of such networks may be relatively small pieces of computer code. Furthermore, even some cyber operations with damaging effects—such as altering data or implanting malware to disable or destroy digital systems—are akin to black bag jobs, propaganda operations, or covert support for proxy paramilitary forces, activities traditionally carried out by US intelligence agencies. A cyber operation like Stuxnet, which targeted militarily significant and sensitive sites and had significant, destructive physical effects, comes closer to an exercise of war powers but bears an even stronger resemblance to past exercises of intelligence powers, such as physical sabotage operations carried out by intelligence operatives or their proxies. Such operations are usually treated as a different constitutional category.

As Foreign Commerce

Yet another possibility is that cyberattacks are a form of meddling with international commerce, implicating the Constitution's allocation of foreign commerce powers. Domestically, telecommunications and other uses of the internet are uncontroversially understood to fall under Congress's Commerce Clause regulatory authority. Internationally, too, operations to halt, redirect, or otherwise interfere in digital information flows could be viewed as interventions into foreign commerce. I highlight this possibility because unlike the categories above, intervention in the flow of commerce is expressly Congress's domain: Article I assigns to Congress the power to regulate foreign commerce. International commerce is also another arena in which the US government often wields tools—in the form of economic and financial sanctions—that impose damage on foreign states, organizations, and individuals in order to advance US foreign policy objectives. Indeed, it is in part because foreign commerce is so connected with national defense that Congress exercises much of its power in this area through broad delegations; it has granted the president wide discretion to take economic measures to deal with foreign emergencies or trade disputes, for example.[41]

For constitutional purposes it might seem like a stretch to analogize manipulating computer code or digital information flows across borders to manipulating trade in goods or services. So is analogizing such activities to dropping bombs or deploying troops, though. Moreover, whereas kinetic military attacks may have incidental effects on private, commercial property, some cyber operations use commercial infrastructure as an integral feature of attack.

A Combination of Powers—and Institutional Conventions

Of course, cyberattacks might involve several or even all of these constitutional powers (non-combat military powers, foreign affairs powers, intelligence powers, commerce powers, and perhaps others). Indeed, depending on the specific facts, cyberattacks should be understood to involve various combinations of them. The main upshot is that while there could perhaps be instances where cyberattacks are exercises of war powers, such instances are exceedingly rare and limited to specific extreme cases. Most cyberattacks, especially ones that do not rise to the level of uses of force or armed attacks under international law, could fit in other categories. They could also form a new constitutional category altogether, for which the respective roles of Congress and the president are not yet established.

Congress and Cyber Strategy

As stated at the outset, one reason to resist categorizing cyberattacks as exercises of war powers—as that concept is commonly understood—is that the doctrinal fit is poor. That is not just rigid formalism; cyberattacks do not implicate the main concerns underlying war powers law, at least not to the same degree as does kinetic force, and they raise other concerns. Another reason to resist that categorization is that it tends to limit thinking about institutional arrangements. In particular, critics of presidential war powers unilateralism tend to focus on specific congressional approval for actions, at least those beyond a certain threshold. It may seem natural, under that view, to demand specific congressional approval for cyberattacks or cyber campaigns beyond a certain threshold, too. Proponents of presidential war powers unilateralism, meanwhile, tend to see congressional regulation of such powers as dangerous, if not constitutionally suspect, meddling.

By contrast, the catalog of constitutional powers in the previous section, each of which involves potent tools of international competition and conflict, brings along a wide array of institutional arrangements. Moreover, to those who worry about executive unilateralism with regard to cyber operations—and who therefore seek to bolster congressional checks and oversight—that catalog offers many more and stronger legal justifications for congressional involvement than does a legal framework rooted primarily in war powers. Congress shapes the use of non-combat military powers through, among other things, legislating military force structures and organizational arrangements, annual appropriations and authorization bills, and oversight processes. The president has a very free hand in exercising some foreign affairs functions, but Congress can shape most of them using powers of its own. Congress regulates intelligence largely through special oversight and statutory procedural requirements, and, especially when national security is involved, it often regulates international commerce through broad delegations of authority to the executive branch.

As Robert Chesney has shown, Congress is already quite engaged in shaping US cyber strategy, including pushing and facilitating more assertive uses of military cyber operations against particular adversaries.[42] That congressional involvement includes a wide range of institutional arrangements typical of coercive tools besides military force.

Congress has pressed the Defense Department to build up its offensive cyber capacity through annual National Defense Authorization Acts (NDAAs),[43] for example. It has clarified the Defense Department's authority to conduct offensive cyber operations,[44] thereby strengthening its position within the executive branch. Congress has also tried to streamline the internal executive-branch approval of cyber operations while setting outer boundaries on how those operations should be conducted. For instance, it has provided clearer statutory authority for the Defense Department to conduct wide-ranging clandestine cyber operations considered short of hostilities, including in areas where hostilities are not occurring, thereby enabling quicker and more flexible action in countering cyber adversaries outside US computer networks.[45]

Congress has acted to enhance oversight of cyberattacks, mandating special reporting requirements to the armed services committees for offensive and "sensitive" military cyber operations.[46] Cyberattacks conducted as covert action by the CIA are reported separately to the intelligence committees under long-standing arrangements, as are other intelligence activities that might fit within this chapter's definition of cyberattacks. Such reporting is foundational to other congressional roles, because it keeps Congress—or at least certain committees—informed of executive-branch actions that would otherwise be largely invisible. As discussed above, cyberattacks are especially invisible compared to other methods of international conflict, so robust congressional oversight is arguably extra-important as a stand-in for public scrutiny. One continuing challenge for Congress, then, is to design more meaningful reporting requirements, especially ones that get at results of cyber operations—that is, that emphasize the outputs (which are difficult to assess) rather than just the inputs of US cyber activities themselves. Congress might partly address this issue by requiring notification of committees not only of operations and targets but also of certain types of collateral damage or effects.

In short, concern that cyber is an area of executive unilateralism is misplaced, especially when it comes to cyber operations conducted by the US military. Congress and the executive are already collaborating on a system built through interbranch deliberation, and invoking war powers—either along with a belief in broad inherent executive-branch authority or along with insistence on case-by-case congressional approval—is neither appropriate nor useful. As Chesney writes: "With little fanfare and less public notice, Congress and the executive branch have cooperated effectively over the past decade to build a legal architecture for military cyber operations."[47]

It is true that this legal architecture leaves the president with a lot of discretion to engage in cyber operations or cyberattacks, at least those that fall below a very high threshold constituting war (if one takes the view that cyberattacks alone could ever meet that bar), without getting additional congressional approval. That discretion is a product of both inherent constitutional power and delegated power from Congress.

At least with regard to Defend Forward, there is a powerful strategic logic to that vast zone of discretion. When it comes to using hostile kinetic military force, strategy usually involves specific breakpoints in time and conflict intensity: as tensions with a specific adversary rise, the United States sustains a military attack, or as a threat grows, the United States moves from not using force to using it. It is often an on/off switch. Normally, the military force switch is off, and at a particular moment the government turns it on. At that moment, constitutional war powers are activated.

In contrast to the on/off nature of most kinetic military intervention, Defend Forward involves a constant level of cyber conflict;[48] the United States must be continually prosecuting it.[49] Cyber Command's chief and a top advisor recently described its implementation this way:

> Cyber Command implements this defend forward strategy through the doctrine of persistent engagement. The idea behind persistent engagement is that so much of the corrosive effects of cyber attacks against the United States occur below the threshold of traditional armed conflict. . . . This doctrine of persistent engagement reflects the fact that one-off cyber operations are unlikely to defeat adversaries. Instead, U.S. forces must compete with adversaries on a recurring basis, making it far more difficult for them to advance their goals over time.[50]

"There is also consensus across the U.S. government that great-power competitors are making strategic gains in and through cyberspace with persistent, targeted campaigns that never rise to the level of a catastrophic cyber attack," writes Emily Goldman, a policy official at Cyber Command and the National Security Agency. Therefore, "Competing below the level of armed conflict and contesting malicious cyber activity in day-to-day competition are consistent themes across the *National Defense Strategy*, the *National Military Strategy*, and the 2018 *Department of Defense Cyber Strategy*."[51]

The type of continuous agility called for in such situations matches especially poorly with the sort of rigid requirements for case-by-case congressional approval that critics of unilateral presidential war powers often call for. The case-by-case model is workable when there is a clear and visible initiation point, or a break from baseline dormancy. The vast majority of US cyberattacks, however, will be part of constant and largely invisible campaigns against multiple adversaries simultaneously. Indeed, in recent years the executive branch has also wrestled with whether and how to delegate decision making on cyber operations to lower levels of command, too, in order to better promote agility.[52] Whereas a war powers framing tends to focus on horizontal allocations of power—between the president and Congress—the vertical allocations of power within the executive branch are especially important in the cyber context.[53]

It may well be that Congress and future presidential administrations will move toward a different strategy. There may also be rare US offensive cyberattacks that look more like discrete applications of military force. For now, though, a war powers framing matches poorly the way the United States actually conducts cyberattacks.

Conclusion

Cyberattacks are a national capability the exercise of which usually involves no direct risk to American lives, is largely invisible to the public eye, could possibly but is relatively unlikely to escalate to conventional military conflict, and for which international law and norms are uncertain and evolving. At the most general level, this chapter is about constitutional analogies: What exercises of power are cyberattacks most like? There are, to be sure, other ways entirely of approaching these issues. One might, for example, ask whether cyber-operations—which will, among other features, be continuous and stealthy—are so fundamentally transforming international conflict that war powers law and institutional arrangements require radical reimagination.

For present purposes, constitutional categorization by analogy is important not just for doctrinal reasons but because how one categorizes cyberattacks triggers certain conventions, practices, and political arguments regarding how overlapping executive and legislative power is shared. Cyberattacks-as-war-powers is one possible answer, but it is rarely—and maybe never—a good fit. There are many other categories that, in combination, better fit most cyberattacks, including operations conducted as part of Defend Forward. Those categories provide better doctrinal justifications for executive action, as well as for congressional regulation. Viewing cyberattacks in those alternative terms also helps to open up a wider array of institutional arrangements that more appropriately match emerging cyber strategy.

Notes

1. This is similar to the way the Defense Department's Joint Publication 3–12 defines "cyberspace attack": "Cyberspace attack actions create noticeable denial effects (i.e., degradation, disruption, or destruction) in cyberspace or manipulation that leads to denial effects in the physical domains." JOINT CHIEFS OF STAFF, JOINT PUB. 3-12, CYBERSPACE OPERATIONS CORE ACTIVITIES II-7 (2018).
2. See Andy Greenberg, *The Untold Story of NotPetya, the Most Devastating Cyberattack in History*, WIRED (Aug. 22, 2018); David E. Sanger, *Obama Order Sped Up Wave of Cyberattacks Against Iran*, N.Y. TIMES (June 1, 2012).
3. *See* Ellen Nakashima, *U.S. Cyber Command Operation Disrupted Internet Access of Russian Troll Factory on Day of 2018 Midterms*, WASH. POST (Feb. 27, 2019).
4. *See, e.g.*, Lyle Denniston, *Constitution Check: Is the War Powers Clause a Dead Letter in the Cyberspace Age?*, NAT'L CONST. CTR. (Feb. 5, 2013); Stephen Dycus, *Congress's Role in Cyber Warfare*, 4 J. NAT'L SEC. L. & POL'Y 155 (2010); Jason Healey & A.J. Wilson, *Cyber Conflict and the War Powers Resolution: Congressional Oversight of Hostilities in the Fifth Domain*, 5 GEO. J. INT'L AFF. 59 (2012); Tyler K. Lowe, *Mapping the Matrix: Defining the Balance Between Executive Action and Legislative Regulation in the New Battlefield of Cyberspace*, 17 SCHOLAR 63 (2015).
5. *See, e.g.*, Eric Talbot Jenson, *Future War and the War Powers Resolution*, 29 EMORY INT'L L. REV. 499 (2015); Oona A. Hathaway, *How to Revive Congress' War Powers*, 3 TEX. NAT'L SEC. REV. 136 (2019).
6. 2 THE RECORDS OF THE FEDERAL CONVENTION OF 1787, at 318 (Max Farrand ed., rev. ed. 1966); *see also, e.g.*, John Hart Ely, WAR AND RESPONSIBILITY: CONSTITUTIONAL LESSONS OF VIETNAM AND ITS AFTERMATH 3-10 (1993); Arthur M. Schlesinger, Jr., THE IMPERIAL PRESIDENCY 1-26 (Mariner Books ed. 2004).

7. *See* 3 Joseph Story, Commentaries on the Constitution of the United States 59–61 (1833).

8. *See generally* Schlesinger, *supra* note 6, at 27–201.

9. *See, e.g.*, Memorandum Opinion from Caroline D. Krass, Principal Deputy Assistant Att'y Gen., Office of Legal Couns., to the Att'y Gen., Authority to Use Military Force in Libya (Apr. 1, 2011); Memorandum Opinion from Steven A. Engel, Office of Legal Couns., to the Couns. to the President, April 2018 Airstrikes Against Syrian Chemical-Weapons Facilities (May 31, 2018).

10. Hon. Paul C. Ney, Jr., DOD General Counsel Remarks at U.S. Cyber Command Legal Conference (Mar. 2, 2020).

11. *Id.*

12. *Id.*

13. *See* sources cited *supra* note 9.

14. *See* Jack Goldsmith & Matthew Waxman, *The Legal Legacy of Light-Footprint Warfare*, 39 Wash. Q. 7, 18 (2016).

15. *See* Engel, *supra* note 9, at 21.

16. *See* Erica D. Borghard & Shawn W. Lonergan, *Cyber Operations as Imperfect Tools of Escalation*, 13 Strategic Stud. Q. 137 (2019). For an excellent discussion of cyberattacks and crisis stability, see also Jason Healey & Robert Jervis, *The Escalation Inversion and Other Oddities of Situational Cyber Stability*, 3 Tex. Nat'l Sec. Rev. (2020).

17. *See* Jacquelyn G. Schneider, *Deterrence in and through Cyberspace*, in Cross-Domain Deterrence: Strategy in an Era of Complexity 95 (Eric Gartzke & Jon R. Lindsay eds., 2019); Jacquelyn G. Schneider, *What War Games Tell Us About the Use of Cyber Weapons in a Crisis*, Council on Foreign Rels. (June 21, 2018).

18. *See* Benjamin Jensen & Brandon Valeriano, Atlantic Council, What Do We Know About Cyber Escalation? Observations from Simulations and Surveys (2019); Brandon Valeriano & Benjamin Jensen, *How Cyber Operations Can Help Manage Crisis Escalation with Iran*, Wash. Post (June 25, 2019).

19. *See* Idrees Ali & Phil Stewart, *U.S. Carried Out Secret Cyber Strike on Iran in Wake of Saudi Oil Attack: Officials*, Reuters (Oct. 15, 2019); Julian E. Barnes & Thomas Gibbons-Neff, *U.S. Carried Out Cyberattacks on Iran*, N.Y. Times (June 22, 2019); Sean Lawson, *What Will Be the Effect of the Latest US Cyberattack on Iran?*, Fifth Domain (Oct. 23, 2019); Anya van Wagtendonk, *Trump Called Off a Military Strike Against Iran. The US Targeted Its Computer Systems Instead*, Vox (June 23, 2019).

20. Vivian Yeo, *Stuxnet Infections Spread to 115 Countries*, ZDNet (Aug. 9, 2010).

21. Greenberg, *supra* note 2.

22. *See generally* Ben Buchanan, The Cybersecurity Dilemma (2017).

23. For a discussion of US government positions on this point, see *Cyber Strategy & Policy: International Law Dimensions: Hearing Before the S. Armed Forces Committee*, 115th Cong. 18 (2017) (statement of Matthew C. Waxman, Liviu Librescu Professor of L., Columbia L. School). The United States and many others also apply *jus in bello* rules to cyberattacks in the course of armed conflict.

24. *See, e.g.*, Matthew C. Waxman, *Cyber-Attacks and the Use of Force: Back to the Future of Article 2(4)*, 36 YALE J. INT'L L. 421 (2011); Michael N. Schmitt, *Noteworthy Releases of International Cyber Law Positions—Part I: NATO*, ARTICLES OF WAR (Aug. 27, 2020).

25. That is especially so if one applies that interpretation of the War Powers Resolution advanced by the Obama administration during the 2011 Libya intervention. In that case, the executive took the position that "hostilities" did not exist because the mission, exposure of US armed forces, risk of escalation, and military means were all limited. *See Libya and War Powers: Hearing Before the S. Comm. on Foreign Relations*, 112th Cong. 89 (2011) (statement of Harold Koh, Legal Advisor, U.S. Dep't. of State).

26. *See* Gary P. Corn, *Cyber National Security: Navigating Gray-Zone Challenges in and through Cyberspace, in* COMPLEX BATTLESPACES: THE LAW OF ARMED CONFLICT AND THE DYNAMICS OF MODERN WARFARE 367 (Christopher M. Ford & Winston S. Williams eds., 2019) (explaining that for many offensive cyber operations "the scope of the President's authority is more nuanced as it implicates the full range of Article II authority, not just the commander-in-chief power, and is further complicated by the novelty and uncertainties surrounding the use of cyber operations as a tool of national power").

27. *See* Erica D. Borghard, *Operationalizing Defend Forward: How the Concept Works to Change Adversary Behavior*, LAWFARE (Mar. 12, 2020).

28. U.S. DEP'T. OF DEF., SUMMARY: DEPARTMENT OF DEFENSE CYBER STRATEGY 1 (2018).

29. *See* W. Taylor Reveley III, WAR POWERS OF THE PRESIDENT AND CONGRESS: WHO HOLDS THE ARROWS AND THE OLIVE BRANCH? 15–16 (1981).

30. Training of British Flying Students in the United States, 40 Op. Att'y Gen. 58, 61 (1941).

31. *See* Julian E. Barnes, *U.S. Cyberattack Hurt Iran's Ability to Target Oil Tankers, Officials Say*, N.Y. TIMES (Aug. 28, 2019).

32. *See* BOLKO J. SKORUPSKI & NINA M. SERAFINO, CONG. RSCH. SERV., R44602, DOD SECURITY COOPERATION: AN OVERVIEW OF AUTHORITIES AND ISSUES (2016).

33. *See* JENNIFER K. ELSEA ET AL., CONG. RSCH. SERV., R41989, CONGRESSIONAL AUTHORITY TO LIMIT MILITARY OPERATIONS (2013).

34. *Cf.* United States v. Curtiss-Wright Export Corp., 299 U.S. 304, 319 (1936) (discussing the president as the sole organ of the nation in its external relations).

35. *Cf.* Joshua Rovner, *Cyber War as an Intelligence Contest*, WAR ON THE ROCKS (Sept. 16, 2019).

36. For a discussion of these perspectives, and a critique of the executive branch view, see Jules Lobel, *Covert War and the Constitution*, 5 J. NAT'L SEC. L. & POL'Y 393 (2011).

37. *See, e.g., Intelligence Oversight Act of 1988 and National Security Reform Act of 1987: Hearing on S. 1721 and S. 1818 Before the S. Select Comm. on Intelligence*, 110th Cong. 93 (1987) (prepared statement of Charles J. Cooper, Assistant Att'y Gen. for the Office of L. Couns.); *Hearings on S. Res. 21 before the S. Select Comm. to Study Governmental Operations with Respect to Intelligence Activities*, 94th Cong. 1730–37 (1975) (statement of Mitchell Rogovin, Special Couns., Dir. of Nat'l Intel.); *see also* Richard O.W. Morgan & Jonathan M. Fredman, *The Law of Foreign and National Intelligence, in* NATIONAL SECURITY LAW & POLICY 1041, 1048 (John Norton Moore,

Guy B. Roberts & Robert F. Turner eds., 3rd ed. 2015) (discussing covert action as a category of intelligence activities with a foundation in the president's Article II powers).

38. 50 U.S.C. § 3093 (2018).

39. *See* M. E. Bowman, *Secrets in Plain View: Covert Action the U.S. Way*, 72 Int'l L. Stud. 1, 10 (1998)("Although the precise authority for covert action is debatable, it is clear that both the Congress and the Executive believe it a necessary option. Both presume that legal authority exists to engage in covert action and each presumes to have a Constitutionally authorized, if not precisely defined, role.").

40. Robert Chesney, *Military-Intelligence Convergence and the Law of the Title 10/50 Debate*, 5 J. Nat'l Sec. L. & Pol'y 539, 580 (2012).

41. *See* Christopher A. Casey, Ian F. Ferguson, Dianne E. Rennack & Jennifer K. Elsea, Cong. Rsch. Serv., R45618, The International Emergency Economic Powers Act: Origins, Evolution, and Use (2020).

42. Robert Chesney, *The Domestic Legal Framework for US Military Cyber Operations* 3 (Hoover Working Group on Nat'l Sec., Tech., and Law, Aegis Series Paper No. 2003, 2020).

43. *See, e.g.*, National Defense Authorization Act for Fiscal Year 2017, Pub. L. No. 114–328, § 923, 30 Stat. 2000, 2357 (2016) (creating a unified combatant command for cyber).

44. *See* National Defense Authorization Act for Fiscal Year 2012, Pub. L. No. 112–81, § 954, 125 Stat. 1298, 1551 (2011); 10 U.S.C.A. § 111 note; National Defense Authorization Act for Fiscal Year 2018, Pub. L. No. 115–91, § 1633(a), (b)(5)(B), 131 Stat. 1283, 1738–39 (2017).

45. National Defense Authorization Act for Fiscal Year 2019, Pub. L. No. 115–232, § 1632, 132 Stat. 1636, 2123–24 (2018); 10 U.S.C. § 394 (2018).

46. The 2013 NDAA required DoD to "provide to the Committees on Armed Services of the House of Representatives and the Senate quarterly briefings on all offensive and significant defensive military operations in cyberspace carried out by the Department of Defense during the immediately preceding quarter." National Defense Authorization Act for Fiscal Year 2013, Pub. L. No. 112–239, § 939, 126 Stat. 1632, 1888 (2013); 10 U.S.C. § 484 (2018). This provision was updated and expanded in the 2017 and 2019 NDAAs to add and amend the required elements of these reports.

47. Chesney, *supra* note 42, at 1.

48. James A. Lewis, Remarks at U.S. Cyber Command Legal Conference: Toward a More Coercive Cyber Strategy 2 (Mar. 4, 2021).

49. One might, however, compare the long-term, constant features of cyber conflict to ongoing counterterrorism operations, especially since 2001.

50. Paul M. Nakasone & Michael Sulmeyer, *How to Compete in Cyberspace: Cyber Command's New Approach*, Foreign Aff. (Aug. 25, 2020).

51. Emily O. Goldman, *From Reaction to Action: Adopting a Competitive Posture in Cyber Diplomacy*, 3 Tex. Nat'l Sec. Rev. (2020).

52. *See* Jacquelyn Schneider, *Are Cyber-Operations a U.S. Retaliatory Option for the Saudi Oil Field Strikes? Would Such Action Deter Iran?*, Wash. Post (Oct. 1, 2019).

53. Ellen Nakashima, *White House Authorizes "Offensive Cyber Operations" to Deter Foreign Adversaries*, WASH. POST (Sept. 20, 2018); Mark Pomerleau, *After Tug-of-War, White House Shows Cyber Memo to Congress*, FIFTH DOMAIN, (Mar. 13, 2020); David E. Sanger, Julian E. Barnes, & Nicole Perlroth, *Preparing for Retaliation Against Russia, U.S. Confronts Hacking by China*, N.Y. TIMES (Mar. 7, 2021).

6

Defend Forward and the FBI

James Baker and Matt Morris

Introduction

In an effort to address an increasingly complex and challenging cyber threat landscape, the United States military's Cyber Command (USCYBERCOM) recently updated its strategy. Instead of assuming a primarily reactive posture, the United States would begin to "defend[] forward[,] as close as possible to the origin of adversary activity,"[1] operating outside of US domestic networks to identify and counter cyber threats proactively. Because this strategy, coined Defend Forward, is outward facing, most discussions surrounding it focus on its international law implications or on the domestic-law basis for cyber operations abroad.[2] There has been insufficient analysis of the legal regime that impacts not only Defend Forward but potentially all US defensive and quasi-offensive operations to maintain cybersecurity, namely, domestic laws, including the United States Constitution, meant to protect privacy, particularly privacy in data and electronic communications. This chapter takes up that understudied but vital issue.

Unlike USCYBERCOM's strategy, this domestic legal regime has not been overhauled for the twenty-first century. As a result, it constrains the ability of the US government to respond effectively to today's cyber threats and at the same time does not adequately protect privacy. The main reason is that while cyber conflict is borderless, the Constitution and laws of the United States are not. When operating on US territory or in situations involving United States persons, the United States government must navigate a complex patchwork of legal restrictions that significantly impede its ability to identify and respond to malicious cyber activity and to do so quickly. But outside of the country, particularly where United States persons are not involved, most of these legal constraints fall away, and US law enforcement, intelligence, and military personnel can act much more freely.

This foreign-domestic dichotomy has significant practical consequences. To detect, understand, and respond to malign cyber activity coming from within the United States, the government must often conduct complicated legal analysis, sometimes appear before courts to obtain search warrants or other legal process, and coordinate operational activity across multiple agencies with distinct legal and policy-based authorities and restrictions. These processes take time, and government officials can face criminal sanctions and civil liability in certain circumstances for failing to adhere to them. By contrast, the legal regime and approval requirements governing the conduct of the exact same activities outside the United States is far less onerous.

What's more, sophisticated US adversaries—foreign nations and non-state actors—are aware of this dynamic and exploit it. Rather than launching cyberattacks or other operations solely from abroad, they intentionally use various techniques to conduct their activities from computers and networks within the geographic United States and/or devices that belong to (or appear to belong to) US persons. In so doing, they make it more difficult for the United States to respond, constrained as it is by domestic law gaps and inefficiencies and the significant protections domestic law provides for digital privacy.

Recent events have brought these problems into sharp relief. In December 2020, a domestic cybersecurity firm uncovered an apparently massive cyber espionage operation, now known as "SolarWinds," the name of the network infrastructure management company whose software the perpetrators infiltrated to launch their operation.[3] SolarWinds apparently compromised systems at the Pentagon, the Department of Homeland Security, the Department of State, the Justice Department, and the Department of the Treasury, alongside other government agencies and private sector firms like Microsoft and Cisco.[4] Russian intelligence services are allegedly responsible. And in March 2021, state-affiliated Chinese hackers allegedly executed a potentially more serious operation. The hack hit tens of thousands of Microsoft Exchange email servers and left them with vulnerabilities that may take years to identify and repair.[5] These malicious actions apparently had two things in common: they may have originated, at least in part, from within the United States, and the US government apparently never found them. While the reasons for both are no doubt complex, it seems likely that the unwieldy legal regime we describe is part of the reason why.

We discuss these problems in more detail below, briefly describing the cyber threat landscape and providing an overview of some of the elements of the applicable legal structure. We then conclude by arguing that it is well past time for the United States to conduct a thorough review of the legal regime applicable to cybersecurity and to comprehensively reform that regime.

But before that, we want to be clear: Our position is not that digital privacy protections within the United States should simply be eliminated or diminished in order to protect national security. To the contrary, we are deeply concerned that our outdated cyber law inadequately protects privacy and fails to address the complex challenges that privacy presents. Moreover, we are not advocating for a massive government surveillance program for the entire US-based internet or substantially expanding the National Security Agency's (NSA) authorities to operate domestically. Such endeavors would obviously raise grave and unprecedented legal, privacy, and economic concerns and could be antithetical to the goal of maintaining a free society. Further, we have substantial doubts about whether such programs would even work. We firmly believe that reform need not and should not be zero-sum. By simplifying and modernizing our law to take account of both the national security *and* privacy vulnerabilities of the digital age we can make headway on both fronts. This chapter focuses on the former, but it is written with full awareness of the latter.

The Problem

In order for the United States to engage in effective offensive and defensive cyber operations (including the nominally defensive but apparently quasi-offensive operations conducted under the Defend Forward mantle), it needs to collect, retain, analyze, and disseminate information that is to, from, or about foreign adversaries—as well as the actual or intended victims of those adversaries—so that it can develop a comprehensive picture of the operational environment in which it is acting. It needs real-time and full scope situational awareness of the cyber environment—who the adversaries are, where they are, what capabilities they have, and what they are doing or have already accomplished. Importantly, it also needs to collect and share pertinent information with all relevant government actors—law enforcement, the intelligence community, and the military—as well as with foreign governmental partners and, at times, with the private sector.

In other words, with respect to the cyber environment, "[t]imely, accurate, and insightful information about the activities, capabilities, plans, and intentions of foreign powers, organizations, and persons, and their agents, is essential to the national security of the United States."[6] It is no mystery why: Hostile cyber actors—whether they are nation-states, terrorist groups, international criminal organizations, or individual hackers—utilize global network infrastructure to conduct malicious activities targeted at the United States and its allies.

It does not appear that foreign nation-state adversaries are constrained by their own domestic law with respect to offensive cyber operations, especially undemocratic and authoritarian states such as China, Russia, Iran, and North Korea. It is also unclear whether, as a practical matter, international law constrains the cyber behavior of those adversaries, although they well may take into account the UN Charter and related legal restrictions, evidenced in part by the limited number of publicly known cyber operations conducted to date that have resulted in kinetic harm that some would consider to be a use of force and/or an armed attack. Further, although international law is generally understood not to regulate cyber espionage operations, it is unlikely that such foreign actors place much weight on respecting international law when conducting offensive operations. United States domestic law also appears to be no serious obstacle to malicious cyber actors operating from abroad; indeed, what they are doing is criminal and US criminal law seems to be a weak deterrent.[7] So from a legal perspective, and as a practical matter, adversaries operating from abroad can generally act unencumbered, constrained only by the operational imperatives of the mission they are trying to accomplish, the limitations of technology, and the defensive measures that their intended victims put into place.

As we explain in detail below, outside of the geographic United States, the legal and policy constraints on the US government's cyber activities are similarly flexible, dynamic, and—in general—relatively limited. International law—including international humanitarian law and the principle of neutrality—does constrain, although, perhaps to a greater degree than most countries, the United States can influence the contours of international law through its own practice in the cyber area. Domestic law also constrains US overseas cyber operations through the application of the Constitution (especially Articles I and II and the Fourth Amendment) and certain federal statutes and executive orders. Moreover, applicable law constrains all governmental actors, including law enforcement and foreign intelligence agencies as well as the military (for example, agencies cannot go beyond their remit as assigned by Congress and the president). Additional statutes impose further restrictions on the military and intelligence community, respectively. Finally, some key laws apply to both public and private sector actors.

But hostile foreign cyber adversaries conduct operations globally, including from within the geographic United States. And domestic law constrains the US government to a far greater degree when it seeks to act within US territory than when it acts abroad.

Which leads to our main thesis: US domestic law significantly impedes the ability of governmental actors in the United States to take timely and effective action against the full range of malicious cyber actors—especially nation-states—who threaten the national and economic security of the United States and its allies. In particular, US law makes it more difficult for the government to collect, retain, and share information related to cyber threats—all fundamental aspects of identifying, understanding, and responding to malicious cyber activity. In various ways, the Constitution and laws of the United States make it unlawful for the government to take these critical actions in certain circumstances, and government actors can face criminal and civil penalties for violating these rules. Adversaries understand this reality and use the restrictions of US law to their advantage to thwart efforts to detect, deter, and defeat them.

One of the reasons the applicable law in this area negatively impacts United States cyber operations is that the law is difficult to understand and apply accurately, quickly, and consistently. As stated in the Obama Administration's 2009 Cyberspace Policy Review:

> [The] [l]aw applicable to information and communications networks is a complex patchwork of Constitutional, domestic, foreign, and international laws that shapes viable policy options. In the United States, this patchwork exists because, throughout the evolution of the information and communications infrastructure, the Federal government enacted laws and policies to govern aspects of what were very diverse industries and technologies.[8]

Thus, the United States has known for more than a decade that its cyber legal framework is flawed. But the United States government has taken only limited action to address this problem, and so it persists.

As a result, operators and the lawyers advising them often have a hard time determining what the law is and how it applies to any particular course of action. Lawyers can correctly determine whether the law permits, prohibits, or restricts a particular operational activity, but it is hard to know that their analysis is right consistently and with high confidence, particularly given the dynamic nature of cyber threats and the speed at which such threats can materialize. As a result, operators may sometimes do things that are unlawful or, conversely, refrain from doing things that are lawful out of fear of getting it wrong and exposing themselves and their organizations to legal and reputational risk. Of course, this type of uncertainty is not a new phenomenon in the area of national security law; it was an acute issue in the counterterrorism context, among others. But that does not make it desirable, particularly given the increasing stakes of cyber conflict.

In addition to the complex and patchwork nature of applicable cyber law, two important reasons that US law has a negative impact on offensive and defensive cyber operations are that it makes critical distinctions between activities that (1) take place in the geographic United States and those that occur abroad; and (2) involve United States persons versus persons who do not have substantial connections to the United States.[9] More specifically, US government agencies are much more restricted with respect to surveillance activities that occur in the geographic United States or involve United States persons than they are when these conditions are not met.

Accordingly, one way for adversaries of the United States and its allies to make it more difficult to counter their malicious cyber activities is to conduct those activities at least in part from computers and other devices that are physically located in the United States. The reasons for doing so are simple: US law applies clearly within the territory and possessions of the United States,[10] and that law is intended to protect the rights of people within these geographic locations. It is to the advantage of adversaries to operate— or appear to be operating—from the geographic United States in order to avail themselves of US legal protections.

To be sure, the challenges of the geographic and identity focus of US law on national security operations is not a problem that is unique to the cyber realm. Officials in the Bush administration complained about the fact that al Qaeda operatives who came into the United States received heightened legal protections even though they were part of an enemy combatant force.[11] General Michael Hayden stated publicly, for example, that if Osama bin Laden was on the Canadian side of the bridge in Niagara Falls, it was substantially easier to target his communications for collection than if he simply crossed the bridge over to the US side.[12] But the ways in which geography and identity constrain US government action loom especially large in the cyber context, as it is simply much easier to operate or appear to operate inside the United States in cyberspace than in actual space, as the Bin Laden example illustrates. Not only that, cyber conflict and cyber security are becoming increasingly central to US national security and law enforcement objectives.

The Threat

Before diving deeper into the specifics of the legal problem outlined above, we provide below a very brief synopsis of the cyber threat environment to better orient the legal discussion. In short, the United States and its allies face a range of sophisticated cyber adversaries who are well-resourced and highly motivated. Those adversaries include nation-states such as the People's Republic of China, the Russian Federation, North Korea, and Iran. They also include various international criminal organizations that operate both independently and at the behest of foreign governments with which they are aligned or to which they are beholden. Terrorist groups are generally thought to have some cyber capabilities, but cyber actions do not appear to be their focus. Hacktivist organizations and small groups or individual hackers round out the list.

In 2019, the United States Intelligence Community issued its annual Worldwide Threat Assessment (the last publicly available such assessment) that discussed at length the cyber threat that the United States and its allies face. The assessment stated:

> Our adversaries and strategic competitors will increasingly use cyber capabilities—including cyber espionage, attack, and influence—to seek political, economic, and military advantage over the United States and its allies and partners. China, Russia, Iran, and North Korea increasingly use cyber operations to threaten both minds and machines in an expanding number of ways—to steal information, to influence our citizens, or to disrupt critical infrastructure.
>
> At present, China and Russia pose the greatest espionage and cyber attack threats, but we anticipate that all our adversaries and strategic competitors will increasingly build and integrate cyber espionage, attack, and influence capabilities into their efforts to influence US policies and advance their own national security interests. In the last decade, our adversaries and strategic

competitors have developed and experimented with a growing capability to shape and alter the information and systems on which we rely. For years, they have conducted cyber espionage to collect intelligence and targeted our critical infrastructure to hold it at risk. They are now becoming more adept at using social media to alter how we think, behave, and decide. As we connect and integrate billions of new digital devices into our lives and business processes, adversaries and strategic competitors almost certainly will gain greater insight into and access to our protected information.[13]

Hostile foreign countries conduct cyber operations against the United States and its allies to achieve a variety of strategic and tactical goals. Because of the immense military, economic, and political strength of the United States, it can be difficult for those adversaries, at least in the short term, to compete directly with the United States across a range of strategic dimensions. But those nations can obtain a variety of short- and long-term advantages through the use of asymmetric means, such as cyber-enabled and covert operations (including disinformation campaigns intended to influence and disrupt elections) that they conduct directly or through proxies.

One of the keys to conducting effective asymmetric cyber operations against a much larger and more powerful adversary is stealth. From the perspective of China, Russia, Iran, and North Korea, for such operations to be maximally successful, it is essential that the United States and its allies have as hard a time as possible determining the nature, scope, and even existence of cyber operations directed against them. Typically, such actors want to make it difficult for a victim to: (i) know whether a cyber operation is under way, (ii) understand how the hostile actor exploited a known, or, even better, unknown system vulnerability and thereby gained access to a network or device, (iii) learn the objectives of the intrusion, (iv) ascertain the systems or data that have been compromised or exfiltrated (v) and attribute the intrusion to a particular hostile adversary.

There are numerous cyber tactics, techniques, and procedures that hostile actors can use to obscure their cyber activities. We are not computer scientists, engineers, or information technology professionals, and this chapter is not intended for a technical audience. But we can assert confidently that one of the methods that prudent cyber actors use to achieve the obfuscation described above is to compromise numerous intermediary networks and devices prior to effecting an intrusion on the ultimate intended target. Such efforts can be quite complex and involve several layers of intermediate compromised systems in order to make it that much harder for the victim to track the intrusion back to its ultimate origin. A sophisticated and careful cyber operation will involve considerable care and planning in developing such a multi-layered intrusion network, and once it is developed, a cyber actor usually will take great efforts to protect that network from identification and compromise.[14]

Various tactical factors go into the design, development, and maintenance of a complex intrusion execution network. And one that the best cyber actors will consider is the particular legal regime that applies to the various elements of such networks and how it might be leveraged to thwart the network defender. Accordingly, when the United States and its allies are the intended victims of malicious cyber operations, hostile foreign powers will endeavor to make the job of the network defenders more difficult by using the legal regimes of the United States and its allies against them—for example, by effectively turning themselves into domestic actors for legal purposes by working through intermediary networks located in the United States.

The Law

The thicket of US laws discussed above that constrain—in our view disadvantageously in certain respects—the cyber operations of the United States applies in the overlapping contexts of surveillance, data collection, privacy, and information sharing. Our basic thesis, outlined above, is that frequently and often without adequate consideration or evaluation, the freedom with which federal agencies can act turns on the geographic location of attacks and government operations, and on the identities of the unknowing victims (ultimate and intermediary) of such attacks and targets of such operations.

Because this chapter focuses on the impact of this legal regime on the cyber activities (primarily defensive) of the United States government, we will direct our attention to the Constitution—particularly the Fourth Amendment—and certain federal statutes that have the greatest impact on cyber operations, including the Foreign Intelligence Surveillance Act (FISA),[15] the Electronic Communications Privacy Act (ECPA),[16] the Posse Comitatus Act,[17] and the Covert Action Statute.[18] We will also discuss some of the provisions of the main executive directive pertaining to the intelligence activities of United States government agencies, Executive Order No. 12,333.[19] Numerous other provisions of law also constrain government actors in the cyber realm, but a comprehensive discussion of all such law is beyond the scope of this chapter. So too is a discussion of the ways in which US law impacts the ability of state and local governments and private sector entities to protect themselves from hostile foreign actors. Instead, we focus only on the legal constraints that we believe most acutely impact the nature and scope of federal government cyber operations, intelligence collection, and information sharing.

The Fourth Amendment

The primary constitutional limit the federal government confronts when responding to a cyberattack is the Fourth Amendment's prohibition on unreasonable searches and seizures.[20] Tracing a cyber intrusion through domestic computer systems and analyzing malware and other techniques used to effect the intrusion can involve activities meeting the Fourth Amendment's search threshold,[21] and as a result the government generally needs a warrant supported by probable cause for such activity to be lawful, unless an exception to the warrant requirement applies.[22] Critically, obtaining a warrant is often infeasible or unattractive in this context, given the speed at which the government must understand and respond to attacks and the significant informational uncertainty that often accompanies them.

Because obtaining a warrant may not be a viable option when responding to a discrete cyberattack, it is of considerable importance whether a warrant exception might apply to the activities comprising such response. There are several candidates, but no perfect ones. The most promising is the "special needs" exception, which permits warrantless searches when (1) the government action implicates concerns "beyond the normal need for law enforcement," and (2) acquiring a warrant is impracticable.[23] There is a strong argument that countering a cyberattack against government entities (or private entities important to national security, such as defense contractors or providers of critical infrastructure) implicates interests beyond the normal need for law enforcement. And as noted, acquiring a warrant may well be impractical where the government needs to access computer networks quickly. But the issue is not clear-cut. Special needs exceptions have generally been recognized for "dragnet" policies, such as bulk NSA communications collection,[24] or searches of sub-populations with a reduced expectation of privacy, such as parolees.[25] Responding to a cyberattack does not fall clearly within either bucket. That said, there is nothing that inherently limits special needs searches to these traditional categories, so the exception remains likely the most attractive option.

The warrant exception for consent might also provide a basis for access.[26] To leverage this exception, the government could potentially obtain some form of ex ante consent to enter certain networks and computer systems in the event of a cyber incident. But while such an approach could be effective in certain circumstances, it is hard to imagine the government acquiring sufficiently broad consent to address the range of cyber threats it faces, particularly where diffuse private-sector networks and machines are involved.

Finally, the Supreme Court has also recognized a warrant exception in cases of exigent circumstances, including where police are actively pursuing a suspect who they have probable cause to believe committed a crime.[27] The prototypical case involves chasing a suspect into a house without stopping to get a search warrant, but one could imagine applying this exception in the cyber context, where the government needs to quickly trace an attack. As is the case with cyber special needs, however, this particular flavor of the exigent circumstances exception is untested and thus uncertain.[28]

In sum, the Fourth Amendment probably does not present an insurmountable barrier to tracing and countering cyberattacks. All the same, the theories on which the government would need to rely are not well established. So at the very least, the government operates with less constitutional certainty than it would prefer to have, and any given attack will present its own Fourth Amendment complexities.

Importantly, the Fourth Amendment's applicability varies based on the link between the search or seizure and the territory of the United States. The basic rule, from *United States v. Verdugo-Urquidez*, is that the Fourth Amendment applies only where the subject of a search or seizure is within US territory or has a "significant voluntary connection" with the United States.[29] Under this regime, United States citizens abroad retain Fourth Amendment protection,[30] although the scope of the *Verdugo-Urquidez* rule for non-citizens abroad remains poorly defined.[31] And even when the Fourth Amendment does apply abroad, a warrant is not presumptively required as it is domestically; the search need only be "reasonable."[32] The upshot is this: Outside US territory, at least where US citizens are not involved, the Fourth Amendment's protections—hurdles, though of course important ones, that law enforcement must surmount—either do not apply or do not apply with the same force as they do domestically or where the government seeks to search the network or device of a US citizen.

The Foreign Intelligence Surveillance Act of 1978 (FISA)

FISA[33] is the next major authority that imposes significant procedural constraints on the government in domestic settings and where US persons are concerned but gives the government a relatively free hand abroad, particularly as against non-US persons. FISA in broad strokes authorizes and creates procedures governing certain types of information collection (such as electronic surveillance and physical searches) for foreign intelligence purposes.

Importantly, FISA makes it a crime for anyone acting under color of law to intentionally engage in "electronic surveillance" or "physical search," as those terms are defined in the Act, except as authorized by FISA or other specified provisions of law, or to knowingly disclose information obtained from such unlawful collection.[34] Persons who engage in such activities also face potential civil liability.[35] Although the risk of prosecution for such felony offenses and related lawsuits resulting in the imposition of monetary damages for FISA violations is low, criminal prohibitions in particular nevertheless act as real constraints on government action and drive prudent lawyers to steer well clear of them when advising clients. The problem is not that lawyers are not keen to push the uncertain limits of a criminal law; it is that the law is not written in a way that clearly provides the government the tools it needs for effective cyber response.

As relevant here, FISA governs "electronic surveillance" and "physical searches" targeting "foreign power[s]" or agents thereof.[36] A "foreign power" includes foreign governments and entities they control as well as "group[s] engaged in international terrorism," and other "foreign-based political organization[s], not substantially composed of United States persons."[37] Similarly, "agent of a foreign power" includes but is not limited to non-United States persons working in the United States for or on behalf of a foreign power as well as "any person," (including US persons), who "knowingly engages in clandestine intelligence gathering activities for or on behalf of a foreign power, which activities involve or may involve a violation of the criminal statutes of the United States."[38]

FISA defines "electronic surveillance" four different ways, and each definition turns on the connection between the surveillance and both the territory of the United States and whether the target is a United States person:[39]

- Definition one covers acquisition of the contents of wire or radio (i.e., wireless) communications "sent or intended to be received by" an intentionally targeted United States person located in the United States.[40]
- Definition two covers the acquisition of the contents of wire communications "to or from a person in the United States," without either party's consent "if such acquisition occurs in the United States."[41]
- Definition three covers acquisition of the contents of radio communications "if both the sender and all intended recipients are located within the United States."[42]
- Definition four covers "the installation or use" of an electronic or similar surveillance device within the United States to monitor or acquire information "other than from a wire or radio communication."[43]

Definitions one, three, and four all require that the surveillance occur "under circumstances in which a person has a reasonable expectation of privacy and a warrant would be required for law enforcement purposes."[44] And in contrast to the first three definitions, the fourth does not require that the relevant information be intercepted while being carried by a radio and/or wire and thus can reach stored communications.

This multi-pronged regime codifies the foreign-domestic divide. Definitions two and four only apply when the act of surveillance—the acquisition of the content of communications or use of a surveillance device—occurs within the United States. Definitions one, two, and three, moreover, require the subjects of surveillance be within the United States, even if the act of surveillance takes place outside of it. So if identifying, tracing, and responding to cyberattacks involves acquiring the contents of electronic communications of foreign powers or agents thereof, the government can act largely uninhibited abroad but, as explained below, it must operate subject to FISA's constraints domestically.

FISA's definition of "physical search" is also geographically limited because it prohibits "any physical intrusion within the United States" that also meets various additional requirements.[45] The provisions of FISA governing physical searches are relevant in the cyber context because they prohibit anyone acting under color of law from searching any stored data except as authorized by statute. To the extent that cyber operators would need to access, for example, emails containing links to malware or malware sets that are stored in the cloud or on systems of innocent victims, FISA would prohibit such actions without a warrant or the use of one of the other permissible mechanisms for obtaining such access under the statute, or through valid consent.

FISA's basic constraint is its requirement that the government obtain a court order before engaging in any of the four categories of "electronic surveillance" (or physical searches) for foreign intelligence purposes.[46] To obtain such an order, the agency engaging in surveillance (the FBI or NSA) must demonstrate probable cause that the prospective target is a foreign power or an agent of a foreign power who is using or about to use the particular "facilit[y]" to be surveilled.[47] The government must also propose and a court must approve certain "minimization procedures" designed to limit the collection and retention of extraneous information about US persons.[48] Moreover, FISA regulates how material obtained through such surveillance may be used and provides procedures to challenge the legality of such surveillance as well as penalties for electronic surveillance or searches not in compliance with FISA.[49] But again, these constraints only kick in when the government's activity meets the definitional criteria above—largely a function of whether the subject or act of surveillance or search occurs within the United States and/or pertains to US persons.

As with the Fourth Amendment's warrant requirement, there are exceptions to FISA's court order requirement. But only two are potentially relevant to cyberattack response, and neither is likely to allow the government to act outside of FISA's constraints domestically in a typical cyber incident situation.[50] The first allows the president or attorney general to authorize electronic surveillance directed at communications solely between or among foreign powers if "there is no substantial likelihood that the surveillance will acquire the contents of any communication to which a United States person is a party."[51] The issue with this exception is that if computers within the United States are implicated in a cyberattack, there may well be a "substantial likelihood" that any resulting surveillance will acquire the contents of "communication[s] to which a United States person is a party."[52] Even if not, the time it takes to make such a determination and for the president or attorney general to sign off may render the exception relatively impractical.

The second relevant exception allows the attorney general to authorize surveillance in "emergency situation[s]" where surveillance must be conducted before a court order can be obtained.[53] In such cases, the attorney general must contemporaneously inform the court and obtain a court order ex post within seven days.[54] Even assuming that authorization could be obtained with sufficient speed for the surveillance to be effective (not a given), it is hardly desirable for an emergency exception to provide the basis for the government's standard cyber response strategy.

In 2008 Congress widened the U.S. versus non-U.S. person and foreign versus domestic territory divides when it expanded the government's authority to target non-US persons "reasonably believed to be located outside the United States"[55] without following the procedures detailed above, an authority commonly known as § 702 of FISA.[56] Section 702 allows surveillance of such targets without a particularized court order or even probable cause; the government need only reasonably believe the nationality and geographic location predicates are satisfied. Additionally, although § 702 only allows the government to *target* persons outside of the United States, it nevertheless permits the government to collect communications between such persons and persons located *within* the United States, as long as the actual target is located abroad and the purpose is "to acquire foreign intelligence information."[57] This incidental collection authority empowers the government to collect the communications of US persons in the United States without a court order for foreign intelligence purposes, so long as the targeted party is outside the country.

Section 702 is a powerful authority, but consider what it does not reach—that is, what collection still requires a court order: Section 702 does not reach collection that intentionally targets any person located within the United States.[58] It does not reach collection targeted at a US person, even when located abroad, and even when the collection is conducted outside the United States.[59] And it does not reach communications where both sender and recipient—US persons or not—are located within the United States.[60] It also specifically forbids the use of incidental collection authority as a loophole to target a US person under the guise of targeting a non-US person abroad on the other end of their communications.[61] Section 702 is thus consistent with the rest of FISA in that it does not constrain the government abroad to the same degree it does within the United States.

Electronic Communications Privacy Act of 1986 (ECPA)

Outside of the foreign intelligence context, the dynamic is much the same. ECPA imposes additional limits on the government's ability to acquire electronic communications, typically for law enforcement purposes. It has three chapters: the first (originally enacted as Title III of the Omnibus Crime Control and Safe Streets Act of 1968,[62] and also known as the Title III or the Wiretap Act) governs the real-time interception of wire, oral, or electronic communications;[63] the second, the Stored Communications Act (SCA), governs the acquisition of stored electronic communications and related metadata;[64] and the third regulates the use of pen registers and trap-and-trace devices (the Pen Register Statute).[65]

All three components restrict particular categories of activity (i.e., using wiretaps or pen registers or accessing stored communications and related metadata) through a combination of criminal prohibitions, civil actions against government officials and private parties (for the Wiretap Act and SCA only), and in some cases, the exclusionary rule.[66] As explained in more detail below, each then exempts from its general prohibition the conduct of the relevant activity in particular circumstances. For example, the government can obtain legal process such as a court order or search warrant for a wiretap or the installation of a pen/trap device or a subpoena for certain communications records. The government can also engage in such activities with consent or, for stored communications, in emergencies.[67]

Except as noted below, all three ECPA chapters are generally understood to apply only within the United States and do not limit the government's ability to acquire real-time or stored electronic communications or related metadata abroad.[68] But because ECPA covers a wide range of both the content of communications (that is, the "substance, purport, or meaning" of communications)[69] and non-content metadata (such as "dialing, routing, addressing, and signaling information"),[70] the impact of its complicated set of prohibitions and exemptions on cyber operations conducted *inside* the United States is significant.

There is a large body of scholarship describing the contours of ECPA and its various provisions.[71] We will not endeavor to summarize that work here. Instead, we provide a brief and high-level overview of the law and highlight a few of the provisions that impact the ability of governmental entities in the United States to engage in cyber-related activities.

Title III
As noted above, Title III generally prohibits the interception of wire, oral, or electronic communications. It then contains three primary exemptions from this prohibition, none of which is especially amenable to the real-time cyber environment.[72] The first two are standard fare: (1) interceptions with

consent of a party to the communication, and (2) interceptions pursuant to a court order supported by probable cause, or in anticipation of such order.[73] The third allows the government to monitor and intercept the communications of a "computer trespasser" (an unauthorized accessor) on a network as part of an investigation, where the network operator consents to such activity.[74] The computer trespasser provision was added to the ECPA as part of the USAPATRIOT Act and, according to some, "seems designed to enable authorities to track intruders who would surreptitiously use the computer systems of others to cover their trail."[75] Although this exception seems promising, there is less to it than meets the eye. One problem is that it still requires consent. Unless such consent is obtained on a general, ex ante basis, the exception is unlikely to solve the government's problems any more than Title III's general consent exception. Another problem is that the exception applies only if "such interception does not acquire communications other than those transmitted to or from the computer trespasser."[76] If the defender needs to acquire the entire contents of a dataflow, for example, including the communications of innocent parties to the communications who are not trespassers, it is unlikely that the defender can rely on the trespasser exception .

The SCA

The SCA's regime governing electronic communications stored by third parties (e.g., emails and other communications stored by internet service providers (ISPs) and other network service providers) similarly consists of broad prohibitions and a set of exceptions. The SCA contains four primary types of restrictions: (1) limits on the government's authority to compel the disclosure of communications absent particular legal process;[77] (2) restrictions on third-party service providers' voluntary disclosure of the contents of their customers' communications;[78] (3) a prohibition on such providers disclosing communications metadata (such as user account information, email header information, etc.) to the government;[79] and (4) a bar on the intentional and unauthorized access of certain stored communications.[80] Stiff civil penalties back the first three prohibitions and violating the fourth is a crime.[81]

Alongside these restrictions are exceptions permitting both voluntary and compelled disclosure in certain circumstances. These exemptions are complex and vary based on, among other things, the nature of the service the third party provides (e-mail communications or data storage and processing); the type of disclosure (voluntary or compelled); the kind information at issue (communications content, communications metadata, or basic subscriber information); how long the communication has been in storage; whether the government is willing to have the subscriber or customer whose privacy the data implicates receive notice about the government's effort to collect the material; whether the data are needed to address an emergency; whether the communicant or customer/subscriber has consented to disclosure; and whether the material constitutes child pornography.[82] The answers to these questions determine whether service providers can voluntarily disclose information or, in the compelled disclosure context, whether the government needs a subpoena, a search warrant, or what is known as a § 2703(d) order—a court order based on "specific and articulable facts"—to compel it.[83]

The permutations of these variables are many—and that is the key point here. The SCA is a complicated statute that restricts in a variety of important ways the ability of the government to obtain information that may be crucial to conducting offensive and defensive cyber operations. The government cannot reliably obtain important information at "network speed" because it cannot quickly compel its production, and service providers must carefully analyze whether they can disclose information voluntarily so as not to expose themselves to civil liability and reputational damage. Put differently, because the SCA makes it hard for public and private sector entities to share information quickly in the cyber context, adversaries benefit from a slower and less complete government response.

As with the rest of the ECPA, the SCA's prohibitions fall away outside the United States.[84] But in 2018, Congress passed the CLOUD Act, which in part clarified that the SCA's grant of authority to the government to compel production with a court order applies to communications stored outside the country.[85] The CLOUD Act thus expressly empowered the government to compel production of overseas data without commensurately extending the general prohibitions on accessing or disclosing such information absent appropriate legal process to cover activities abroad. While the CLOUD Act did not make it any easier for the US government to access electronic communications domestically, in certain ways it narrowed the gap between the legal regimes governing data stored domestically versus data stored abroad.

Pen Register Statute

The Pen Register Statute governs the use of certain devices to intercept communications metadata while an electronic communication is in transit. Metadata—"dialing, routing, addressing, or signaling information"—does not represent the content of communications but instead is information that can be used to determine the identity of the source and recipient—telephone numbers dialed, email and internet protocol addresses, and the like.[86] Originally a telephone law, the Pen Register Statute was amended through the USAPATRIOT Act to reach internet communications.[87]

Analogous to FISA and Title III (and to some extent the SCA), the Pen Register Statute makes it a crime (a misdemeanor offense) for anyone to install or use a pen register or trap-and-trace device except as authorized by law.[88] Consistent with the less intrusive, non-content nature of the information pen registers and trap-and-trace devices collect, the permissible uses of such tools are less restrictive than those for wiretaps and stored communications access.[89] The relevant court orders need only be based on a certification that the information to be collected "is relevant to an ongoing criminal investigation,"[90] a standard lower than both probable cause and the SCA's § 2703(d) court order. The statute also contains certain exceptions, including to permit service providers to use such devices to operate, maintain, and protect their services as well as one for consent. As with the rest of ECPA, the pen register and trap-and-trace provisions do not apply extraterritorially[91] except as they relate to the provisions of the CLOUD Act as discussed above.

Executive Order 12,333

Executive Order 12,333 is the long-standing primary executive branch directive that governs the activities of the US Intelligence Community. The order, as amended, sets out certain authorizations for and rules governing foreign intelligence operations by the executive branch, and it retains the now-familiar US-person and geographic dynamics. Among other things, E.O. 12,333 authorizes the intelligence community to "conduct intelligence activities necessary for the conduct of foreign relations and the protection of the national security of the United States."[92] Such activities include "[c]ollection of information concerning, and the conduct of activities to protect against, intelligence activities directed against the United States . . . and other hostile activities directed against the United States by foreign powers, organizations, persons, and their agents."[93] Of particular relevance here, 12,333 assigns broad roles and responsibilities to, and places limitations on, all of the members of the US intelligence community.

For better or worse, when applied to cyber-related operations (both defensive and offensive), the order assigns overlapping responsibilities to NSA, CIA, the FBI, and other intelligence community members, and also limits their authorities in important ways. Although a complete analysis of the cyber-related contours of the order is beyond the scope of this chapter, below we discuss some of the limitations that the order places on (a) all agencies with respect to the collection of information of or concerning United States persons; and (b) agencies other than the FBI with respect to domestic activities. But first we address the relationship between 12,333 and FISA.[94]

Because FISA controls the authorizations and restrictions on foreign intelligence collection where it applies, and ECPA restricts other government collection activities domestically, 12,333's foreign intelligence collection provisions are most relevant in areas outside of the scope of those statutes.[95] Recall that FISA's definition of electronic surveillance is limited: FISA typically governs surveillance that intentionally targets either a US person (whether within the United States or abroad) and/or a non-US person located inside the United States where the surveillance is conducted in the United States.[96] And, as discussed above, ECPA generally has been construed as applying only in the United States. As a result, where surveillance does not intentionally target a US person or is conducted abroad, 12,333 is generally the primary source of authority and constraint.[97]

At the outset, it is important to stress that unlike FISA and ECPA 12,333 cannot impose criminal or civil penalties on anyone for violations of its terms, because it is an executive order. While 12,333 is law and executive branch agencies and officers must comply with it, the risks associated with violations of its provisions are substantially lower and agencies and their lawyers are more likely to be willing to interpret it aggressively in a variety of contexts, including cyber.

Executive Order 12,333 authorizes and constrains the collection, retention, and dissemination of "information concerning United States persons"[98] but generally provides fewer limits on these activities regarding information concerning non-US persons. Specifically, 12,333 provides that where information of or concerning US persons is involved, collection, retention, and dissemination activities may only be conducted according to procedures established by the relevant agency and approved by the attorney general.[99] While such procedures vary agency to agency, 12,333 provides that they shall in general permit the collection of certain information, including information "constituting foreign intelligence,"[100] so long as such collection is not "undertaken for the purpose of acquiring information concerning the domestic activities of United States persons" by agencies other than the FBI.[101] Similarly, electronic surveillance within the United States or targeting US-persons abroad pursuant to 12,333 requires the approval of both the agency head and the attorney general, and must be conducted using the "least intrusive collection techniques feasible."[102] Collection activities intentionally targeting US persons abroad are now also significantly constrained by Title VII of FISA and generally require an order from the FISC except in emergency circumstances.[103] By contrast, such approvals and procedures are not required for procedures governing signals intelligence targeting non-US persons and targets abroad.[104]

In general, but with important exceptions, 12,333 assigns the FBI primary responsibility domestically for collecting foreign intelligence information and undertaking other intelligence and counterintelligence activities.[105] To the extent that elements of the intelligence community other than the FBI may engage in some domestic intelligence activities in certain circumstances, 12,333 provides that "no foreign intelligence collection by such elements may be undertaken for the purpose of acquiring information concerning the domestic activities of United States persons."[106] This latter restriction is particularly important in cyber-related operations because it is often very difficult to assess in real time the true identity of a malicious cyber actor. As a result, when such an actor is operating in the United States, it is risky for the intelligence community to assume that the actor is a non-United States person. Even if an intelligence agency other than the FBI were to take on that risk and potentially violate 12,333 by collecting foreign intelligence information regarding the domestic activities of the malicious cyber actor, it would quickly run into collection problems as a result of the criminal prohibitions set forth in FISA and ECPA.

On their face, both 12,333 and Title VII of FISA permit incidental collection of the communications of US persons who are located either in the United States or abroad, so long as such persons are not intentionally targeted for collection and appropriate minimization procedures are in place to minimize such collection's impact on the privacy of US persons. This is a significant authority, and the extent to which 12,333 allows the incidental collection, retention, and analysis of the communications of US persons has been criticized from certain quarters.[107] But whatever the normative implications of 12,333-authorized incidental collection of US person communications, the relative freedom that 12,333, FISA, and ECPA give US intelligence agencies abroad disappears when those agencies confront adversaries whose activities, in whole or in part, occur within the United States or require the intentional targeting of US persons (or what appear to be US persons) to address the threat. This could be the case, for instance, when a malicious cyber actor has compromised and is utilizing an identifiable US person facility as part of its activities.

Domestic Military Activity

The law governing the domestic use of the armed forces of the United States—including active duty military, the reserves, and the national guard—is complicated and a full analysis of that legal regime is beyond the scope of this chapter. Nevertheless, as we will explain briefly, we assess that the military is not well positioned to fill the legal gaps facing the law enforcement and intelligence communities in the cyber realm. For starters, unless martial law is in effect or the military is responding to a use of force or armed attack, the same laws that limit law enforcement and intelligence agencies domestically also apply to the military. Indeed, even if the military was called into action to suppress an insurrection, it would be acting "to enforce [United States] law[] or to suppress the rebellion."[108] In other words, the Constitution and laws of the United States do not go out the window merely because the president has decided to use the armed forces domestically in some capacity.

But before such restrictions even become relevant, there is a threshold question: Can the military as a general matter operate domestically in a law enforcement or intelligence collection capacity, setting aside other more specific prohibitions? The answer is typically no. The Posse Comitatus Act[109] makes it unlawful for anyone to "willfully use[] any part of the Army or the Air Force as a posse comitatus or otherwise to execute the laws" "except in cases and under circumstances expressly authorized by the Constitution or Act of Congress."[110] This Act, combined with 10 U.S.C. § 275, which restricts all branches of the military from "direct participation . . . in a search, seizure, arrest, or other similar activity," as well as related DoD policies,[111] broadly prohibits military involvement in domestic law enforcement.

There are two exceptions to the Posse Comitatus Act that may allow the military to respond to cyber activities domestically, but neither is easily read to permit the military to, in general, serve as the primary actor tracing, attributing, and responding to malicious cyber activities in the United States. The first is less an exception than a DoD interpretation that the act does not apply to "[a]ctions taken for the primary purpose of furthering a DOD or foreign affairs function of the United States, regardless of incidental benefits to civil authorities."[112] While this interpretation might initially seem to permit substantial DoD activity—particularly where a hostile state actor is involved—it also states that such actions do not "include actions taken for the primary purpose of aiding civilian law enforcement officials,"[113] arguably proscribing the very conduct with which we are concerned. This is in part because it can be difficult in real time to determine the identity of malicious cyber actors and their purpose. For example, it can be hard to assess quickly whether a particular intrusion on the network of a public utility is being undertaken by a hostile foreign intelligence service to lay the groundwork for a damaging cyberattack in the future on critical infrastructure or whether it is a criminal actor seeking to gain access to steal credit card information and other personally identifiable information from customers. As such, it is simply not viable to rely on the military to respond to such incidents that all would agree fall short of a use of force or an armed attack.

Moreover, as a general matter, actions taken to "further[] a DOD or foreign affairs function of the United States" within the meaning of the statute likely involve only actions related to DoD personnel and facilities. DoD provides an enumerated list of such actions and it includes, for example, investigations related to the enforcement of the Uniform Code of Military Justice, actions related to "a commander's inherent authority to maintain law and order on a DoD installation or facility," and protection of DoD personnel and equipment.[114] While this list has a broad catch-all provision covering "[s]uch other actions that are undertaken primarily for a military or foreign affairs purpose," a fair reading of this clause likely limits it to actions similar to those listed. Still, the list includes "[p]rotection of classified defense information or equipment or controlled unclassified information," which could potentially allow the military to act in response to attacks on defense contractors and other private-sector entities possessing such information.[115]

The second exception—understood to be constitutionally based[116]— allows the military "to engage temporarily in activities that are necessary to quell large-scale, unexpected civil disturbances" if doing so is "necessary to prevent significant loss of life or wanton destruction of property and . . . to restore governmental function and public order," or when other authorities are unable to protect federal property and governmental functions.[117] The second of these justifications would seem to authorize the military to respond to cyber activities directed at federal property and is understood to do so.[118] The scope of the first justification is less clear. Some commentators argue that any attack on critical cyber infrastructure—even private networks—would permit the military to respond under the first justification, but others disagree.[119] Either way, the military's authority to respond domestically to cyberattacks on private networks is at best contested.[120]

Covert Action Statute

The regime governing covert action provides a final example of the foreign-domestic cyber activity response dichotomy. In general, the covert action statute—currently codified at 50 U.S.C. § 3093—represents a congressional grant of broad authority to the executive branch to conduct certain intelligence activities pursuant to presidential authorization and with notice to Congress. Covert action comprises government activities to "influence political, economic, or military conditions abroad, where it is intended that the role of the United States Government will not be apparent or acknowledged publicly."[121] The president may authorize such activities, contingent on making a "finding" and subject to certain requirements to report such activities to the congressional intelligence committees.[122]

While potentially a relevant authority for *offensive* cyber operations,[123] covert action is a poor fit for tracing and responding defensively to domestic cyber intrusions. By definition, covert activities are not conducted to influence "political, economic, or military conditions" within the United States. So, once again, the rules change at the border. And in any event, the statute expressly carves out from the definition of covert action "traditional law enforcement activities conducted by United States Government law enforcement agencies or routine support to such activities."[124] Presumably this would sweep in typical and long-standing efforts by agencies such as the FBI and other federal domestic law enforcement agencies (such as the US Secret Service) to identify and trace cyber intrusions within the United States and prosecute cyber criminals.

Public-Private Collaboration

Across a range of constitutional and statutory authorities and constraints, then, the government operates more freely on international networks than on domestic ones. In the important area of public-private collaboration, the equation is more complicated.

From taking down botnets[125] to defending critical private sector network infrastructure,[126] the government and some private sector actors at times work collaboratively, or at least in a mutually supportive fashion, to protect against and identify the parties responsible for malicious cyber activities. In particular, this can take the form of information sharing regarding potential threats, a function the importance of which recent experience makes clear: According to news reports, private firms—not the government—first identified the recent SolarWinds and Microsoft Exchange hacking operations.[127] And public-private collaboration may increase, in substantial part because of the legal constraints on government action described above.[128]

Information sharing is relatively straightforward as a legal matter where the government shares information with private companies (apart from issues regarding the sharing of classified information, which can be addressed by granting private sector actors clearances or having them sign non-disclosure agreements). But where the government seeks information *from* private companies, these companies must comply not only with their own policies and terms of service but also with US law (in particular, ECPA) as well as that of other jurisdictions (such as US state laws and the laws of foreign countries) in which the information the government seeks might be processed or stored. Legal regimes, such as EPCA, permit private sector entities to share information in some circumstances and empower the government to compel those entities to disclose information in others if it obtains appropriate legal process (such as a warrant or subpoena). But as explained above, the rules are complex and require some amount of time and effort to analyze and implement, resulting inevitably in delay. And such delay plays to the advantage of malicious cyber actors, which is exactly why they seek to conduct at least some of their activities from the United States.

Non-US law can create additional complications, by prohibiting information disclosure that the US government seeks to compel. Particularly after the CLOUD Act, the US government will generally have the means to compel production of information that companies store both domestically and abroad. But international legal regimes, most notably the EU's Global Data Protection Regulation (GDPR), are at times more protective of user data than is US law. As a result, complying with US legal process might violate the GDPR, and private sector lawyers must analyze the situation to ensure compliance with all applicable law, resulting in delay that benefits adversaries.[129]

While both the CLOUD Act and GDPR contain provisions that may at times resolve such conflicts,[130] US and non-US law may be irreconcilable in certain circumstances, and there is no guarantee US law will win out. As a result, data the US government could plainly get access to with appropriate process domestically may at times be out of reach where it is located abroad—a reversal of the typical pattern described above.

Conclusion

The concerns we raise are not hypothetical. In recent months Russia and China apparently conducted two of the most serious hacking operations the United States has ever seen. The SolarWinds hackers may have had access to highly sensitive government and private sector systems for over nine months before detection.[131] And the fallout from the Microsoft Exchange hack may only be beginning. Hackers apparently have begun to exploit the security vulnerabilities it created, leading to a rash of ransomware attacks and other predatory actions.[132] These incidents are in part consequences of gaps in US law.

By far the most sophisticated tools in the US cyber arsenal—the sorts of capabilities that might have detected these hacks—sit with the US intelligence community. And as explained, Executive Order 12,333 prohibits certain elements of the intelligence community, such as the NSA and CIA, from conducting domestic surveillance directed at US persons. As former NSA director Admiral Michael Rogers put it: "The N.S.A. cannot operate in the domestic infrastructure[, and] [y]ou can't defend something you can't see."[133] Microsoft, for its part, believes the Exchange hack was specifically designed with these considerations in mind. Its vice president for customer security explained that the operation was committed by "a sophisticated actor that apparently took the time to research legal authority . . . [and] knew that by operating from servers in the United States, it could evade some of the US government's best threat hunters."[134]

And, of course, the legal complications do not stop there. The FBI and Department of Homeland Security, the agencies that are more empowered to operate domestically, face their own constraints. Most fundamentally, they simply lack the capabilities and resources that the rest of the US intelligence community has. But they must also abide by the Fourth Amendment, ECPA, and FISA, and that often means getting a warrant before acting, something former NSA General Counsel Glenn Gerstell described in the aftermath of the SolarWinds and Microsoft Exchange events as impractical: "Someone's got to be able to take that information from the N.S.A. and instantly go take a look at [suspicious] computer[s]. But the F.B.I. needs a warrant to do that, and that takes time by which point the adversary has escaped."[135]

In Gerstell's view, "It can't possibly be the case that the Fourth Amendment ties our hands in such a way that we just have to sit there and watch the Chinese romp through our infrastructure."[136] Whether or not Gerstell's constitutional analysis is correct, malicious cyber actors are able to conduct offensive cyber operations in the United States in ways that all should agree are unacceptable. The Biden administration has signaled its intent to increase its collaboration with the private sector as a first step to shoring up the United States' defenses.[137] That is a welcome first step, but we submit that substantial legal reform is needed as well in order to protect both security and privacy. Society must find a way, consistent with the Constitution's protections of civil liberties, to better defend itself against the full range of cyber threats while, at the same time, protecting privacy in an era of Big Data, advanced data analytics, and high-speed computing. The politics of any such reform will be challenging, and balancing security and privacy has never been easy. But recent events should be yet another wake-up call, and we hope to see the conversation accelerate.

Notes

1. U.S. CYBER COMMAND, ACHIEVE AND MAINTAIN CYBERSPACE SUPERIORITY 6 (2018).
2. See, e.g., Ashley Deeks, Defend Forward and Cyber Countermeasures (Hoover Inst. Working Group on Nat'l Sec., Tech., and L., Aegis Series Paper No. 2004, 2020); Robert Chesney, The Domestic Legal Framework for US Military Cyber Operations (Hoover Inst. Working Group on Nat'l Sec., Tech., and L., Aegis Series Paper No. 2003, 2020).
3. Kevin Paulsen, Robert McMillan, and Dustin Volz, SolarWinds Hack Victims: From Tech Companies to a Hospital and University, WALL ST. J. (Dec. 21, 2020); Isabella Jibilian and Katie Canales, Here's A Simple Explanation of How the Massive SolarWinds Hack Happened and Why It's Such a Big Deal, BUS. INSIDER (Feb. 25, 2021).
4. Id.
5. Nicholas Weaver, The Microsoft Exchange Hack and the Great Email Robbery, LAWFARE (Mar. 9, 2021).

6. Exec. Order No. 12,333, 3 C.F.R. § 200 (1982), *reprinted as amended in* 50 U.S.C. § 3001 note (preamble).

7. *See, e.g.*, Computer Fraud and Abuse Act (CFAA), 18 U.S.C. § 1030 (2018).

8. FED'N OF AM. SCI, CYBERSPACE POLICY REVIEW: ASSURING A TRUSTED AND RESILIENT INFORMATION AND COMMUNICATIONS INFRASTRUCTURE 10 (2009).

9. The term "United States person" generally includes citizens, permanent resident aliens, and U.S.-based corporations and organizations. *See, e.g.*, 50 U.S.C. § 1801(i) (2018) ("'United States person' means a citizen of the United States, an alien lawfully admitted for permanent residence (as defined in section 1101(a)(20) of title 8), an unincorporated association a substantial number of members of which are citizens of the United States or aliens lawfully admitted for permanent residence, or a corporation which is incorporated in the United States, but does not include a corporation or an association which is a foreign power, as defined in subsection (a)(1), (2), or (3) [of title 50].").

10. The various titles of the United States Code relevant to this discussion contain definitions of the term "United States" in a geographical sense that differ slightly from each other, but the basic point remains regardless of the particulars. *See, e.g.*, 18 U.S.C. § 5 (2018) ("'United States' . . . includes all places and waters, continental or insular, subject to the jurisdiction of the United States, except the canal zone"); 10 U.S.C. § 101(a) (2018) ("'United States,' in a geographic sense, means the States and the District of Columbia," *id.* § 101(a)(1), "[and] [t]he term 'possessions' includes the Virgin Islands, Guam, American Samoa, and the Guano Islands, so long as they remain possessions, but does not include any Commonwealth, *id.* § 101(a)(3)); 50 U.S.C. § 1801(j) (2018) ("'United States' . . . means all areas under the territorial sovereignty of the United States and the Trust Territory of the Pacific Islands.").

11. *Joint Inquiry into the Terrorist Attacks of September 11, 2001 by the H. Permanent Select Comm. on Intelligence and the S. Select Comm. on Intelligence*, 107th Cong. 793 (2002) (Statement of Lieutenant Gen. Michael Hayden, Dir. NSA / Chief, Central Sec. Serv.)

12. *Id.*

13. *Worldwide Threat Assessment of the U.S. Intelligence Community: Hearing Before the S. Select. Comm. on Intel*, 116th Cong. 15 (2019) (Statement for the Record of Daniel R. Coats, Director of National Intelligence).

14. *See, e.g.*, DAVID A. WHEELER AND GREGORY N. LARSEN, INSTITUTE FOR DEFENSE ANALYSES, TECHNIQUES FOR CYBER ATTACK ATTRIBUTION 2-4 (2003); Susan W. Brenner, *"At Light Speed": Attribution and Response to Cybercrime/Terrorism/Warfare*, 97 J. CRIM. L. & CRIMINOLOGY 379, 409 (2007)("It is common for online attackers to use 'stepping stones'—computers the attacker controls but that are owned by innocent parties—in their assaults.")

15. Pub. L. No. 95-511, 92 Stat. 1783 (codified as amended in scattered sections of 50 U.S.C.).

16. Pub. L. No. 99-508, 100 Stat. 1848 (codified as amended in scattered sections of 18 U.S.C.).

17. Army Appropriations Act, ch. 263, § 15, 20 Stat. 145, 152 (1878) (codified as amended at 18 U.S.C. § 1385 (2018)).

18. 50 U.S.C. § 3093 (2018).

19. Exec. Order No. 12,333, 3 C.F.R. § 200 (1982), *reprinted as amended in* 50 U.S.C. § 3001 note.

20. U.S. CONST. amend IV ("The right of the people to be secure in their persons, houses, papers, and effects, against unreasonable searches and seizures, shall not be violated, and no warrants shall issue, but upon probable cause, supported by oath or affirmation, and particularly describing the place to be searched, and the persons or things to be seized.").

21. *See* United States v. Heckenkamp, 482 F.3d 1142, 1146–47 (9th Cir. 2007).

22. *See* Katz v. United States, 389 U.S. 347, 357 (1967).

23. *See* Griffin v. Wisconsin, 483 U.S. 868, 873 (1987).

24. Memorandum from the U.S. Dep't of Justice, Legal Authorities Supporting the Activities of the National Security Agency Described by the President 37–38 (Jan. 19, 2006).

25. *See* Samson v. California, 547 U.S. 843, 857 (2006); *see also* Eve Brensike Primus, *Disentangling Administrative Searches*, 111 COLUM. L. REV. 254, 259 (2011).

26. Davis v. United States, 328 U.S. 582, 593–94 (1946).

27. Warden v. Hayden, 387 U.S. 294 (1967).

28. *See* Jay P. Kesan and Carol M. Hayes, *Mitigative Counterstriking: Self-Defense and Deterrence in Cyberspace*, 25 HARV. J. L. & TECH. 429, 535 (2012).

29. United States v. Verdugo-Urquidez, 494 U.S. 259, 260 (1990).

30. *See* Reid v. Covert, 354 U.S. 1, 6 (1957) (plurality opinion) ("[T]he shield which the Bill of Rights and other parts of the Constitution provide to protect [one's] life and liberty should not be stripped away just because [one] happens to be in another land"); United States v. Stokes, 726 F.3d 880, 890–91 (7th Cir. 2013) ("[I]f U.S. agents substantially participate in an extraterritorial search of a U.S. citizen . . . the Fourth Amendment generally applies.").

31. *Compare e.g.*, American Immigration Lawyers Ass'n v. Reno, 18 F. Supp. 2d 38 (D.D.C. 1998), *aff'd*, 199 F.3d 1352 (D.C. Cir. 2000) (holding that frequent visits to the United States do not create the requisite connection for constitutional protections to apply), *with* Martinez-Aguero v. Gonzalez, 459 F.3d 618 (5th Cir. 2006) (holding the opposite). *See also* Orin Kerr, *The Fourth Amendment and the Global Internet*, 67 STAN. L. REV. 285, 293 (2015).

32. *In re* Terrorist Bombings of U.S. Embassies in East Africa, 552 F.3d 157, 171 (2d. Cir. 2008). There is no consensus regarding how to determine whether a search abroad was reasonable. *Compare id.*, *with*, United States v. Peterson, 812 F.2d 486, 490 (9th Cir. 1987).

33. Pub. L. No. 95-511, 92 Stat. 1783 (codified as amended in scattered sections of 50 U.S.C.).

34. 50 U.S.C. §§ 1809(a) and 1827(a) (2018).

35. *Id.* §§ 1810 and 1828.

36. *Id.* §§ 1804(a)(3)(A), 1822, and 1823(a)(3).

37. *Id.* § 1801(a).
38. *Id.* § 1801(b).
39. "United States person" encompasses citizens, lawful permanent residents, domestically incorporated entities and unincorporated entities that have a substantial number of members who are US citizens or lawfully permanent residents. *Id.* § 1801(i).
40. *Id.* § 1801(f)(1).
41. *Id.* § 1801(f)(2).
42. *Id.* § 1801(f)(3).
43. *Id.* § 1801(f)(4).
44. *Id.* § 1801(f).
45. *See id.* § 1821(5), which provides in full:

> "Physical search" means any physical intrusion within the United States into premises or property (including examination of the interior of property by technical means) that is intended to result in a seizure, reproduction, inspection, or alteration of information, material, or property, under circumstances in which a person has a reasonable expectation of privacy and a warrant would be required for law enforcement purposes, but does not include (A) "electronic surveillance", as defined in section 1801(f) of this title, or (B) the acquisition by the United States Government of foreign intelligence information from international or foreign communications, or foreign intelligence activities conducted in accordance with otherwise applicable Federal law involving a foreign electronic communications system, utilizing a means other than electronic surveillance as defined in section 1801(f) of this title.

46. *Id.* § 1803. Applications for FISA warrants go through a dedicated court: the Foreign Intelligence Surveillance Court (FISC). *Id.*
47. *Id.* § 1805(a)(2).
48. *Id.* § 1805(a)(3); § 1801(h).
49. *Id.* § 1806; § 1809; § 1810.
50. One of the other two is only applicable within fifteen days of a declaration of war, *id.* § 1811, and the other is limited to testing equipment and training personnel, *id.* § 1805(g).
51. *Id.* § 1802(a)(1). The government must still use minimization procedures. *Id.*
52. *Id.*
53. *Id.* § 1805(e)(1).
54. *Id.* § 1805(e)(1)(C)-(D).
55. 1881a(a). This amendment came through the FISA Amendments Act of 2008, Pub. L. No. 110-261, 122 Stat. 2436 (codified as amended in scattered sections of 18 and 50 U.S.C.).
56. Referencing § 702 of the FISA Amendments Act (FAA).
57. *Id.*
58. 50 U.S.C. § 1881a(b)(1).
59. *Id.* § 1881a(b)(3).
60. *Id.* § 1881a(b)(4).
61. *Id.* § 1881a(b)(2).

62. Pub. L. No. 90-351, 82 Stat. 197 (codified as amended in scattered sections of the U.S. Code).

63. 18 U.S.C. §§ 2510-2521 (2018).

64. *Id.* §§ 2701-2713.

65. *Id.* §§ 3121-3127.

66. Specifically, there is no exclusionary remedy for the use of pen registers, *see Smith v. Maryland*, 442 U.S. 735, 745–46 (1979) (relying on the third party doctrine), or the collection of non-content (i.e., to, from, and similar information for emails, ISP addresses disclosed through electronic communication with another party, etc.) information under the SCA, *see United States v. Forrester*, 512 F.3d 500, 509–11 (9th Cir. 2008) (analogizing to pen registers and to/from information on letters). The SCA itself does not have a suppression remedy, but lower courts have held that the content of both emails, *Warshak v. United States*, 490 F.3d 455, 473 (6th Cir. 2007), *vacated en banc*, 532 F.3d 521 (6th Cir. 2008) (holding claim not ripe for judicial determination), and text messages, *Quon v. Arch Wireless Operating Co.*, 529 F.3d 892, 904 (9th Cir. 2008), are protected by the Fourth Amendment, so violating the SCA to obtain this information could also result in exclusion.

67. *See, e.g.*, 18 U.S.C. § 2702(b)(3), (b)(8), (c)(2), and (c)(4) (2018).

68. *See, e.g.*, United States v. Peterson, 812 F.2d 486, 492 (9th Cir. 1987) ("Title III has no extraterritorial force."); David Kris, *Preliminary Thoughts on Cross-Border Data Requests*, LAWFARE (Sept. 28, 2015, 9:00 AM).

69. 18 U.S.C. § 2510(8) (2018).

70. 18 U.S.C. § 3127(3)-(4) (2018).

71. *See, e.g.*, Orin S. Kerr, *The Next Generation Communications Privacy Act*, 162 U. PENN. L. REV. 373 (2014).

72. The statute also contains a number of other highly specific exceptions to allow, among other things, telecommunications firms and the Federal Communications Commission to conduct routine business without violating the law. 18 U.S.C. § 2511(2)(a)-(b) (2018).

73. *Id.* § 2511(2)(c) (2018); *id.* § 2516.

74. *Id.* § 2511(2)(i).

75. CHARLES DOYLE, CONG. RSCH. SERV., R41733, PRIVACY: AN OVERVIEW OF THE ELECTRONIC COMMUNICATIONS PRIVACY ACT 29 (2012) (citing *Implementation of the USA PATRIOT Act: Crime, Terrorism and the Age of Technology: Hearing Before the Subcomm. on Crime, Terrorism, and Homeland Security of the House Comm. on the Judiciary*, 109th Cong., 2d sess. 30-1 (2005) (prepared statement of FBI Dep. Ass't Director Steven M. Martinez)).

76. 18 U.S.C. § 2511(i)(IV).

77. 18 U.S.C. § 2703 (2018).

78. *Id.* § 2702(a)(1)-(2).

79. *Id.* § 2702(a)(3).

80. *Id.* § 2701(a). This criminal prohibition is largely redundant with the Computer Fraud and Abuse Act (CFAA), 18 U.S.C. § 1030 (2018), but the CFAA expressly does not apply to the government in general, *id.* § 1030(f).

81. 18 U.S.C. § 2707(a)-(d) (2018); id. § 2701(b).

82. *Id.* § 2702(b)-(c); *id.* § 2703.

83. *Id.*

84. *See* Zheng v. Yahoo! Inc., No. C-08-1068, 2009 WL 4430297, at *2-*5 (N.D. Cal. Dec. 2, 2009) (holding that ECPA did not apply to Yahoo! China's release of data stored in China); *see also* Jennifer Daskal, *The Un-Territoriality of Data*, 125 Yale L.J. 326, 362 (2015)("The legislative history, coupled with the presumption against extraterritoriality, overwhelmingly supports the conclusion that the SCA does not apply extraterritorially"); *cf.* Suzlon Energy Ltd. v. Microsoft Corp, 671 F.3d 726, 729–30 (9th Cir. 2011) (holding that the ECPA applies to non-citizens "at least . . . whenever the requested documents are stored in the United States" but reserving the question "whether the ECPA applies to documents stored or acts occurring outside of the United States" and citing *Zheng*).

85. Clarifying Lawful Overseas Use of Data (CLOUD) Act, Pub. L. No. 115-141, 132 Stat. 348, 1213 (2018).

86. Modern pen registers and trap-and-trace devices can intercept the content of communications in certain circumstances, in which case Title III, rather than 18 U.S.C. §§ 3121–3127 (2018), governs their use.

87. The USAPATRIOT Act, Pub. L. No. 107-56, 115 Stat. 272, 288–91 (2001) (codified in relevant part at 18 U.S.C. § 3127(3) (2018)) (defining "pen register" to include devices that record "dialing, routing, addressing, or signaling information" transmitted electronically)

88. 18 U.S.C. § 3121(a) (2018) provides:

> Except as provided in this section, no person may install or use a pen register or a trap and trace device without first obtaining a court order under section 3123 of this title or under the Foreign Intelligence Surveillance Act of 1978 (50 U.S.C. 1801 et seq.) or an order from a foreign government that is subject to an executive agreement that the Attorney General has determined and certified to Congress satisfies section 2523.

89. *Id.* § 3121(b).

90. *Id.* § 3122.

91. *Zheng v. Yahoo! Inc.*, 2009 WL 4430297 (N.D. Cal. Dec. 2, 2009).

92. Exec. Order No. 12,333, 3 C.F.R. § 200 (1982), § 1.4, *reprinted as amended in* 50 U.S.C. § 3001 note.

93. *Id.* § 1.4(c).

94. *Id.* § 1.7(c).

95. 50 U.S.C. § 1812(a) (2018) (providing that except as specifically authorized by statute, FISA "shall be the exclusive means by which electronic surveillance and the interception of domestic wire, oral, or electronic communications may be conducted"); *see also* Mark M. Jaycox, *No Oversight, No Limits, No Worries: A Primer on Presidential Spying and Executive Order 12,333*, 12 Harv. Nat'l Sec. J. 58, 79 (2021).

96. Axel Arnbak & Sharon Goldberg, *Loopholes for Circumventing the Constitution: Unrestrained Bulk Surveillance on Americans by Collecting Network*

Traffic Abroad, 21 MICH. TELECOMM. & TECH. L. REV. 317, 321 (2015). While FISA technically sweeps broader than this description, see text accompanying notes 33–61; it is a useful framework for thinking about FISA's scope, and one consistent with how the NSA analyzes which authorities authorize particular kinds of surveillance. *See* NAT'L SEC. AGENCY, SIGINT AUTHORITY DECISION TREE (2014).

97. *See* Arnbak & Goldberg, *supra* note 97, at 321.

98. For example, § 2.8 of the order provides that "[n]othing in this Order shall be construed to authorize any activity in violation of the Constitution or statutes of the United States." Exec. Order 12,333, 3 C.F.R. 200, § 2.8.

99. *Id.* § 2.3. Section 2.3 is not a model of clarity, and provides in subsection (b):

> Collection within the United States of foreign intelligence not otherwise obtainable shall be undertaken by the Federal Bureau of Investigation (FBI) or, when significant foreign intelligence is sought, by other authorized elements of the Intelligence Community, provided that no foreign intelligence collection by such elements may be undertaken for the purpose of acquiring information concerning the domestic activities of United States persons.

100. "Foreign intelligence" has been most recently defined for this purpose in Obama Administration Presidential Policy Directive, PPD-28, as "information relating to the capabilities, intentions, or activities of foreign governments or elements thereof, foreign organizations, foreign persons, or international terrorists." Press Release, Off. of the Press Sec'y, Presidential Policy Directive—Signals Intelligence Activities (Jan. 17, 2014). This definition supersedes but largely tracks the definition in 12,333.

101. Exec. Order 12,333, 3 C.F.R. 200, § 2.3(b).

102. *Id.* § 2.4.

103. 50 U.S.C. §§ 1881b-1881c (2018).

104. *See* Jaycox, *supra* note 96, at 85–86; Arnbak & Goldberg, *supra* note 97, at 321.

105. Exec. Order 12,333, 3 C.F.R. 200, § 2.6.

106. *Id.* § 2.3(b).

107. *See, e.g.*, John Napier Tye, *Meet Executive Order 12333: The Reagan Rule that Lets the NSA Spy on Americans*, WASH. POST (July 18, 2014).

108. 10 U.S.C. § 252 (2018).

109. Army Appropriations Act, ch. 263, § 15, 20 Stat. 145, 152 (1878) (codified as amended at 18 U.S.C. § 1385 (2018)).

110. § 1385. The term "posse comitatus" stems from the "common law power of state agents to call forth the *posse*—or power—of their *comitatus*—a medieval term meaning both an armed retinue and an administrative unit of government." William O. Scharf, *Cybersecurity, Cyber Command, and the Posse Comitatus Act* (MIT Computer Science & Artificial Intelligence Lab Working Paper, 2010) (on file with author).

111. DOD INSTRUCTION 3025.21 (updated Feb. 8, 2019) [hereinafter DOD 3025.21].

112. *Id.* Enclosure 3, para. 1(b)(1).

113. *Id.* Enclosure 3, para. 3(a)-(b).

114. *Id.* Enclosure 3, para. 1(b)(1).

115. *Id.* Enclosure 3, para. 1(b)(1)(d).

116. Sean M. Cordon, *Getting It Right: Protecting American Critical Infrastructure in Cyberspace*, 20 HARV. J. L. & TECH. 403, 420 (2007). Cordon relied on language in 32 C.F.R. § 215.4 suggesting that the following exceptions are constitutionally based. Those regulations have since been repealed, but DOD 3025.21 contains identical language.

117. DOD 3025.21, Enclosure 3, para. (1)(b)(3).

118. Scharf, *supra* note 111, at 10; Cordon, *supra* note 117, at 420.

119. *Compare* Scharf, *supra* note 111, at 19, *with* Cordon, *supra* note 117, at 420.

120. Other Posse Comitatus carve outs allow military personnel to assist law enforcement in the operation of equipment, 10 U.S.C. § 272 (2018), and share information collected in the course of lawful military activities with domestic law enforcement, *id.* at § 271. While these exceptions may be useful to the overall project of cyber defense, they are likely to be of limited use in the immediate response to any given cyber event that clearly falls short of a use of force or armed attack.

121. 50 U.S.C. § 3093(e) (emphasis added).

122. *Id.*

123. *See, e.g.*, Chesney, *supra* note 2, at 8–10; Aaron P. Brecher, Note, *Cyberattacks and the Covert Action Statute: Toward a Domestic Legal Framework for Offensive Cyberoperations*, 111 MICH. L. REV. 423 (2012).

124. 50 U.S.C. § 3093(e)(3).

125. Kristen Eichensehr, *Public-Private Cybersecurity*, 95 TEX. L. REV. 467, 479 (2017); Robert M. Chesney, *Persistently Engaging TrickBot: USCYBERCOM Takes on a Notorious Botnet*, LAWFARE (Oct. 12, 2020).

126. Eichensehr, *supra* note 126, at 494–99.

127. *See, e.g.*, David E. Sanger, Julian E. Barnes, and Nicole Pelroth, *White House Weighs New Cybersecurity Approach After Failure to Detect Hacks*, N.Y. TIMES (Mar. 14, 2021) [hereinafter Sanger et al., *White House Weighs New Cybersecurity Approach*].

128. *Id.*

129. For example, Article 48 of GDPR, which governs compelled transfers of data to non-EU states, makes clear that "a foreign court order does not, as such, make a transfer lawful under the GDPR." Brief of the European Commission on behalf of the European Union as Amicus Curiae in support of neither party, at 14, United States v. Microsoft Corp., 138 S. Ct. 1186 (2018) (per curiam) (No. 17-2). Instead, such transfers are only lawful under GDPR "if based on an international agreement, such as a mutual legal assistance treaty, in force between the requesting third country and the Union or a Member State." GDPR art. 48. The warrants the CLOUD Act contemplates are not necessarily consistent with the requirements of mutual legal assistance treaties, setting up the potential for conflict.

130. *See, e.g.*, 18 U.S.C. § 2713 (2018) (the CLOUD Act's quash provisions); GDPR art. 49(1)(d) (allowing transfers "necessary for important reasons of public interest"); GDPR art. 49(1) (authorizing transfers "necessary for the purposes of compelling legitimate interests pursued by the controller which are not overridden by the interests or rights and freedoms of the data subject").

131. *SolarStorm Supply Chain Attack Timeline*, UNIT 42 (Dec. 23, 2020); Craig Timberg and Ellen Nakashima, *The U.S. Government Spent Billions on a System for Detecting Hacks. The Russians Outsmarted It*, WASH. POST. (Dec. 15, 2020).

132. *See, e.g.*, Threatpost Podcast, *Microsoft Exchange Server Attack Onslaught Continues*, THREATPOST (Mar. 23, 2021); Dan Goodin, *Ransomware Operators Are Piling On Already Hacked Exchange Servers*, ARS TECHNICA (Mar. 23, 2021).

133. Sanger et al., *White House Weighs New Cybersecurity Approach*, *supra* note 128.

134. Dustin Volz and Robert McMillan, *Massive Hacks Linked to Russia, China Exploited U.S. Internet Security Gap*, WALL ST. J. (Mar. 10, 2021).

135. Sanger et al., *White House Weighs New Cybersecurity Approach*, *supra* note 128.

136. Volz and McMillan, *supra* note 135.

137. Sanger et al., *White House Weighs New Cybersecurity Approach*, *supra* note 128.

PART III
INTERNATIONAL LAW FRAMEWORK

7

Defend Forward and Sovereignty

Jack Goldsmith and Alex Loomis[*]

Damaging state-sponsored cross-border cyber operations beyond mere espionage have long been on the rise and appear to many to be on the verge of spinning out of control. While there has been much talk about how international law might regulate this dangerous behavior, no concrete rules have emerged. The governments of the world tried to hammer out a legal consensus on such rules in a United Nations process that lasted two decades but ended in failure in 2017.[1] A related process that began in 2018 ended in March 2021, once again without any agreement by governments on "how international law applies to State use of" information and communications technologies across borders.[2]

Against the background of these failures, and in the face of growing and seemingly more dangerous cross-border cyber operations, it is understandable that norm entrepreneurs would step in to try to do better. This in a nutshell is the aim of the *Tallinn Manual*, which argues that customary international law imposes a variety of binding rules on state behavior related to cyber operations. The first version, *Tallinn Manual 1.0*, published in 2013, proposed to describe international law on cyber operations involving the use of force and in armed conflict more generally.[3] *Tallinn Manual 2.0*, published in 2017, builds on and supersedes the original.[4] It covers peacetime cyber operations as well as ones related to armed conflict, and it revises some of its earlier rules.

Among the most discussed provisions of the *Tallinn Manual 2.0* is Rule 4 on "Violation of sovereignty." Rule 4 provides: "A State must not conduct cyber operations that violate the sovereignty of another State."[5] Considered alone, Rule 4 is banal and unobjectionable, since there are many established sovereignty-based international-law rules that cyber operations might violate. For example, the UN Charter's prohibition on certain uses of force and the customary international-law rule of non-intervention constrains cyber operations by one state in another. The hard question is whether international law related to sovereignty requires anything more. Here the commentary to Rule 4 is quite ambitious. It argues that a stand-alone customary international-law concept of state sovereignty operates to regulate and render illegal certain cyber operations that would not otherwise be illegal under any of the specific and acknowledged sovereignty-based rules of international law.

The rules articulated in the Rule 4 commentary, if valid, have important implications for non-consensual cyber operations in many contexts. As the *Tallinn Manual 2.0* editors note, "[T]he vast majority of hostile cyber operations attributable to states implicate only the prohibition of violation of sovereignty."[6] Thus, "[T]he rule represents the most significant red line between lawful and internationally wrongful conduct"[7]—assuming, that is, it truly represents customary international law.

In this chapter we argue that the discrete rules articulated in the Rule 4 commentary do not reflect customary international law. The Rule 4 commentary cites very little legal authority in support of its bold conclusions and lacks any practical connection to the complex interplay of extensive state practice and *opinio juris* that constitutes customary international law.

We consider the validity of the Rule 4 commentary primarily in the context of the United States' "Defend Forward" (DF) strategy for disrupting cyber threats. The United States of course is not the only nation to engage in cross-border cyber operations that might implicate Rule 4. But the DF concept is the most prominent public example of a nation announcing its intention to conduct cyber operations that might violate the rules articulated in the Rule 4 commentary. DF is thus proper to study in this context.

Part I summarizes and critiques the discrete rules in the Rule 4 commentary on their own terms. Part II provides broader reasons to doubt that these rules have a plausible basis in customary international law. Part III engages the policy aims of Rule 4 and speculates on how international-law rules in this context may develop in the future.

Tallinn Manual 2.0 and Sovereignty

This part examines and critiques the commentary to Rule 4 of the *Tallinn Manual 2.0*.

The *Tallinn Manual*

The *Tallinn Manual 2.0* consists of rules followed by commentary. The rules all purport to "reflect customary international law" and thus to be "binding on all States, subject to" any persistent objector exceptions.[8]

The rules were formulated by a group of "distinguished international law practitioners and scholars, the so-called 'International Group of Experts.' "[9] The *Tallinn Manual 2.0* "is not an official document," the editors emphasize, "but rather the product of two separate endeavors undertaken by groups of independent experts acting solely in their personal capacity."[10] It does, however, purport to reflect international law "as it existed at the point of the Manual's adoption" in 2016.[11] It disclaims any intention to be a "progressive development of the law," insists it is "policy and politics-neutral," and asserts that it "is intended as an objective restatement of the *lex lata*."[12]

The commentary accompanying each rule in the *Tallinn Manual 2.0* aims "to identify the rule's legal basis, explain its normative content, address practical implications in the cyber context, and set forth differing positions as to scope or interpretation."[13] Sometimes the commentary reflects the experts' unanimous views, while at other times the experts disagree and the commentary explains the majority and minority views.

Despite claiming to discern and describe customary international law, the *Tallinn Manual 2.0* says practically nothing about how the publicly known cross-border state-sponsored cyber activity, and significant public discussion by states about this activity, informs its rules and commentary. The *Tallinn Manual 2.0* notes that "[s]tate cyber practice is mostly classified and publicly available expressions of *opinio juris* are sparse."[14] But it never explains why known state practice and the "sparse" *opinio juris* should not be relevant to the content of customary international law.

Rule 4

Chapter 1 of the *Tallinn Manual 2.0* is entitled "Sovereignty." It contains five rules, of which Rule 4—"Violation of sovereignty"—is the most pertinent to this chapter.[15] Rule 4 states: "A State must not conduct cyber operations that violate the sovereignty of another State."[16] By itself, this statement is unremarkable, since it says nothing about which cyber operations violate sovereignty. And indeed, as the manual goes on to analyze in later rules, there are many specific sovereignty-based restrictions that might apply to cross-border cyber operations, including the prohibition on the use of force, the prohibition on coercive intervention, sovereign immunity, neutrality, the limits on enforcement and prescriptive jurisdiction, diplomatic law, the law of the sea, air law, space law, and international telecommunications law.[17]

It is in the commentary to Rule 4 where the novel claims appear. The commentary is filled with interesting insights and analysis. It purports to derive from the general principle of sovereignty a number of discrete prohibitions that govern state behavior independent of and in addition to the established specific doctrines. It is the legal status of these discrete rules, and not the practically empty formulation in Rule 4, that is important. Our analysis focuses on the discrete prohibitions in the commentary that are supported by either all of the experts or a majority of them. These discrete rules rest on legal authority at a very high level of generality, misinterpret or overinterpret some legal authorities, or (most often) constitute *ipse dixits*, lacking any basis at all.

Consider comment 6 to Rule 4. It provides that "it is a violation of territorial sovereignty for an organ of a State . . . to conduct cyber operations while physically present on another State's territory."[18] The *Tallinn Manual 2.0* offers no authority for this proposition but appears to derive it from two more general principles of international law: a state's sovereignty over its territorial integrity, and the international-law rules pertaining to "enforcement jurisdiction."[19]

The experts assert without legal citation that "a violation of sovereignty occurs whenever one State physically crosses into the territory or national airspace of another State without either its consent or another justification in international law."[20] But this proposition is overbroad to the point of being erroneous. Sometimes a state (or its agents) crossing into foreign territory violates international law (when, for example, a state's fighter aircraft or reconnaissance drone trespasses foreign airspace), and other times it does not (such as when a state's spy crosses a border with stealth but engages in no internationally unlawful activity, or when a state sends propaganda digitally into another state). The naked principle of "sovereignty" cannot tell us why some border crossings are unlawful and some not. As we explain in the next part, one needs to look at state practice and *opinio juris* in discrete contexts to figure that out. This the manual does not do.

The Rule 4 commentary's reliance on enforcement jurisdiction commits a different type of error. Comment 6 to Rule 4 states correctly that "the non-consensual exercise of enforcement jurisdiction in another State's territory . . . is a violation of that State's sovereignty."[21] It then concludes that "*therefore*," international law prohibits one nation from "[conducting] cyber operations while physically present on another State's territory."[22] This reliance on enforcement jurisdiction is a category mistake. Enforcement jurisdiction is a specific sovereignty-based prohibition on a specific type of activity with a specific purpose: "to induce or compel compliance or punish noncompliance with its laws or regulations."[23] As James Crawford explains, the "governing principle of enforcement jurisdiction is that a state cannot take measures on the territory of another state *by way of enforcement of its laws* without the consent of the latter."[24] The rule prohibits law enforcement–related actions such as arrest, summons, police actions, and production orders on the territory of another state.[25] Rule 11 of the manual covers this specific prohibition. A cross-border cyber operation that is not in aid of law enforcement does not implicate this particular sovereignty-based rule any more than does a black-bag job in furtherance of espionage or the firing of a cruise missile in anticipatory self-defense.

The Rule 4 commentary next asserts, in comment 7, that a majority of its experts concluded that the sovereignty rule prohibits one state's cyber espionage conducted while physically present in another state "without its consent or other legal justification."[26] They did not, however, believe that espionage conducted by remote cyber operations violated international law.[27] The *Tallinn Manual 2.0* provides no legal authority at all for this supposed prohibition (or distinction) other than the opinions of most of its experts. And yet it acknowledges a "widespread State practice of engaging in non-consensual espionage while present on another State's territory."[28] (We consider the relevance of state practice in the next part.)

The Rule 4 commentary next moves to the issue of "remote cyber operations that manifest on a State's territory," which is an issue likely implicated by the bulk of what goes on under DF.[29] Comment 10 states that the issue is "somewhat unsettled in international law" and then offers a two-part framework for assessing lawfulness: "(1) the degree of infringement upon the target State's territorial integrity; and (2) whether there has been an interference with or usurpation of inherently governmental functions."[30]

Applying the "degree of infringement" criterion, most experts agreed that a remote cyber operation causing "physical damage" violates Rule 4, while some thought that physical damage was one factor to be considered.[31] No legal authority or analysis is provided for either the degree-of-infringement criterion or these specific conclusions. Comment 10 does state that the "degree of infringement" criterion "is based on the premise that a State controls access to its sovereign territory."[32] This explanation suffers from the overgenerality problem noted above. It is thus little surprise that the experts disagreed on its application to "physical damage," and that the manual does not explain the nature of or reasons for the disagreement.

The experts further agreed that "the remote causation of loss of functionality of cyber infrastructure located in another State sometimes constitutes a violation of sovereignty, although no consensus could be achieved as to the precise threshold at which this is so due to the lack of expressions of *opinio juris* in this regard."[33] We will consider the relevance of *opinio juris* in the next part. For now, we simply note again that the commentary to Rule 4 provides no authority for its normative claims. Finally, comment 14 states that "no consensus could be achieved as to whether" a cyber operation falling below the physical-damage and loss-of-functionality thresholds (such as "a major DDoS [distributed denial of service] operation" or "emplacing malware into a system") would violate Rule 4.[34] The manual again fails to explain any legal or practical basis, if any, for the disagreement.

As for the second criterion, the experts in comment 15 state that Rule 4 prohibits "one State's cyber operation [that] interferes with or usurps the inherently governmental functions of another State."[35] They could not agree on a definition of "inherently governmental functions," but they concluded that "a cyber operation that interferes with data or services that are necessary for the exercise of inherently governmental functions is prohibited as a violation of sovereignty."[36] Most experts believed these activities would violate Rule 4 irrespective of the cyber operation's direct effects in the affected state. Comments 17 through 21 apply this test to various hypotheticals, such as inhibiting communications between a state's leadership (illegal) and inhibiting a state's communication to the public (legal).[37]

The experts' only legal basis for these fine-grained rules comes from "the sovereign right of a State to exercise within its territory, 'to the exclusion of any other State, the functions of a State.'"[38] The internal quotation is from the 1928 *Island of Palmas* arbitration award. That award involved a dispute between the United States and the Netherlands over the Island of Palmas, a tiny piece of land in the Pacific Ocean fifty or so miles southeast of the island of Mindanao, Philippines. The case was resolved on the basis of international law concepts of discovery, possession, competing state activity, and other propositions about title to land under international law.[39] Along the way the arbitrator made "some general remarks on *sovereignty in its relation to territory,*" one of which was the following: "Sovereignty in the relations between States signifies independence," which "in regard to a portion of the globe is the right to exercise therein, to the exclusion of any other State, the functions of a State."[40] This dictum from a century-old, colonial maritime territory dispute is the only legal authority even in the neighborhood of Rule 4's claim that "a cyber operation that interferes with data or services that are necessary for the exercise of inherently governmental functions is prohibited as a violation of sovereignty."[41] Yet again, state practice and *opinio juris* go unmentioned.[42]

In sum, the Rule 4 commentary maintains that the customary international-law principle of sovereignty forbids a variety of cyber operations by one state in another. It makes these claims often without citing any legal authority, sometimes on the basis of inapt or very general legal authority, and always without ever seriously examining state practice or *opinio juris*.

Tallinn Manual 2.0 and the Identification of Customary International Law

As noted above, Rule 4 and the sub-rules in its commentary purport to be "an objective restatement of the *lex lata*," or "the law as it currently exists."[43] The *Tallinn Manual 2.0* experts, we are told, "assiduously avoided including statements reflecting *lex ferenda*," or the law as it should be.[44] These are surprising statements with respect to the Rule 4 commentary, which purports to identify fine-grained rules of customary international law yet cites very little legal authority and mentions state practice even less. The commentary to Rule 4 adopts an unorthodox method for identifying customary international law—so unorthodox, we argue in this part, that it is entirely implausible that it reflects *lex lata*.

Why State Practice and *Opinio Juris* Matter

Customary international law, says the Restatement (Third) of Foreign Relations Law, "results from a general and consistent *practice* of states followed by them from a sense of legal obligation."[45] The International Law Commission recently stated: "To determine the existence and content of a rule of particular customary international law, it is necessary to ascertain whether there is a general practice among the States concerned that is accepted by them as law (*opinio juris*) among themselves."[46] As these and every other canonical definition of customary international law make plain, the identification of customary international law that binds states turns on the right kind of state practice and the presence of *opinio juris*, the sense of legal obligation that attaches to practice.[47]

Governments in their statements about and analyses of customary international law take these traditional two-element criteria very seriously.[48] International and domestic courts are in practice less rigorous. They sometimes elevate the *opinio juris* requirement over state practice and discern *opinio juris* in multi-lateral treaties, domestic and international case law, and authoritative non-binding instruments (such as UN General Assembly resolutions).[49] They sometimes rely in part on secondary sources, including the work of scholars, even though the opinion of experts without probative supporting legal materials obviously cannot count.[50] And they sometimes use what some have described as a deductive method for identifying customary international law but tend to do so only after considering state practice and *opinio juris*.[51]

A serious analysis of customary international law must at least be attentive to extant state practice and expressions of *opinio juris*, and it is very rare for a rule to develop and become binding without any consideration of either ingredient. The commentary in Rule 4, however, is almost entirely oblivious to state practice and *opinio juris* and proceeds instead to derive discrete fine-grained rules of ostensible *lex lata* based on the mostly unexplained votes of its experts. Its only justification for ignoring state practice and *opinio juris* is that the former is "mostly classified" and the latter is sparse. But even in the stealthy world of adverse cyber operations, there is plenty of both if one looks, and they cut against the Rule 4 commentary.

Before turning to this real world of cyber operations and state commentary about them, a brief word is in order on the debate in the scholarly literature about whether "sovereignty is . . . a primary rule of international law susceptible to violation," and not just a "principle" from which other rules of international law "derive."[52] The rule-versus-principle debate is mainly about the question of whether Rule 4 as formulated is a stand-alone rule of customary international law, rather than a generalization about specific, recognized rules such as limitations on enforcement jurisdiction or the prohibition on intervention. This academic debate has obscured the settled legal test for determining which state cyber operations below recognized thresholds violate customary international law. That test turns entirely on how nations behave and what they say and believe about the legality of such behavior.[53] It is to that task that we now turn.

The Real World

States have not been oblivious to the problems raised by cross-border cyber operations. The news for over a decade has been filled with weekly reminders that states are intensively engaged on both the sending and receiving ends of damaging or disruptive cross-border cyber operations. And of course, the news reflects only the activities that have been made public. We can safely assume that there are many more state-sponsored cross-border cyber operations that cause damage or disruption below the use-of-force level but that are not in the news. Any assessment of the customary law claims in the Rule 4 commentary must examine what states have done and said.

Begin with state practice. To make the analysis concrete and manageable, we will consider two of the manual's proposed rules on "remote cyber operations that manifest on a State's territory" that likely implicate DF.[54] The Rule 4 commentary claims that such operations violate the customary international law of sovereignty (1) if they cause physical damage or "loss of functionality of cyber infrastructure"; or (2) if they "[interfere] with or [usurp] the inherently governmental functions of another State," regardless of whether the interference results in "physical damage, injury, or loss of functionality."[55] There have been many examples in the news in the last fifteen years that plausibly fit these categories, some of which we list in the appendix.[56]

By our (no doubt incomplete) count, between 2007 and 2020, at least sixteen cyberattacks caused a loss of functionality, and twelve cyberattacks interfered with or usurped inherent government functions.[57] (Some cyber operations did both.) As Sean Watts and Theodore Richard put it in 2018, "State cyber practice is brimming with examples of what the *Manual* would consider violations of sovereignty."[58]

Moreover, in none of these examples, not a single one, have we found evidence that the victim state complained about a violation of a customary international-law rule of sovereignty. The closest case is Russia's 2019 cyber operation against Georgia that took offline or defaced Georgia's government sites and damaged its government servers, thus violating Rule 4's prohibition against interfering with inherent government functions.[59] More than twenty countries formally attributed the attack to Russia and condemned it in the strongest terms.[60] None labeled it a violation of international law. Georgia accused Russia only of going "against international norms and principles" and "[violating its] sovereignty," but it did not contend that Russia had violated international law.[61]

States often publicly denounce cyber operations as violations of sovereignty generally. Yet they don't make claims that cyber operations violate an international law of sovereignty, much less ones that align with the Rule 4 commentary. Many cyber operations have caused harm or disruption; many have been attributed to specific aggressors, either officially or by credible news outlets and experts; many were strongly condemned—though not as violations of international law; and some even prompted retaliation.[62] States' failure to condemn these cyberattacks under international law contrasts sharply with the long history of states labeling extraterritorial law enforcement and certain non-cyber breaches of territorial integrity as violations of international law.[63] All of this strongly suggests that Rule 4 does not reflect international practice or *opinio juris*.

States' failure to link their condemnations of cross-border cyber operations to anything like an international-law rule of sovereignty is all the more striking because states have been formally discussing these principles *for almost two decades*. In 2003, the United Nations established a state-based "Group of Governmental Experts on Developments in the Field of Information and Telecommunications in the Context of International Security" (GGE) to develop rules and norms governing the harmful uses of information technologies in international relations.[64] After about the first decade of work, the third GGE concluded that "international law" applies to information and communication technologies (ICT) and that "State sovereignty and international norms and principles that flow from sovereignty apply to State conduct of ICT-related activities."[65] It said nothing about whether "sovereignty" prescribes anything beyond the acknowledged sovereignty-based prohibitions (such as the principle of non-interference), much less what that something more might be. And neither the 2013 report nor its successor 2015 report reached any conclusion on how this or other norms constrain state behavior.[66]

The fifth GGE working group was commissioned to fill this gap in 2015.[67] It failed. The GGE met around the same time that the Tallinn experts were formulating their rules and was supposed to issue its report shortly after the manual published its views on extant international law. But in contrast to the confident assertions of the *Tallinn Manual 2.0* experts, the state-led GGE process collapsed one year after publication of *Tallinn Manual 2.0* because it "failed to agree on a draft for a consensus report."[68] It ostensibly broke down over differences about whether and how *jus ad bellum* applies to the legality of cross-border cyber operations, and over the contention by some states that it was "premature" to decide "*how* international legal rules and principles apply" in cyberspace.[69] Given this lack of consensus on the applicability of well-accepted sovereignty-based international law, such as the prohibition of the use of force in the UN Charter, and the stated uncertainty by states about how any international law applies in cyberspace, it is inconceivable that, as *Tallinn Manual 2.0* claimed, there was at the same time a settled customary international-law rule that prohibits various types of cross-border cyber operation far below the use-of-force threshold.[70]

Events since the manual was published call the validity of the Rule 4 commentary into greater question. In 2018, the United Nations created a new GGE and an adjacent Open-Ended Working Group (OEWG) that is open to all states.[71] The final OEWG and GGE reports, issued in March and July 2021, reveal the current diminished state of consensus among nations.[72] Both are modest and defensive documents that seeks to preserve the 2015 GGE report's thin consensus. The OEWG report's main international-law concern was preserving the minimalist notion that "international law, and in particular the Charter of the United Nations, is applicable and essential to maintaining peace and stability" in the digital environment.[73] Governments could agree on nothing regarding international law below the use-of-force threshold beyond that minimalist statement about the charter, and indeed they acknowledged that "further common understandings need to be developed on how international law applies to State use of" the digital realm.[74] The 2021 GGE Report went further, stating that the non-intervention principle and prohibition on the use of force apply in cyberspace and offering some guidance for state responsibility over cyber operations; but it said nothing else about how (or if) international law governs cyber operations below the use of force threshold.[75] In short, these reports, issued in the four-year period after *Tallinn Manual 2.0*, show that the nations of the world have reached no consensus on anything approaching the Rule 4 commentary.[76]

To be sure, individual nations have in various contexts issued statements expressing more concrete views about how international law applies to the digital realm. Some of these statements were issued on an ad hoc basis. More than fifty statements came in the context of the OEWG process; fifteen were in connection with the 2021 GGE.[77] All of these statements came after the *Tallinn Manual 2.0*'s claims about sovereignty had been made public and widely discussed. The vast majority did not come close to endorsing anything like Rule 4 and its commentary.

A few states have appeared to embrace something like Rule 4 and its commentary—some in the OEWG process, and some not. The Czech Republic and Finland have embraced Rule 4.[78] The Netherlands has "in general . . . endorse[d]" Rule 4, but acknowledged that the "precise interpretation" of the commentary principles "is a matter of debate,"[79] and later explained that there is a "clear gap" in how international law "applies in cyberspace," including on matters related to the international law of sovereignty.[80] Norway and Switzerland seem to hold the same basic view.[81] Citing Rule 4 and its commentary, Germany takes the view that any cyber operations that "lead to physical effects and harm" or "functional impairments" in another state violate an international-law rule of sovereignty.[82] But, apart from stating that "interference in the conduct of elections of a State may under certain circumstances constitute a breach of sovereignty" (which may be entirely coextensive with the prohibition on coercive intervention),[83] it does not embrace the "inherently governmental functions" prong of the Rule 4 commentary.[84] By contrast, Romania adopted the inherently governmental functions prong only (but not physical or functional impairments).[85] Three states—Iran, Guatemala, and Brazil—have gone further than Rule 4 and its commentary by claiming that all cross-border cyber operations violate an international-law rule of sovereignty (Brazil goes further still and claims that all "[i]nterceptions of telecommunications ... violate state sovereignty).[86] France takes the view that all unauthorized cross-border cyber operations "[constitute] a violation of sovereignty" but does not assert that such violations are contrary to international law, and has elsewhere described sovereignty as a "principle," not a rule of international law.[87]

These statements are probative of these nations' views about the content of customary international law, but so too are their practices, which often do not match the statements. For example, Germany's interior minister and the head of Germany's cyber agency have both defended the use of "active cyberdefense" cyber operations to "delete data" in hostile networks and "shut down enemy servers."[88] France's intelligence agencies have used cyber operations to spy on foreign countries and to disable botnets in foreign countries without their permission, which is inconsistent with its seemingly absolutist position.[89] And Iran has conducted several cyber operations that disregard Rule 4.[90]

Far more states have demurred on Rule 4 and its commentary. At least six states (New Zealand, Israel, Austria, Guyana, Bolivia, and Japan) have claimed that sovereignty is in some respects a rule of international law that applies in cyberspace. But none of these states claim that the content of international law reflects Rule 4 and its commentary, or even offer an example of a cyber operation below the use-of-force or non-intervention threshold that has violated or would violate an ostensible international-law rule of sovereignty.[91] The United Kingdom has rejected Rule 4 outright.[92]

The United States has not rejected Rule 4 outright but has not embraced it either, and has never endorsed any part of the commentary. It claims that its Defend Forward operations, which at a general level seem hard to square with the Rule 4 commentary, are consistent with international law.[93] And it has further stated that "it does not appear that there exists a rule that all infringements on sovereignty in cyberspace necessarily involve violations of international law," and that "there is not sufficiently widespread and consistent State practice resulting from a sense of legal obligation to conclude that customary international law generally prohibits such non-consensual cyber operations [below the use-of-force and prohibited-intervention thresholds] in another State's territory."[94]

And finally, many states (including Iran, despite its absolutist position) have made public statements—consistent with decades of GGE and OEWG gridlock—that note a lack of consensus as to "how provisions of international law apply" in cyberspace.[95]

The bottom line is this: During the three years after the failure of the GGE process, and the four years after publication of the *Tallinn Manual 2.0*, damaging cross-border cyber operations seem to have grown and grown, and during this period states have conducted intensive formal and informal discussions, in domestic and international fora, about the international law governing cyber operations. Yet only two states (the Czech Republic and Finland) have clearly embraced Rule 4 and its commentary, three (the Netherlands, Norway, and Switzerland) nod in that direction (though their statements are ambiguous); one (Germany) has endorsed Rule 4 and one half its commentary (but may disregard it in practice);

another (Romania) has endorsed the other half of its commentary; per-haps four others (if one includes France, an ambiguous case) have gone further in their statements (if not their practice); two states appear to have rejected it; and the vast majority of states have been either silent or non-committal. All of this has taken place against the background of contin-uous debate and discussion by the nations of the world in the OEWG and GGE processes about how international law might apply to cyberspace. The final OEWG and GGE reports' call for yet more future discussion about how international law applies to cyberspace—and the inability to reach any further concrete conclusion—confirms the utter lack of con-sensus on Rule 4 and its commentary.

The *Tallinn Manual 2.0*'s defenders have not sufficiently credited these developments. Some commentators claim that states may secretly agree with Rule 4 but are afraid to say so, and that they ignore it in practice because ag-gressor states think "the benefits of nonconsensual intrusions outweigh the costs," while victim states fear accusations of hypocrisy.[96] We do not see how states' private, unexpressed beliefs might be credited in discerning a rule of customary international law. But in any event, this explanation is belied by the decades of discussion and negotiation by the nations of the world in the GGE and OEWG processes, and by the scores of affirmative statements by states acknowledging a lack of consensus about how international law applies in cyberspace.[97] The *Tallinn Manual 2.0* advocates maintain that state ac-tors "bear the burden of justifying the non-applicability of the existing sov-ereignty rule to cyber operations."[98] We doubt any such burden exists: As explained above, the Rule 4 commentary does not come close to establishing that its purported rules flow from well-established international-law prin-ciples. In any case, states' collective refusal to embrace anything like Rule 4 and its commentary—after decades of discussion and debate, and amidst growing state practice of cross-border cyber operations—more than meets any such burden.[99]

The simple fact is that Rule 4's commentary does not align with how states practice or talk about international law. That is dispositive because interna-tional law is constituted by what states do, say, and agree to. Private individ-uals' judgments about how abstract legal principles apply to new domains, which side has the burden of proof, and states' implicit motivations for ignoring their analysis are beside the point. There is, to be sure, an impor-tant role for private norm entrepreneurship when developing new rules of international law. But we should recognize that the Rule 4 commentary fits squarely in that category.

In sum, the legal status of the rules articulated in Rule 4 is not a hard question: They are (at most) *lex ferenda*, not *lex lata*. States have intensively engaged in cyber operations below the use-of-force line for a long time and have failed after decades of efforts to reach consensus about whether and how better-established, sovereignty-based rules of international law, such as use of force, apply in cyberspace. Many of these admittedly unresolved and still-hard questions would be irrelevant if the much lower threshold for illegality posited by the Rule 4 commentary were valid. It clearly is not.

The Bigger Picture

The argument thus far has been internal to the logic of international law—that the Rule 4 commentary employs an improper international-law standard and does not in fact reflect customary international law. This argument entails no view on what the content of international law in this context should be in an ideal world. That is a very hard question that requires consideration of, among other things, the broader strategic context in which the debate over the Rule 4 commentary has been taking place. Which brings us back to DF.

The United States has prominently engaged in cyberspace operations, from using cyberattacks in armed conflict and in self-defense to various sorts of operations below the use-of-force threshold and pervasive global cyber exploitation and espionage. It has also prominently been on the losing end of many notorious cyber operations. President Barack Obama bragged in the fall of 2016 that the United States has greater offensive and defensive cyber capabilities than any other nation.[100] He said this right in the middle of Russia's consequential intervention in the US election, after years of cyber disruptions in the US domestic sphere below the use-of-force threshold that exposed the United States' weak cyber defenses. DF is a direct response to this history.

The Russian operation violated the Rule 4 commentary, but no US government official claimed that it violated international law—because in the US view it didn't. It is entirely understandable, even if we don't like it, that Russia would use its cyber capabilities against the United States to serve its interests. The United States engages in analogous operations, including against Russia. The Russian operation may have been deeply damaging to the United States and, from the perspective of global stability, a bad act. But the same can probably be said of some US cyber operations abroad.

In an ideal world, nations should want rules that constrain cyber operations in ways that promote global harmony. But, of course, this is much easier said than done, because every rule has distributional consequences due to vast differences in national capacities and interests. Generalizing quite a lot, the United States is likely dominant in using cyber in military conflict situations and in cyber exploitation on the whole (and Israel is very good at cyber for military operations as well). Russia seems to dominate in the gray zone. China is by far the world's leader in commercial cyber theft and is also adept, as is Russia, at large-scale cyber exploitations of government networks. Many weaker countries are on the losing end of these sticks, though some—notably, Iran and North Korea—are using cyber operations to their asymmetrical advantage.[101]

Against this background, the primary strategic logic behind the *Tallinn Manual 2.0* is that a firm, customary international-law rule of sovereignty that bans Defend Forward–type operations would permit nations to condemn those operations as unlawful, "ostracize the state that launched them," and presumably deter such harmful cross-border digital operations.[102] But matters are much more complex than this. As Gary Corn observes, using countermeasures—that is, actions otherwise illegal under international law—in response to cyber operations that violate Rule 4 and its commentary might heighten escalation.[103] Moreover, states (especially powerful ones) benefit too much from deploying cyber operations opportunistically to yield to criticism about violating novel, top-down legal rules that are divorced from the reality of their interests.

Relatedly, any powerful nation that obeyed Rule 4 tomorrow would be put at an enormous disadvantage vis-à-vis its adversaries. These are but some of the reasons to think that ostracization would not work in this context, even if Rule 4 somehow reflected customary international law, especially against the powerful nations that act contrary to Rule 4 the most in practice. As President Obama said in response to the Russian electoral hack in 2016, "The idea that somehow public shaming is going to be effective I think doesn't read the thought process in Russia very well."[104]

The DF strategy takes a very different approach to influencing mischievous cyber behavior below the use-of-force threshold. Rather than seeking to shame nations into refraining from certain cyber operations, it aims to alter their capacities and material incentives to engage in such operations. This approach poses at least two dangers. First, it might provoke bilateral escalation that will leave the digitally dependent United States worse off on balance. And second, it might spark a global escalation in the use of such techniques, to the detriment of all or at least most nations. (This is an especial danger since DF probably involves below-the-threshold cyber operations in another country that mirror in some respects the below-the-threshold cyber operations it seeks to check.)

Presumably the United States considered these risks and decided that, given its capabilities, weaknesses, and recent run of damaging cyber losses, DF made sense on balance. Yet it remains far from clear that the DF strategy will work. Perhaps it is best seen as a first step in altering adversary incentives on a path toward mutually beneficial confidence-building measures or soft or hard cooperative agreements.[105]

Conclusion

Whether DF, diplomatic approaches, or any similar state-driven approach will successfully forge a better global cyber order remains very much an open question. It is also unclear which strategy—carrot, stick, or some combination of the two—has the best chance of success. Top-down entrepreneurial sovereignty theories such as Rule 4 and its commentary might well influence customary international law, depending on what states subsequently do and say.[106] But as developments since it was published in 2017 underscore, it does not reflect customary international law today.

Appendix

This is a selective list of some of the publicly known state-sponsored cross-border cyber operations below the use-of-force level from 2007-2020 that implicate two of the rules articulated in the commentary to Rule 4. Category 1 concerns such operations that cause "loss of functionality of cyber infrastructure."[107] Category 2 concerns operations that "[interfere] with or [usurp] the inherently governmental functions of another State," regardless of whether the interference results in "physical damage, injury, or loss of functionality."[108]

Year	Category 1	Category 2
2020	Israeli cyberattack resulted in explosion at Natanz nuclear facility.[109]	Israeli cyberattack disabled Iranian port computers, in response to April 2020 Iranian cyberattack on Israeli water-distribution networks.[110] In July 2020 Iranian cyberattacks shut down Israeli water distribution networks.[111] Iranian actors hacked voter rolls to obtain voter information and sent voter-intimidation emails to US voters during presidential election.[112] Three-year-long campaign by Russian hackers to compromise news sites in Eastern Europe attributing false quotations to government officials was disclosed.[113]
2019	US government "wiped" computers and shut down communications networks of Iranian government officials used to plot attacks on oil tankers.[114]	Russian cyberattacks in Georgia in October 2019 disabled and defaced state websites.[115]
2018	Russian hackers wiped computers that were part of the 2018 South Korea Olympics.[116] Cyber Command removed Russia's Internet Research Agency's online capabilities during the US midterms elections.[117]	

Year	Category 1	Category 2
2017	North Korean WannaCry attack encrypted data on every computer it reached, leaving hundreds of thousands of computers unusable around the world.[118] Russia's NotPetya attack rendered millions of computers around the world unusable, causing more than $10 billion in damages and devastating giants like Maersk, FedEx, and Merck.[119] "Shamoon 4" attack by Iran wiped computers belonging to Saudi government offices as well as Saudi and American companies.[120]	WannaCry also crippled the United Kingdom's National Health Service, interrupting the delivery of medical services.[121] NotPetya effectively wiped 10 percent of Ukrainian computers, forcing health care providers and government ministries to shut down or disconnect from the internet.[122] United Arab Emirates hacked Qatari government and media sites to attribute false quotations to the Qatari emir.[123]
2016	Russia used cyberattacks to cause power outages in Ukraine, affecting millions of people.[124] "Shamoon 3" attack by Iran against Saudi Arabia erased data in Saudi government computers.[125]	Russia interfered in the 2016 US election by generating social media content without disclosing its source, and hacking and leaking the Democratic National Committee and chairman of the Clinton campaign John Podesta's emails. Many have argued that this changed the result in what was an extremely close election.[126]
2015	Russia used cyberattacks to cause power outages in Ukraine, affecting hundreds of thousands of people.[127]	Russian cyberattack on Germany forced the Bundestag to shut down its internal parliamentary network and reinstall software on many of its computers.[128]

Year	Category 1	Category 2
2014	Attack by North Korea against the United States wiped 70 percent of Sony's computing power.[129] Attack by Iran against the United States permanently wiped data on thousands of Sands Casinos computers and servers.[130]	
2012	"Wiper" attack by United States against Iran erased data on computers connected to Iran's oil industry.[131] "Shamoon 2" attack by Iran against Qatar forced the oil company RasGas to shut down its internal network.[132] "Shamoon" attack by Iran against Saudi Arabia wiped tens of thousands of hard drives belonging to Saudi Aramco.[133]	"Wiper" attack shut down six of Iran's oil terminals, which were responsible for most of its exports.[134]
2010	United States and Israel attacked Iran with the Stuxnet virus, physically disabling centrifuges.[135]	
2007		Russian DDoS (distributed denial of service) attack on Estonia disrupted government networks and banks.[136]

Notes

* The authors wish to thank Elena Chachko, Robert M. Chesney, Gary P. Corn, Eric Talbot Jensen, Sean Watts, and participants in a Hoover Institution workshop for outstanding comments; and Casey Corcoran, Matthew Gluck, Katarina Krasulova, and Jacques Singer-Emery for outstanding research assistance. The opinions expressed are those of the authors and do not necessarily reflect the views of Quinn Emanuel or its clients.

1. See Anders Henriksen, The End of the Road for the UN GGE Process: The Future Regulation of Cyberspace, 5 J. CYBERSECURITY 1, 1 (2019).

2. Open-Ended Working Grp. on Devs. in the Field of Info. and Telecomms. in the Context of Int'l Sec., Final Substantive Report, U.N. Doc. A/AC.290/2021/CRP.2, at ¶ 34 (2021) [hereinafter OEWG Final Substantive Report].

3. See TALLINN MANUAL ON THE INTERNATIONAL LAW APPLICABLE TO CYBER WARFARE 3–4 (Michael N. Schmitt ed., 2013) [hereinafter TALLINN MANUAL 1.0]. ("This project was launched in the hope of bringing some degree of clarity to the complex legal issues surrounding cyber operations, with particular attention paid to those involving the *jus ad bellum* and the *jus in bello*.")

4. See generally TALLINN MANUAL 2.0 ON THE INTERNATIONAL LAW APPLICABLE TO CYBER OPERATIONS (Michael N. Schmitt & Liis Vihul eds., 2017) [hereinafter TALLINN MANUAL 2.0].

5. Id. at 17.

6. Michael N. Schmitt & Liis Vihul, Sovereignty in Cyberspace: Lex Lata Vel Non, 111 AJIL UNBOUND 213, 214 (2017).

7. Id. at 213.

8. TALLINN MANUAL 2.0, supra note 4, at 4.

9. Id. at 1.

10. Id. at 2.

11. Id. at 2–3.

12. Id. at 3.

13. Id.

14. Id.

15. Id. at v, 17. Rules 1–3 articulate general principles of international law related to sovereignty but say nothing concrete about how they regulate operations in cyberspace. Rule 5 is about sovereign immunity.

16. Id. at 17.

17. See id. at 27–29, 51–78, 212–83, 294–98, 312–25, 329–39, 555–62.

18. Id. at 19, ¶ 6.

19. Id.

20. Id.

21. Id.

22. See id. (emphasis added). Tallinn offers as an example one state using a flash drive to introduce malware into cyber infrastructure in another state as a violation of the rule.

23. RESTATEMENT (THIRD) OF FOREIGN RELATIONS LAW § 431 (*Am. L. Inst.* 1987). *Tallinn* confirms this scope for enforcement jurisdiction when it cites the Eichmann Security Council resolution. *See* TALLINN MANUAL 2.0, *supra* note 4, at 19 n.22.

24. James Crawford, BROWNLIE'S PRINCIPLES OF PUBLIC INTERNATIONAL LAW 462 (9th ed. 2019) (emphasis added).

25. *Id.* at 462.

26. TALLINN MANUAL 2.0, *supra* note 4, at 19, ¶ 7.

27. *Id.* at 169, ¶ 5.

28. *Id.* at 19, ¶ 7.

29. *Id.* at 20, ¶ 10.

30. *Id.*

31. *Id.* at 20, ¶ 11.

32. *Id.* at 20, ¶ 10.

33. *Id.* at 20–21, ¶ 13.

34. *Id.* at 21, ¶ 14.

35. *Id.* at 21, ¶ 15.

36. *Id.* at 22, ¶ 16. The examples of what the experts have in mind include "changing or deleting data such that it interferes with the delivery of social services, the conduct of elections, the collection of taxes, the effective conduct of diplomacy, and the performance of key national defence activities." *Id.*

37. *Id.* at 22–23, ¶¶ 17–21.

38. *Id.* at 20, ¶¶ 10 & n.24 (quoting Island of Palmas (Neth. v. U.S.), 2 R.I.A.A. 829, 838 (1928)).

39. *See* Island of Palmas (Neth. v. U.S.), 2 R.I.A.A. 829, 867–69.

40. *Id.* at 838 (emphasis in original).

41. TALLINN MANUAL 2.0, *supra* note 4, at 22, ¶ 16. A footnote suggests that when "assessing the inherently governmental nature of cyber activities . . . the notion of *acta jure imperii*, used in the context of State immunity, could prove helpful," but it does not explain why the two concepts connect. *Id.* at 22, ¶ 17 n.26. Otherwise, it seems to vaguely connect usurpation of government functions with the prohibition on extraterritorial exercise of jurisdiction, as discussed above. *See id.* at 22–23, ¶ 18.

42. The rest of Rule 4's commentary addresses other interstitial applications of Rule 4. Comment 23, for example, states that "a State's cyber operations may constitute a violation of another State's sovereignty . . . irrespective of [where] the operations are launched from," and comments 24 and 25 make clear that a state's intent to violate (or not to violate) sovereignty is irrelevant. *See id.* at 24, ¶¶ 23–25. Cyber operations targeting one country would "generally not violate the sovereignty" of a state that suffers incidental spillover effects, nor would cyber operations that just "result in severe economic loss," propaganda, crimes committed by private actors, or operations taken with the target state's consent. *See id.* at 24–27, ¶¶ 26, 28–32.

43. *Id.* at 2–3.

44. *Id.* at 3.

45. RESTATEMENT (THIRD) OF FOREIGN RELATIONS LAW § 102(2) (Am. L. Inst. 1987) (emphasis added).

46. Int'l Law Comm'n, Draft Conclusions on Identification of Customary International Law, with Commentaries, U.N. Doc. A/73/10, at 154 (2018).

47. *See* Statute of the International Court of Justice, art. 38(1), June 26, 1945, 59 Stat. 1055, 3 Bevans 1179 (explaining that the Court shall apply "international custom, as evidence of a general practice accepted as law"); SHABTAI ROSENNE, PRACTICE AND METHODS OF INTERNATIONAL LAW 55 (1984) (stating that customary international law "consists of rules of law derived from the consistent conduct of States acting out of the belief that the law required them to act that way"); Int'l L. Ass'n London Conference, *Statement of Principles Applicable to the Formation of General Customary International Law*, at 8 (2000).

48. Int'l Law Comm'n, *supra* note 46, at 126; Noora Arajärvi, *The Requisite Rigour in the Identification of Customary International Law: A Look at the Reports of the Special Rapporteur of the International Law Commission*, 19 INT'L COMM. L. REV. 9, 11–12 (2017).

49. *See, e.g.*, Ryan M. Scoville, *Finding Customary International Law*, 101 IOWA L. REV. 1893, 1917 (2016); Cedric M. J. Ryngaert & Duco W. Hora Siccama, *Ascertaining Customary International Law: An Inquiry into the Methods Used by Domestic Courts*, 65 NETH. INT'L L. REV. 1, 2 (2018); Alberto Alvarez-Jimenez, *Methods for the Identification of Customary International Law in the International Court of Justice's Jurisprudence: 2000–2009*, 60 INT'L & COMPAR. L. Q. 681, 687 (2011); Curtis A. Bradley & Jack L. Goldsmith, *Customary International Law as Federal Common Law: A Critique of the Modern Position*, 110 HARV. L. REV. 815, 839–42 (1997).

50. As the ILC recently explained, the writings of scholars "are not themselves a source of international law," but their teachings may be valuable "in collecting and assessing State practice; in identifying divergences in State practice and the possible absence or development of rules; and in evaluating the law." Int'l Law Comm'n, *supra* note 46, at 151. The ILC noted caution when drawing on these writings, since the writings are of uneven quality, sometimes reflect national or personal viewpoints, and sometimes "seek not merely to record the state of the law as it is (lex lata) but to advocate its development (lex ferenda)." *Id.* It then quoted favorably from *The Paquete Habana*, which noted that the writings of jurists "are resorted to by judicial tribunals, not for the speculations of their authors concerning what the law ought to be, but for trustworthy evidence of what the law really is." 175 U.S. 677, 700 (1900).

51. Stefan Talmon, *Determining Customary International Law: The ICJ's Methodology between Induction, Deduction and Assertion*, 26 EUR. J. INT'L L. 417, 418 (2015); William Thomas Worster, *The Inductive and Deductive Methods in Customary International Law Analysis: Traditional and Modern Approaches*, 45 GEO. J. INT'L L. 445 (2014).

52. Michael N. Schmitt, *In Defense of Sovereignty in Cyberspace*, JUST SECURITY (May 8, 2018); *see also, e.g.*, Schmitt & Vihul, *supra* note 6, at 214. *But see* Gary P. Corn & Robert Taylor, *Sovereignty in the Age of Cyber*, 111 AJIL UNBOUND 207, 211 (2017) (arguing that sovereignty is a principle only).

53. *Cf.* Eric Talbot Jensen, *The Tallinn Manual 2.0: Highlights and Insights*, 48 GEO. J. INT'L L. 735, 741–42 (2017)("[S]overeignty is a principle that depends on the domain

and the practical imperatives of states and is subject to adjustment in interstate application.").

54. TALLINN MANUAL 2.0, *supra* note 4, at 20, ¶ 10.

55. *Id.* at 20–22, ¶¶ 13–15.

56. We focus here on examples that fall below the use-of-force threshold and take no position on whether they implicate any other established rule of international law below the use-of-force level, such as prohibited coercive intervention. These examples are based on one nation accusing another nation of the cyber operation, or credible sources in credible publications confirming them. We borrow, in part, from the list compiled by Dan Efrony & Yuval Shany, *A Rule Book on the Shelf? Tallinn Manual 2.0 on Cyberoperations and Subsequent State Practice*, 112 AM. J. INT'L L. 583, 655–57 (2018), though we disagree with some of their conclusions.

57. *See infra* Appendix.

58. *See* Sean Watts & Theodore Richard, *Baseline Territorial Sovereignty and Cyberspace*, 22 LEWIS & CLARK L. REV. 771, 869 (2018).

59. *Georgia Hit by Massive Cyber-Attack*, BBC NEWS (Oct. 28, 2019).

60. Przemyslaw Roguski, *Russian Cyber Attacks against Georgia, Public Attributions and Sovereignty in Cyberspace*, JUST SECURITY (Mar. 6, 2020).

61. *Georgia Blames Russia for Cyberattack, US, UK Agree*, ASSOCIATED PRESS (Feb. 20, 2020).

62. For example, the United States attributed 2016 election interference to Russia, condemned it for undermining "international norms," imposed sanctions, and even indicted (under domestic law) Russians responsible for the operation; but it never labeled the operation a violation of international law. Press release, Office of the Press Sec'y, Statement by the President on Actions in Response to Russian Malicious Cyber Activity and Harassment (Dec. 29, 2016).

63. A paper by the lead editors of the *Tallinn Manual 2.0* offers many revealing examples. *See* Michael N. Schmitt & Liis Vihul, *Respect for Sovereignty in Cyberspace*, 95 TEX. L. REV. 1639, 1656–63 (2017)(giving the examples of Pakistan complaining about US drone strikes, Iran complaining about US breaches of its territorial waters, Canada complaining about radioactive debris on its territory from a Russian satellite, and Argentina complaining about Israel's abduction of Adolph Eichmann—all by reference to international law rules related to sovereignty).

64. For a thorough summary of the history of the GGE, *see generally* Henriksen, *supra* note 1.

65. Rep. of the Group of Governmental Experts on Developments in the Field of Information and Telecommunications in the Context of International Security (2013), transmitted by Letter dated 7 June 2013 from the Chair of the Group Established Pursuant to G.A. Res. 66/24 (2012) Addressed to General Assembly, ¶ 20, U.N. Doc. A/68/98 (June 24, 2013) [hereinafter 2013 GGE Report]. Apart from an admission in the Secretary-General's foreword that states had "only begun to develop the norms, laws and modes of cooperation needed for this new information environment," the 2010 GGE report ignored international law and sovereignty entirely. Rep. of the Group of Governmental Experts on Developments in the Field of Information

and Telecommunications in the Context of International Security (2010), transmitted by Letter dated 16 July 2010 from the Chairman of the Group Established Pursuant to G.A. Res. 60/45 (2006) Addressed to General Assembly, at 4, U.N. Doc. A/65/201 (July 31, 2010). The first GGE working group, by contrast, reached "no consensus" on any issue. U.N. Secretary-General, *Group of Governmental Experts on Developments in the Field of Information and Telecommunications in the Context of International Security*, ¶ 5, U.N. Doc. A/60/202 (Aug. 5, 2005).

66. *See* 2013 GGE Report, *supra* note 65, at ¶ 16; *see also id.* at 25 ("Member states should consider how best to cooperate in implementing the above norms and principles of responsible behavior."). The 2015 GGE noted that states "must observe, among other principles of international law, State sovereignty, sovereign equality, the settlement of disputes by peaceful means and non-intervention in the internal affairs of other States" but again offered no specifics. Rep. of the Group of Governmental Experts on Developments in the Field of Information and Telecommunications in the Context of International Security (2015), transmitted by Letter dated 26 June 2015 from the Chair of the Group Established Pursuant to G.A. Res. 68/243 (2014) Addressed to General Assembly, ¶ 28, U.N. Doc. A/70/174 (July 22, 2015) [hereinafter 2015 GGE Report].

67. G.A. Res. 70/237, ¶ 5 (Dec. 30, 2015) ("*Requests* the Secretary-General, with the assistance of a group of governmental experts . . . to continue to study . . . how international law applies to the use of information and communications technologies by States.") (emphasis in original).

68. Henriksen, *supra* note 1, at 3.

69. Michele G. Markoff, Deputy Coordinator for Cyber Issues, Off. of the Coordinator for Cyber Issues, U.S. Dep't of State, Remarks at the U.N. GGE: Explanation of Position at the Conclusion of the 2016–2017 UN Group of Governmental Experts (GGE) on Developments in the Field of Information and Telecommunications in the Context of International Security (June 23, 2017) (emphasis in original).

70. *Cf.* Oona Hathaway & Alasdair Phillips-Robins, *COVID-19 and International Law Series: Vaccine Theft, Disinformation, the Law Governing Cyber Operations*, JUST SECURITY (Dec. 4, 2020)("[T]he very fact of wide disagreement among States about a potential rule of cyber sovereignty itself forecloses the existence of such a norm—at least at present").

71. Samuele De Tomas Colatin, *A Surprising Turn of Events: UN Creates Two Working Groups on Cyberspace*, NATO COOP. CYBER DEF. CTR. EXCELLENCE.(last visited Apr. 12, 2021), https://ccdcoe.org/incyder-articles/a-surprising-turn-of-events-un-creates-two-working-groups-on-cyberspace/.

72. OEWG Final Substantive Report, *supra* note 2, at ¶ 7; Rep. of the Group of Governmental Experts on Advancing Responsible State Behaviour in Cyberspace in the Context of International Security (2021), transmitted by Letter dated 28 May 2021 from the Chair of the Group Established Pursuant to G.A. Res. 73/266 (2018) Addressed to General Assembly, ¶¶ 71-72, U.N. Doc. A/76/135 (May 28, 2021) [hereinafter 2021 GGE Report].

73. *Id.* at ¶ 34.

74. *Id.*

75. 2021 GGE Report, *supra* note 73, ¶¶ 70-72.

76. *Inside Cyber Diplomacy: Discussing the UN OEWG with Mother of Norms*, CSIS (Mar. 2021) (interviewing US State Department official Michelle Markhoff who concludes that the 2021 OEWG Report "doesn't break new ground" and "doesn't add new norms").

77. For countries' submissions to the OEWG, see *Open-Ended Working Group*, U.N., https://www.un.org/disarmament/open-ended-working-group/. While the states were formally asked to comment on the draft proposals, many states' submissions touched on their views on international law related to cyber operations. For countries' submissions to the 2021 GGE, see Official compendium of voluntary national contributions on the subject of how international law applies to the use of information and communications technologies by States submitted by participating governmental experts in the Group of Governmental Experts on Advancing Responsible State Behaviour in Cyberspace in the Context of International Security established pursuant to General Assembly resolution 73/266, U.N. Doc. A/76/136 (July 13, 2021) [hereinafter 2021 GGE Compendium].

78. *See* Special Envoy of Czech Republic for Cyberspace, Director of Cybersecurity Department, Statement dated Feb. 11, 2020 from the Special Envoy of Czech Republic for Cyberspace, Director of Cybersecurity Department at the 2nd Substantive Session of the Open-Ended Working Group on Developments in the Field of Information and Telecommunications in the Context of International Security of the First Committee of the General Assembly of the United Nations (Feb. 11, 2020); International Law and Cyberspace: Finland's National Positions (Oct. 15, 2020).

79. Appendix: International Law in Cyberspace (2019), transmitted by Letter dated 5 July 2019 from the Minister of Foreign Affairs to the President of the House of Representatives on the International Legal Order in Cyberspace (Sept. 26, 2019) (Neth.).

80. The Kingdom of the Netherlands' Response to the Pre-Draft Report of the OEWG, at ¶ 17 (April 2020).

81. 2021 GGE Compendium, *supra* note 78, at 68 (Norway) ("The precise threshold of what constitute a cyber operation in violation of sovereignty is not settled in international law, and will depend on a case-by-case assessment."); *id.* at 87 (Switzerland) ("A precise definition of these criteria is a question of interpretation and subject to debate").

82. German Federal Foreign Office, German Federal Ministry of Defence, & German Federal Ministry of the Interior, Building and Community, On the Application of International Law in Cyberspace: Position Paper 4 (Mar. 2021).

83. *Cf.* Brian J. Egan, Legal Advisor, U.S. Dep't of State, Remarks on International Law and Stability in Cyberspace, BERKELEY LAW (Nov. 10, 2016) (noting that "a cyber operation by a State that interferes with another country's ability to hold an election or that manipulates another country's election results would be a clear violation of the rule of non-intervention").

84. *Id.* at 3. *But see* Michael Schmitt, *Germany's Positions on International Law in Cyberspace Part I*, JUST SECURITY (Mar. 9, 2021) (arguing that Germany embraces both bases for violation).

85. 2021 GGE Compendium, *supra* note 78, at 76 (Romania).

86. MINISTRY OF THE ARMED FORCES OF FRANCE, INTERNATIONAL LAW APPLIED TO OPERATIONS IN CYBERSPACE 7, 18 (2019); *General Staff of Iranian Armed Forces Warns of Tough Reaction to Any Cyber Threat*, NOURNEWS (Aug. 18, 2020, 5:59 AM); Letter from Gabriel Juárez Lucas, Fourth Vice Minister, Interior Ministry, Government of the Republic of Guatemala, to the honorable Department of International Law, General Secretariat of the Organization of American States, Washington, D.C. (July 9, 2019); 2021 GGE Compendium, *supra* note 78, at 18 (Brazil).

87. French Ministry of Defense, International Law Applied to Operations in Cyberspace 7, 18 (2019); France's response to Resolution 73/27 "Developments in the field of information and telecommunications in the context of international security" and Resolution 73/266 "Advancing responsible State behaviour in cyberspace in the context of international security" 8; *see also* Gary Corn, *Punching on the Edges of the Grey Zone: Iranian Cyber Threats and State Cyber Responses*, JUST SECURITY (Feb. 11, 2020).

88. Naomi Conrad & Nina Werkhäuser, *Germany Debates Stepping Up Active Cyberoperations*, DEUTSCHE WELLE (June 26, 2019); Maria Sheahan, *German Cyber Agency Calls for Authority to Hack Back: Spiegel*, REUTERS (Nov. 22, 2017, 7:17 AM).

89. See Jack Kenny, *France, Cyber Operations and Sovereignty: The "Purist" Approach to Sovereignty and Contradictory State Practice*, LAWFARE (Mar. 12, 2021, 8:01 AM); Pierluigi Paganini, ANIMAL FARM APT AND THE SHADOW OF FRENCH INTELLIGENCE, INFOSEC RESOURCES (July 8, 2015).

90. *See infra* Appendix.

91. *See* NEW ZEALAND MINISTRY OF FOREIGN AFFAIRS & TRADE, THE APPLICATION OF INTERNATIONAL LAW TO STATE ACTIVITY IN CYBERSPACE ¶¶ 11–15 (Dec. 2020); Roy Schondorf, Israeli Deputy Attorney General (International Law), Keynote Address at the U.S. Naval War College conference on Disruptive Technologies and International Law: Israel's Perspective on Key Legal and Practical Issues Concerning the Application of International Law to Cyber Operations (Dec. 8, 2020); Comments by Austria on the Pre-Draft Report of the OEWG–ICT (Mar. 3, 2020); Permanent Mission of the Republic of Guyana to the Organization of American States, Note No: 105/2019 (July 30, 2019) ("Whether a violation occurs depends on the degree of infringement and whether there has been an interference with Government functions."); Office of the Commander-in-Chief of the State Inspector General of the Armed Forces of Bolivia, OAS Inter-American Juridical Committee Questionnaire (July 17, 2019); 2021 GGE Compendium, *supra* note 78, at 46 (Japan) ("[I]t can be presumed that, in some cases, a violation of sovereignty constitutes a violation of international law even when it does not fall within the scope of unlawful intervention. . . . [I]t is desirable that a common understanding be forged through State practices and future discussions.").

Some have argued that NATO's *Allied Joint Doctrine for Cyberspace Operations* recognized sovereignty as a rule of international law, but they are wrong. NATO's publication merely noted that cyber operations below the threshold of use of force or armed attack may "constitute a violation of international law as a breach of sovereignty or other internationally wrongful act." N. ATL. TREATY ORG., ALLIED JOINT PUBICATION-3.20: ALLIED JOINT DOCTRINE FOR CYBERSPACE OPERATIONS, at 20 n.26 (2020). That statement does not affirmatively embrace anything approaching the Rule 4 commentary and might refer simply to cyber operations that violate one of the many sovereignty-based rules, such as the prohibition against intervention. At a minimum, the NATO report does not comment on the scope of any such sovereignty-based rules below the use-of-force threshold.

92. Jeremy Wright QC MP, U.K. Att'y Gen., Address at Chatham House Royal Institute for International Affairs: Cyber and International Law in the 21st Century (May 23, 2018).

93. *See* CYBERSPACE SOLARIUM COMM'N, FINAL REPORT 2, 24, 29 (2020).

94. Paul C. Ney, Jr., Dep't of Def. Gen. Couns., DOD General Counsel Remarks at U.S. Cyber Command Legal Conference (Mar. 2, 2020). Previously, the United States had stated that a "cyber operation [could violate] the sovereignty of another State." TALLINN MANUAL 2.0, *supra* note 4, at 17. But it has not elaborated or specified whether it was referring to a stand-alone international law rule or what that rule was. Harold Koh, Legal Advisor, US Dep't of State, Remarks at the U.S. Cyber Command Inter-Agency Legal Conference: International Law in Cyberspace (Sept. 18, 2012) (transcript available at Chris Borgen, *Harold Koh on International Law in Cyberspace*, OPINIO JURIS [Sept. 19, 2012]); Egan, *supra* note 82. On April 15, 2021, President Biden by Executive Order imposed sanctions on various Russian entities for a variety of real-space and cyberspace activities. Exec. Order No. 14,024, 86 Fed. Reg. 20,249 (Apr. 19, 2021). The Order stated that the "specified harmful foreign activities of the Government of the Russian Federation" that formed the basis for the sanctions included interference in U.S. and foreign elections, "malicious cyber-enabled activities against the United States" and allies, transnational corruption to influence foreign governments, extraterritorial activities targeting dissidents or journalists, *and* violation of "well-established principles of international law, including respect for the territorial integrity of states." The listing of malicious cyber activities separate from the well-established violations of international law related to territorial integrity, among other things, indicates that the statement does not mark an implicit change of the US position on the topic of this chapter. Moreover, the White House Fact sheet on the sanctions make plain that many of the new sanctions related to Russia's "occupation . . . [of] Crimea." The White House, Fact Sheet: Imposing Costs for Harmful Foreign Activities by the Russian Government (Apr. 15, 2021).

95. Estonia's Comments to the OEWG Pre-Draft Report, at 9 (Apr. 16, 2020); *see, e.g.,* Intervention by Delegation of the Islamic Republic of Iran on International Law (Oct. 1, 2020); *see also* Statement by the Representative of the Russian Federation at the Online Discussion of the Second "Pre-Draft" of the Final Report of the UN Open-Ended Working Group on Developments in the Field of Information and Telecommunications in the Context of International Security (June 15, 2020); Permanent Mission of Denmark to the United Nations, Denmark's Response to the Initial "Pre-Draft" Report of the Open-Ended Working Group on Developments in the Field of Information and Telecommunications in the Context of International Security, Ref. no. 2019-36843 (Apr. 16, 2020).

96. Watts & Richard, *supra* note 58, at 837–38.

97. *See supra* note 96 and accompanying text.

98. Michael Schmitt, *The Defense Department's Measured Take on International Law in Cyberspace*, JUST SECURITY (March 11, 2020); *see also* Schmitt & Vihul, *supra* note 63, at 1670.

99. *See supra* note 96 and accompanying text.

100. Joe Uchill, *Obama: US Government Has Largest Capacity to Hack*, THE HILL (Sept. 6, 2016, 9:55 AM).

101. *See generally* DAVID SANGER, THE PERFECT WEAPON: WAR, SABOTAGE, AND FEAR IN THE CYBER AGE (2018).

102. Schmitt, *supra* note 52. Another justification, also presumably related to deterrence, is that violation of a low-level sovereignty rule would permit a broader array of countermeasures. *Id.*

103. Corn, *supra* note 88.

104. President Barack Obama, Press Conference by the President (Dec. 16, 2016).

105. See, e.g., Jack Goldsmith, ON THE RUSSIAN PROPOSAL FOR MUTUAL NONINTERFERENCE IN DOMESTIC POLITICS, LAWFARE (Dec. 11, 2017, 9:30 AM); Jack Goldsmith, *Contrarian Thoughts on Russia and the Presidential Election*, LAWFARE (Jan. 10, 2017, 11:30 AM); *see also, e.g.,* BEN BUCHANAN, THE CYBERSECURITY DILEMMA: HACKING, TRUST AND FEAR BETWEEN NATIONS 157–86 (2017).

106. *Cf.* Henriksen, *supra* note 1, at 2 ("[D]espite what many international lawyers seem to believe, the discussion about how ICT should be regulated is as much about strategy, politics and ideological differences (if not more so) than it is about law. And at present, states' interests and normative preferences are simply too diverse for consensus on anything but the most basic of such issues to arise.").

107. TALLINN MANUAL ON THE INTERNATIONAL LAW APPLICABLE TO CYBER WARFARE 20, ¶ 13 (MICHAEL N. SCHMITT ED., 2013).

108. *Id.* at 21–22, ¶ 15.

109. Kate O'Flaherty, *Stuxnet 2? Iran Hints Nuclear Site Explosion Could Be a Cyberattack*, FORBES (July 4, 2020, 7:03 AM). While Iran acknowledged there was some ambiguity about whether the explosion was caused by a cyber operation, it did not suggest that any such cyber operation would be unlawful under international law.

110. Joby Warrick & Ellen Nakashima, *Officials: Israel Linked to a Disruptive Cyberattack on Iranian Port Facility*, WASH. POST (May 18, 2020, 2:48 PM).

111. Toi Staff, *Cyber Attacks Again Hit Israel's Water System, Shutting Agricultural Pumps*, TIMES ISR. (July 17, 2020, 1:18 AM).

112. CYBERSECURITY & INFRASTRUCTURE SEC. AGENCY, *Alert (AA20-304A): Iranian Advanced Persistent Threat Actor Identified Obtaining Voter Registration Data* (Oct. 30, 2020).

113. Mandiant, "Ghostwriter" Influence Campaign: Unknown Actors Leverage Website Compromises and Fabricated Content to Push Narratives Aligned with Russian Security Interests 3 (2020).

114. Julian E. Barnes, *U.S. Cyberattack Hurt Iran's Ability to Target Oil Tankers, Officials Say*, N.Y. TIMES (Aug. 28, 2019).

115. Ryan Browne, *US and UK Accuse Russia of Major Cyber Attack on Georgia*, CNN (Feb. 20, 2020, 1:19 PM).

116. Andy Greenberg, *The Untold Story of the 2018 Olympics Cyberattack, the Most Deceptive Hack in History*, WIRED (Oct. 17, 2019, 6:00 AM).

117. Garrett M. Graff, *The Man Who Speaks Softly—and Commands a Big Cyber Army*, WIRED (Oct. 13, 2020, 6:00 AM).

118. *See* BEN BUCHANAN, THE HACKER AND THE STATE 280–81 (2020).

119. *See id.* at 289–90, 295–96, 299; Kimberly Crawley, *NotPetya Development May Have Started Before EternalBlue*, INFOSECURITY MAG. (June 30, 2017).

120. Nicole Perlroth & Clifford Krauss. *A Cyberattack in Saudi Arabia Had a Deadly Goal. Experts Fear Another Try*, N.Y. TIMES (Mar. 15, 2018).

121. Ellen Nakashima & Philip Rucker, *U.S. Declares North Korea Carried Out Massive WannaCry Cyberattack*, WASH. POST (Dec. 19, 2017); *see generally* UNITED KINGDOM NATIONAL AUDIT OFFICE, DEPARTMENT OF HEALTH, INVESTIGATION: WANNACRY CYBER ATTACK AND THE NHS (2018).

122. *See* BUCHANAN, *supra* note 119, at 300–01.

123. Karen DeYoung & Ellen Nakashima, *UAE Orchestrated Hacking of Qatari Government Sites, Sparking Regional Upheaval, According to U.S. Intelligence Officials*, WASH. POST (July 16, 2017).

124. *See* BUCHANAN, *supra* note 119, at 188.

125. Michael Riley, Glen Carey & John Fraher, *Destructive Hacks Strike Saudi Arabia, Posing Challenge to Trump*, BLOOMBERG (Dec. 1, 2016, 3:21 AM).

126. SANGER, *supra* note 102, at 201, 205, 212, 232; NICOLE PERLROTH, THIS IS HOW THEY TELL ME THE WORLD ENDS: THE CYBERWEAPONS ARMS RACE 318–19 (2021) (speculating that this might have swayed the election); Michael N. Schmitt, *"Virtual" Disenfranchisement: Cyber Election Meddling in the Grey Zones of International Law*, 19 CHI. J. INT'L L. 30, 46–47 (2018)(arguing that the operation violated Rule 4, at least in part).

127. *See* BUCHANAN, *supra* note 119, at 188.

128. *Russia "Was Behind German Parliament Hack,"* BBC NEWS (May 13, 2016); *Bundestag Counting Cost of Cyberattack*, DEUTSCHE WELLE (Nov. 6, 2015); *see also* Efrony & Shany, *supra* note 56, at 617–19, 640 (outlining the operation and noting that Germany responded by beefing up its cyber capabilities).

129. John P. Carlin, DAWN OF THE CODE WAR: AMERICA'S BATTLE AGAINST RUSSIA, CHINA, AND THE RISING GLOBAL CYBER THREAT 310 (2019) ("The company's computers had, it turned out, been nuked—not just frozen, but wiped clean, turned into expensive bricks sitting across 3,000 desks."); SANGER, *supra* note 102, at 141.

130. Benjamin Elgin & Michael Riley, *Nuke Remark Stirred Hack on Sands Casinos That Foreshadowed Sony*, BLOOMBERG (Dec. 11, 2014, 9:01 PM). The *Tallinn Manual* 2.0 says that a cyberattack that wipes computers like this would violate Rule 4 because it causes computers to lose "functionality." TALLINN MANUAL 2.0, *supra* note 4, at 20, ¶ 13.

131. BUCHANAN, *supra* note 119, at 143.

132. Nicole Perlroth, *In Cyberattack on Saudi Firm, U.S. Sees Iran Firing Back*, N.Y. TIMES (Oct. 23, 2012).

133. SANGER, *supra* note 102, at 52; *see also* Efrony & Shany, *supra* note 56, at 624 (noting that Saudi Arabia never condemned it).

134. *Id.*

135. *See generally* Kim Zetter, COUNTDOWN TO ZERO DAY: STUXNET AND THE LAUNCH OF THE WORLD'S FIRST DIGITAL WEAPON (2015).

136. Lucas Kello, *The Meaning of the Cyber Revolution: Perils to Theory and Statecraft*, 38 INT'L SEC. 7, 24 (2013).

8

Defend Forward and Cyber Countermeasures

*Ashley Deeks**

When a state suffers an internationally wrongful act at the hands of another state, international law allows the injured state to respond in a variety of ways. Depending on the nature, scope, and severity of the initial wrongful act, lawful responses can range from a demand for reparations in response to a low-level violation to a forcible act of self-defense in response to an armed attack. Countermeasures offer an additional way for a state to respond to an internationally wrongful act. Countermeasures are acts that would in general be considered internationally wrongful but are justified to address the wrongdoing state's original international law violation. The goal of countermeasures is to prompt the wrongdoing state to cease its legal violation. The countermeasures regime can help deter international law violations ex ante and mitigate those violations ex post, offering an avenue by which states can—at least in theory—de-escalate disputes.

As states increasingly employ cyber tools to commit hostile acts against their adversaries, countermeasures are poised to play a growing role in inter-state relations. While states disagree about the precise threshold for either a use of force or an armed attack in the cyber context, most have nevertheless treated it as a high bar. In contrast, many inter-state activities in cyberspace fall below the force threshold but nevertheless may violate international law and warrant responses from the targeted states.[1] Understanding when and how states lawfully may deploy countermeasures and which customary limits govern the use of countermeasures is critical for states operating in the cyber arena, not only to understand their own options when injured but also to anticipate the responses that their cyber activities may trigger from other states.

This chapter explores the role that countermeasures can play in the US cyber strategy known as Defend Forward. This strategy calls for US forces to "defend forward to disrupt or halt malicious cyber activity at its source, including activity that falls below the level of armed conflict."[2] The United States appears to believe that most, if not all, of the Defense Department's (DoD's) activities under this strategy are consistent with international law. But it is possible that some of DoD's activities might be legally controversial, particularly because the content of some customary international law norms, such as the norm of non-intervention, is both vague and contested.[3] As a result, it is worth evaluating whether and when DoD might be able to defend such actions as countermeasures under international law.

Part I identifies the background rules of countermeasures in international law. Part II discusses how states and scholars have interpreted the law of countermeasures in the cyber context and highlights areas in which the law may be changing. It is straightforward to apply some traditional requirements of countermeasures to cyberspace, but directly applying others produces illogical or unsatisfying outcomes. For this reason, some states seem to be developing a *lex specialis* of cyber countermeasures. Part III lays out a hypothetical to illustrate when and how the US government could justify as cyber countermeasures certain actions taken under the Defend Forward strategy. It also suggests ways in which the United States should use countermeasures to avoid other states perceiving such actions as unlawful (and potentially taking their own countermeasures in response). Part IV identifies ways in which key actors can help develop the law of cyber countermeasures in a direction consistent with the US Defend Forward strategy.[4]

Countermeasures: A Primer

Countermeasures are acts that a state can take in response to a wrong committed against it by another state. These acts would otherwise be considered internationally wrongful but are justified to address the wrongdoing state's original international law violation.[5] Countermeasures must be non-forcible and proportional, and they are limited to a temporary non-performance of the injured state's international obligations toward the wrongdoing state.[6] The injured state's conduct is not deemed wrongful if the conditions justifying countermeasures are satisfied, though this is true only for such time as the responsible state continues its wrongful act.[7] The purpose of countermeasures is not to punish but to bring the wrongdoing state back into compliance with its international obligations.[8] Once the wrongdoing state has complied with its obligations of cessation and reparation, the injured state must terminate the countermeasures.[9] For example, if a state wrongfully denies its treaty partner the right to provide air services in its territory, the injured treaty partner could deny the wrongdoing state the right to provide air services in the injured state's territory as long as the original treaty violation continued.[10] That said, the injured state need not undertake its countermeasures within the same body of international law as that of the violation.[11]

There are limited public examples of injured states clearly imposing countermeasures on wrongdoing states. Nevertheless, many states accept the basic legal parameters of countermeasures.[12] The most prominent articulation of the countermeasures regime is the International Law Commission's (ILC's) 2001 Draft Articles on Responsibility of States for Internationally Wrongful Acts (DARS). Many states view the DARS as reflecting customary international law.[13] The United States has cited the DARS in pleadings before international courts and tribunals but believes that certain articles do not constitute customary international law.[14] Further, the US government has expressed a preference for leaving the articles in draft form, resisting recent efforts to convert them into a treaty.[15]

The DARS defines countermeasures and articulates various conditions that attach to their use. States generally accept that countermeasures are a necessary option in an international system that lacks a supreme arbiter or other vertical mechanism to enforce compliance with international law.[16] Countermeasures are a useful way for an injured state to impose costs on another state that is engaged in a wrongful act against it and can (at least theoretically) deter such violations ex ante.

States have placed important substantive and procedural limits on countermeasures to ensure that their use remains consistent with the goal of reestablishing legal compliance by the wrongdoing state. The injured state is responsible for properly attributing the wrongdoing and implementing countermeasures that comply with the law. In making these judgments unilaterally, the injured state acts at its own risk. If an injured state does not abide by these limits when taking countermeasures, the original wrongdoing state or the international community may later judge it responsible for committing a wrongful act itself.[17] The most significant limitations are outlined below.

Limitations on Categories of Countermeasures

Countermeasures must not amount to a use of force and may not contravene the injured state's obligations to protect fundamental human rights, obligations "of a humanitarian character prohibiting reprisals," or obligations under peremptory norms of international law, such as those prohibiting genocide, slavery, and torture.[18] These limitations may change over time as states' understandings of human rights obligations evolve. When using countermeasures, states must respect the inviolability of diplomatic missions, agents, archives, and documents and may not derogate from their dispute settlement obligations to the wrongdoing state.[19] These limits help ensure that channels of communication remain open between states and offer core protections to individuals who might otherwise be adversely affected by an injured state's reciprocal international law violation.

Notice and Negotiation Requirements

Procedurally, the DARS requires that before undertaking countermeasures, an injured state must call upon the wrongdoing state to fulfill its international law obligations, notify the wrongdoing state that it intends to take countermeasures, and offer to negotiate with that state.[20] The notice obligation ensures that the wrongdoing state is aware of the injured state's claim and understands the injured state's actions as an attempt to correct the wrongdoing state's behavior. The DARS notes an exception for cases in which an injured state must take such "urgent countermeasures as are necessary to preserve its rights."[21] The DARS commentaries offer as an example of urgent countermeasures a decision to temporarily freeze the wrongdoing state's assets to prevent the wrongdoer from immediately withdrawing those assets from its accounts.[22]

Proportionality Requirement

Countermeasures must be proportional, considering the injury suffered and the "quality or character of the rights in question."[23] As in other areas of international law, the proportionality requirement regulates the scope and intensity of a state's response to wrongful conduct, improves predictability among states, and mitigates the risk of abuse by the injured state. A level of indeterminacy inheres in the proportionality principle, and international tribunals have not fully developed the concept.[24] However, states generally accept that proportionality does not require that the quantitative effects of the countermeasure be equal to those of the initial wrongful act, nor does it mean that an injured state must respond with behavior that mirrors that of the wrongdoing state.[25]

Reversibility Requirement

A state taking countermeasures should attempt to make them reversible, meaning that it should use them in a way that "permit[s] the resumption of performance of the obligations in question" after the countermeasures are finished.[26] For example, in the Gabčíkovo-Nagymaros Project case before the International Court of Justice, Slovakia's decision to divert the Danube in response to a treaty violation by Hungary was likely not a lawful counter-measure, in part because it was not reversible.[27] The reversibility requirement is not absolute, as it may be impossible to ensure that all consequences of a particular countermeasure are reversible.[28] If a state has a choice between two effective countermeasures, though, choosing the one that produces the least irreversible damage can help ensure the countermeasure's proportionality.

The Effect of Countermeasures on Third States

The injured state may direct its countermeasures only against the state that is responsible for the internationally wrongful act.[29] But indirect effects on third parties will not automatically render a countermeasure unlawful as long as it does not constitute an independent breach of a legal obligation to the third party.[30] The DARS leaves open whether countermeasures may be taken by third states that are not directly injured by the wrongdoer's actions but are owed the same obligation that the wrongdoing state breached—for example, in cases implicating general international obligations, where all states might have an interest in compliance.[31] An injured state should not use countermeasures to coerce a wrongdoing state to violate obligations to third states; it should use them only to achieve cessation and reparation for itself.[32]

As noted above, there are few public examples in which injured states have imposed countermeasures on wrongdoing states. One reason for this scar-city may be the high procedural bars that the DARS creates.[33] As discussed in the next part, some of these procedural bars pose particular challenges in the context of cyber operations.

The *Lex Specialis* of Countermeasures in Cyberspace

As traditional methods of statecraft migrate to digital platforms, states and experts have spent considerable time assessing how international law does or should apply in the cyber context. While scholars initially debated whether it was possible to translate existing international law into a workable legal framework governing cyber operations, most states now accept that the pre-cyber rights and obligations of states under international law attach in the cyber realm—albeit with some modifications.[34] While many states have expressed general support for the proposition that international law regulates cyber operations, clear articulations about how specific rules apply are still somewhat rare.[35]

To fill this gap, state officials and international law experts have begun to give speeches and produce manuals and other documents that set forth their views about how international law—including the law of countermeasures—does or should apply to cyber operations. In particular, the United States, the United Kingdom, the Netherlands, France, Australia, and Israel have articulated their views about the relevance and application of international law to cyber countermeasures.[36] Further, in 2017 a group of non-state experts, facilitated by the NATO Cooperative Cyber Defence Centre of Excellence, published the *Tallinn Manual 2.0*, a non-binding but comprehensive analysis that attempts to articulate how international law applies to cyber operations, including how countermeasures function.

Governments that have made statements about the applicability of international law to cyber operations generally accept that the international law of countermeasures applies to those operations. However, significant questions remain about when and how states may use countermeasures in response to wrongful acts in cyberspace. This section first discusses aspects of traditional countermeasures that translate easily into the cyber domain. It then turns to aspects of countermeasures that do not translate sensibly or neatly into the cyber arena. It argues that to deal with these areas of disconnect, states have begun to shape a *lex specialis* of cyber countermeasures—that is, a subset of rules regarding countermeasures that adjusts the traditional requirements to take account of the novel aspects of cyber operations.

Countermeasures Rules That Apply Straightforwardly to Cyber

States and scholars have applied some aspects of the DARS's countermeasures rules to cyber operations with minimal controversy. These aspects include the permissibility of an asymmetrical response, the need for appropriate attribution, the general requirement to provide notice to the wrongdoing state, and the constraints of proportionality and reversibility. Importantly, the purpose of countermeasures in response to an international wrong in cyberspace remains the same: not to punish but to compel the wrongdoing state to resume compliance with its international obligations.[37] Further, all states that have spoken on this issue, as well as the *Tallinn Manual 2.0*, have affirmed that countermeasures may not violate fundamental human rights or peremptory norms of international law.[38]

Asymmetry of Response

In 2016, State Department legal advisor Brian Egan expressed the US view that a state may respond to wrongful cyber activity using either cyber or non-cyber-based countermeasures.[39] Shortly thereafter, UK Attorney General Jeremy Wright stated that there is "no requirement in the doctrine of countermeasures for a response to be symmetrical to the underlying un-lawful act."[40] Australia and France likewise have signaled that victim states that suffer malicious cyber activity may take countermeasures outside the cyber realm.[41] The *Tallinn Manual 2.0* similarly maintains that a state may use cyber countermeasures in response to non-cyber wrongful acts and vice versa.[42] Tallinn also notes, however, that "the requirement of proportionality is less likely to be contravened" when countermeasures responding to cyber activity are in kind.[43]

Head: Attribution

States taking countermeasures in response to wrongful cyber activity bear the burden of attributing the wrongful activity to which they are responding to the proper actors—just as they do when responding to wrongful activity outside of cyberspace. The evidentiary standard for proof has never been de-finitively established.[44] But the elevated risk of misattribution in the cyber context suggests that states should have high levels of confidence before taking countermeasures in response to malicious cyber operations. In March 2020, DoD General Counsel Paul Ney emphasized the importance of proper attribution, stating that an inability to establish that "the act is internationally wrongful and attributable to a state" within the time frame in which DoD needed to respond would render countermeasures unavailable.[45] Leaders from the United Kingdom and France, as well as the *Tallinn Manual 2.0*'s group of experts, have stressed the importance and practical difficulties of attribution. On the other hand, each has also emphasized that there is no international legal obligation to *publicly* attribute internationally wrongful cyber acts or, when making such attributions publicly, to reveal the under-lying information on which that attribution is based.[46]

Proportionality

Though states may encounter technical difficulties in ensuring the propor-tionality of their cyber countermeasures, they generally accept that the pro-portionality principle applies. For example, the United States, the United Kingdom, Japan, Estonia, and Australia have explicitly stated that cyber countermeasures must be proportionate.[47] The *Tallinn Manual 2.0* also affirms the principle but cautions that injured states must take into account that cyber systems are often interconnected. Interconnection creates the risk that a cyber countermeasure directed at a hostile state's server could affect innocent actors whose servers happen to be connected to the targeted server. Tallinn suggests that a reviewing tribunal would consider which effects were foreseeable if asked to decide whether a given countermeasure was proportional.[48]

Reversibility

States have said little about the need to make countermeasures reversible. Tallinn's group of experts was unable to reach consensus about whether states must simply select feasibly reversible options when taking countermeasures, or if states bear an additional burden to choose the option that is most easily reversed.[49] In light of the ambiguity in the law, it seems that states should approach the reversibility question through the lens of reasonableness and feasibility—that is, favoring a reversible option over a non-reversible option when feasible.[50]

Countermeasures Rules Complicated by the Features of Cyberspace

Other requirements associated with traditional countermeasures trans-late less easily into the cyber setting, such as the requirement that an in-jured state give the wrongdoing state notice ex ante that it intends to impose countermeasures. Some states also have discussed the possibility of using other forms of countermeasures that the ILC either chose not to address or failed to consider, such as collective or anticipatory countermeasures, be-cause the states see such measures as increasingly relevant or necessary in the cyber domain.[51] These states may be starting to develop a specialized body of law for cyber operations—a *"lex specialis* of cyber countermeasures"— that attempts to adjust the existing requirements of countermeasures to the unique features of the cyber setting.

Ex Ante Notification and Negotiations

As noted in Part I of this chapter, the traditional approach to countermeasures is to require the injured state to call on the wrongdoing state to cease its violation, to provide notice to the wrongdoing state ex ante of its decision to take countermeasures, and to offer to negotiate with the wrongdoing state.[52] The traditional rule also acknowledges that the injured state may take "urgent countermeasures" where necessary to preserve its rights. States have signaled a willingness to reinterpret these requirements in the cyber setting.

The US perspective on the notice requirement in the cyber context may be growing more flexible. In 2016, State Department legal adviser Brian Egan did not dispute the "prior demand" requirement but noted that "[t]he sufficiency of a prior demand should be evaluated on a case-by-case basis in light of the particular circumstances of the situation at hand and the purpose of the requirement."[53] DoD General Counsel Paul Ney's 2020 remarks continued to acknowledge the traditional notice requirement but indicated that "there are varying State views on whether notice would be necessary in all cases in the cyber context because of secrecy or urgency"[54]—suggesting some skepticism on DoD's part about how stringently this requirement does or should apply to cyber operations.[55]

The United States is not alone in this skepticism. UK Attorney General Jeremy Wright, discussing covert cyber intrusions, stated that he did not agree that states are always legally obliged to give prior notice before taking countermeasures against wrongdoing states, and that it would "not be right for international law to require a countermeasure to expose highly sensitive" defense capabilities.[56] The French Ministry of the Armies also rejected an absolute duty of prior notice before taking countermeasures, stating that a state could derogate from this rule where there is a "need to protect its rights" in urgent cases—a premise that will play a significant role in high-speed cyber operations.[57] The Dutch Minister of Foreign Affairs affirmed the general notification requirement "in principle," even in the cyber setting, but emphasized that it may be dispensed with when immediate action is necessary.[58] And the Israeli Deputy Attorney General indicated Israel's agreement with the US and UK that there is no absolute duty under international law to notify the wrongdoing state in advance of a cyber countermeasure.[59]

The *Tallinn Manual 2.0* reiterates the DARS's requirement that a state intending to take countermeasures must first notify the target state and offer to negotiate.[60] But it also carries forward and expands the exception for urgent circumstances, noting that the notification requirement is not categorical, not necessary when injured states must act immediately, and not required when notice would render countermeasures meaningless.[61] In light of the heightened speed of cyber interactions, the limited effect that public warnings have had on hostile states such as Russia and China, and the recent public statements by Western states, this exception has the potential to become the norm.[62]

Collective Countermeasures

The debate over the right to engage in collective countermeasures is not a new one. However, several states and scholars have become newly interested in the concept's application to the cyber setting. In the DARS commentaries, the ILC left open whether a state could take countermeasures in response to a violation of international law that injured another state.[63] During the ILC's deliberations, some experts favored an article explicitly authorizing collective countermeasures while others opposed the idea for fear that it would lead to abuse by major powers or undermine the security regime contained in Chapter VII of the UN Charter.[64]

Discussions of "collective countermeasures" sometimes conflate two concepts. One version of collective countermeasures echoes the UN Charter's concept of "collective security": the idea that there are some international harms so problematic that they injure the international community as a whole, and that the whole community of states therefore may react to them as injured parties.[65] The other version of collective countermeasures is more modest and parallels the concept of collective self-defense. Collective self-defense allows non-injured states to provide assistance to an injured state that requests help in responding to an armed attack. Although scholars have tended to focus on "collective security"–type collective countermeasures, recent state speeches seem to envision collective (non-forcible) countermeasures that are closer in conception to collective self-defense.

Recently, Estonia became the first state to publicly endorse the idea of collective countermeasures in the cyber context. In a May 2019 speech,

President Kersti Kaljulaid of Estonia cited the inherent right to self-defense, noting: "Among other options for collective response, Estonia is furthering the position that states which are not directly injured may apply countermeasures to support the state directly affected by the malicious cyber operation."[66] The Estonian approach views collective countermeasures as an extension of collective self-defense and deems the approach to be appropriate in light of the need for collective diplomatic responses to malicious cyber activities. The US Deputy Assistant Secretary of Defense for Cyber Policy told a reporter that he thought Estonia's approach was "the general [direction] of international law" and that "states are in the process of moving international law in that direction."[67] In the 2018 US National Cyber Strategy, the United States announced that it would launch a Cyber Defense Initiative, stating: "The United States will work with like-minded states to coordinate and support each other's responses to significant malicious cyber incidents, including through intelligence sharing, buttressing of attribution claims, public statements of support for responsive actions taken, and joint imposition of consequences against malign actors."[68] Although the strategy does not expressly mention countermeasures, the idea of coordinating attribution and imposing joint consequences against malign actors may well include such activities.

In support of the direction in which Estonia and the United States seem to be heading, some scholars have argued that states generally should embrace the idea of collective countermeasures, citing the interconnected and persistent nature of cyber threats, technological disparities between states, and a desire to reduce the risk of escalation by discouraging the wrongdoing state from further hostile acts.[69] At least one state has rejected the idea outright, however.[70] The *Tallinn Manual 2.0*'s group of experts failed to reach consensus on whether states may take countermeasures on behalf of injured states that request their assistance.[71]

Although some of the ILC members who drafted the DARS were concerned that collective countermeasures might exacerbate, rather than suppress, interstate tensions, there is something counterintuitive about allowing collective acts of forcible self-defense but not collective measures that do not rise to the level of force. That is, if the international community benefits from efforts to suppress interstate tensions at the earliest possible stage, then the possibility of collective countermeasures offers both a stronger deterrent against the initial violation by the wrongdoing state ex ante and a more potent ability to bring to bear appropriate pressure against the wrongdoing state ex post, as long as the countermeasures remain proportional and the underlying wrongdoing is clear. This is particularly so when the state assisting the victim state has cyber capabilities that the victim state lacks. A researcher who reviewed recent statements by Western states summarized those statements as reflecting a shift in emphasis from self-defense to countermeasures, a "general approval of collective response," and a sense that the *opinio juris* in national strategies "is currently bent towards overriding the prohibition on collective countermeasures."[72]

Anticipatory Countermeasures

As in traditional domains, the purpose of countermeasures in the cyber domain is to stimulate the wrongdoing state to cease its wrongful acts. In light of this goal, the *Tallinn Manual 2.0*'s drafters emphasized that countermeasures are reactive, not proactive, and so assessed that states may not use countermeasures in an anticipatory or preemptive posture.[73] But some commentators consider the speed of cyber operations and the need for a persistent presence on the targeted systems to weigh in favor of allowing some level of anticipatory countermeasures to derail impending illegal actions.[74] This argument parallels conversations regarding anticipatory self-defense; states generally view anticipatory self-defense as permissible in the face of a threat of an imminent armed attack. Some states and scholars have recognized that changing technologies require an expansion of the interpretation of "imminence," including in cyber operations.[75] Many of the same arguments that have driven this expanded approach to imminence resonate in the call to accept some limited set of anticipatory countermeasures. So far, no state has advocated this position explicitly, but—to the extent we are able to identify it—state practice may begin to show that states are unwilling to allow adversaries to complete wrongful operations against them simply to justify a belated countermeasure. Without clear messaging, however, the target of anticipatory countermeasures may well interpret those countermeasures as stand-alone international law violations.

In sum, the United States and a number of its allies have begun to articulate a *lex specialis* of cyber countermeasures in an effort to modernize traditional countermeasures for use in cyberspace. Although to date there is insufficient state practice and *opinio juris* to treat these new approaches to countermeasures as having crystallized into customary international law, a number of Western states appear to see advantage in using the countermeasures concept in cyber settings to suppress growing numbers of international law violations there.

Using Countermeasures While Defending Forward

How might DoD's Defend Forward strategy fit with these existing—and, in some cases, evolving—rules regulating the use of cyber countermeasures? Countermeasures will be relevant when the United States is the victim of an internationally wrongful act by another state and it wishes to respond in a way that would at least arguably constitute an international law violation. Such a situation might arise, for instance, when the United States (or one of its allies) is the victim of a violation of the customary rules of non-intervention or due diligence, a cyber use of force, or a cyber-based effort to interfere with a US freedom of navigation exercise. This part sets out a hypothetical case study to help illustrate when and how the United States might justify as countermeasures certain actions taken under the Defend Forward umbrella.

Consider a hypothetical operation involving Russian interference that affects the casting and recording of votes in a US election. The rule of non-intervention provides that one state may not take forcible or coercive measures against the interests of another state that fall within the latter state's *domaine réservé*.[76] The "domaine réservé is generally understood to refer to those matters reserved in international law to the sole prerogative of States, matters such as the right to choose a political, economic, social, and cultural system, and to formulate and execute foreign policy."[77]

Although it is commonplace to highlight the vagueness of the concept of non-intervention, many states and scholars have concluded that interference with the physical conduct of US elections would constitute a violation of the non-intervention rule. The United States has stated: "[A] cyber operation by a State that interferes with another country's ability to hold an election or that manipulates another country's election results would be a clear violation of the rule of non-intervention."[78] UK Attorney General Jeremy Wright noted that the "precise boundaries" of non-intervention "are the subject of ongoing debate between states" but offered "the use by a hostile state of cyber operations to manipulate the electoral system to alter the results of an election in another state" as an example that "surely" constituted intervention.[79]

Imagine that in 2016 the Russian military intelligence agency (the GRU) was able to insert malware into the voter rolls of twenty counties in North

Carolina.[80] When election workers at polling places used their laptops to check in registered voters, the malware would have reflected that certain people already had voted (although they had not) and prevented the election workers from allowing those people to vote. The malware in some of the systems also would have informed the election workers that the voters were required to show identification, even though the North Carolina courts had struck down such a requirement. As a result of the malware, twenty thousand North Carolinians would have been unable to vote in the election.[81] Such an operation would constitute a coercive action intended to deprive the United States of its ability to make decisions that it is entitled to decide freely—to wit, a decision to conduct credible elections to select the leadership of its political system, and the actual decision about which leader to elect.

Alternatively, imagine that private actors within Russia direct botnets or distributed denial of service attacks against the actual functioning of US electoral systems in several states, preventing thousands of US citizens from having their votes properly counted in the 2020 election. Imagine further that the United States has a high level of confidence that Russian government officials are aware of these attacks and have the capacity to stop them but choose not to. In such a scenario, Russia would violate its international law obligation to undertake due diligence to stop cyber harms from emanating from Russian territory, triggering the US right to impose countermeasures on Russia.

What steps could the United States lawfully take as countermeasures to respond to the GRU's malware attack, particularly if it had reason to believe that Russia continued such attacks through the 2018 elections and planned to undertake additional, even more aggressive operations in 2020? The United States could take actions that would otherwise violate US international legal obligations to Russia with the goal of persuading Russia to stop these malicious operations. Either because it perceives an urgent need to respond or because it believes that giving Russia notice ex ante of the United States' intent to take cyber countermeasures would defeat their effect, the United States might choose not to inform Russia in advance that it considers Russia's operations to violate international law, to offer to negotiate, or to give Russia advance notice of its plan to impose countermeasures. Even if it does not give Russia advance notice, however, the United States must somehow make clear that its action is a countermeasure that is responding to Russia's wrong. A US official could, for instance, give a speech in advance stating that the United States intends to impose countermeasures on states that interfere with the physical processes or outcomes of US elections. The United States could then send a message to Russia shortly after the United States had inflicted countermeasures, informing Russia that it had taken specific actions as countermeasures and that Russia should not treat those actions as stand-alone violations of international law.

In terms of the countermeasures' parameters, the United States might well decide that engaging in a similar operation in response, while lawful as a countermeasure, would be inconsistent with US values. That is, the United States might want to signal its strong condemnation of election interference and avoid interfering with Russian elections. The United States instead might choose to respond against a different Russian governmental function. The United States might penetrate a Russian government system and render the hard drive of the control server that facilitates Russian Foreign Ministry communications temporarily inoperable, for example, something that easily would be proportional to the harm inflicted on US elections. Indeed, even encrypting the servers, so that Russia would need to replace them, might be proportional, even if not reversible. If the victim of Russia's election interference had been Montenegro rather than the United States,[82] the United States might be able to help Montenegro properly attribute the unlawful interference, develop possible countermeasures options, and offer guidance to Montenegro on how to execute its countermeasures.

The Way Forward

This Part identifies ways in which key US actors and other states can continue to develop the law of cyber countermeasures in a direction that is consistent with US cyber strategy. The first section discusses unilateral steps that the United States might take; the second section considers multilateral approaches.

Unilateral Steps

First, senior US officials should continue to give detailed speeches about which cyber acts constitute violations of international law and about the applicability of countermeasures in cyberspace. Doing so may increase predictability and (possibly) deterrence for adversaries while maintaining allies' confidence that the United States is committed to acting in a manner consistent with international law. In these speeches, the United States might include hypothetical examples of violations of the rules of non-intervention and due diligence, plus examples of countermeasures that the United States would and would not consider to be proportional in response to those violations.

The requirements to call on the wrongdoing state to comply with international law, to give notice ex ante, and to offer to negotiate seem particularly inappropriate in light of the cyber operations to which Defend Forward is responding. Many of these incoming acts constitute intentional, hostile operations and, in some cases, international law violations. Announcing the violation and one's willingness to negotiate may defeat the effectiveness of a countermeasure entirely by allowing the wrongdoing state to prepare for and circumvent a US response. To respect the purpose of the notice requirement without defeating the efficacy of countermeasures, the United States should consider making a general statement that it will treat specific cyber activities as international law violations to which it is entitled to respond using countermeasures. It could further indicate that the United States will provide notice to the wrongdoing state shortly after the United States has undertaken the countermeasure. Although this approach would not guarantee that a wrongdoing state could not misinterpret a US operation against it as an independent international law violation—rather than a US countermeasure—a widely publicized US announcement could minimize the chance of confusion by the wrongdoing state.

If the United States believes that collective and anticipatory cyber countermeasures are (or should be) lawful under international law, it should articulate the conditions under which states may take such countermeasures. For example, it should explain whether the victim state must request assistance before another state may intervene to impose collective countermeasures. Given the nature of cyberspace, we might expect that third states often will not know about international law violations against their allies' systems without a discussion with those allies. However, a state with advanced cyber capabilities might be in a position to witness a hostile cyber operation against a victim state of which the victim itself might be unaware. The United States should state whether it views a victim state's request as a requirement for engaging in collective cyber countermeasures. To address situations in which time is of the essence and the victim state is unaware of the internationally wrongful act against it, the United States and its allies might also consider providing one another with advance consent to undertake collective countermeasures on the others' behalf in certain well-defined circumstances.

Further, the United States should articulate whether its view about the permissibility of collective or anticipatory cyber countermeasures extends to traditional countermeasures and, if not, why cyber operations are different. Even if the United States thinks that pursuing collective or anticipatory cyber countermeasures today would push the boundaries of international law too far, the United States could assist allies in a range of ways—both generally and in the face of specific hostile operations—that would not run afoul of a rule prohibiting a state from taking a countermeasure directly on behalf of another state.[83]

This discussion assumes that US activities in cyberspace are consistent with international law. If the United States is engaged in cyber operations that clearly or arguably violate international law, there will be costs to more clearly articulating the kinds of views set out above. If other states observe the United States violating the norms it has articulated, the United States will (fairly) face charges of hypocrisy, and those violations will weaken the very norms that it has tried to establish. Further, the United States will be unable to resist claims by victim states that the victims are entitled to undertake countermeasures—possibly including anticipatory and collective countermeasures—against the United States for those violations. The United States will need to weigh the benefits and costs of seeking clearer international norms, taking into account both its defensive and offensive postures.

Multilateral Approaches

One obvious multi-lateral forum in which to advance cyber norms is the North Atlantic Treaty Organization (NATO). NATO, which established a Cyber Operations Center in 2017, was scheduled to discuss countermeasures at the 2018 NATO Summit, though it is not clear whether it did so.[84] The US State Department reportedly has been lobbying twenty-six countries (many of which are NATO states) to agree that they are willing to impose "joint costs on hostile actors in cyberspace."[85] Although news reports are not explicit about whether this means that these states have accepted the concept of collective countermeasures, the United States should continue to use this forum of like-minded states to engage in granular discussions about the acceptability and parameters of collective cyber countermeasures, as well as the other legal questions identified in Part II of this chapter.

The United States should not limit its discussions to friendly interlocutors, however. In bilateral discussions with adversaries such as Russia and China, the United States should articulate its interpretations of international law and put these states on notice—as it has already begun to do using criminal indictments—about which behaviors in cyberspace the United States will not tolerate. More specifically, the United States should specify which behaviors it considers to violate international law and underline its general policy about conducting countermeasures in response to hostile cyber operations. These efforts will mitigate the chance of misunderstandings when these states are on the receiving end of US operations.

Conclusion

Various aspects of Defend Forward are clearly consistent with international law and require no special legal justification. Other aspects of the strategy may be more contested under international law. As this chapter has shown, this does not necessarily mean that they are unlawful. If these US acts are in fact proportional responses to international law violations by other states and are intended to prompt the wrongdoing states to cease their wrongful behavior, the United States may frame its acts as countermeasures. The United States and a range of other states have made clear their views that cyber countermeasures are permissible, even as they begin to craft a *lex specialis* of cyber countermeasures that is responsive to the unique features of cyber operations. Only time will tell, though, whether cyber countermeasures are an effective way to de-escalate cyber hostilities among states.

Notes

* The author wrote this chapter while serving as a professor at the University of Virginia Law School, but edited it while on leave to work in the US government. Nothing herein should be construed to reflect the position or views of the US government.
1. *See, e.g.*, Paul M. Nakasone, *A Cyber Force for Persistent Operations*, 92 JOINT FORCE Q. 10, 11 (2019).

2. US Dep't of Defense, Summary: Department of Defense Cyber Strategy 2018, at 1 (2018).

3. See, e.g., Hon. Paul C. Ney Jr., General Counsel, Department of Defense, DoD General Counsel Remarks at the US Cyber Command Legal Conference, March 2, 2020.

4. Certain US allies (such as Australia) have articulated a strategy that involves offensive cyber operations. See Mike Burgess, Director-General, Australian Signals Directorate, Speech to the Lowy Institute (March 27, 2010).

5. Int'l Law Comm'n, Rep. of the Int'l Law Comm'n on the Work of Its Fifty-Third Session, Draft Articles on Responsibility of States for Internationally Wrongful Acts, with Commentaries, art. 22, UN Doc. A/56/10, at 75 (2001) [hereinafter DARS].

6. Id. art. 50(1)(a), 51, 49(2).

7. Id. art. 52(3)(a).

8. Id. art. 49(1).

9. Id. art. 53. If a state has ceased its wrongful act but still owes reparations, the injured state need not terminate its countermeasures until reparations are made. Also, if a wrongful act is part of a pattern or series of similar acts from the same state, the injured state may impose countermeasures that extend beyond the cessation of a single act to induce a state to cease its pattern of conduct. See Michael N. Schmitt, "Below the Threshold" Cyber Operations: The Countermeasures Response Option and International Law, 54 VA. J. OF INT'L L. 697, 697–715 (2014).

10. See Case Concerning the Air Service Agreement of 27 Mar. 1946 (US v. Fr.), 18 R.I.A.A. 417, 445–46 (Perm. Ct. Arb. 1978).

11. DARS, supra note 5, Chapter II, cmt. 5.

12. Julian Simcock, Deputy Legal Advisor, US Mission to the UN, Remarks at a UN General Assembly Meeting of the Sixth Committee on Agenda Item 75: Responsibility of States for Internationally Wrongful Acts (October 14, 2019).

13. See Noble Ventures, Inc. v. Romania, ICSID Case No. ARB/01/11, Award, ¶ 69 (Oct. 12, 2005).

14. Sean D. Murphy, Contemporary Practice of the United States Relating to International Law: US Comments on ILC Draft Articles on State Responsibility, 95 AM. J. OF INT'L L. 626, 627 (2001).

15. Simcock, supra note 12.

16. Daniel Bodansky, John R. Crook, and David J. Bederman, Counterintuiting Countermeasures, 96 AM. J. OF INT'L L. 817, 818 (2002).

17. DARS, supra note 5, art. 49, cmt. 3.

18. Id. art. 50(1).

19. Id. art. 50(2).

20. Id. art. 52(1).

21. Id. art. 52(2).

22. Id. art. 52, cmt. 6.

23. Id. art. 51, cmt. 4.

24. See, e.g., Gabčíkovo-Nagymaros Project (Hung. v. Slovk.), Judgment, 1997 I.C.J. Rep. 7, ¶¶ 71, 85 (Sept. 25). Scholars have criticized the ICJ for failing to conduct an in-depth proportionality analysis and missing an opportunity to develop its proportionality

jurisprudence. *See* Eliza Fitzgerald, *Helping States Help Themselves: Rethinking the Doctrine of Countermeasures*, 16 MACQUARIE L. J. 67, 75 (2016); Thomas M. Franck, *On Proportionality of Countermeasures*, 102 AM. J. OF INT'L L. 715, 739 (2008).

25. *See* Case Concerning the Air Service Agreement of 27 Mar. 1946 (US v. Fr.), 18 R.I.A.A. 417, 443 (Perm. Ct. Arb. 1978); Murphy, *supra* note 14, at 628.

26. DARS, *supra* note 5, art. 49(3).

27. Gabčíkovo-Nagymaros Project, 1997 I.C.J. Rep. 7, at ¶ 87. Although the Court did not decide whether Slovakia's act satisfied the reversibility requirement, it emphasized the "often irreversible character of damage to the environment and of the limitations inherent in the very mechanism of reparation of this type of damage." *Id.* at ¶ 140.

28. DARS, *supra* note 5, art. 49, cmt. 9.

29. *Id.* art. 49(1).

30. The Cysne Case (Port. v. Ger.), 2 R.I.A.A. 1035, 1052 (Perm. Ct. Arb. 1930).

31. DARS, *supra* note 5, art. 54, cmt. 1.

32. *See id.* art. 18.

33. *See* Gary Corn and Eric Jensen, *The Use of Force and Cyber Countermeasures*, 32 TEMPLE INT'L & COMP. L. J. 127, 129 (2018); Rebecca Crootof, *International Cybertorts: Expanding State Accountability in Cyberspace*, 103 CORNELL L. REV. 565, 585–86 (2018).

34. *See, e.g.*, Group of Governmental Experts on Developments in the Field of Information and Telecommunications in the Context of International Security, ¶ 24, UN Doc. A/70/174 (July 22, 2015); Group of Governmental Experts on Developments in the Field of Information and Telecommunications in the Context of International Security, ¶ 19, UN Doc. A/68/98 (June 24, 2013). Despite the failure to reach consensus in the GGE for its 2017 report, competing groups nevertheless agreed on a baseline understanding that international law applies to the cyber domain in general. See UN General Assembly, 73rd Sess., First Committee, Developments in the Field of Information and Telecommunications in the Context of International Security, Revised Draft Resolution, UN Doc. A/C.1/73/L.27/Rev.1 (Oct. 29, 2018); UN General Assembly, 73rd Sess., First Committee, Advancing Responsible State Behaviour in Cyberspace in the Context of International Security, Draft Resolution, UN Doc. A/C.1/73/L.37 (Oct. 18, 2018).

35. *Cf.* Dan Efrony and Yuval Shany, *A Rule Book on the Shelf? Tallinn Manual 2.0 on Cyberoperations and Subsequent State Practice*, 112 AM. J. OF INT'L L. 583 (2018).

36. For Australia's perspective, see generally Dep't of Foreign Affairs and Trade, AUSTRALIA'S INTERNATIONAL CYBER ENGAGEMENT STRATEGY, 2019 Progress Report, Annex A: 2019 International Law Supplement (2019) (Austl.) [hereinafter DFAT CYBER STRATEGY]. For Israel's perspective, *see* Roy Schondorf, Israeli Deputy Attorney General (International Law), Keynote Address at the US Naval War College Conference on Disruptive Technologies and International Law: Israel's Perspective on Key Legal and Practical Issues Concerning the Applications of International Law to Cyber Operations (Dec. 9, 2020).

37. Brian J. Egan, *International Law and Stability in Cyberspace*, BERKELEY J. OF INT'L L. 169, 178 (2017); see also DFAT CYBER STRATEGY, *supra* note 36, at 91.

38. TALLINN MANUAL 2.0 ON THE INTERNATIONAL LAW APPLICABLE TO CYBER OPERATIONS 122–23 (Rule 22) (Michael N. Schmitt ed., 2nd ed. 2017) [hereinafter TALLINN MANUAL 2.0].

39. Egan, *supra* note 37, at 178.

40. Jeremy Wright, Attorney General of the United Kingdom, Speech: Cyber and International Law in the 21st Century (May 23, 2018).

41. Ministry of the Armies, INTERNATIONAL LAW APPLICABLE TO OPERATIONS IN CYBERSPACE 8 (2019) (Fr.) [hereinafter FRENCH MINISTRY OF THE ARMIES]; DFAT CYBER STRATEGY, *supra* note 36.

42. TALLINN MANUAL 2.0, *supra* note 38, at 111 (Rule 20).

43. *Id.* at 129 (Rule 23) cmt. 7.

44. *See* Kristen E. Eichensehr, *The Law & Politics of Cyberattack Attribution*, 67 UCLA L. REV. 520, 524 (2020).

45. Ney, *supra* note 3.

46. Wright, *supra* note 40; FRENCH MINISTRY OF THE ARMIES, *supra* note 41, at 10; TALLINN MANUAL 2.0, *supra* note 38, at 83 cmt. 13.

47. JAPAN, CYBERSECURITY STRATEGY § 4.3.2(2)(i) (July 27, 2018) (provisional English translation); Kersti Kaljulaid, President, Republic of Estonia, Speech at the Opening of the International Conference on Cyber Conflict (CyCon) 2019 (May 29, 2019); DFAT CYBER STRATEGY, *supra* note 36, at 91; Egan, *supra* note 37, at 178; Wright, *supra* note 40.

48. TALLINN MANUAL 2.0, *supra* note 38, at 128 (Rule 23) cmt. 6.

49. *Id.* at 119 (Rule 21) cmt. 9.

50. *Id.*

51. Some scholars additionally have suggested that states should be allowed to take countermeasures against non-state actors that violate international law in cyberspace. However, because Defend Forward is largely directed at state actors, this chapter does not consider the interplay between countermeasures and non-state actors.

52. DARS, *supra* note 5, art. 52(1).

53. Egan, *supra* note 37, at 178.

54. Ney, *supra* note 3.

55. *See* Robert M. Chesney, *The Pentagon's General Counsel on the Law of Military Operations in Cyberspace*, LAWFARE (Mar. 9, 2020).

56. Wright, *supra* note 40.

57. FRENCH MINISTRY OF THE ARMIES, *supra* note 41, at 8.

58. Letter from the Minister of Foreign Affairs to the President of the House of Representatives, Letter to the Parliament on the International Legal Order in Cyberspace, Appendix at 7 (July 5, 2019) (Neth.).

59. *See* Schondorf, *supra* note 36.

60. TALLINN MANUAL 2.0, *supra* note 38, at 120 (Rule 21) cmt. 10.

61. *Id.* at cmts. 11, 12.

62. A minority of Tallinn Manual 2.0 experts disagreed and believed that customary international law requires the injured state to seek negotiations before taking countermeasures in all circumstances. *Id.* at 120–21 (Rule 21) cmt. 13.

63. DARS, *supra* note 5, at Ch. II cmt. 8.

64. *See* Otto Spijkers, *Bystander Obligations at the Domestic and International Level Compared*, 6 GOETTINGEN J. OF INT'L L. 47, 75–76 (2014)(internal citations omitted).

65. DARS Article 48 anticipates that states other than injured states may invoke the responsibility of the wrongdoing state where the obligation breached "is owed to the international community as a whole." *See* DARS, *supra* note 5, art. 48(1)(b).

66. Kaljulaid, *supra* note 47.

67. Shannon Vavra, *Pentagon's Next Cyber Policy Guru Predicts More Collective Responses in Cyberspace*, CYBERSCOOP (Nov. 21, 2019).

68. OFFICE OF THE PRESIDENT, NATIONAL CYBER STRATEGY OF THE UNITED STATES OF AMERICA 21 (2018).

69. *See, e.g.*, Samuli Haataja, *Cyber Operations and Collective Countermeasures Under International Law*, 25 J. OF CONFLICT AND SECURITY L. 33, 48–49 (2020); Jeff Kosseff, *Collective Countermeasures in Cyberspace*, 10 NOTRE DAME J. OF INT'L & COMP. L. 18 (2020); Corn and Jensen, *supra* note 33, at 130.

70. FRENCH MINISTRY OF THE ARMIES, *supra* note 41, at 7.

71. TALLINN MANUAL 2.0, *supra* note 38, at 132 (Rule 24) cmt. 7.

72. Ann Väljataga, NATO COOPERATIVE CYBER DEFENCE CENTRE OF EXCELLENCE, TRACING OPINIO JURIS IN NATIONAL CYBER SECURITY STRATEGY DOCUMENTS 15 (2018).

73. TALLINN MANUAL 2.0, *supra* note 38, at 118 (Rule 21) cmt. 5.

74. *See* Corn and Jensen, *supra* note 33, at 130–31. In certain circumstances, a state alternatively might invoke the principle of necessity as a justification for violating an international law obligation to another state. It could do so, however, only when the violation was the only way for the state to safeguard an essential interest against a grave and imminent peril. *See* DARS, *supra* note 5, at art. 25. The application of countermeasures faces a lower bar.

75. *See, e.g.*, Jay P. Kesan and Carol M. Hayes, *Mitigative Counterstriking: Self-Defense and Deterrence in Cyberspace*, 25 HARVARD J. OF L. & TECH. 429, 528–29 (2012); Michael N. Schmitt, *Peacetime Cyber Responses and Wartime Cyber Operations Under International Law: An Analytical* Vade Mecum, 8 HARVARD NAT'L SECURITY J. 239, 246–47 (2017); David E. Sanger, *Pentagon Announces New Strategy for Cyberwarfare*, N.Y. TIMES (Apr. 23, 2015).

76. Philip Kunig, "Prohibition of Intervention," in *Max Planck Encyclopedia of Public International Law* ¶ 3 (2008).

77. Gary P. Corn, *Cyber National Security*, in COMPLEX BATTLESPACES: THE LAW OF ARMED CONFLICT AND THE DYNAMICS OF MODERN WARFARE 411, ed. Winston S. Williams and Christopher M. Ford (Oxford: Oxford University Press, 2019) (emphasis removed).

78. Egan, *supra* note 37, at 175.

79. Wright, *supra* note 40. *See also* Nicholas Tsagourias, *Electoral Cyber Interference, Self-Determination and the Principle of Non-Intervention in Cyberspace*, EJIL:TALK! (Aug. 26, 2019); Jens David Ohlin, *Did Russian Cyber Interference in the 2016 Election Violate International Law?*, 95 TEX. L. REV. 1579, 1594 (2017).

80. These facts are largely drawn from actual incidents during the 2016 election. See Kim Zetter, *How Close Did Russia Really Come to Hacking the 2016 Election?*, POLITICO (Dec. 26, 2019).

81. This is hypothetical; there is no indication that this actually occurred in the 2016 US election.

82. The United States recently sent personnel to Montenegro in order to observe and better prepare for Russian cyber operations in the lead-up to the 2020 election. Shannon Vavra, *Pentagon Again Deploying Cyber Personnel Abroad to Gather Intel for 2020 Elections*, CYBERSCOOP (Nov. 1, 2019).

83. *See* Kosseff, *supra* note 69, at 33; *see also* TALLINN MANUAL 2.0, *supra* note 38, at 132 (Rule 24) cmt. 8 (noting that one group of experts thought that it would be lawful to provide assistance to a victim state that is engaged in countermeasures, which it distinguished as different from taking countermeasures on behalf of another state).

84. Martina Calleri and Samuele Dominioni, *NATO's Stance on Cyber Defense ahead of the Brussels Summit*, ISPI (Jul. 10, 2018).

85. Vavra, *supra* note 67.

9

Covert Deception, Strategic Fraud, and the Rule of Prohibited Intervention

Gary P. Corn[*]

All warfare is based on deception.[1]

It clearly follows from the liberty and independence of Nations that each has the right to govern itself as it thinks proper, and that no one of them has the least right to interfere in the government of another.[2]

If information is power, then the corruption of information is the erosion, if not the outright usurpation, of power. This is especially true in the information age, where developments in the technological structure and global interconnectedness of information and telecommunications infrastructure have enabled states to engage in malicious influence campaigns at an unprecedented scope, scale, depth, and speed. The Digital Revolution and the attendant evolution of the global information environment have intensified, if not generated, what one expert describes as "one of the greatest vulnerabilities we as individuals and as a society must learn to deal with."[3] The relative explosion of digital information and telecommunications technology (ICT) and the modern information environment it has enabled "have resulted in a qualitatively new landscape of influence operations, persuasion, and, more generally, mass manipulation."[4]

As evidenced by Russia's continual efforts at election interference in the United States and Europe, the role of information conflict in global strategic competition has evolved and taken on new weight.[5] A number of revisionist states, Russia and China chief among them, have fully embraced the new reality of the modern information environment, deftly adapting their capabilities and strategies to exploit the societal vulnerabilities it exposes. They have incorporated sustained, hostile influence campaigns as a central part of their destabilizing strategies to cause or exacerbate societal divisions, disrupt political processes, weaken democratic institutions, and fracture alliances, all with a broader aim of undermining the rules-based international order and gaining competitive advantage.

The anchor for these campaigns is the extensive and deep use of ICTs to conduct covert deception and disinformation operations at an extraordinary scale. Deployed at a strategic level, malign influence and disinformation operations have the very real potential to undermine and disrupt a targeted state's independent exercise of core governance prerogatives. Along with the advent of hostile cyber operations, these ICT-enhanced deception campaigns have raised challenging questions about whether and how international law applies to these novel state interactions. This chapter focuses on the customary international law prohibition against intervening in the internal and external affairs of another state—a rule intended to protect the cardinal right of states to conduct their affairs without outside interference. It considers the rule's applicability to the murky and evolving landscape of information conflict. Drawing on general principles of law, it argues for an interpretation of the non-intervention rule better suited to the realities of the information age, where undermining the exercise of sovereign free will is the specific aim of strategic covert deception and disinformation campaigns.

The non-intervention rule is important because US adversaries see the information environment as fertile ground for subverting the United States and the rules-based international order. Among the reasons for this perspective is the tremendous ambiguity surrounding the international legal framework applicable to states' use of ICTs, especially in the gray zone below traditionally recognized use-of-force thresholds and outside of armed conflict. To date, efforts to achieve greater clarity regarding international law's applicability to states' use of ICTs, whether led by states or otherwise, have focused almost exclusively on the problem of harmful cyber effects operations—the use of cyber capabilities to disrupt, deny, degrade, destroy, or manipulate computers or information systems or the data resident thereon. With the exception of some limited scholarship and commentary on the international law implications of Russia's 2016 election interference, little work has been done to analyze the use of ICTs as a platform for covert deception.

The primary conflict-regulation mechanism in international law is the UN Charter prohibition on states using force against the political independence or territorial integrity of other states. While a small number of states have recently signaled a willingness to consider some cyber operations involving serious financial or economic harm as amounting to uses of force, they have thus far not indicated the same openness with regard to influence operations. For good reason, they are unlikely to do so. Overly expansive invocation of the use-of-force prohibition has obvious escalatory implications. In contrast, the non-intervention rule, which governs both forcible and non-forcible measures, is far more suited to regulating the sub-use-of-force threats posed by the nuanced sphere of information conflict and covert deception.

With respect to cyber effects operations, there is little if any dissent from the view that the rule of prohibited intervention applies to states' use of ICTs.[6] Consensus quickly breaks down, however, over the rule's content. The rule is generally described as prohibiting coercive measures against a limited but important zone of sovereign interests falling within what is commonly referred to as a state's *domaine réservé*. Unfortunately, substantial definitional and conceptual uncertainty clouds understandings of the "elements" of this rule and how they apply in practice, especially in the context of cyber and information conflict. The International Court of Justice (ICJ) has described the element of coercion as "defin[ing], and indeed form[ing] the very essence of, prohibited intervention."[7] Many commentators have treated this statement as canonical and have applied it dogmatically, notwithstanding the court's failure to offer a definition of the term. Both the ICJ's statement and the undue weight many afford it misapprehend the true objective of the rule—to prevent states from employing measures aimed at depriving a targeted state of the free exercise of its will over protected sovereign matters. They also fail to capture significant modes of state action, strategic covert deception in particular, that should be considered internationally wrongful.

As the attorney general of the United Kingdom has noted, achieving greater clarity as to the non-intervention rule's force and effect is of "particular importance in modern times when technology has an increasing role to play in every facet of our lives, including political campaigns and the conduct of elections."[8] Adapting the concept of coercion to account for the realities of modern information conflict is a necessary step toward achieving the clarity he seeks. Deception is frequently regulated in domestic legal regimes, either directly in the form of criminal fraud provisions, or indirectly through the recognition that deception can substitute constructively for the actual force and coercion elements of other crimes. In both cases, it is the subversion of free will that is considered the cognizable harm. States should draw on these general principles of law to inform the concept of coercion in international law and thereby better define the non-intervention rule's applicability to information conflict.

This chapter's efforts to reinforce the existing international legal architecture are not offered as a panacea to the ill of foreign influence campaigns. International law has its limits, and countering hostile foreign influence will require a far more holistic and concerted approach than simply evolving or achieving greater clarity as to the scope of applicability of any particular rule of international law. But as one important study notes, the United States "needs an updated framework for organizing its thinking about the manipulation of infospheres by foreign powers determined to gain competitive advantage."[9] The US Department of Defense's implementation of a new cyber strategy in 2018 with its operational concept of Defend Forward is a step in the right direction, as evidenced by the success of US Cyber Command's reported operations to counter Russian election interference in 2018 and 2020. Accurately characterizing covert influence campaigns as a matter of international law would add additional tools to the defend-forward toolbox, and doing so should figure prominently in a broader effort to develop a coherent strategy and framework to counter foreign influence efforts while reinforcing the rules-based international order.

The Problem—Covert Deception and Disinformation Operations at Scale

Information conflict is not new. Propaganda is a truly ancient human endeavor, and states have leveraged information—truthful, manipulated, and fabricated—for influence purposes since the inception of the Westphalian order. Hostile influence campaigns have historically assumed many monikers and taken many forms but generally share the common characteristic of disseminating overt and covert propaganda (including facts, opinions, rumors, half-truths, and lies) in pursuit of a competitive advantage over an opponent. Suasion, including the use of propaganda, is a staple of statecraft and has long been viewed as falling outside of international law's reach.

The Cold War provides a relatively recent example. Political warfare was the defining characteristic of the conflict, and a primary weapon in the Soviet Union's arsenal was its use of "active measures"—subversive practices including political influence efforts, the surreptitious use of Soviet front groups and foreign communist parties, and the core element of *dezinformatsiya* (disinformation).[10] One former KGB general described the use of active measures as "the heart and soul of the Soviet intelligence" apparatus, specifically designed to subvert the United States and "drive wedges" in the West's alliances.[11] To be sure, the United States also employed deception during the Cold War. But Russia has reinvigorated such efforts in the post–Cold War era; according to recent US intelligence assessments, Russia's campaign to interfere in the 2016 presidential elections "demonstrated a significant escalation in directness, level of activity, and scope of effort" to undermine "the US-led democratic order."[12]

Russia's efforts in 2016 were aimed directly at the US presidential election. The objective was to undermine public faith in the democratic process and to denigrate and harm the electability of one candidate and boost the candidacy of another. Although unprecedented in scope and scale, Russia's campaign "followed a longstanding . . . messaging strategy that blends covert intelligence operations—such as cyber activity—with overt efforts by Russian Government agencies, state-funded media, third-party intermediaries, and paid social media users or 'trolls.'"[13] Russia employed a multi-faceted approach to its interference campaign that involved cyber espionage against both political parties; the weaponization of sensitive information collected through those operations—specifically the timed release through intermediaries of personal emails and other damaging information belonging to Democratic Party officials and political figures; hacking into state and local electoral boards and voting systems; and a deep and extensive propaganda effort, both overt and covert.[14]

Russia's use of "quasi-government trolls" to covertly propagandize and spread mis- and disinformation played a central role in its election interference efforts and demonstrated Russia's broader goals of undermining public faith in the democratic process and institutions and generally seeding and cultivating political discord. The Internet Research Agency (IRA), an entity in St. Petersburg, Russia, financed by a Russian oligarch and close Putin ally with ties to Russian intelligence, ran an extensive and well-organized social-media *dezinformatsiya* campaign.[15] Among other tactics, the IRA used false personas and the stolen identities of real Americans to purchase millions of dollars of advertising on social media platforms such as Facebook, Twitter, and Instagram to plant propaganda, and used false accounts and bots to amplify its messaging. The IRA also used these false social media accounts to stage political rallies in the United States and to solicit and pay unwitting US persons to promote or disparage candidates.

Based on these well-documented interference efforts, in 2018 the grand jury in Special Counsel Robert Mueller's investigation returned an indictment of thirteen Russian individuals and three companies associated with the covert deception campaign.[16] Each was accused, *inter alia*, of conspiring "to defraud the United States by impairing, obstructing, and defeating the lawful functions of the government through fraud and deceit for the purposes of interfering with the U.S. political and electoral process, including the presidential election of 2016."[17] The indictment lays out in detail the IRA's, and by extension Russia's, extensive covert influence activities aimed at swaying the 2016 election and "sow[ing] discord in the U.S. political system."[18] In 2020, the Senate Select Committee on Intelligence released an extensive three-volume report on *Russian Active Measures Campaigns and Interference in the 2016 U.S. Election*, confirming the Intelligence Community's assessment.[19]

Russia's interference and covert influence campaigns are not limited to targeting the United States. Europe has been on the receiving end of Russia's disruptive efforts perhaps longer than has the United States.[20] In addition to targeting an array of European states with destabilizing disinformation campaigns generally, Russia has targeted elections in Ukraine, France, Germany, and the United Kingdom, to name a few, as well as the European Parliament election in 2019.

Russia's interference in the 2016 presidential election served as a wake-up call. In response, the United States mounted a concerted, government-wide effort to protect the 2018 midterm elections against Russian interference operations, taking measures that reportedly included Department of Defense cyber operations. But Russia's covert influence operations have not abated. Russian covert deception operations were again at play in 2020 seeking to "denigrat[e] President Biden's candidacy and the Democratic Party, support[] former President Trump, undermin[e] public confidence in the electoral process, and exacerbate[] sociopolitical divisions in the US."[21] Evidence is also mounting that Russia has been disseminating disinformation regarding the COVID-19 pandemic in order "to aggravate the public health crisis in Western countries, specifically by undermining public trust in national healthcare systems—thus preventing an effective response to the outbreak."[22]

Russia is not alone in this regard. Although arguably several steps behind, China has also moved aggressively into the information conflict arena. The Chinese Communist Party "has used ideology and propaganda as governing tools 'since the People's Republic was established in 1949,' and this can even be dated to the Party's founding in 1921."[23] While traditionally these efforts were more internally focused, China now views influence and information operations as a "magic weapon" for achieving its foreign policy goals.[24] Indications are that it has learned from Russia's disinformation campaigns. China is testing those lessons and refining its influence capabilities in Taiwan and Southeast Asia and has moved beyond spreading, for example, COVID-19-related disinformation.[25]

Russia and China present the most advanced information-conflict threats, but they are not the only threats. Iran and other US adversaries are studying, emulating, and adapting the Russian and Chinese models to advance their own disruptive goals. According to the 2020 Worldwide Threat Assessment, "US adversaries and strategic competitors almost certainly will use online influence operations to try to weaken democratic institutions, undermine US alliances and partnerships, and shape policy outcomes in the United States and elsewhere."[26] In each case, these campaigns extend beyond open influence activities, employing sophisticated deception operations to achieve strategic aims. Countering these efforts is and should be a stated US policy goal, along with strengthening the international rules-based order and the applicability of international law to states' use of ICTs, other emerging technologies, and state interactions in the information environment.[27] The rule of prohibited intervention is the most pertinent rule of international law available to confront the harm of election interference and covert deception campaigns.

International Law and the Principle of Non-Intervention

State sovereignty and the principle of sovereign equality form the foundation upon which the rules-based international order rests.[28] At its core, sovereignty signifies independence in relations between states, with independence being the right to exercise the functions of a state within a defined portion of the globe—the territory under the state's lawful jurisdiction—to the exclusion of any other state.[29] These organizing principles underlie the most important rules of international law governing interstate relations, such as the *jus ad bellum* prohibition on states using force against the territorial integrity or political independence of other states.[30]

States have also developed the customary international law principle of non-intervention as a safeguard against impairments of their sovereignty.

The principle is considered a "corollary of every state's right to sovereignty, territorial integrity and political independence."[31] It protects the "right of every sovereign State to conduct its [internal and external] affairs without outside interference."[32] The non-intervention principle is written into numerous international instruments, and states frequently invoke it, albeit with imprecision and under disparate circumstances.

The customary status of the non-intervention rule is not controversial, and the proposition that it applies to states' use of ICTs, at least in the context of cyber operations, is gaining increased acceptance among states.[33] Further, it is widely recognized that the rule can be violated by both forcible and non-forcible means.[34] Unfortunately, outside of relatively clear examples of forcible interventions—which concurrently violate the prohibition on the use of force—the rule's content is commonly recognized as ill-defined.[35] This makes it difficult to discern the line between non-forcible but unlawful interventions on the one hand, and lawful influence activities on the other.

States routinely employ various means of statecraft with the intent of shaping other states' policy decisions or actions, and there is no general prohibition in international law against states engaging in suasion. And although states frequently invoke the terms intervention and interference to complain about such activities, they are not the same normatively. International law proscribes only the former as wrongful; "[i]nterference pure and simple is not intervention."[36] It is an important distinction, setting apart what states view as legitimate from illegitimate forms of statecraft, itself an expression of sovereign will. Unfortunately, the indeterminate line between mere interference and prohibited intervention weakens the non-intervention rule's value as a guard against impairments of sovereign rights and "risks permitting coercive policies that undermine the political independence of states or impair the right to self-determination," especially in the context of information conflict.[37]

Although the precise content and scope of the non-intervention principle are unclear, certain core aspects of the rule are evident. The general contours can be gleaned from the ICJ's description of the principle in its *Nicaragua* judgment:

> [T]he principle [of non-intervention] forbids all States or groups of States to intervene directly or indirectly in internal or external affairs of other States. A prohibited intervention must accordingly be one bearing on matters in which each State is permitted, by the principle of State sovereignty, to

decide freely. One of these is the choice of a political, economic, social and cultural system, and the formulation of foreign policy. Intervention is wrongful when it uses methods of coercion in regard to such choices, which must remain free ones. The element of coercion, which defines, and indeed forms the very essence of, prohibited intervention, is particularly obvious in the case of an intervention which uses force, either in the direct form of military action, or in the indirect form of support for subversive or terrorist armed activities within another State.[38]

This passage is often cited for the proposition that interference is internationally wrongful only when two constituent elements are present. First, the measures employed must be directed against the *domaine réservé* of the targeted State. Second, such measures must be coercive.[39]

The ambiguity that plagues the non-intervention rule generally also infects these two elements. Unfortunately, the ICJ has offered little by way of additional explanation. This should not be surprising. The court's discussion of non-intervention in the *Nicaragua* judgment was narrowly confined to the specific facts of the case, which primarily concerned forcible measures.[40] Further, the court's entire *sua sponte* discussion of the non-intervention principle was only for the purpose of ruling out whether the forcible measures attributed to the United States were justified as countermeasures.[41] As such, its broader pronouncements on the elements of the rule—or lack thereof—were unnecessary and should be considered with circumspection.[42] Still, convention holds that the concept of coercion demarcates the line between mere interference and wrongful intervention.[43]

The ICJ's focus on coercion as the touchstone of prohibited intervention likely reflects the evolution of the rule over time from one that traditionally served to protect only the territorial integrity of states against military force, to one aimed at also shielding political independence against non-forcible infringements.[44] In this regard, the term is perhaps equally inapt and unhelpful since in common parlance the concept of coercion is generally considered to involve force or the threat of force to impose one's will on another.[45] As set out below, overreliance on coercion as a defining element of intervention distorts the focus of the rule and risks excluding from its scope non-forcible means of subverting protected sovereign interests. Before turning to the element of coercion, however, a brief discussion of the concept of *domaine réservé* is useful.

The Concept of *Domaine Réservé*

As noted, the non-intervention rule does not reach all forms of state interference in the internal affairs of other states. It is a rule of finite scope as to both the object and means of outside state action. And states have generally rejected proposals to prohibit their use of propaganda to influence other states. With respect to the object of prohibited intervention, the zone of sovereign interests or state functions protected by the rule has never been well understood or defined.

Oppenheim describes intervention generally as "a form of interference by one state in the affairs, internal or external, of another" by either direct or indirect means.[46] By "affairs," Oppenheim is referring loosely to the prohibited object of intervention—matters which, as a function of sovereignty, are reserved in international law to the sole prerogative of states. This zone of protected interests is often referred to, imprecisely, as the state's *domaine réservé*. As Jens Ohlin has noted, "despite the patina of precision in its French rendering, the concept has little internally generated content" as a concept.[47]

Strictly speaking, *domaine réservé* refers only to matters within a state's internal jurisdiction and therefore does not speak to the full range of protected sovereign functions that also include a state's external affairs.[48] According to the ICJ, these matters include, but are not limited to, the right to choose a political, economic, social, and cultural system, and to formulate and execute foreign policy.[49] The right of states to independence over these matters is not conferred by international law but rather is inherent in the concepts of statehood and sovereignty. Therefore, the rule's protection is better understood as extending to those matters in which each state has the right, "by the principle of State sovereignty, to decide freely."[50] Restrictions on states' independence over these sovereign matters cannot be presumed.[51]

Perhaps the most frequently cited example of a matter falling within the scope of the *domaine réservé*, and thus within the non-intervention rule's protection, is a state's choice of both its political system and organization.[52] In contrast, purely commercial government activities are generally considered to fall outside of the *domaine réservé*.[53] Between these extremes, uncertainty lingers, and the rule's scope depends on a number of variables, including, perhaps most importantly, the degree to which a particular state's discretion over a matter is subject to its specific international obligations. To the extent that a state's policy choices are governed by international law, the state is considered to have surrendered its discretion over the matter. That is, the concept of sovereign prerogative is not without limits, and those "domains or activities" not strictly reserved to the state are said to be potentially subject to foreign action.[54] Accordingly, in light of the ever-expanding subjects of international regulation, some commentators argue that the concept of *domaine réservé* is diminishing, and therefore so too is the utility of the non-intervention rule.

These are exaggerated claims. First, since international legal obligations vary from state to state, the "margin of liberty" each exercises will differ accordingly.[55] International legal obligations differ widely as to content and may apply differently depending on the state involved and the given circumstances. Further, states often retain significant independent authority even with respect to matters committed to international law.[56] The scope of another state's authority to intervene in a matter regulated by international law will generally be defined by the source of the obligation at issue. Most often, available remedies are narrow and specifically defined in applicable treaties. Outside of such treaty-based measures, the customary law of state responsibility sets a high bar for an intervening state to claim that the wrongfulness of its employment of coercion against a targeted state should be excused or precluded as a legitimate countermeasure.[57] Therefore, the fact that a matter is in some way the subject of international regulation does not equate to a license for other states to coerce decisions or conduct with respect thereto.

Ultimately, like many aspects of international law, whether a matter falls within the protective ambit of the non-intervention rule involves a fact-specific inquiry, considering state practice and *opinio juris* prevalent at the time.[58] Suffice to say that, notwithstanding the increasing degree to which states surrender some degree of sovereignty to international regulation, there exists a strong presumption that matters of state governance fall to the sole prerogative of states and are protected from external intervention. That is, "it is in the expression of [the] idea" that sovereignty equates to "the exclusion of the authority of other states, but not international law," that "the principle of nonintervention has its primary function."[59] Holding elections and implementing public health measures, two areas that Russia has specifically targeted in the last several years, certainly fall within this protective umbrella. Elections are frequently cited as a quintessential matter falling within a state's *domaine réservé*.[60] Similarly, the adoption and implementation of public health policies and measures, especially in the face of a global pandemic, are widely recognized as legitimate matters of governance within a state's internal sovereign jurisdiction.[61]

The Elusive Element of Coercion

As with the concept of *domaine réservé*, little interpretive guidance exists in international law regarding the element of coercion. In *Nicaragua*, the ICJ described as a particularly obvious case "an intervention which uses force, either in the direct form of military action, or in the indirect form of support for subversive or terrorist armed activities within another State."[62] Equally obvious is that neither propaganda nor aggressive diplomacy qualify as prohibited interventions, at least not per se.[63] Between these extremes, the standard lacks clarity, making it difficult to map to the realm of information conflict.

The principle of non-intervention has been described as a "doctrinal mechanism to express the outer limits of permissible influence that one state may properly exert upon another."[64] Since the principle's inception, locating the demarcation between permissible and impermissible influence has proved exceedingly difficult. The vagueness in the rule's scope and meaning traces back to the principle's conceptual roots and the differences in the early naturalist and positivist approaches to international law generally, and to the principle's definition and evolution specifically—differences beyond the scope of this chapter.[65] It is enough to note that a significant aspect of these early debates centered on whether the principle was absolute or was subject to exception, for example, as a matter of self-preservation.[66] The latter view ultimately held sway, shifting the focus of the debate to the issue of when interventions might be justified, and, more important to the present discussion, how to define the "outer limits" of permissible influence.

Historically, armed force, described as "dictatorial interference," was considered the dividing line between permissible and impermissible influence.[67] In fact, well into the twentieth century, many states and commentators, including the United States, held the view that prohibited intervention and the prohibition on the threat or use of force were equivalent.[68]

Over time, however, the concept of intervention expanded, and coercion evolved as a broader but inapt benchmark for denominating the boundary between lawful influence and prohibited intervention.

Thus, according to Oppenheim "to constitute intervention [an] interference must be forcible or dictatorial, *or otherwise coercive*," and can take the form of direct or indirect military action, as well as non-military actions such as economic or political measures "where they have the necessary coercive effect."[69] This expanded concept of intervention also finds expression in a number of treaties, declarations, and General Assembly resolutions concluded in the latter half of the twentieth century—instruments that the ICJ has cited as reflective of customary international law.[70] For example, the Friendly Relations Declaration recalls "the duty of States to refrain in their international relations from military, political, economic or any other form of coercion aimed against the political independence or territorial integrity of any State."[71] However, beyond reinforcing the notion that prohibited interventions can be effected by non-forcible means, these sources offer little guidance on the meaning of coercion as the term is used in the specific context of intervention, and in certain respects are at odds with state practice. States routinely use sanctions and other economic means to pressure or compel other states and have frequently rejected proposals that would deem the use of economic pressure as internationally wrongful.

The ICJ's rendering of the non-intervention principle in its *Nicaragua* judgment is often cited as offering a definitive description of the rule's content. According to the court:

> Intervention is wrongful when it uses methods of coercion in regard to such choices, which must remain free ones. The element of coercion, which defines, and indeed forms the very essence of, prohibited intervention, is particularly obvious in the case of an intervention which uses force, either in the direct form of military action, or in the indirect form of support for subversive or terrorist armed activities within another State.[72]

However, as noted above, the court specifically limited the scope of its review, confining its description to "only those aspects of the principle which appear to be relevant to the resolution of the dispute."[73] By and large, the dispute was over measures the court separately determined to constitute direct and indirect uses of force that it deemed "particularly obvious" examples of intervention.[74] Beyond this discussion, the court intimates that coercion can involve non-forcible measures, but offers no guidance on how.

Undue weight is often ascribed to the court's discussion of the non-intervention rule. Its account of the rule is non-binding and general in description.[75] In this regard, its comment that coercion "defines" and "forms the very essence" of the rule is overbroad and misleading. As set out below, the essence of the non-intervention rule is the prevention of measures intended to subvert a state's independence over protected sovereign prerogatives, or free will. The court's reference to coercion is better understood as illustrative of the fact that not all modes of interference are internationally wrongful, and a loosely conceived concept of coercion specific to the non-intervention context has emerged over time as a reference point for distinguishing between permissible and impermissible influence.[76]

Defining a sensible limit to the principle's reach is no doubt important, otherwise the rule risks sweeping within its ambit "any act which ha[s] an effect on another state."[77] However, over-inclusiveness is not currently the problem. As reflected in the ICJ's emphasis in *Nicaragua* on the concept of coercion, the non-intervention rule is mired in the past and therefore tethered to force as the *sine qua non* of its violation. This raises legitimate questions as to the rule's utility in light of the separate prohibition on the use of force. And while there is general agreement that the rule now comprehends non-forcible modes of coercion, what that means in practice remains clouded in uncertainty. Owing to the historical force-prohibition emphasis of the rule, efforts to elucidate the meaning of coercion frequently miss the mark on correlating this "element" to the underlying purpose of the non-intervention principle—to protect against the subversion of a targeted state's independent sovereign choices—making under-inclusiveness a far greater risk. This dynamic has become particularly evident in the context of information conflict.

Some also consider the *Nicaragua* judgment to imply that to constitute coercion, one state's actions must involve an actual threat against the affected state, and the threatened consequence of non-compliance must itself be unlawful.[78] However, nothing in the judgment or international law more broadly requires that an intervention be effected by threat of consequence, lawful or otherwise. To the extent that a threat is involved, the threatened consequence must be judged contextually to determine whether it crosses the line between prohibited coercion and lawful, albeit "corrosive," pressure.[79] Furthermore, interpreting non-intervention as being premised on a compelled *quid pro quo* again misapprehends the interest protected by the rule—unimpeded sovereign prerogative and the right of independence in governance. As discussed further below, threats of negative consequence are not the only means for undermining this interest.

It is well recognized that the principle of non-intervention is an outgrowth, or corollary, of the principles of sovereignty and the sovereign equality of states. "Sovereignty in the relations between States signifies independence,"[80] and independence has long been understood as "the power of giving effect to the decisions of a will which is free" from external restraint.[81] Where a state employs measures "calculated to impose certain conduct or consequences" on a targeted state that if successful would "in effect depriv[e] the state intervened against of control over [] [a sovereign] matter," the line between interference and intervention is implicated and likely crossed.[82] Non-intervention is far more about potential consequence than it is about the means employed. While the choice of means is a relevant factor, as in the case of forcible measures which are presumptively employed to compel an outcome, it is not definitive. Thus, the rule is better understood as prohibiting measures calculated and likely to deprive, subordinate, or substantially impair the right of independence in governance, and such interventions are wrongful even if inchoate or unsuccessful.[83]

In her recent Chatham House paper on sovereignty and non-intervention, Harriet Moynihan reaches a similar conclusion. She describes coercion as the application of pressure or compulsion by one state sufficient to subordinate the sovereign will of the targeted state.[84] Thus, in her view, "the non-intervention principle is in practice capable of broader application" than a narrow interpretation of the ICJ's description of coercion would suggest.[85] According to Moynihan:

[S]ources suggest[] that the coercive behaviour could extend beyond forcing a change of policy to other aims, such as preventing the target state from implementing a policy or restraining its ability to exercise its state powers in some way. At the same time, as noted above, the attempt to deprive the target state of its free will over its sovereign powers is carried out for the benefit of the perpetrating state in some way: the unauthorized exercise of authority is not incidental. The benefit sought need not relate to a specific policy issue; it may suffice for the target state's control over the underlying policy area to be impaired in a way that adversely affects the target state. In light of this, the coercive behaviour is perhaps best described as pressure applied by one state to deprive the target state of its free will in relation to the exercise of its sovereign rights in an attempt to compel an outcome in, or conduct with respect to, a matter reserved to the target state.[86]

This approach correctly places emphasis on the non-intervention rule's central focus of protecting states' independence over core sovereign prerogatives.[87] Actions calculated to subvert a state's free will undermine the sovereign equality of states and the international order, and present a direct threat to international stability, peace, and security.

The *Tallinn Manual 2.0* also appears to take a similar approach. Rejecting the idea that coercion requires physical force, the manual states that coercion "refers to an affirmative act designed to deprive another State of its freedom of choice, that is, to force that State to act in an involuntary manner or involuntarily refrain from acting in a particular way."[88] Not surprisingly, Michael Schmitt, the general editor, also recognizes that the primary focus of the non-intervention rule and the "core" function of the element of coercion is to prevent subordination of sovereign free will. In his view, "a coercive action is intended to cause the State to do something, such as take a decision that it would otherwise not take, or not to engage in an activity in which it would otherwise engage."[89]

The evolving realm and nature of information conflict is providing states with lucrative opportunities to undermine the sovereign decisions of adversaries, yet how the non-intervention principle applies to propaganda and influence campaigns remains unclear. Debates over whether Russia's reported hack into the Democratic National Committee's (DNC) servers and subsequent "meddling" in the 2016 presidential election constituted a prohibited intervention are a case in point. Some argue that in the aggregate, Russia's actions sufficiently manipulated the election process to qualify.[90] Others view them as espionage and propaganda, which are not violations of international law by themselves, at least not per se.[91]

Some scholars and commentators considering the question of whether influence operations or propaganda alone can violate the rule have converged on the view that the use of covert deception crosses the intervention line, but little analysis is offered in support of this conclusion.[92] For example, Schmitt suggests that Russia's covert "troll" operation may have violated the non-intervention rule because "[a]rguably, the covert nature of the troll operation deprived the American electorate of its freedom of choice" when exercising the franchise. But he does not elaborate on how this aligns with more rigid interpretations of coercion, such as those that would require an interaction premised on a threat of consequence.[93]

The answer is twofold. First, as set out above, the non-intervention rule has never been premised on the existence of a threat-based transaction. It is a rule meant to prevent states from engaging in measures calculated to subvert sovereign free will. Second, measures of deception are commonly recognized in domestic legal systems as cognizable harms precisely because they are a means of undermining the exercise of free will. States frequently regulate deception either directly in the form of fraud-based proscriptions, or indirectly by making deception a constructive substitute for force or coercion elements of other crimes. States can draw on these general principles to adapt the non-intervention rule to the realities of the modern information environment.

General principles of law common to the principal legal systems of the world are recognized as valid subsidiary sources for determining the scope and meaning of primary treaty and customary international law rules such as the rule of prohibited intervention.[94] Admittedly, the means of identifying general principles of law and the normative weight to be accorded them is an open question, and a fulsome review of states' domestic legal regimes is beyond the scope of this chapter.[95] What follows are illustrative examples with an emphasis on US domestic law. Like all states, the United States can draw on these principles to inform its views on the meaning of coercion as applied in the context of the non-intervention rule and, by extension, the scope of application of the rule more generally.

Deception as a Means of Undermining Free Will

The indictment of the thirteen Russians and three Russian organizations stemming from the Special Counsel's investigation into Russian election meddling in 2016 is a compelling exposition, albeit in the vernacular of US domestic law, of a prohibited intervention into the US electoral process. The indictment lays out in great detail Russia's extensive covert deception campaign intended to impair, obstruct, and defeat the lawful functions of the US government "for the purpose of interfering with the U.S. political and electoral processes."[96] Significantly, the gravamen of the indictment was that the Russians carried out their scheme of interference by non-forcible means of fraud and deceit.

Specifically, the defendants were charged, *inter alia*, with conspiring to defraud the United States in violation of 18 U.S.C. § 371 by impeding the lawful functions of the Federal Election Commission, the Department of Justice, and the Department of State to administer federal requirements for disclosure of foreign involvement in certain domestic activities.[97] Section 371, the general federal conspiracy statute, prohibits two or more persons from conspiring to obstruct or interfere with a legitimate government activity "by deceit, craft or trickery, or at least by means that are dishonest."[98] This portion of the statute is intended to "protect governmental functions from frustration and distortion through deceptive practices."[99] While cheating the government out of money or property can serve as one means by which someone can defraud the United States, prosecution under Section 371 is not limited to financial crimes.[100] Actions "calculated to frustrate the functions of an entity of the United States will suffice."[101]

The fraud provisions encompassed in Section 371 are not unique. They reflect long-standing common law fraud concepts that proscribe both pecuniary and non-pecuniary harm, including depriving victims of a legal right. Fraud is also criminalized at the state level throughout the United States, and similar concepts can be found in the legal systems of most, if not all nations. Fraud is a crime of deceit that traces its roots in both common and civil law systems to the early Roman *lex Cornelia de Falsi*.[102] Fraud and similar provisions recognize that deception can be both a means to a harmful end and a legally cognizable harm in and of itself.[103] As such, legal systems universally regulate deception directly by criminalizing fraud and other *crimen falsi*. Fraud and similar provisions are ultimately grounded in the recognition that at its core, deception is a non-forcible means of undermining free will.

In addition to proscribing *crimen falsi*, legal systems commonly regulate deception indirectly as well, prescribing it as a constructive substitute for elements of actual force and coercion in other crimes. This legal principle has deep historical roots. For example, the common law has long recognized that for the crime of burglary, the element of breaking can be effected not just by actual force but also constructively through deceit.[104] Constructive force is recognized in other areas of law as well: deception can substitute for force as the *actus reus* of larceny. Larceny by trick is a common law species of larceny dating back at least to 1779 in English common law,[105] where the element of trick substitutes for the wrongful taking element required by larceny.[106] The rationale behind including larceny by trick within the crime of larceny is that "fraud vitiates the property owner's consent to the taking."[107] As such, the common law developed so that, to satisfy the requirements for larceny, "actual trespass or actual violence is not necessary. Fraud may take the place of force."[108]

Rape law offers another example of constructive force through deception. Although the traditional definition of rape required force or threat of force to satisfy the *actus reus*, the common law developed to embrace situations "in which the defendant employed deception rather than force."[109] Traditional common law distinctions between fraud in the factum and fraud in the inducement have steadily fallen away, with states trending toward adoption of the Model Penal Code approach, which states that consent is ineffective if "it is induced by force, duress or deception of a kind sought to be prevented by the law defining the offense."[110] Consistent with this trend, states have allowed specific instances of fraud in the inducement to serve as the basis for a rape conviction, including fraud in the context of certain professional relationships, spousal impersonation, impersonation of another, fraud as to the nature of the act, and "a few newer provisions more generally making consent obtained by fraud insufficient."[111] In each of these cases, the salient point is the recognition that deceit vitiates consent, the ultimate expression of free will.

Consider also the federal Trafficking Victims Protection Act (TVPA).[112] Passed as part of the Victims of Trafficking and Violence Protection Act of 2000, it was the first comprehensive federal law to address human trafficking. Recognizing that deception can "have the same purpose and effect" as actual threats of or use of physical coercion, Congress criminalized "severe forms" of human trafficking, which it defines as sex and labor trafficking induced by, *inter alia*, force, fraud, or coercion.[113] As one court recognized, "the TVPA not only protects victims from the most heinous human trafficking crimes, but also various additional types of fraud and extortion leading to forced labor."[114]

The idea that deception is a legally cognizable harm, in the form of fraud or as a constructive substitute for force or coercion, is not unique to United States law. These are precepts of law commonly reflected in domestic legal systems.[115] Drawing on these precepts, some states have also begun passing legislation specifically addressing foreign influence, disinformation, and election interference.[116]

Australia, for example, passed comprehensive legislation in 2018 in response to the growing threat of foreign interference. As part of this legislation, the National Security Legislation Amendment (Espionage and Foreign Interference) Act 2018 amended Australia's Criminal Code Act 1995 to create several new criminal offenses related to national security, espionage, and foreign influence. The two most relevant offenses are general foreign interference and foreign interference involving a targeted person.[117] For purposes of these new offenses, Australia distinguishes between foreign influence, which it deems permissible, and foreign interference, describing the latter as conduct which "goes beyond the routine diplomatic influence that is commonly practised by governments [and] . . . includes covert, deceptive and coercive activities intended to affect an Australian political or governmental process."[118] This distinction tracks closely with general understandings of the divide between lawful interference and prohibited intervention in international law, and it specifically recognizes covert deception as a means of intervention.

Australia is not alone in its efforts to combat foreign interference and adapt its domestic legal structure to account for the evolving nature of information conflict. France and other countries have either adopted or are considering laws to protect against foreign interference, disinformation, and election meddling. Many of these approaches similarly recognize the significance and threat of covert deception. These concepts are often reflected in international instruments as well. For example, Congress's approach to sex trafficking finds a direct analog in international law, which also recognizes that coercion need not be limited to physical force for purposes of human trafficking, defining trafficking to include inducement "by means of the threat or use of force or other forms of coercion, of abduction, of fraud, [or] deception."[119] The war crime of prohibited perfidy, which is predicated on an act of treachery, offers another example of international law criminalizing deception, albeit under very narrow and particular circumstances.[120]

The foregoing examples are illustrative, not exhaustive. They demonstrate how deception operates as a legally operative harm with direct relevance to the principle of non-intervention. States can and should take account of these principles as legitimate subsidiary tools for elaborating the meaning of coercion in the context of non-intervention, better defining the scope of the rule, and adapting it to the realities of modern cyber and information conflict.

Calibrating the Pendulum

Applying these general principles to the element of coercion will better align the non-intervention rule with its underlying purpose and adapt it to the realities of the information age. As Watts notes: "As States consider and weigh the merits and costs of various modes of interaction in the international system, charting options on this legal spectrum with some specificity becomes a prudent, if not always a simple exercise."[121] This is notably true with respect to the increasingly complex dynamics of inter-state relations in the cyber and information environments. States should leverage the non-intervention rule as a legitimate tool for deterring and regulating inimical action in these contexts.

Adopting the approach suggested here does not come without risk, however. Overbroad application of the rule would capture legitimate forms of statecraft and influence in its scope and raise collateral concerns regarding free expression that should be accounted for. States are rightfully unlikely to subscribe to a framework that sweeps too wide. Overt influence is a staple of international relations. It provides states an effective means of peacefully advancing their individual and collective interests on the world stage in a way that, even when aggressive, affords the targeted state the opportunity to contextualize and counter the influence in ways that covert deception campaigns are specifically intended to prevent. As Ohlin correctly asserts: "[T]here must be a line between being coercive and being corrosive to the proper functioning of a democracy."[122] Clarifying how best to identify where that line falls is one thing. Blurring it further or erasing it altogether is another. Recognizing covert deception and disinformation campaigns as qualitatively and normatively distinct from overt influence, and as such a means of actual or constructive coercion, is a necessary step in drawing that line. However, additional limiting principles are warranted.

It is important to reemphasize at this point that to be wrongful, like any means or method of statecraft, covert deception must be intended "to influence outcomes in, or conduct with respect to, a matter reserved to a target State."[123] Clarifying or recasting the meaning of coercion would have no impact on defining the object of the rule's protection—states' *domaine réservé*. It would simply place the emphasis back on the ends that the principle of non-intervention is concerned with, with less dogmatic focus on the means employed. Ultimately, whatever means are employed, they "must have the potential for [actually or constructively] compelling the target State to engage in an action that it would otherwise not take (or refrain from taking an action that it would otherwise take)."[124]

Noting that coercion might fall along a broad spectrum from minimally invasive to "exceptionally aggressive" actions, any of which might or might not amount to intervention, Watts, borrowing from McDougal and Feliciano, proposes a test of "consequentiality" for determining wrongfulness.[125] This test would consider "three dimensions of consequentiality" including, "the importance and number of values affected, the extent to which such values are affected, and the number of participants whose values are so affected."[126] Under this approach, he suggests consideration of the scale of an operation, the effects it produces in the target state, and its reach in terms of actors involuntarily affected.[127]

There is merit to Watts's approach, perhaps with slight modification and clarification. First, as is often the case, it presupposes a consummated intervention. For the rule to have any true force and effect, it needs to operate prophylactically—both as a deterrent and potentially as a justification for measures intended to thwart an actual or anticipated intervention before it works its harm. Responding to an intervention after the fact is sub-optimal, because it may be too late at that point to prevent harm. Thus, the consequentiality test, or any other, must consider potential, not actual, harm.[128]

Second, the number of participants whose values are affected is not a particularly helpful dimension. It is just one measure of the extent to which sovereign values are affected and is a highly dependent variable. This is apparent in the case of election interference through covert deception, where the populace, or subsets thereof, are the primary targets of an operation or campaign, and swaying or dissuading votes or generally causing distrust in the results is the aim. In general terms, the degree to which the sovereign value of a free and fair election will be affected will likely be a function of the number of voters deceived. One can imagine how the viral spread of false reports of a candidate's withdrawal from a closely contested race on the eve of election could swing the results. On the other hand, where such close margins are at play, it might only require a handful of voters to alter the outcome. In either case, the consequence is the same.

Thus, consequentiality, or perhaps better stated, potential impact, is better understood as an assessment of the inverse relationship between the relative value of the targeted interest and the anticipated extent to which the interest will be affected. Even among the bundle of rights falling within the *domaine réservé*, there are necessarily qualitative differences. As evidenced by recent state pronouncements, independence over the choice of a state's political system, that is, election processes and results, is at the core of protected sovereign interests.[129] For heavily weighted interests such as elections, there should be lower tolerance for interventions aimed at undermining their independence. In such cases, there should be a strong presumption that covert deception measures targeting the electorate and election processes constitutes a prohibited intervention.

Some states have recently expressed a view that cyber operations intended to disrupt the fundamental operation of legislative bodies or that would destabilize financial systems would violate the non-intervention principle.[130] It is for those states to assign the relative weight of these sovereign interests, and they must bear responsibility for those assessments.

Determining whether a covert disinformation campaign constitutes a prohibited intervention must also account for intent. As noted in the *Tallinn Manual 2.0*, actions that "have a *de facto* coercive effect must be distinguished from those in which a State intends to coerce *de jure*."[131] While discerning adversary intent is always a challenge, where a campaign of covert deception is involved intent is perhaps most easily assessed based on the nature of the deception and the target or targets of the covert propaganda being spread. For example, it is apparent from the record that the objective of Russia's disinformation campaign during the last several election cycles was at least to corrupt the process and alter the results. But Russia has not confined its disinformation efforts to disrupting elections. It is also evident from the nature of its deception operations that Russia has engaged in a broader, systematic campaign to sow division throughout Western democracies, demoralize cultural values, and alter the populations' perceptions of reality. These actions meet almost any definition of subversion, where intent is fairly apparent.[132]

Finally, assessing the potential consequentiality or impact of anticipated or ongoing interference should be done holistically, considering the full context of an action or set of actions and their potential impact on the affected state.[133] Information is but one element of state power and is rarely employed in isolation. For example, analyses that attempt to disaggregate the conglomeration of actions Russia took to impact the 2016 presidential elections ignore context and miss the mark. Russia's actions were synchronized over time and space and mutually supportive—exactly the types of composite acts that "defined in the aggregate" are internationally wrongful.[134]

Conclusion

The advent of the modern, digital information environment has introduced the phenomenon of cyber conflict and has fundamentally recast the nature of information conflict. Taking cues from Russia's covert influence efforts, China and other revisionist states are more actively stepping into the information conflict arena, and the United States national-security apparatus is rightfully taking note. The recognition of this emerging threat is beginning to drive the United States' strategic orientation and efforts to better defend against hostile foreign influence campaigns. International law can and should play a role in these efforts.

The rise of hostile cyber operations and the resurgence and evolution of information conflict have placed renewed emphasis on the principle of non-intervention as a tool for regulating interstate relations in the gray zone below and outside of armed hostilities. This renewed emphasis on the rule has also highlighted its definitional weaknesses—flaws that limit its immediate value as a means for regulating cyber and information conflict and risk casting it as an anachronism. Effective adaptation of the rule to account for the realities of cyber and information conflict will require states to establish greater clarity on the core concept of coercion and the boundaries between legitimate and illegitimate non-forcible measures of influence and statecraft. This is difficult terrain, but states should start the process by refocusing on the central interest the non-intervention rule is intended to protect—sovereign equality and independence. Drawing a line between covert deception and overt influence is a sound starting point, consistent with general principles of law common to many domestic legal regimes that recognize and regulate deception as a legally cognizable harm in myriad ways.

A cornerstone of the rules-based international order, international law has played an important role in regulating interstate relations and achieving some semblance of stability and security in the post–World War II era—a proposition reflected in the United States' long-standing commitment to the framework of international law and its contribution to the peaceful resolution of disputes. Any US strategy aimed at effectively addressing ICT-enabled national security threats, including covert influence and deception campaigns, should include the United States taking a lead on advancing the role of international law and norms development. Drawing more definitive lines with respect to the role of the rule of non-intervention will serve the dual purpose of deterring adversary states from crossing articulated red lines, and, where deterrence fails or is ineffective, underpinning the legitimacy of US counter-cyber and counter-influence responses.

Notes

* The opinions expressed herein are those of the author and do not necessarily reflect the views of the Department of Defense or any other organization or entity with which the author is affiliated. Special thanks to Dillon Chepp (Washington College of Law, JD 2020) and Matthew Kahn (Harvard Law School, JD Candidate, 2022) for their excellent research support to this chapter.

1. Sun Tzu, *The Art of War* ¶ 18, INTERNET CLASSICS ARCHIVE, http://classics.mit.edu/Tzu/artwar.html (Lionel Giles trans.) (last visited Jul. 14, 2020).

2. E. DE VATTEL, THE LAW OF NATIONS OR THE PRINCIPLES OF NATURAL LAW 131 (James Brown Scott ed., Charles G. Fenwick trans., Carnegie Institute of Washington 1916) (1758).

3. Rand Waltzman, *The Weaponization of Information: The Need for Cognitive Security: Hearing Before the Subcomm. on Cybersec. of the S. Comm. on Armed Services*, 115th Cong. 1 (2017) [hereinafter Waltzman Testimony] (testimony of Rand Waltzman, Senior Information Scientist, RAND Corp.).

4. *Id.* at 2.

5. For purposes of this chapter, information conflict refers to the strategic use of information to influence, disrupt, corrupt, or usurp the decisions and actions of an adversary's government, military, private sector, general population, or a combination thereof.

6. *See, e.g.*, Group of Governmental Experts on Developments in the Field of Information and Telecommunications in the Context of International Security, ¶ 28(b), U.N. Doc. A/70/174 (July 22, 2015) [hereinafter U.N. GGE Report].

7. Military and Paramilitary Activities in and Against Nicaragua (Nicar. V. U.S.), Judgment, 1986 I.C.J. Rep. 14, ¶ 205 (June 27).

8. Jeremy Wright QC MP, *Cyber and International Law in the 21st Century*, GOV.UK (May 23, 2018).

9. MICHAEL J. MAZARR ET AL., HOSTILE SOCIAL MANIPULATION: PRESENT REALITIES AND EMERGING TRENDS xii (2019).

10. Dennis Kux, *Soviet Active Measures and Disinformation: Overview and Assessment*, 15 PARAMETERS—J. U.S. ARMY WAR C. 19 (1985). By some counts, the Soviets carried out over 10,000 individual disinformation operations during the Cold War. S. SELECT COMM. ON INTELLIGENCE, RUSSIAN ACTIVE MEASURES CAMPAIGNS AND INTERFERENCE, VOLUME II: RUSSIA'S USE OF SOCIAL MEDIA WITH ADDITIONAL VIEWS, S. Rep. No. 116-XX, at 11–12 (2020).

11. *Inside the KGB: An Interview with Maj. Gen. Oleg Kalugin*, CNN (Jan. 1998).

12. OFFICE OF THE DIR. OF NAT'L INTELLIGENCE, ASSESSING RUSSIAN ACTIVITIES AND INTENTIONS IN RECENT US ELECTIONS ii (2017) [hereinafter ODNI REPORT].

13. *Id.* at 2.

14. *Id.* at 1–4.

15. *See id.* at 4.

16. Indictment, United States v. Internet Research Agency, LLC, No. 1:18-cr-00032-DLF (D.D.C. Feb. 16, 2018).

17. *Id.* at 5. Specifically, the indictment alleges the defendants obstructed the lawful functions of the Federal Election Commission, the US Department of Justice, and the US Department of State.

18. *Id.* at 4.

19. S. SELECT COMM. ON INTELLIGENCE, *supra* note 10, at 11–12.

20. Margaret L. Taylor, *Combatting Disinformation and Foreign Interference in Democracies: Lessons from Europe*, BROOKINGS INSTITUTE: TECHTANK (July 31, 2019).

21. NATIONAL INTELLIGENCE COUNCIL, INTELLIGENCE COMMUNITY ASSESSMENT: FOREIGN THREATS TO THE 2020 US FEDERAL ELECTIONS i (Mar. 10, 2021).

22. James Frater et al., *EU Says Pro-Kremlin Media Trying to Sow 'Panic and Fear' with Coronavirus Disinformation*, CNN (Mar. 18, 2020, 1:13 PM).

23. MAZARR, *supra* note 9, at 107 (quoting Murong Xuecun, *The New Face of Chinese Propaganda*, N.Y. TIMES (Dec. 20, 2013).

24. *Id.* at 114 (quoting President Xi Jinping).

25. Julian E. Barnes, Matthew Rosenburg, and Edward Wong, *As Virus Spreads, China and Russia See Openings for Disinformation*, N.Y. TIMES (Apr. 10, 2020).

26. DANIEL R. COATS, STATEMENT FOR THE RECORD ON THE WORLDWIDE THREAT ASSESSMENT OF THE US INTELLIGENCE COMMUNITY FOR THE SENATE SELECT COMMITTEE ON INTELLIGENCE 7 (2019).

27. OFFICE OF THE PRESIDENT, CYBER STRATEGY OF THE UNITED STATES OF AMERICA 41 (2018).

28. U.N. Charter, art. 2, ¶ 1.

29. Island of Palmas (Neth. v. U.S.), 2 R.I.A.A 829, 838 (Perm. Ct. Arb. 1928).

30. The *jus ad bellum* refers to the body of customary international law that governs the conditions under which states may resort to force and is reflected in the United Nations Charter. *See* U.N. Charter, art. 2, ¶ 4; *id.* art. 51.

31. 1 LASSA OPPENHEIM, OPPENHEIM'S INTERNATIONAL LAW 428 (Sir Robert Jennings & Sir Arthur Watts, eds., 9th ed. 1992).

32. Military and Paramilitary Activities in and Against Nicaragua (Nicar. V. U.S.), Judgment, 1986 I.C.J. Rep. 14, ¶ 202 (June 27). Some assert that sovereignty is itself a primary rule of international law. That issue is beyond the scope of this chapter.

33. *See, e.g.*, U.N. GGE Report, *supra* note 6, at ¶ 28(b) ("In their use of ICTs, States must observe, among other principles of international law . . . non-intervention in the internal affairs of other States.").

34. TALLINN MANUAL 2.0 ON THE INTERNATIONAL LAW APPLICABLE TO CYBER OPERATIONS 317 (Rule 66) cmt. 18 (Michael Schmitt ed., 2d ed. 2017) [hereinafter TALLINN MANUAL 2.0].

35. *See* Sean Watts, *Low-Intensity Cyber Operations and the Principle of Non-intervention*, *in* CYBERWAR: LAW AND ETHICS FOR VIRTUAL CONFLICTS 255 (Jens David Ohlin, Kevin Govern & Claire Finkelstein eds., 2015) (noting that jurists and commentators "have struggled to identify the precise contours of the principle and to apply those delineations to ever-evolving and increasingly inter-tangled international relations").

36. OPPENHEIM, *supra* note 31, at 432.

37. Mohamed Helal, *On Coercion in International Law*, 52 N.Y.U. J. INT'L L. & POL. 1, 55 (2019).

38. Military and Paramilitary Activities in and Against Nicaragua (Nicar. V. U.S.), Judgment, 1986 I.C.J. Rep. 14, ¶ 205 (June 27).

39. TALLINN MANUAL 2.0, *supra* note 34, at 314 (Rule 66) cmt. 6.

40. *Nicaragua*, 1986 I.C.J. Rep. at ¶ 205 (noting that with regard to "the content of the principle of non-intervention—the Court will define only those aspects of the principle which appear to be relevant to the resolution of the dispute").

41. *Id.* at ¶ 201. (noting that its analysis of the principle of non-intervention served only to "enquire whether there is any justification for the activities in question, to be found not in the right of collective self-defence against an armed attack, but in the right to take counter-measures in response to conduct of Nicaragua which is not alleged to constitute an armed attack").

42. *See* HARRIET MOYNIHAN, CHATHAM HOUSE, THE APPLICATION OF INTERNATIONAL LAW TO STATE CYBERATTACKS: SOVEREIGNTY AND NON-INTERVENTION 27 (2019) (noting that the court's discussion of non-intervention should be considered non-prescriptive dicta).

43. OPPENHEIM, *supra* note 31, at 432.

44. Philip Kunig, *Prohibition of Intervention, in* MAX PLANCK ENCYCLOPEDIA OF PUBLIC INTERNATIONAL LAW (2008).

45. *See, e.g., Coercion,* USLEGAL, https://definitions.uslegal.com/c/coercion/ (last visited July 25, 2020) ("Coercion generally means to impose one's will on another by means of force or threats.").

46. OPPENHEIM, *supra* note 31, at 430.

47. *See* Jens David Ohlin, *Did Russian Cyber Interference in the 2016 Election Violate International Law?,* 95 TEX. L. REV. 1579, 1588 (2017) (discussing the concept of *domaine réservé*).

48. MOYNIHAN, *supra* note 42, at 34.

49. *See id.;* OPPENHEIM, *supra* note 31, at 430–31. The *Tallinn Manual 2.0* draws a distinction between inherently governmental functions (protected by the purported rule of sovereignty) and the narrower class of protected interests falling within the *domaine réservé* (protected by the rule of non-intervention). *See* TALLINN MANUAL 2.0, *supra* note 34, at 24 (Rule 4) cmt. 22 ("Usurpation of an inherently governmental function differs from intervention in that the former deals with inherently governmental functions, whereas the latter involves the *domaine réservé,* concepts that overlap to a degree but that are not identical."). The *Tallinn Manual 2.0* offers no further explanation to support this schema of distinct sovereign functions, which makes little sense in light of the broad presumptions of independent internal governance that flow from the principle of sovereignty. *See* MOYNIHAN, *supra* note 42, at 34 ("In any event, since the non-intervention principle derives from and is a reflection of the principle of sovereignty, the better view is that there are not two different standards of matters reserved to a state.").

50. Military and Paramilitary Activities in and Against Nicaragua (Nicar. V. U.S.), Judgment, 1986 I.C.J. Rep. 14, ¶ 205 (June 27).

51. S.S. "Lotus" (Fr./Turk.), Judgment, 1927 P.C.I.J. (ser. A) No. 10, at 18 (Sept. 7).

52. *See, e.g.,* TALLINN MANUAL 2.0, *supra* note 34, at 315 (Rule 66) cmt. 10.

53. Michael N. Schmitt, *Grey Zones in the International Law of Cyberspace,* 42 YALE L.J. ONLINE 1, 7 (2017).

54. Ohlin, *supra* note 47, at 1588.

55. Helal, *supra* note 37, at 66–67 ("The *domaine réservé* . . . is not static. Its breadth is ever-changing depending on the extent of the international legal obligations of a state, the growth of international law, and the intrusiveness of international regulatory and adjudicatory bodies.").

56. MOYNIHAN, *supra* note 42, at 34.

57. Int'l Law Comm'n, Rep. of the Int'l Law Comm'n on the Work of Its Fifty-Third Session, Draft Articles on Responsibility of States for Internationally Wrongful Acts, with Commentaries, art. 22, U.N. Doc. A/56/10, at 75 (2001).

58. *See* TALLINN MANUAL 2.0, *supra* note 34, at 314 (Rule 66) cmt. 7.

59. R. J. VINCENT, NONINTERVENTION IN THE INTERNATIONAL ORDER 40 (2015).

60. *See, e.g.*, Military and Paramilitary Activities in and Against Nicaragua (Nicar. V. U.S.), Judgment, 1986 I.C.J. Rep. 14, ¶ 205 (June 27).

61. *See, e.g.*, Jacobson v. Massachusetts, 197 U.S. 11 (1905) (upholding as within the general police power the authority of states to enact and enforce compulsory vaccination laws).

62. *Nicaragua*, 1986 I.C.J. Rep. at ¶ 205. These actions would also constitute prohibited uses of force in violation of Article 2(4) of the Charter, triggering the victim state's inherent right of self-defense under the US view of the *jus ad bellum. See id.* Some argue that, implicit in the *Nicaragua* judgment's description is the notion that to constitute coercion, the threatened consequence must itself be unlawful.

63. Schmitt, *supra* note 53, at 8; TALLINN MANUAL 2.0, *supra* note 34, at 318 (Rule 66) cmt. 21 ("[C]oercion must be distinguished from persuasion, criticism, public diplomacy, [and] propaganda . . . .").

64. VINCENT, *supra* note 59, at 15.

65. For a discussion of the origins of the principle of non-intervention, see *id.* at 20–44

66. *Id.* at 35–37.

67. *See* Helal, *supra* note 37, at 56 (quoting Tomislav Mitrovic, *Non-Intervention in the Internal Affairs of States, in* PRINCIPLES OF INTERNATIONAL LAW CONCERNING FRIENDLY RELATIONS AND COOPERATION 224–25 (Milan Šahović ed., 1972)); Watts, *supra* note 35, at 256 ("Twentieth-century commentators observed that non-intervention prohibits only acts that are 'dictatorial' by nature or effect.").

68. See Helal, *supra* note 37, at 56.

69. OPPENHEIM, *supra* note 31, at 432 (emphasis added), 434.

70. Military and Paramilitary Activities in and Against Nicaragua (Nicar. V. U.S.), Judgment, 1986 I.C.J. Rep. 14, ¶ 203 (June 27).

71. Declaration on Principles of International Law Concerning Friendly Relations and Cooperation among States in Accordance with the Charter of the United Nations, G.A. Res. 2625, U.N. GAOR 6th Comm., 25th Sess., Supp. No.28, U.N. Doc a/8082 (1970).

72. *Nicaragua*, 1986 I.C.J. Rep. at ¶ 205.

73. *Id.*

74. *Id.*

75. MOYNIHAN, *supra* note 42, at 34.

76. *See, e.g., id.* at 29 (noting that in the context of non-intervention, coercion bears a different meaning than in normal usage); Watts, *supra* note 35, at 256 ("In this sense, it is likely that the best understanding of non-intervention appreciates a nuanced and particularized notion of coercion.").

77. Maziar Jamnejad and Michael Wood, *The Principle of Non-intervention*, 22 LEIDEN J. INT'L L. 345, 381 (2009).

78. *See* Ohlin, *supra* note 47, at 1589.

79. *See id.*

80. Island of Palmas (Neth. v. U.S.), 2 R.I.A.A 829, 838 (Perm. Ct. Arb. 1928).

81. WILLIAM EDWARD HALL, A TREATISE ON INTERNATIONAL LAW 50 (1895).

82. OPPENHEIM, *supra* note 31, at 430, 432.

83. TALLINN MANUAL 2.0, *supra* note 34, at 322 (Rule 66) cmt. 29 ("The fact that a coercive cyber operation fails to produce the desired outcome has no bearing on whether [the non-intervention rule] has been breached.").

84. MOYNIHAN, *supra* note 42, at 28 (quoting Jamnejad and Wood, *supra* note 77, at 348).

85. Harriet Moynihan, *The Application of International Law to Cyberspace: Sovereignty and Non-intervention,* JUST SECURITY (Dec. 13, 2019).

86. MOYNIHAN, *supra* note 42, at 30 (internal citations omitted).

87. Moynihan's effective substitution of "pressure and compulsion" for coercion to distinguish between interference and intervention is less helpful. According those terms their common meaning, it is unclear whether she uses them simply as synonyms for coercion, or also to include persuasion and influence which standing alone, risks over-inclusion.

88. TALLINN MANUAL 2.0, *supra* note 34, at 317 (Rule 66) cmt. 18.

89. Michael N. Schmitt, *"Virtual" Disenfranchisement: Cyber Election Meddling in the Grey Zones of International Law,* 19 CHI. J. INT'L L. 30, 51 (2018).

90. *See, e.g.,* Schmitt, *supra* note 53, at 8; Ohlin, *supra* note 47, at 1579–80.

91. *See* TALLINN MANUAL 2.0, *supra* note 34, at 168 (Rule 32) cmt. 5.

92. *See* Schmitt, *supra* note 89, at 51 ("[T]he deceptive nature of [Russian] trolling is what distinguishes it from a mere influence operation."); Helal, *supra* note 37, at 115 ("[I]n times of peace, *covert* or *black* IO, IW, or PSYOPs, are unlawful under the prohibition on intervention if these activities are undertaken to interfere with the domaine réservé of a state."); Steven J. Barela, *Cross-Border Cyber Ops to Erode Legitimacy: An Act of Coercion,* JUST SECURITY (Jan. 12, 2017).

93. Schmitt, *supra* note 89, at 51; *see also* Ohlin, *supra* note 47, at 1589 ("In order to count as illegal intervention, the structure of the interaction must have the following form: engage in this action; otherwise you will suffer a particular consequence.").

94. *See* Statute of the International Court of Justice, June 26, 1945, Art. 38(1)(c), 59 Stat. 1055, 33 U.N.T.S. 933; *see also* Restatement (Third) of The Foreign Relations Law of the United States § 102(c)(4) (1987) (recognizing general principles as those "common to the major legal systems, even if not incorporated or reflected in customary law or international agreement, [that] may be invoked as supplementary rules of international law where appropriate").

95. *See generally* Int'l L. Comm'n, Second Report on General Principles of Law, U.N. Doc. A/CN.4/741 (2020) (describing the concept and means of identifying general principles of law).

96. Indictment, United States v. Internet Research Agency, LLC, No. 1:18-cr-00032-DLF, at ¶ 2 (D.D.C. filed Feb. 16, 2018). The Department of Justice has since

decided to dismiss charges against two of the corporate defendants due to their "ephemeral presence and immunity to just punishment, the risk of exposure of law enforcement's tools and techniques, and the post-indictment change in the proof available at trial." Motion to Dismiss Concord Defendants, United States v. Internet Research Agency, No. 1:18-cr-00032-DLF, at 9 (D.D.C. filed Mar. 16, 2020).

97. Indictment, United States v. Internet Research Agency, LLC, No. 1:18-cr-00032-DLF, at ¶ 9 (D.D.C. filed Feb. 16, 2018).

98. Hammerschmidt v. United States, 265 U.S. 182, 188 (1924).

99. U.S. Dep't of Justice, Criminal Resource Manual, 18 U.S.C. § 371—Conspiracy to Defraud the United States (last updated Jan. 21, 2020) [hereinafter DOJ Criminal Resource Manual, 18 U.S.C. § 371].

100. See Hammerschmidt, 265 U.S. at 188.

101. Charles Doyle, Cong. Research Serv., R41223, Federal Conspiracy Law: A Brief Overview 9 (2020). Although the Special Counsel's indictment does not allege that the defendants' actions altered the outcome of the 2016 presidential election, it is sufficient that there was an injury to the integrity of the government. DOJ Criminal Resource Manual, 18 U.S.C. § 371, supra note 99.

102. See Stuart P. Green, Deceit and the Classification of Crimes: Federal Rules of Evidence 609(A)(2) and the Origins of Crimen Falsi, 90 J. Crim. L. & Criminology 1087, 1095–99 (2000).

103. See id. at 1093–94.

104. See, e.g., State v. Abdullah, 967 A.2d 469, 476–77 (R.I. 2009); Davis v. State, 910 So. 2d 1228, 1231 (Miss. Ct. App. 2005).

105. People v. Williams, 305 P.3d 1241, 1245 (Cal. 2013) (citing Rex v. Pear, 168 Eng. Rep. 208 (1779)).

106. Reid v. Commonwealth, 781 S.E.2d 373, 375 n.1 (Va. Ct. App. 2016); see also Williams, 305 P.3d at 1241; State v. Barbour, 570 S.E.2d 126, 128 (N.C. Ct. App. 2002).

107. Williams, 305 P.3d at 1245.

108. Id. (quoting People v. Edwards, 236 P. 944, 948 (Cal. Dist. Ct. App. 1925)).

109. Wayne R. LaFave, 2 Subst. Crim. L. § 17.3(c) (3d ed.), Westlaw (last updated Oct. 2019).

110. Model Penal Code § 2.11(3)(d) (Am. Law Inst., Proposed Official Draft 1962); see LaFave, supra note 109, at § 17.3(C) n.108 (collecting statutes).

111. LaFave, supra note 109, at § 17.3(c) n.98, n.99 (collecting statutes).

112. Pub. L. 106–386, 114 Stat. 1464 (2000) (codified as amended in scattered sections of the U.S. Code).

113. 22 U.S.C. §§ 7101(b)(13), 7102(11) (2018). The TVPA directly prohibits sex trafficking obtained by force, fraud, or coercion. 18 U.S.C. § 1591 (2018). The TVPA's prohibitions on forced labor, § 1589, and human trafficking to further forced labor, § 1590, extend to involuntary servitude obtained by fraud, see Mairi Nunag-Tanedo v. E. Baton Rouge Parish Sch. Bd., 790 F. Supp. 2d 1134, 1144, 1147 (C.D. Cal. 2011) (refusing to dismiss plaintiffs' claims that defendants violated 18 U.S.C. §§ 1589, 1590 where defendants' fraudulent scheme coerced plaintiffs into performing forced labor).

114. *Mairi Nunag-Tanedo*, 760 F. Supp. 2d at 1145.

115. For example, in the United Kingdom, deception or "dishonesty" forms the basis of numerous criminal and civil proscriptions. *See* Ivey v. Genting Casinos [2018] AC 391 (defining dishonesty for purposes of acquisitive crimes). Brazil's public corruption statute similarly identifies fraud or deception as a means of harming government administration. Lei Anticorrupção [Anticorruption Law] (Lei n. 12.846/ 2013), art. 5 (Braz.). A number of states also recognize deception as a substitute for force or coercion in sex-related crimes. *See, e.g.*, CÓDIGO PENAL [C.P.] [Penal Code] art. 215 (Braz.); R.v. Cuerrier, [1998] 2 S.C.R. 371, 374 (Can.); CrimA 5734/ 10 Kashour v. State of Israel (Jan. 25, 2012) (Isr.); *Crimes Act 1900* (NSW) s61HE(6) (Austl.); Assange v. Swedish Prosecution Authority [2011] EWHC (Admin) 2849 [87–90] (Eng.).

116. *See, e.g.*, Ruth Levush, *Government Responses to Disinformation on Social Media Platforms: Comparative Summary*, LAW LIBRARY OF CONG. (last updated Mar. 16, 2020); Luis Acosta, *Regulation of Foreign Involvement in Elections: Comparative Summary*, LAW LIBRARY OF CONG. (last updated Nov. 8, 2019); SAMANTHA BRADSHAW ET AL., NATO STRATEGIC COMMS. CTR. EXCELLENCE, GOVERNMENT RESPONSES TO MALICIOUS USE OF SOCIAL MEDIA (2018).

117. *National Security Legislation Amendment (Espionage and Foreign Interference) Act 2018* (Cth) div. 92.2(1)(a)-(c) (intentional), 92.3(1)(a)-(c) (reckless) (Austl.); *id.* at 92.2(2), 92.3(2). Additionally, the actor's conduct must be covert or deceptive, or involve a threat to cause serious harm or a demand "with menaces." *Id.* at 92.2(1)(d), 92.3(1)(d).

118. ATT'Y-GEN.'S DEP'T, FOREIGN INFLUENCE TRANSPARENCY SCHEME: FACTSHEET 2 (2019) (Austl.).

119. Protocol to Prevent, Suppress and Punish Trafficking in Persons, Especially Women and Children, Supplementing the United Nations Convention Against Transnational Organized Crime art. 3(a), G.A. Res. 55/25, U.N. Doc. A/55/383 (Nov. 15, 2000).

120. For a general discussion of the crime of perfidy in the cyber context, see Colonel Gary P. Corn & Commander Peter Pascucci, *The Law of Armed Conflict Implications of Covered or Concealed Cyber Operations—Perfidy, Ruses, and the Principle of Passive Distinction, in* THE IMPACT OF EMERGING TECHNOLOGIES ON THE LAW OF ARMED CONFLICT (Maj. Ronald T.P. Alcala & Eric Talbot Jensen eds., 2019).

121. Watts, *supra* note 35, at 249.

122. Ohlin, *supra* note 47, at 1593.

123. TALLINN MANUAL 2.0, *supra* note 34, at 318 (Rule 66) cmt. 19.

124. *Id.* at 319 (Rule 66) cmt. 21.

125. Watts, *supra* note 35, at 257.

126. *Id.*

127. *Id.*

128. This approach undoubtedly raises legitimate challenges with respect to available intelligence and the ability to assess attribution and prejudge the intent, design, causal connection to a protected aspect of sovereignty, and the likely impact a planned or ongoing influence operation will have. But these are neither unique

nor insurmountable obstacles. States routinely face similar intelligence challenges when evaluating adversary activities and considering responses, such as in the jus ad bellum context.

129. *See, e.g.*, Letter from the Minister of Foreign Affairs to the President of the House of Representatives, Letter to the Parliament on the International Legal Order in Cyberspace, Appendix at 3 (July 5, 2019) (Neth.); Honorable Paul C. Ney, Jr., DOD General Counsel Remarks at U.S. Cyber Command Legal Conference (Mar. 2, 2020); Wright, *supra* note 8.

130. Wright, *supra* note 8.

131. TALLINN MANUAL 2.0, *supra* note 34, at 321 (Rule 66) cmt. 27.

132. Some consider subversion a distinct category of intervention. *See* Watts, *supra* note 35, at 255–56.

133. *See* TALLINN MANUAL 2.0, *supra* note 34, at 319 (Rule 66) cmt. 21 (noting the view of some experts that actions can rise to the level of an intervention based on the context and consequences).

134. See Int'l Law Comm'n, Rep. of the Int'l Law Comm'n on the Work of Its Fifty-Third Session, Draft Articles on Responsibility of States for Internationally Wrongful Acts, with Commentaries, art. 15, U.N. Doc. A/56/10, at 62 (2001).

10

Due Diligence and Defend Forward

Eric Talbot Jensen and Sean Watts

Introduction

As its name implies, the 2018 US Department of Defense (DoD) Defend Forward strategy is principally reactive.[1] The strategy assumes that the United States will continue to suffer harm from competitors and malign actors through cyberspace. Accordingly, it outlines US reactions to preempt threats, defeat ongoing harm, and deter future harm.[2] Previous strategies have instructed similarly, but the 2018 National Cyber Strategy purports to reflect a strategic evolution in its overt commitment to countering cyber harm at its origin and to doing so not intermittently or episodically but on a day-to-day basis.[3] Defending forward involves a wide range of cyber activities, but a defining feature will likely be routine non-consensual cyber operations in the networks of hostile foreign governments and private actors.

These operations are sure to require technical, doctrinal, political, and even diplomatic reevaluations. But they also call for review of supporting international legal justifications. While a host of international law doctrines will be relevant to Defend Forward, the principle of due diligence is likely to play a significant role, in light of both the reactive nature of Defend Forward and the interconnected yet shadowy domain of cyberspace.

Well before the Defend Forward strategy or even cyberspace itself emerged, states developed the international law obligation of due diligence as an important regulation of international relations. In the incomplete and fragmented international legal system, due diligence has served as a general policing regime to manage and redress harm between states. At its most general level, due diligence requires states to take reasonable measures to put a stop to activities, whether private or public, within their borders that cause serious adverse consequences to other states.[4] International tribunals and publicists have repeatedly confirmed that breaches of due diligence entitle injured states to relief and reparations from offending states. Just as important, breaches of due diligence authorize victim states to react with a wide range of measures of self-correction from non-diligent states, including resort to countermeasures.[5]

In these respects, breaches of due diligence resemble other international wrongs that give rise to self-help. Breaches of due diligence are distinct, however, in that wrongfulness arises not from attribution of harm to organs or agents of the offending state but rather from the emanation of harm itself. A victim state can establish a breach of due diligence without establishing the territorial state's responsibility for the harm; the victim state need only determine that the offending state knew of and failed to quell harm coming from its territory. In this respect, breaches of due diligence most often involve omissions rather than affirmative acts by states. Alleged breaches of due diligence can potentially justify reactive measures of self-help such as those envisioned by the Defend Forward strategy, particularly in situations where cyber harm emanates from another state's territory but cannot be attributed directly to that state.[6]

Despite the doctrine's potential utility to curb harmful omissions by states and justify remedial measures, due diligence remains an ambiguous concept in international law. Some detect reluctance on the part of states, including the United States, to publicly support or clarify the concept of due diligence.[7] Others question whether due diligence is a freestanding obligation at all, perceiving it instead as a secondary rule that merely informs the implementation of other primary rules of conduct.[8] It is also unclear whether the duty of due diligence extends to an obligation to monitor and prevent harm ex ante. Moreover, the precise threshold or degree of harm required to establish a breach remains unsettled. Adding complexity, the concept of due diligence has developed to include regime-specific standards and duties applicable to various domains and conditions of international relations.

This chapter evaluates perceived US hesitance concerning due diligence in light of the Defend Forward cyber strategy. We begin with a brief review of due diligence as an obligation of general international law. We highlight a broad base of support from international tribunals and commentators for due diligence as a freestanding rule of conduct. We then recount recent efforts to apply due diligence to activities in cyberspace. Next, we review past US foreign relations experience with due diligence, including its invocation in international litigation and its use to generate favorable diplomatic outcomes. We conclude that positive US diplomatic and legal precedent counsel in favor of renewed recognition of due diligence as an obligation under general international law. We then examine how conceptions of due diligence may complement the Defend Forward strategy in cyberspace. Specifically, we suggest how the United States might best tailor a view on due diligence specific to activities in cyberspace and offer doctrinal refinements that might be acknowledged in light of the US Defend Forward strategy.

Due Diligence in International Law

General Due Diligence

A state's obligation not to permit activities within its territory that harm other states finds classic international legal expression in the phrase *sic utere tuo et alienum non laedas* (use your own property in such a manner as not to injure that of another).[9] By the late nineteenth century, influential commentators had begun to refine the no harm maxim into a concept of due diligence. In 1871, the former British Majesty's advocate Robert Phillimore observed, "[a] Government may by *knowledge* and *sufferance*, as well as by direct *permission*, become responsible for the acts of subjects whom it does not prevent from the commission of an injury to a foreign State."[10] Although Phillimore's formulation suggests a theory of liability as much as one of international wrong, later publicists, including Lassa Oppenheim and Hersch Lauterpacht, soon translated the concept into an international obligation of conduct. Oppenheim identified "international delinquency," in the form of "culpable negligence" resulting in injury to another state, as a violation of general international law.[11] Meanwhile, Lauterpacht endorsed notions of due diligence as means by which to hold a "defaulting State to the possible consequences of its negligence."[12]

By the mid-twentieth century, states increasingly invoked due diligence in diplomatic practice and litigation.[13] Modern recitations of the obligation most often cite the 1949 International Court of Justice (ICJ) decision in the *Corfu Channel* case. After two of its destroyers lawfully present in Albanian waters struck naval mines, the United Kingdom alleged that Albania had wrongfully failed to honor its legal duty to alert the ships to the presence of the mines. The United Kingdom framed Albania's failure as a breach of international law specifically addressed to maritime mines. But UK advocates also characterized the Albanian omission as a breach of "general principles of international law."[14]

Although the ICJ could not attribute the placement of the mines to Albania, the court held that Albania must have been aware of the mines and affirmed the United Kingdom's claim with respect to due diligence as a principle of international law. Offering the clearest and now most recited expression of due diligence, the court confirmed "every State's obligation not to allow knowingly its territory to be used for acts contrary to the rights of other States."[15]

The court's statement on due diligence as a matter of general international law has been criticized as obiter dictum. Some suggest that the court should have decided the case on the narrower legal grounds of a breach of the international law applicable to naval mines.[16] True, states had developed specific international law to govern naval mines by the time of the *Corfu Channel* case. For example, the Hague Convention VIII of 1907 required states to take "every possible precaution" to render mines harmless and to notify shipowners of the presence of mines off their coasts.[17] But as both the judgment of the court and the dissent observed, the Hague Convention and its regime of precaution and notice applied only during war between state parties.[18] The United Kingdom and Albania were not at war, nor was Albania a party to the convention. As a result, the general duty of diligence cited by the court and alleged by the UK filings was inescapably before the court.

Two recent ICJ cases have confirmed the *Corfu Channel* court's observation on due diligence. In the *Pulp Mills* case, Argentina alleged Uruguay's construction of a pulp mill along a shared river breached both a treaty obligation to prevent harm along the river as well as the latter's duty of due diligence. In its judgment, the court clearly embraced due diligence as a matter of general international law.[19] Although the case implicated a treaty specifically addressed to the situation between the parties, the court observed, regarding general international law: "[T]he principle of prevention, as a customary rule, has its origins in the due diligence that is required of a State in its territory. It is 'every State's obligation not to allow knowingly its territory to be used for acts contrary to the rights of other States.'"[20]

Just five years later, the ICJ revisited due diligence in the *Border Area* case.[21] The case arose from cross claims between Costa Rica and Nicaragua related to dredging and road construction, respectively, along the San Juan River. Each side cited the international law principle of due diligence as well as specific duties under international environmental law. In its judgment, the court reiterated its *Pulp Mills* conclusions on law, reemphasizing that due diligence is a general international law principle and confirming its application to international environmental claims.

Two important points concerning the present state of due diligence can be drawn from these ICJ cases. First, the filings of the several states party to each case demonstrate clear support for the notion of due diligence both in a general international legal sense and in specific contexts of international relations involving transboundary harm. No states party to any of the three cases, nor any justice hearing them, rejected due diligence as either an international legal principle or as a regime-specific rule of conduct. Second, in the two more recent cases, the court not only reaffirmed earlier observations concerning a general duty of due diligence. It also discerned refinements to the duty, most obviously in the form of a duty not merely to suppress ongoing harm but also to prevent it.

Yet significant uncertainty surrounds the obligation of due diligence both as a principle of general international law and in the specific contexts in which it operates as a separate rule. Private organizations and scholars have attempted to elicit greater state attention to these ambiguities. On the heels of the *Pulp Mills* judgment, during proceedings in the *Border Area* litigation, and in response to growing academic and diplomatic attention to the principle of due diligence, the International Law Association (ILA) commissioned a study group "to consider the extent to which there is a commonality of understanding between the distinctive areas of international law in which the concept of due diligence is applied."[22] In a pair of reports, the ILA noted sector-specific iterations of due diligence alongside an "overarching concept of increasing[] relevance in international law."[23] Still, the reports concluded further work was necessary to refine the principle of due diligence and its numerous sector-specific variations.

Cyber Due Diligence

The ILA's conclusion that a "broad principle of due diligence can be understood as underlying more specific rules of due diligence" invites consideration of how due diligence might be applied in the rapidly developing domain of cyberspace.[24] Beginning in 2004, the United Nations (UN) General Assembly convened a Group of Governmental Experts (GGE) for a discussion of this topic: "Developments in the Field of Information and Telecommunications in the Context of International Security." Over time, the GGE has become the leading forum for states to debate, develop, and confirm international regulations and norms of conduct in cyberspace.[25]

In addition to issuing a number of important consensus declarations, including a determination that "[i]nternational law, and in particular the Charter of the United Nations, is applicable and is essential to maintaining peace and stability and promoting an open, secure, peaceful and accessible ICT environment," the GGE has commented on the application of due diligence to the cyber domain.[26] In its most recent consensus document, issued in 2015, the GGE adopted "recommendations for consideration by states for voluntary, non-binding norms, rules or principles of responsible behaviour of states aimed at promoting an open, secure, stable, accessible and peaceful ICT environment."[27] Among those recommendations was the observation that "states should not knowingly allow their territory to be used for internationally wrongful acts using ICTs."[28] This clear recitation of the *Corfu Channel* case's notion of general due diligence stands as a prominent, if aspirational, reference to cyber due diligence.

Other multi-state organizations have more clearly endorsed cyber due diligence as an international legal matter. Most recently, the European Council published a statement concerning "malicious cyber activities exploiting the coronavirus pandemic."[29] The statement noted:

> The European Union and its Member states call upon every country to exercise due diligence and take appropriate actions against actors conducting such activities from its territory, consistent with international law and the 2010, 2013 and 2015 consensus reports of the United Nations Groups of Governmental Experts (UNGGEs) in the field of Information and Telecommunications in the Context of International Security.[30]

Duncan Hollis has also collected views of states on cyber due diligence under the auspices of the Organization of American States in a report titled *International Law and State Cyber Operations: Improving Transparency (Fourth Report)*.[31] Hollis found that Chile, Ecuador, Guatemala, Guyana, and Peru have all agreed that due diligence applies to cyber operations, with Bolivia somewhat more equivocal in its approach.[32] Meanwhile, France, the Netherlands, and Estonia have also expressed support for the obligation of cyber due diligence in detailed public statements.[33]

Private commentators echo these views. For example, the authors of the 2017 *Tallinn Manual on the International Law Applicable to Cyber Operations* note that "[the] due diligence principle has long been reflected in jurisprudence [and] it is a general principle that has been particularized in specialized regimes of international law."[34]

The group further agreed that "[a] State must exercise due diligence in not allowing its territory, or territory or cyber infrastructure under its governmental control, to be used for cyber operations that affect the rights of, and produce serious adverse consequences for, other States."[35]

The willingness of select states, international organizations, and private commentators to extract from international law a rule on cyber due diligence seems indicative of trends respecting due diligence in other domains of international relations. However, there are signs of dissent as well. After his survey of views, including those of states that expressed positive views, Hollis concluded that "there are competing views on whether due diligence is a requirement of international law in cyberspace," and there is not yet a consensus among states on how the due diligence principle will apply in the sector-specific area of cyber operations.[36] Thus, despite more than a century of repeated confirmation by accepted sources of international law, there remain signs that some states harbor reservations about due diligence and how, if at all, the principle applies to cyberspace.

US Approaches to Due Diligence

The United States and General Due Diligence

The United States played a conspicuous role in the early development of due diligence as a principle of international law. From the mid-nineteenth century to the mid-twentieth century, the United States was involved in three prominent disputes involving early conceptions of the duty of due diligence. In this same period, the US Supreme Court accepted international law notions of due diligence as well. In each case, the US government cited or acknowledged breach of due diligence as a freestanding cause of action or international law obligation. Yet today, the US position on due diligence is unclear. In his report, Hollis evaluated US legal policy toward due diligence specifically. He surmised:

> [T]he United States has tended to describe any obligations to respond to requests for assistance in non-binding terms. The lack of any public US

endorsement of due diligence as a legal rule in either the GGE context or elsewhere may be indicative of US doubts as to its legal status.[37]

This recent US hesitance with respect to due diligence warrants a review of US diplomatic practice and outcomes relating to the concept.

The US experience with due diligence extends to the early days of the republic. In 1837, during an insurrection in Canada against the British, Canadian rebels hired a US-flagged steamer, the *Caroline*, to deliver supplies from the United States across the Niagara River. Unsatisfied with the response to its complaints about the United States' failure to stem the flow of supplies to the Canadian rebels, Great Britain took matters into its own hands and destroyed the *Caroline*.[38] The incident generated a now famous legal correspondence between the US government and Great Britain. Because the Canadian rebels had not met the conditions of belligerency, the United States had not declared itself to be a neutral party and therefore did not incur the obligations a neutral state owes to belligerents in a conflict. Thus the United States' failure to cut off rebel supply chains could not be characterized as a breach of neutrality. Instead, the *Caroline* incident involved a general, peacetime duty of due diligence in the form of a freestanding obligation independent of duties relating to neutrality or any other sector-specific rule of international law. In their diplomatic resolution of the dispute, the parties agreed: "[A]ll that can be expected from either government in these cases is good faith, a sincere desire to preserve peace and do justice, [and] the use of *all proper means of prevention*."[39]

A further episode involving international law due diligence arose between the United States and Great Britain during the American Civil War. Although Great Britain declared its neutrality early in the conflict, British-built ships supplied to the Confederacy sank more than 150 Union merchant ships around the world. After protracted and heated diplomatic exchanges, the United States and Great Britain agreed to resolve US claims from the sinkings at an ad hoc international tribunal known as the *Alabama* arbitration. Among other claims, the United States alleged that Great Britain's failure to seize the ships amounted to a breach of due diligence.

Although the law of neutrality seemed to offer an adequate and relevant legal ground on which to address the situation, both the parties and the tribunal resorted to the international law principle of due diligence to resolve the US claims. In the treaty that formed the tribunal, the United States and Great Britain agreed:

A neutral Government is bound—

First, to use due diligence to prevent the fitting out, arming, or equipping, within its jurisdiction, of any vessel which it has reasonable ground to
believe is intended to cruise or to carry on war against a Power with which
it is at peace; and also to use like diligence to prevent the departure from its
jurisdiction of any vessel intended to cruise or carry on war as above, such
vessel having been specially adapted, in whole or in part, within such jurisdiction, to warlike use. . . .

Thirdly, to exercise due diligence in its own ports and waters, and, as to
all persons within its jurisdiction, to prevent any violation of the foregoing
obligations and duties.[40]

The tribunal unanimously concluded that Great Britain had violated its duty
of diligence as a neutral state and awarded the United States $15 million in
damages. Importantly, the tribunal did not attribute construction or transfer
of the ships to the British government as acts of state.[41] Instead, it found
that Great Britain had "failed, by omission, to fulfil the duties" of a neutral
state.[42] Although frequently regarded as a narrow ruling on the obligations
of neutral states during armed conflict, the tribunal's decision also stands as
an early articulation of states' general international obligations with respect
to due diligence. The tribunal based its legal conclusions on the Treaty of
Washington but also cited "principles of international law."[43] In this respect,
the tribunal appears to have adopted the US position that "a reasonable
ground [for believing that an international law violation might occur] . . . is
an element of the question of *due diligence* always fairly to be considered"
in judging the conduct of states and the extent of their knowledge of harm
emanating from their territory.[44] Guided by the parties' own consensus
statements of law codified in a treaty, the tribunal clearly framed British conduct as both a breach of its due diligence duty to safeguard other states against
harm emanating from its own territory as well as a failing of neutrality. The
tribunal, at the repeated urging of the United States, laid the groundwork for
due diligence as a general and freestanding obligation of conduct in international law.

No doubt inspired by the *Alabama* arbitration, the Supreme Court of the
United States soon recognized the legal principle of due diligence as well.
In 1887, the court upheld a federal statute prohibiting the counterfeiting
of foreign financial instruments.[45] Citing de Vattel's *The Law of Nations*,
the court identified both a specific international law prohibition on

tolerating counterfeiters as well as a general international law duty of due diligence to cease and redress such harm. The court held that Congress had authority to enact the statute under its power to define the law of nations, in this case the duty of due diligence. The court observed: "The law of nations requires every national government to use 'due diligence' to prevent a wrong being done within its own dominion to another nation with which it is at peace, or to the people thereof."[46] A breach of due diligence with respect to counterfeiting, the court noted, "may not, perhaps, furnish sufficient cause for war, but it would certainly give just ground of complaint."[47]

Finally, in 1937, the United States returned to international arbitration and to due diligence to address pollution from the Canadian zinc smelter at Trail, British Columbia, near the border with Washington State. The treaty that committed the issue to the tribunal instructed the arbitrators to apply US law as well as "international law and practice."[48] After confirming that pollution from the smelter caused extensive damage to US farms and forests, the tribunal issued two decisions. The first came in 1938, in an opinion that applied US tort law to calculate and award damages to the United States. The first opinion also held that Canada had a duty to the United States to cease polluting and refrain from permitting future harm. In addition, it ordered the installation of mitigation measures and pollution detectors, but it cited no international legal authority.

In the second decision, issued in 1941 and relying on readings from the pollution detectors, the tribunal returned to the question of a Canadian duty of due diligence to cease harm. The tribunal announced that "under the principles of international law . . . no State has the right to use or permit the use of its territory in such a manner as to cause injury by fumes in or to the territory of another."[49] Quoting a then contemporary treatise on state responsibility, the tribunal also noted:

> "A State owes at all times a duty to protect other states against injurious acts by individuals from within its jurisdiction." A great number of such general pronouncements by leading authorities concerning the duty of a State to respect other states and their territory have been presented to the Tribunal. These and many others have been carefully examined. International decisions, in various matters, from the Alabama case onward, and also earlier ones, are based on the same general principle, and, indeed, this principle, as such, has not been questioned by Canada. But the real difficulty

often arises rather when it comes to determine what, *pro subjecta materie*, is deemed to constitute an injurious act.[50]

Addressing the relevant threshold of harm, the tribunal held that principles of international law identified a "serious consequence . . . established by clear and convincing evidence" as the relevant injury threshold for purposes of diligence.[51]

The significance of early US legal and diplomatic encounters with the principle of due diligence is clear on several points. First, on three occasions in its international legal relations, and in its domestic law as upheld by its highest court, the United States relied on or confirmed a general duty of due diligence with respect to harm emanating from a state's territory. From the early nineteenth century through the middle of the twentieth century, the United States steadfastly supported a general duty of territorial due diligence. Second, in two momentous international arbitrations, breach of due diligence claims successfully vindicated significant US national and private interests. In both the *Alabama* and *Trail Smelter* arbitrations, international tribunals adopted US arguments about due diligence and used these arguments to justify substantial awards under international law.

And finally, in all three international legal episodes, the vindication of due diligence claims contributed to a peaceful resolution of diplomatic tension between powerful states. In each case, due diligence operated as a sort of relief valve in international relations. The *Alabama* claims arose in the highly charged context of recognition by Great Britain of a condition of belligerency between the northern Union and the southern Confederacy. Paired with this diplomatic and international legal insult, the harm resulting from British-built ships to US merchant fleets nearly brought the parties to war. Broader political and economic considerations perhaps best explain how the United States and Great Britain avoided war. Yet the availability of a claim for breach of due diligence based on mere omissions to give rise to liability for an internationally wrongful act may also have played a part in the peaceful and successful resolution of the *Alabama* claims. Casting British conduct as a failure of due diligence permitted the United States to raise the issue early, in effect freezing the facts of the dispute and reducing the likelihood of escalatory exchanges of retorsions or even reprisals.

Similarly, although damage from the Trail smelter significantly soured US-Canadian relations for more than a decade, the fact that the United States alleged a lapse of diligence—an omission or oversight rather than an affirmative act that intended harm—may explain the successful and peaceful resolution of the issue. Again, the nature of a due diligence breach as a lapse of oversight and control rather than as a deliberate harm or a form of imputed responsibility may have played a part in the peaceful and successful resolution of the claims.

These legal and diplomatic precedents warrant consideration in present and future US perspectives on due diligence generally. The nascent US misgivings concerning due diligence detected by Hollis suggest a change from the United States' historical legal and diplomatic embrace of the principle. Whether the law and conditions that informed prior US practice with respect to due diligence have changed sufficiently to warrant this shift is relevant to the formation of US legal policy. Similarly, whether US security interests, including those identified in the US Defend Forward strategy, call for a change in policy toward due diligence is worthy of examination.

As noted previously, although legally distinct from each other, the general international law principle of due diligence and various regime-specific expressions of due diligence have experienced a developmental cross-pollination of sorts. Clearly the broader principle of due diligence has inspired and informed more specific notions of the concept. Meanwhile, doctrinal elaborations, originally developed for specific contexts of international interaction, have found their way into academic and even judicial descriptions of the general principle of due diligence. For instance, although the regime-specific notion of prevention of harm presents most clearly in international environmental law, it has featured in a number of prominent articulations of the general obligation of due diligence. Such accounts of the due diligence principle recite a general, as opposed to a merely regime-specific, duty on the part of states to prevent rather than just respond to and cease transboundary harm. To preserve the traditional, unembellished principle of due diligence (i.e., without the gloss imported from particularized applications), the United States might reject refinements such as a duty of prevention or a threshold of harm lower than what has traditionally been required for a breach, reserving such questions for regime-specific incarnations of the principle.

The United States and Cyber Due Diligence

As detailed above, the United States has remained conspicuously silent on the application of due diligence to cyberspace. Although the United States joined the 2015 UN GGE consensus document stating that "States should not knowingly allow their territory to be used for internationally wrongful acts using ICTs," this statement was couched in terms of voluntary, non-binding recommen`1ons.[52] Moreover, in its submissions to both the 2013 and 2015 UN GGEs, the United States evidently made no assertions as to the application of due diligence to cyber activities.

Likewise, none of the recent US government statements on cyber operations has expressly and unequivocally embraced a doctrine of cyber due diligence. For example, the 2018 National Cyber Strategy does not comment on due diligence.[53] While subsequent cyber strategy employed by the Department of Defense briefly recites the due diligence principle, noting recent international consensus on a prohibition "against allowing national territory to be used for intentionally wrongful cyber activity," it does not announce any conclusion on the role of cyber due diligence in US policy.[54] Nor does it indicate how breaches of due diligence by adverse actors might justify US cyber responses under the Defend Forward strategy. In the recent Cyberspace Solarium Commission report, the commission had the opportunity to endorse due diligence as a means of fixing legal responsibility for harm to US interests both at home and abroad, but it did not do so. A statement to that effect would have been an important step in supporting the Defend Forward approach to national security, but the commission did not take it.[55]

It is unclear at this point if the lack of comment on cyber due diligence was an intentional decision or simply reflected a lack of full consideration by the government. Importantly, future US legal policy toward due diligence generally may not mirror in all respects policy toward cyber due diligence. As preceding sections have demonstrated, due diligence has lived something resembling two lives in international law: one as a general provision of international law, and another as a sector-specific notion tailored to the norms and demands of various domains and conditions of international relations. While the rejection of a general principle of due diligence and embrace of cyber due diligence would seem inconsistent, the same would not be true if the United States supported the general principle and rejected its application to cyber activities. As argued next, the DoD specifically, and the United States more broadly, ought to accept a tailored doctrine of cyber due diligence and advocate its adoption throughout the international community.

Cyber Due Diligence and Defending Forward

In a recent speech, the Honorable Paul C. Ney, general counsel of the DoD, described the Defend Forward strategy. He explained:

> A key element of the US military's strategy in the face of these cyber-threats is to "defend forward." Implementing this element of the strategy begins with continuously engaging and contesting adversaries and causing them uncertainty wherever they maneuver—which we refer to as "persistent engagement." Persistent engagement recognizes that cyberspace's structural feature of interconnectedness and its core condition of constant contact creates a strategic necessity to operate continuously in cyberspace. As General [Paul M.] Nakasone has said, "If we find ourselves defending inside our own networks, we have lost the initiative and the advantage." In short, the strategy envisions that our military cyber forces will be conducting operations in cyberspace to disrupt and defeat malicious cyber activity that is harmful to US national interests.[56]

The United States has thus concluded that operating outside of domestic cyber infrastructure is essential to effectively respond to significant cyber harm and to preserve national security. The strategy clearly indicates that the United States will maintain a presence and conduct operations in cyber networks outside its own borders, on the sovereign territory of other states. Although neither the strategy itself nor Ney's remarks expressly couples Defend Forward with specific international legal justifications, it is clear that Persistent Engagement on foreign networks requires such legal work. Due diligence, particularly as expressed in past US diplomatic and legal practice, presents an enticing legal basis to support operations that respond to harm emanating from foreign networks and cyber infrastructure.

Endorsing cyber due diligence would provide a number of direct and immediate benefits to the Defend Forward approach. First, legal and technical attribution have always been vexing in the cyber context. The internet facilitates anonymity, at least in the short term, and allows states and nonstate actors to operate without fear of immediate accountability. Further, the legal regime of state responsibility sets a high bar for attributing the actions of no-nstate proxy actors to states themselves.[57] In fact, it is likely that the difficulties associated with attribution in cyberspace motivated the

US Defend Forward strategy. We have previously addressed this subject and argued:

> [A] primary rule of conduct requiring diligent management of territorial cyber infrastructure could give rise to responsibility on the part of nondiligent states as proxies for unidentified or unreachable malicious actors. Legal recognition of such breaches of diligence permits State victims of cyber harm to take action to induce compliance and terminate harm without necessarily tracing attribution to the original, difficult-to-identify source.[58]

In other words, reaffirming and clarifying the duty of due diligence would permit the United States to hold territorial states responsible for transboundary cyber harms and react using self-help measures, regardless of whether the United States could accurately identify the actual source of the harm—whether the government of the territorial state itself, a state proxy, or a non-connected entity or individual. Such an approach, appropriately applied, would relieve the United States, and other states, of significant forensic difficulties and dramatically strengthen accountability across the international community.

Additionally, endorsing due diligence would support the GGE process of clarifying cyber obligations under international law. Due diligence did receive a mention, though aspirational, in the GGE's 2015 consensus document. The participating states, including cyber superpowers, offered "recommendations for consideration by states for voluntary, non-binding norms, rules or principles of responsible behaviour of states aimed at promoting an open, secure, stable, accessible and peaceful ICT environment."[59] By reaffirming the principle of due diligence and clarifying its approach in cyberspace, the United States would not only set a marker for the international community during norm development. It would also provide notice to allies and adversaries alike of US intentions as they formulate their own approaches to this question, including their reactions to the US Defend Forward policy.

These considerations provide ample reason for the United States to embrace cyber due diligence as a legal justification for its Defend Forward approach to national security. However, skepticism remains among other nations concerning the general application of due diligence to cyber operations. For example, Israel's deputy attorney general, Roy Schondorf, recently stated that the 2015 UN GGE Report described due diligence as a non-binding, voluntary norm to purposely reflect that it was not "a binding rule of International law in the cyber context."[60] He continued that "we have not seen widespread State practice beyond this type of voluntary cooperation, and certainly not practice grounded in some overarching opinio juris, which would be indispensable for a customary rule of due diligence, or something similar to that, to form."[61]

Acknowledging this skepticism, as the United States crafts its international legal policy toward due diligence, four doctrinal aspects deserve special consideration. First, some recitations of cyber due diligence have included an obligation to proactively monitor and prevent transboundary harmful activities. This is not the prevailing approach and should not be the approach the United States adopts. Rather, the United States should make clear that neither the general principle of due diligence nor any obligation of cyber-specific due diligence includes a duty to monitor and prevent. Second, any endorsement of cyber due diligence should require a threshold of harm amounting to "serious adverse consequences" before liability attaches. Third, acceptance of cyber due diligence should be understood only to require feasible measures on the part of territorial states. Finally, the United States should bear in mind and warn of the potential escalatory nature of cyber due diligence—particularly with respect to the potential use of countermeasures—and take affirmative steps to build safeguards against such danger.

In addition to the basic due diligence duty that states quell harm emanating from their territories, some sources have referred to an ex ante duty to prevent such harm from starting in the first place. Under a sector-specific conception of due diligence, some advocates of cyber due diligence have argued that this means states have a duty to monitor and prevent transboundary cyber harms. The ICJ, for instance, has repeatedly endorsed a duty to exercise due diligence to prevent transboundary harm in the international environmental law context.[62] By contrast, the *Tallinn Manual 2.0* drafters did not identify a duty to monitor and prevent transboundary cyber harms. They agreed that the duty of due diligence extends to cyberspace but indicated that this duty "is not to be interpreted as including a requirement of monitoring or taking other steps designed to alert authorities to misuse of cyber infrastructure located on the State's territory."[63] Indeed, the drafters concluded that "it would be unreasonable to assert that an obligation of prevention exists in the cyber context[;] [s]uch a requirement would impose an undue burden on States, one for which there is no current basis in either the extant law or current State practice."[64] They noted inadequate evidence that states had expressed either in statements or practice a sense of legal obligation to take preventive measures. Nor had states legally condemned failures to take preventive measures.

In addition to their practical and precedential reasons for rejecting a duty of prevention, states have not adopted this duty out of a concern that "obligations of States under international human rights law could run counter to such a duty, depending on how it was fulfilled."[65] For example, an authoritarian state might monitor electronic communications, allowing the repression or censorship of unfriendly or politically non-supportive communications, under the guise of the duty to prevent transboundary harm. The United States, in adopting a duty of cyber due diligence, should be clear that this duty does not justify a country's monitoring all cyber communications within its territory, nor does it provide any excuse for potential human rights (or more likely domestic constitutional) violations.

In the same regard, the United States might dampen the obligation of cyber due diligence by indicating that not all cyber harm triggers it. To this end, the United States should advocate a relatively high threshold of harm as a prerequisite to a breach of due diligence. The United States has already expressed support for this view in multiple contexts, including in the 2018 National Cyber Strategy, which lists one of the DoD's cyberspace objectives as "[d]efending U.S. critical infrastructure from malicious cyber activity that alone, or as part of a campaign, could cause a *significant* cyber incident."[66] The document then defines a "significant cyber incident" as "an event occurring on or conducted through a computer network that is . . . likely to result in demonstrable harm to the national security interests, foreign relations, or economy of the United States or to the public confidence, civil liberties, or public health and safety of the American people."[67]

The *Tallinn Manual 2.0* drafters agreed that a high threshold of harm was a prerequisite for the onset of the due diligence obligation in cyber operations. They further noted:

> The precise threshold of harm at which the due diligence principle applies is unsettled in international law. All of the Experts agreed that the due diligence requirement arises when the situation involves a cyber operation that results in "serious adverse consequences", [*sic*] although they could identify no bright line threshold for the identification of such consequences.[68]

By simultaneously embracing a duty of cyber due diligence and making clear that the duty is subject to a threshold of harm such as "serious adverse consequences," the United States can help ensure that the duty is appropriately circumscribed while preserving operational prerogative with respect to the kinds of minimally intrusive operations the Defend Forward strategy envisions.

Some detractors of the due diligence obligation argue that the standard of conduct is too high and will impose unachievable demands on states. A robust conception of due diligence, such as that emerging in the context of international environmental law, might indeed implicate this concern. However, consistent with international precedent (including the US experience), the *Tallinn Manual 2.0* requires that a state have actual or constructive knowledge of transboundary harm before a due diligence obligation attaches.[69] With respect to Defend Forward operations, the United States should not be required to have conclusive or even direct evidence that a territorial state had knowledge of the harm coming from its territory in order for a breach of due diligence assertion to be applicable on the part of that state. Circumstantial or indirect evidence should suffice. The requirement of knowledge, combined with the lack of an obligation to monitor or prevent harm ex ante, removes some of the affirmative obligations sometimes associated with due diligence. These limits on the due diligence principle would also place states in a position of potentially cooperative remediation, particularly in the face of non-state cyber activities. If the United States adopts cyber due diligence, it should do so with the same caveats.

Once knowledge is established, due diligence requires a state to take actions to cease or put a stop to the transboundary harm. This might also seem like a potentially arduous standard for states to achieve, even for the United States, with its immense technological resources and capabilities. However, again in accord with the *Tallinn Manual 2.0*, the standard is not one of strict liability. States are only required to take feasible actions necessary to prevent further harm.[70] In this context, feasibility is understood to mean that which is practicable or practically possible. In other words, a state with knowledge of harm emanating from its territory must take feasible actions to try to cease further harm, but it is not required to take all possible actions. If the United States embraces the principle of cyber due diligence, it should likewise clarify for both the international community and its allies and partners that feasibility is the appropriate standard for compliance.

Finally, the United States should draw particular attention to the potentially escalatory nature of responses to failures to exercise cyber due diligence and take affirmative steps to guard against such danger. If an obligation of cyber due diligence is adopted as an international norm, failure to honor the obligation would amount to an internationally wrongful act, allowing the victim state to respond with countermeasures. Cyber countermeasures are adapting to modern state interaction, and continue to provide a very effective tool to encourage violating states toresume compliance with international law.[71] However, aggressive countermeasures also risk escalation and instability.[72] Because countermeasures are adapting alongside cyber capabilities, the United States should engage with like-minded members of the international community to appropriately limit countermeasures in response to cyber offenses as part of its Defend Forward strategy.

The obligation of cyber due diligence and the approach advocated here are not without significant potential drawbacks for the United States. For example, the United States is among the leading countries of origin for transnational cyber hacks.[73] The United States' extensive computer infrastructure is also a desirable target for establishing botnets controlled from outside the United States. McAfee recently reported that the United States was host to more botnets than Russia and China combined.[74]

Both of these facts have significant implications for the United States' adoption of due diligence obligations. Because so much transboundary harm originates from within the United States, victim states would be able to invoke United States failures of diligence and take appropriate actions based on that attribution. Even given the "serious adverse consequences" and "feasibility" limitations discussed above, the sheer volume of transboundary harm emanating from the United States would impose a significant remediation requirement on the government.

Despite these potential issues, we still recommend that the United States endorse due diligence in the manner described above. It is our view that the benefits from adopting cyber due diligence, in an appropriately limited form, would result in greater gains than drawbacks for the United States. Adoption of cyber due diligence obligations would provide meaningful benefits, including but not limited to adding clarity for state practice, accelerated norm development, and a partial resolution to the issue of cyber attribution.

Conclusion

The Defend Forward strategy clearly communicates an evolution in the US approach to emerging threats in cyberspace. No longer content to merely fortify domestic networks and infrastructure, the United States envisions a proactive and externally focused response regime. US reactions to harm emanating from foreign territory will likely include persistent, non-consensual operations on foreign government and private cyber infrastructure. Perhaps just as important as the technical effects of these responses is the fact that the United States has put the world on notice regarding its intent to undertake them. The strategy is not just an administrative instruction to US agencies. It is a deliberate strategic message to US competitors and adversaries in cyberspace.

Threats in cyberspace and US reactions to those threats call for equally clear and effective legal messaging. To be credible to both adversaries and allies, the US cyber strategy requires sound, unambiguous legal justifications. Among other international law provisions relevant to cyberspace, due diligence offers promising legal support for Defend Forward operations. Confronted with harm emanating from foreign territory, states have resorted to due diligence for both legal redress and to justify self-help responses. In many cases, the non-consensual and intrusive cyber operations that likely form the core of the Defend Forward strategy could be justified as measures of self-help undertaken in response to breaches of due diligence.

However, there is increasing evidence that the US position on due diligence is at least circumspect and at worst cynical. The United States should carefully evaluate these views and their motives. There is extraordinarily strong support among a variety of accepted sources of international law for due diligence as a freestanding obligation of state conduct. Extensive and consistent US foreign relations practice played a critical role in the formation of this norm, and throughout its history, the United States has enjoyed peaceful and profitable diplomatic outcomes by invoking the due diligence doctrine. In light of this experience and the promising legal utility of cyber due diligence to the Defend Forward strategy, the United States should endorse due diligence as a general obligation of international law. Further, it should clearly express the legal duties as well as the doctrinal limits associated with due diligence in cyberspace. A clearly defined US legal policy toward due diligence, incorporating the provisions outlined in this chapter, will both support the vital US security interests identified in its cyber strategy and reassert influence on a critical component of the regulation of modern international relations.

Notes

1. US Dep't of Defense, Summary: Department of Defense Cyber Strategy 2018, at 1 (2018) [hereinafter 2018 Strategy Summary]. Only a summary of the strategy is available publicly. Presumably, the full strategy is circulated in government as a classified document.
2. *Id.* at 2.
3. *Id.* at 1.
4. Commentators also refer to a "no harm principle" in this respect. *See* Timo Koivurova, *Due Diligence, in* Max Planck Encyclopedia of Public International Law ¶¶ 2, 11 (Rüdiger Wolfrum ed. 2010).
5. *See* Ashley Deeks, "Defend Forward and Cyber Countermeasures," Hoover Working Group on National Security, Technology, and Law, Aegis Series Paper No. 2004 (examining countermeasures and associated doctrinal limits as a legal facet of the US Defend Forward strategy), August 4, 2020.
6. *See* Eric Talbot Jensen and Sean Watts, *A Cyber Duty of Due Diligence: Gentle Civilizer or Crude Destabilizer?*, 95 Tex. L. Rev. 1555, 1557–58 (2017).
7. *See* Duncan B. Hollis, International Law and State Cyber Operations: Improving Transparency: Fourth Report 24–26 (2020).
8. *See e.g.*, Greg Lynham, *The Sic Utere Principle as Customary International Law: A Case of Wishful Thinking*, 2 James Cook U. L. Rev. 172, 184–86 (1995).
9. Jutta Brunnée, *Sic utere tuo ut alienum non laedas, in* Max Planck Encyclopedia of Public International Law (Rüdiger Wolfrum ed. 2010).
10. Robert Phillimore, 1 Commentaries upon International Law xxi (2d ed. 1871).
11. Lassa Oppenheim, 1 International Law: A Treatise 203, 211 (1905).
12. Hersch Lauterpacht, Private Law Sources and Analogies of International Law 217 (1927) (internal citation omitted).
13. In the 1925 *British Claims in the Spanish Zone of Morocco* arbitration, Max Huber ruled that a state that "failed to exercise due diligence in preventing or punishing the unlawful actions of armed groups could be held responsible for such failure." British Claims in the Spanish Zone of Morocco (Gr. Brit. v. Spain), 2 R.I.A.A. 617, 642–46 (1925).
14. Corfu Channel (U.K. v. Alb.), Merits, 1949 I.C.J. Rep. 4, 10 (Apr. 9).
15. *Id.* at 22.
16. *Cf.* Jörg Schildknecht, *Belligerent Rights and Obligations in International Straits, in* Operational Law in International Straits and Current Maritime Security Challenges 78 (Jörg Schildknecht et al., eds., 2018).

17. Convention Relative to the Laying of Automatic Submarine Contact Mines (Hague No. VIII), art. 3–4, Oct. 18, 1907, 36 Stat. 2332.

18. *Corfu Channel*, 1949 I.C.J. Rep. at 78, 84 (dissenting opinion of Azevedo, J.); *see also* Memorial Submitted of United Kingdom, *Corfu Channel*, 1949 I.C.J. Pleadings at 19, 36–38 (Sept. 30).

19. Pulp Mills on the River Uruguay (Arg. v. Uru.), Judgment, 2010 I.C.J. Rep. 14, ¶ 101, 197 (Apr. 20). Ultimately the Court did not find Uruguay had breached its duty of diligence as a matter of fact. *Id.* at ¶ 265.

20. *Id.* at ¶ 101 (quoting *Corfu Channel*, 1949 I.C.J. Rep. at 22).

21. Certain Activities Carried Out by Nicaragua in the Border Area (Costa Rica v. Nicar.), Judgment, 2015 I.C.J. Rep. 665 (Dec. 16).

22. ILA, ILA Study Group on Due Diligence in International Law: First Report 1 (2014).

23. ILA, ILA Study Group on Due Diligence in International Law: Second Report 47 (2016).

24. *Id.* at 6.

25. Anders Henriksen, *The End of the Road for the UN GGE Process: The Future Regulation of Cyberspace*, J. Cyber Sec., 1–2 (2019) (quoting Martha Finnemore & Kathryn Sikkink, *International Norm Dynamics and Political Change*, 52 Int Org. 887, 896 [1998]).

26. Group of Governmental Experts on Developments in the Field of Information and Telecommunications in the Context of International Security, ¶ 19, UN Doc. A/68/98 (June 24, 2013).

27. Group of Governmental Experts on Developments in the Field of Information and Telecommunications in the Context of International Security, ¶ 13, UN Doc. A/70/174 (July 22, 2015) [hereinafter 2015 UN GGE Report].

28. *Id.*

29. European Council and Council of the EU, "Declaration by the High Representative Josep Borrell, on Behalf of the European Union, On Malicious Cyber Activities Exploiting the Coronavirus Pandemic" press release, August 12, 2020.

30. *Id.*

31. Hollis, *supra* note 7, at 24–26.

32. *Id.* at 25.

33. Ministry of the Armies, International Law Applicable to Operations in Cyberspace 10 (2019) (Fr.); Letter from the Minister of Foreign Affairs to the President of the House of Representatives, Letter to the Parliament on the International Legal Order in Cyberspace, Appendix at 4 (Jul. 5, 2019) (Neth.); Kersti Kaljulaid, President, The Republic of Estonia, Speech at the Opening of the International Conference on Cyber Conflict (CyCon) 2019 (May 29, 2019).

34. Tallinn Manual 2.0 on the International Law Applicable to Cyber Operations 31 (Rule 6) cmt. 4 (Michael N. Schmitt ed., 2d ed. 2017) [hereinafter Tallinn Manual 2.0]. Both authors were members of the international group of experts who drafted the Tallinn Manual. The general editor of the Tallinn Manual has also written separately on due diligence in cyberspace. *See* Michael N. Schmitt, *In Defense of Due Diligence in Cyberspace*, 125 Yale L.J.F. 68 (2015).

35. TALLINN MANUAL 2.0, *supra* note 34, at 30 (Rule 6).

36. HOLLIS, *supra* note 7, at 20.

37. *Id.* at 25–26.

38. *See* JOHN BASSETT MOORE, 7 A DIGEST OF INTERNATIONAL LAW 919–20 (1906) (describing the incident and the US secretary of state's instructions to district attorneys in northern states to abstain from involvement in the rebellion); *see also* MAURICE G. BAXTER, ONE AND INSEPARABLE: DANIEL WEBSTER AND THE UNION 321 (1984) (describing President Van Buren's strict policy of neutrality in the rebellion).

39. Elizabeth Chadwick, *The British View of Neutrality in 1872, in* NOTIONS OF NEUTRALITIES 87, 93 (Pascal Lottaz & Herbert R. Reginbogin eds., 2019) (emphasis added). In response to the incident, the United States amended its domestic neutrality laws to better authorize federal interventions and seizures. *Id.* at 93 (citing Act of March 10, 1838, Ch. 31, 5 Stat. 212); *see also* BASSETT MOORE, *supra* note 40, at 920 (describing events, including a request from President Van Buren, leading to amendment of US neutrality laws).

40. Treaty of Washington, US-U.K., art. VI, May 8, 1871, 17 Stat. 863, T.S. No. 13

41. *See generally* Ala. Claims Arbitration (US v. Gr. Brit.) 29 R.I.A.A. 125 (1872).

42. *Id.* at 131.

43. *Id.* at 129, 132.

44. William Evarts, *Counsel of the United States, Argument Addressed to the Tribunal of Arbitration at Geneva, on the 5th and 6th August 1872, in Reply to the Special Argument of the Counsel of Her Britannic Majesty,* SUPPLEMENT TO THE LONDON GAZETTE, Oct. 4, 1872, at 4643.

45. *United States v. Arjona,* 120 US 479 (1887).

46. *Id.* at 484.

47. *Id.* at 487.

48. Convention for the Final Settlement of the Difficulties Arising through Complaints of Damage Done in the State of Washington by Fumes Discharged from: The Smelter of the Consolidated Mining and Smelting Company, Trail, British Columbia, US-Can., art. IV, Apr. 15, 1935, 162 L.N.T.S 73.

49. Trail Smelter Arbitration (US v. Can.), 3 R.I.A.A. 1905, 1965 (1941).

50. *Id.* at 1963 (quoting CLYDE EAGLETON, RESPONSIBILITY OF STATES IN INTERNATIONAL LAW 80 [1928]).

51. *Id.* at 1965.

52. 2015 UN GGE Report, *supra* note 27, at ¶ 13(c).

53. *See* OFFICE OF THE PRESIDENT, NATIONAL CYBER STRATEGY OF THE UNITED STATES OF AMERICA (2018).

54. 2018 STRATEGY SUMMARY, *supra* note 1, at 5.

55. US CYBER SOLARIUM COMMISSION, FINAL REPORT (2020).

56. Hon. Paul C. Ney Jr., Gen. Counsel, Dep't of Defense, DOD General Counsel Remarks at the US Cyber Command Legal Conference (Mar. 2, 2020) (some internal quotations omitted).

57. Int'l L. Comm'n, Rep. of the Int'l Law Comm'n on the Work of Its Fifty-Third Session, Draft Articles on Responsibility of states for Internationally Wrongful Acts, art. 8, UN Doc. A/56/10, at 47 (2001).

58. Jensen and Watts, *supra* note 6, at 1558.

59. 2015 UN GGE Report, *supra* note 27, at ¶ 13.

60. Roy Schondorf, Israeli Deputy Attorney General (International Law), Keynote Address at the U.S. Naval War College conference on Disruptive Technologies and International Law: Israel's Perspective on Key Legal and Practical Issues Concerning the Applications of International Law to Cyber Operations (Dec. 9, 2020).

61. *Id.*

62. *See, e.g.,* Pulp Mills on the River Uruguay (Arg. v. Uru.), Judgment, 2010 I.C.J. Rep. 14, ¶ 101 (Apr. 20).

63. The *Tallinn Manual 2.0* states: "A State must exercise due diligence in not allowing its territory, or territory or cyber infrastructure under its governmental control, to be used for cyber operations that affect the rights of, and produce serious adverse consequences for, other states." TALLINN MANUAL 2.0, *supra* note 34, at 30 (Rule 6); *Id.* at 42 (Rule 6) cmt. 42.

64. *Id.* at 45 (Rule 7) cmt. 8.

65. *Id.*

66. 2018 STRATEGY SUMMARY, *supra* note 1, at 3 (emphasis added).

67. *Id.* at 3, n. 3 (internal citation omitted).

68. TALLINN MANUAL 2.0, *supra* note 34, at 36–37 (Rule 6) cmt. 25.

69. *Id.* at 40 (Rule 6) cmts. 37–39.

70. *Id.* at 43 (Rule 7).

71. *See generally* Deeks, *supra* note 5.

72. Jensen and Watts, *supra* note 6, at 1569–74.

73. *Top 10 Countries with Most Hackers in the World,* CYWARE SOCIAL (Sept. 7, 2016); *The Top 5 Countries Where Cyber Attacks Originate From,* ARK SYSTEMS (Mar. 16, 2017).

74. Emil Protalinski, *McAfee: US Hosts More Botnet Servers than Any Other Country, More than Russia and China Combined,* TNW, January 24, 2013.

11

Defend Forward and Attribution

Kristen E. Eichensehr

Introduction

When a state seeks to defend itself against a cyberattack, must it first identify the perpetrator responsible? The US policy of "Defend Forward" and "Persistent Engagement" in cyberspace raises the stakes of this attribution question as a matter of both international and domestic law.

International law addresses in part the question of when attribution is required. The international law on state responsibility permits a state that has suffered an internationally wrongful act to take countermeasures, but only against the state responsible. This limitation implies that attribution is a necessary prerequisite to countermeasures. But international law is silent about whether attribution is required for lesser responses, which may be more common. Moreover, even if states agree that attribution is required in order to take countermeasures, ongoing disagreements about whether certain actions, especially violations of sovereignty, count as internationally wrongful acts are likely to spark disputes about when states must attribute cyberattacks in order to respond lawfully.

Under domestic US law, attributing a cyberattack to a particular state bolsters the authority of the executive branch to take action. Congress has authorized the executive to respond to attacks from particular countries and non-state actors in both recent cyber-specific statutory provisions and the long-standing Authorizations for Use of Military Force (AUMFs) related to 9/11 and the Iraq War. Attribution to one of these congressionally designated sources of attack ensures that the executive branch need not rely solely on the president's independent constitutional authority as commander in chief when responding, but instead can act with the combined authority of Congress and the president.[1]

Common across international and US law is the fact that cyberattack attribution serves as both a potential source of empowerment and a potential constraint on governmental action. In both systems, attribution of a cyberattack to another state bolsters the US executive branch's authority to respond, and conversely, the absence of attribution can place the executive on less certain legal footing.

This chapter proceeds in three parts. It first explains cyberattack attribution and attribution's interaction with existing international law on the use of force and state responsibility. The next section turns to the US Defend Forward policy and explores how it may spur disagreements about when states must attribute cyberattacks, even if they agree on the general legal framework set out in the first part. The chapter then briefly addresses US domestic law and explains how congressional authorizations for certain military actions depend on attribution. The conclusion discusses how attribution can shape, not just be shaped by, the international and domestic legal systems.

Attribution and International Law

Cyberattack attribution is the process of assigning responsibility for the commission of a cyberattack.[2] Attribution has technical, legal, and policy aspects, and it can proceed at different levels. Cyberattack attributors might identify one or some combination of (1) the machine from which an attack was launched, (2) the individual who operated the machine, and (3) the organization or entity (if any) that directed the individual's actions.[3] As Herb Lin has noted, "although these three types of attribution are conceptually distinct, they are often related" because attributing an attack to a particular machine "may provide some clues that can help uncover the identity of the human perpetrator," which can in turn "help identify the party ultimately responsible for setting the entire intrusion into motion."[4]

In practice, the technical challenges of making attributions are significant, and attackers can make attributions more difficult by deliberately disguising their identities in so-called false flag operations.[5] Although the US government has signaled that its technical attribution capabilities have improved in recent years, tying a particular cyberattack to an individual and especially to a state raises legal and political issues, not just technical ones.[6]

International law on state responsibility uses the term *attribution* to "denote the operation of attaching a given action or omission to a state."[7] The international law on state responsibility sets out specific requirements for when actions are attributable to a state. Although not codified in a treaty, many provisions of the International Law Commission's Draft Articles on Responsibility of States for Internationally Wrongful Acts are understood to reflect customary international law.[8] Most basically, the articles specify that the conduct of "any State organ" is attributable to the state.[9] A state cannot, however, avoid international responsibility by outsourcing governmental functions. The "conduct of a person or entity which is not an organ of the State . . . but which is empowered by the law of that State to exercise elements of the governmental authority" is attributable to the state so long as "the person or entity is acting in that capacity in the particular instance."[10] Similarly, a state is responsible for the actions of persons or groups if they act "on the instructions of, or under the direction or control of, that State in carrying out . . . conduct."[11] The International Court of Justice has interpreted this standard to mean that a state is responsible if it exercises "effective control" over the actions of a non-state actor.[12] "Effective control" means directing or controlling specific operations involving wrongful acts by a non-state actor; providing generalized support or direction is not sufficient to render a non-state actor's wrongful actions attributable to a state.[13]

While the Draft Articles on State Responsibility provide detailed answers to when states *may* attribute conduct to other states and the relationships that suffice for such attribution, the articles and customary international law are less clear about the question on which this chapter focuses, namely, when *must* states attribute cyberattacks to another state? International law answers this question only implicitly. In the current context, states must attribute internationally wrongful acts, including cyberattacks, if they want to take responsive action that would otherwise violate international law, including using force in self-defense or engaging in countermeasures.

Above the use-of-force threshold, the UN Charter recognizes states' customary international law right to engage in forcible self-defense in the face of an armed attack.[14] But in order for such use of force to be lawful, it must respond to an actual or imminent armed attack and be directed against the attacking entity.[15] Otherwise, the victim state's use of force would be offensive, not defensive, and thus prohibited by the UN Charter.[16]

The same logic underlies the requirement for a state to attribute an internationally wrongful act in order to take countermeasures. Countermeasures are actions that would be illegal under international law in general but are legally permissible for a state to take if it is responding to a prior unlawful act by another state.[17] The International Court of Justice has explained that a countermeasure "must be taken in response to a previous international wrongful act of another State and *must be directed against that State.*"[18] Similarly, the ILC Draft Articles specify: "An injured State may only take countermeasures against a State which is responsible for an internationally wrongful act in order to induce that State to comply with its [legal obligations]."[19] They further clarify that the "only" "is intended to convey that countermeasures may only be adopted against a State which is the author of the internationally wrongful act."[20]

In discussing countermeasures in response to cyberattacks, states have acknowledged the necessity of attributing a given cyberattack to a particular state. Then–State Department legal advisor Brian Egan noted in a 2016 speech that "the availability of countermeasures to address malicious cyber activity requires a prior internationally wrongful act that is attributable to another State."[21] UK attorney general Jeremy Wright made the link to attribution even clearer in explaining that "[a] countermeasure can only be taken in response to a prior internationally wrongful act committed by a state, and must only be directed towards that state," which "means that the victim state must be confident in its attribution of that act to a hostile state before it takes action in response."[22]

The lawfulness of a countermeasure thus depends not only on attributing the cyberattack to another state but also on doing so accurately. A countermeasure launched based on an erroneous attribution turns the acting state from a victim into a perpetrator,[23] making its countermeasure not a countermeasure at all but an internationally wrongful act that could itself justify countermeasures.[24] The lawfulness of any countermeasure, then, depends on the accuracy of the attribution of the initial internationally wrongful act.

While states must attribute cyberattacks or other internationally wrongful acts in order lawfully to respond using countermeasures, states can also react in ways that do not require such attribution. For example, instead of countermeasures, a state that suffers an internationally wrongful act may choose not to respond at all or to engage only in retorsion—"'unfriendly' conduct which is not inconsistent with any international obligation of the State engaging in it."[25] Traditional examples of retorsion include severing diplomatic relations, declaring diplomatic personnel *persona non grata*, and imposing economic sanctions.[26] Some retorsion may be specific to the cybersecurity context. For example, the Netherlands has suggested that "a state may consider . . . limiting or cutting off the other state's access to servers or other digital infrastructure in its territory, provided the countries in question have not concluded a treaty on mutual access to digital infrastructure in each other's territory."[27] There is no extant international law requirement to engage in attribution as a predicate to retorsion.[28] States may engage in such unfriendly acts whenever and against whomever they please, so long as they comply with their treaty and customary international law obligations. Thus, a state engaging in retorsion need not identify a prior wrongdoing state in order to legally justify its own behavior. By definition, retorsion is always lawful.

Importantly, a legal requirement to attribute an internationally wrongful act in order to justify self-defense or countermeasures is not the same as a requirement to attribute *publicly*. States have reserved the right *not* to attribute publicly.[29] They may instead communicate a cyberattack attribution to the perpetrator state privately, or quietly share the attribution with allies or other states.[30] Conversely, states may choose to attribute even lawful actions to other states if they believe the behavior is malign. In other words, a public attribution does not mean that the attributed behavior is necessarily unlawful, nor does the absence of a public attribution mean that the victim state considers the behavior to be lawful.

However, even though public attribution is not presently legally required, there can be advantages to going public.[31] Prominent among them is avoiding confusion about the legal basis for a state's action. Consider a state that suffers a cyberattack that it understands to constitute an internationally wrongful act but that does not cause publicly observable effects. If the victim state engages in countermeasures that *are* publicly observable or otherwise discoverable, then unless it publicly attributes the initial wrongful act and explains that its actions are countermeasures, it risks having its own conduct misunderstood as an internationally wrongful act. Such misunderstandings may be especially likely with respect to cyberattacks and cyber countermeasures because their effects are often less easily observable than are more conventional intrusions, and a cyber tit-for-tat exchange is less easily understood by outside observers than is a more tangible and traditional one.

Attribution in the Era of Defend Forward

Even if states agree that attribution is required before a victim state takes countermeasures, disagreements about what counts as an internationally wrongful act triggering a right to countermeasures raise the prospect of conflicts over when states must make attributions. The lack of clarity about what is lawful and what is unlawful is particularly acute below the use-of-force threshold, where the bounds of prohibited intervention are unclear,[32] and states openly disagree about the existence of a stand-alone rule barring violations of sovereignty. The US Department of Defense's Defend Forward policy puts significant pressure on these areas of disagreement and stakes out a US position setting a high bar for activity in cyberspace to be considered unlawful. It remains to be seen whether the US view will prevail, and in the meantime, states with a different view of the legal lines could well demand attribution in cases where the United States would argue attribution is not required. This section briefly explains the Defend Forward policy and then addresses how disagreements over the primary rules of state behavior below the use-of-force threshold interact with attribution. In short, where states disagree about whether a particular action violates international law, they will also disagree about whether countermeasures are available and thus about whether attribution is required.

The United States announced its Defend Forward policy in 2018 in a new Department of Defense (DoD) Cyber Strategy and a US Cyber Command (CYBERCOM) "Command Vision" document.[33] The strategy has both locational and temporal aspects. The DoD Cyber Strategy explains: "We will *defend forward* to disrupt or halt malicious cyber activity at its source, including activity that falls below the level of armed conflict," and it states that "defend forward" requires "leveraging [the Defense Department's] focus outward to stop threats before they reach their targets."[34] CYBERCOM's Command Vision makes clear that DoD's policy is not purely defensive in the sense of taking defensive activity only on DoD or US networks. Rather, it focuses on taking actions "as close as possible to adversaries and their operations," wherever they may be.[35] Consistent with the goal of meeting adversaries where they are, the policy also encompasses a temporal component of persistent or continuous engagement.[36] The Command Vision explains:

> Defending forward as close as possible to the origin of adversary activity extends our reach to expose adversaries' weaknesses, learn their intentions and capabilities, and counter attacks close to their origins. Continuous engagement imposes tactical friction and strategic costs on our adversaries, compelling them to shift resources to defense and reduce attacks.[37]

Together, Defend Forward and Persistent Engagement make clear that the US strategy for cyberspace is to act consistently and around the world to disrupt hostile cyber activities aimed at the United States.

The Defend Forward policy's emphasis on actions outside of DoD and US networks runs headlong into an ongoing debate about whether international law prohibits violations of sovereignty that do not amount to a prohibited intervention or use of force. The debate is often framed as one between those who argue that sovereignty is a principle in international law that informs other rules,[38] and those who argue instead that sovereignty is a stand-alone rule, such that violations of sovereignty constitute an independent violation of international law even when they do not amount to intervention or use of force.[39] The influential *Tallinn Manual 2.0* controversially sided with the sovereignty-as-a-rule camp,[40] and states have increasingly lined up on one side of the debate or the other.

The United Kingdom has definitively taken the position that sovereignty is a principle, not a rule.[41] The US government also seems to lean in that direction. In a March 2020 speech at the US Cyber Command Legal Conference, DoD general counsel Paul Ney Jr. asserted: "For cyber operations that would not constitute a prohibited intervention or use-of-force, the Department believes there is not sufficiently widespread and consistent State practice resulting from a sense of legal obligation to conclude that customary international law generally prohibits such non-consensual cyber operations in another State's territory."[42] He cited the example of espionage, which states prohibit in domestic law but which "international law, in our view, does not prohibit ... *per se* even when it involves some degree of physical or virtual intrusion into foreign territory."[43] If international law did treat sovereignty as a rule, it would be difficult to explain how at least some instances of espionage would not run afoul of a prohibition on violations of sovereignty.

An increasing number of states have taken the opposite position. In a 2019 white paper, "International Law Applied to Operations in Cyberspace," France's Ministry of the Armies asserted that "any unauthorised penetration by a State of French systems or any production of effects on French territory ... may constitute, at the least, a breach of sovereignty."[44] Similarly, the Netherlands has asserted that "respect for the sovereignty of other countries is an obligation in its own right, the violation of which may in turn constitute an internationally wrongful act."[45] Austria, the Czech Republic, and Iran also appear to endorse the sovereignty-as-a-rule position,[46] and Finland, Germany, and New Zealand recently joined the sovereignty-as-a-rule camp as well.[47] Even among states that endorse sovereignty-as-a-rule, however, the exact boundaries of what such a rule encompasses remain unclear.[48]

States' divergent views on the sovereignty question may cause disagreements over when states must attribute cyberattacks. Consider a hypothetical US operation to take down a botnet.[49] Botnets are networks of malware-infected computers that can be used for a variety of purposes, such as distributed denial of service attacks and launching of ransomware. The hypothetical botnet—let's call it "Hypobot"—deploys ransomware against US small businesses, and the United States believes that Hypobot's operators are Russian-speaking cybercriminals, affiliated in some way with the Russian government. The United States could launch a counter-botnet operation that takes control of the botnet's command and control servers around the world and effectively severs communication to infected computers, disabling the botnet's operation.[50] From the US perspective, which seems to favor sovereignty-as-a-principle, neither the actions of the botnet operators against US businesses nor the US botnet takedown operation to access servers in countries around the world would violate international law. Neither action would constitute a use of force or prohibited intervention, and because sovereignty is a principle, not a rule, there is no internationally wrongful act and thus no need to invoke countermeasures or engage in attribution.

Consider the same operation, however, from the perspective of a state that endorses the sovereignty-as-a-rule view. Such a state would likely recognize the botnet's actions against US institutions as violations of US sovereignty— internationally wrongful acts—and thus conclude that the United States is entitled to take countermeasures *if the United States attributes the botnet's operations to the Russian government.* Countermeasures can only be taken against states, so a sovereignty-as-a-rule state's view of the lawfulness of the US operation would depend on whether or not the United States attributed the botnet to the Russian government.[51] If it did not, then the sovereignty-as-a-rule approach could categorize the US counter-botnet operation as itself perpetrating unlawful violations of sovereignty and entitling affected states to take countermeasures against the United States.[52]

Because relatively few states have declared their position on the sovereignty question, considerable uncertainty remains about whether the majority of countries around the world that have yet to announce a view would regard the US actions as lawful or unlawful. Such uncertainty could cause friction or unintended escalation if, for example, the United States took actions to Defend Forward in or affecting a state that subscribed to (but had not announced) its adherence to the sovereignty-as-a-rule approach and then took countermeasures against the United States.[53]

DoD has made clear that it considers divergences in states' legal views in assessing available options for cyber actions. DoD general counsel Paul Ney Jr. noted in his March 2020 speech that in evaluating possible cyber operations, "even if a particular cyber operation does not constitute a use of force, it is important to keep in mind that the State or States targeted by the operation may disagree, or at least have a different perception of what the operation entailed."[54] With respect to countermeasures, Ney explained:

> In a particular case it may be unclear whether a particular malicious cyber activity violates international law. And, in other circumstances, it may not be apparent that the act is internationally wrongful and attributable to a State within the timeframe in which the DoD must respond to mitigate the threat. In these circumstances, which we believe are common, countermeasures would not be available.[55]

At first blush, this statement appears to be more definitive than Ney's statement about uses of force, going so far as to admit that countermeasures are not available if there is uncertainty or presumably disagreement about whether the triggering act is an international law violation.

But it raises the question: Who determines what counts as a countermeasure? Is a countermeasure defined by the sovereignty-as-a-rule camp or by the sovereignty-as-a-principle proponents? The United States would presumably argue that its cyber actions short of prohibited intervention or a use of force are simply retorsion, not internationally wrongful acts that would have to be justified as countermeasures. As noted above, retorsion does not require attribution to a state or compliance with the procedural and other limitations placed on countermeasures.[56] This leaves considerable room to Defend Forward against actions around the world that may not be attributed or attributable to states and to do so in ways that *other* states consider a violation of their sovereignty. This approach may well explain the reported US Cyber Command operation to disrupt the TrickBot botnet—a ransomware botnet allegedly operated by Russian-speaking cybercriminals that has been used to disrupt health care providers and local governments, among others.[57] Although "what connection, if any, TrickBot's operators share with the Kremlin remains an open question," US officials were reportedly concerned that the botnet might be used to disrupt the 2020 election, on a state's orders or otherwise.[58] Consistent with the US view of sovereignty, the TrickBot takedown would not require attribution to a state and would not itself violate international law.

The other possible interpretation of Ney's statement about the unavailability of countermeasures is that the United States applies Defend Forward differentially depending on the state in which a cyber operation would occur or cause effects. For example, the United States may refrain from taking actions to counter cyber threats short of intervention or uses of force in states that endorse sovereignty-as-a-rule in instances where it cannot or does not wish to attribute the threat to a state actor. One problem with this approach, however, is that it would incentivize gamesmanship. If sovereignty-as-a-principle states were to defer to sovereignty-as-a-rule states' view about when attribution is required, states would have an incentive to declare their support for sovereignty-as-a-rule opportunistically in order to deter operations in their territory. It seems more likely that the United States follows its own sovereignty-as-a-principle view of what counts as an internationally wrongful act and thus when attribution is required, though doing so may well put it in a position of "defending forward" in ways that other states would consider internationally wrongful.

The Domestic Law Overlay

Although the implications of attribution are more significant with respect to international law, the executive branch's ability and willingness to attribute cyberattacks to particular states affects its domestic legal authorities as well. As part of the Article II Commander-in-Chief powers, the president has consistently claimed authority to deploy US armed forces without congressional authorization in situations short of war.[59] This extends to cyber-based actions as well as conventional ones.[60] Executive authority is understood to be "at its maximum," however, "when the President acts pursuant to an express or implied authorization of Congress."[61] Congress has passed several statutes authorizing executive actions in cyberspace, impliedly and expressly, but all depend on attribution.[62]

Congress expressly authorized cyber operations in the John S. McCain National Defense Authorization Act (NDAA) for Fiscal Year 2019.[63] Section 1642 specifies that if "the National Command Authority determines that" Russia, China, North Korea, or Iran "is conducting an active, systematic, and ongoing campaign of attacks against the Government or people of the United States in cyberspace, including attempting to influence American elections and democratic political processes," then the National Command Authority may authorize Cyber Command "to take appropriate and proportional action in foreign cyberspace to disrupt, defeat, and deter such attacks."[64] As stated, this authority depends on attribution of cyber operations to a particular set of states. If the executive does attribute cyber intrusions to Russia, China, North Korea, or Iran, then it need not act based solely on the president's constitutional powers but rather can proceed with the combined constitutional authority of the executive and Congress.[65]

The executive can also invoke congressional authorization for cyber operations if they fall within existing general AUMFs. In particular, the 2001 AUMF, passed in the wake of the 9/11 attacks, authorizes the president "to use all necessary and appropriate force against those nations, organizations, or persons he determines planned, authorized, committed, or aided the terrorist attacks that occurred on September 11, 2001, or harbored such organizations or persons."[66] The 2002 Iraq AUMF authorizes the president "to use the Armed Forces of the United States as he determines to be necessary and appropriate in order to . . . defend the national security of the United States against the continuing threat posed by Iraq."[67] The broad authorizations in the AUMFs logically include force exercised via cyber means, but the extra authority they provide once again depends on attribution of attacks (whether cyber or otherwise) to those involved with the 9/11 attacks or to Iraq.[68]

Given the executive's capacious understanding of its constitutional authority to use force independent of congressional authorization,[69] the cyber-specific and more general authorizations for cyberattacks against particular perpetrator states may not materially change the executive's behavior. The 2019 NDAA cyber provision may simply "[function] as a belt-and-suspenders provision, mooting separation-of-powers objections that might otherwise arise."[70] Nonetheless, it is notable that when Congress specifically considered and passed legislation to empower Cyber Command, it chose to make the authorization dependent on attribution to particular states, rather than generally authorizing Cyber Command to respond in "foreign cyberspace" to *any* "active, systematic, and ongoing campaign of attacks against the Government or people of the United States in cyberspace" by state or non-state actors.[71]

The 2019 NDAA is likely not Congress's last word on the subject of cyberattack attributions. As part of a report on cyberspace policy required by the 2019 NDAA, Congress specified that the president must provide "information relating to the Administration's plans, including specific planned actions, regulations, and legislative action required, for . . . advancing technologies in attribution."[72] Similarly, the Senate Select Committee on Intelligence Report on Russian election interference, released in July 2019, argues that the government "should invest in capabilities for rapid attribution of cyber attacks, without sacrificing accuracy" and that "timely and accurate attribution is not only important to defensive information sharing, but will also underpin a credible deterrence and response strategy."[73] Both Congress's enactments and international law ensure that attribution is indeed key to responding to cyberattacks.

Conclusion

Attributing a cyberattack to a state can empower the victim state by allowing it to take lawful countermeasures, and in US domestic law, attributions of particular kinds of attacks to specific states bolster the legal authority for executive action. But the requirement to attribute also functions as a constraint: victim states cannot engage in countermeasures unless they make an attribution to a state, and in the US system, the executive cannot rely on congressional authorization unless it attributes to a particular set of states.

This legal analysis, however, is not the end of the story on attributions. Public attributions of cyberattacks can play a role beyond justifying responsive actions. They can help to shape, not just be controlled by, international and domestic US law. Public attributions of cyberattacks to governments bring to light the often murky world of state practice in cyberspace, and by declaring certain behaviors to be unacceptable, they can help to develop the rules of the road for state behavior going forward.[74] Attributions, especially if coordinated among groups of countries and accompanied by real consequences such as economic sanctions, can play a constitutive role, solidifying and enforcing norms of responsible behavior in cyberspace that might eventually crystallize into customary international law. Attributions can also shape domestic US authorities by revealing which states are operating against the United States in cyberspace and perhaps prompting Congress to authorize additional operations.

Notes

1. *See* Youngstown Sheet & Tube Co. v. Sawyer, 343 U.S. 579, 635 (1952) (Jackson, J., concurring) (describing Category 1 in which "the President acts pursuant to an express or implied authorization of Congress," and therefore "his authority is at its maximum, for it includes all that he possesses in his own right plus all that Congress can delegate"); *see also infra* section 3 "The Domestic Law Overlay."

2. Kristen E. Eichensehr, *The Law and Politics of Cyberattack Attribution*, 67 UCLA L. Rev. 520, 522 (2020

3. *See, e.g.*, Herbert Lin, *Attribution of Malicious Cyber Incidents* 5 (Hoover Inst. Working Group on Nat'l Sec., Tech., and L., Aegis Series Paper No. 1607, 2016) (explaining that the question of "who is responsible" for a cyberattack "can be answered in three ways . . . a machine, a specific human being pressing the keys or otherwise setting the intrusion into motion, and an ultimately responsible party").

4. *Id.* at 13.

5. For discussions of the technical side of attribution, including types of evidence that can lead to identification of individual and state perpetrators, see *id.* at 5–11; Thomas Rid & Ben Buchanan, *Attributing Cyber Attacks*, 38 J. STRAT. STUD. 4, 14–23 (2015). For discussion of Russian false flag operations, see, for example, Andy Greenberg, *A Brief History of Russian Hackers' Evolving False Flags*, WIRED (Oct. 21, 2019), and Michael S. Schmidt & Nicole Perlroth, *U.S. Charges Russian Intelligence Officers in Major Cyberattacks*, N.Y. TIMES (Oct. 19, 2020).

6. *See, e.g.*, Eichensehr, *supra* note 2, at 531 (detailing US government statements about improvements in its attribution capabilities).

7. Int'l L. Comm'n, Draft Articles on Responsibility of States for Internationally Wrongful Acts, with Commentaries, UN Doc. A/56/10, at 36 (2001).

8. *See, e.g.*, Ashley Deeks, *Defend Forward and Cyber Countermeasures* 2 (Hoover Inst. Working Group on Nat'l Sec., Tech., and L., Aegis Series Paper No. 2004, 2020) (noting that "many states view the [Draft Articles] as reflecting customary international law"). Although the United States has taken issue with some provisions, *see infra* note 56, the State Department's understanding of international law appears to track the Draft Articles on the basic rules for attributing actions to states and states' entitlement to take countermeasures, *see, e.g.*, U.S. Submission to Group of Governmental Experts on Developments in the Field of Information and Telecommunications in the Context of International Security (Oct. 2014), *in* Digest of U.S. Practice in International Law 732, 738–39 (2014).

9. Int'l L. Comm'n, *supra* note 7, at 40.

10. *Id.* at 42; *see also id.* at 42–43 (discussing examples of entities that fall within Article 5). A state remains responsible for the actions of state organs and entities empowered to exercise governmental functions even if "the organ, person, or entity . . . exceeds its authority or contravenes instructions." *Id.* at 45. A state also incurs international responsibility for the conduct of organs of another state that are placed at its disposal and exercising governmental authority on its behalf. *Id.* at 43–44.

11. *Id.* at 47.

12. Military and Paramilitary Activities in and Against Nicaragua (Nicar. v. U.S.), Judgment, 1986 I.C.J. Rep. 14, ¶ 115 (June 27) (explaining that for conduct of a non-state armed group to be attributed to a state "it would in principle have to be proved that that State had effective control of the military or paramilitary operations in the course of which the alleged violations were committed").

13. Case Concerning the Application of the Convention on the Prevention and Punishment of the Crime of Genocide (Bosn. and Herz. v. Serb. and Montenegro), 2007 I.C.J. Rep. 43, ¶ 400 (Feb. 26) (clarifying that in order for state responsibility to attach, a state must exercise "effective control" or give instructions "in respect of each operation in which the alleged violations occurred, not generally in respect of the overall actions taken by the persons or groups of persons having committed the violations"). *But see* Prosecutor v. Tadic, Case No. IT-94-1-A, Judgment, ¶ 145 (Int'l Crim. Trib. for the Former Yugoslavia, July 15, 1999) (adopting a lower standard of "overall control" for state responsibility for the actions of non-state armed groups).

14. UN Charter Art. 51.

15. *See, e.g.,* Letter from the Minister of Foreign Affairs to the President of the House of Representatives on the Int'l Legal Order in Cyberspace, Appendix at 8–9 (July 5, 2019) (Neth.) [hereinafter Netherlands Letter] ("The burden of proof for justifiable self-defence against an armed attack is a heavy one. . . . States may . . . use force in self-defence only if the origin of the attack and the identity of those responsible are sufficiently certain.").

16. UN Charter Art. 2(4).

17. Int'l L. Comm'n, *supra* note 7, at 128 (defining countermeasures as "measures that would otherwise be contrary to the international obligations of an injured State vis-à-vis the responsible State, if they were not taken by the former in response to an internationally wrongful act by the latter in order to procure cessation and reparation").

18. Case Concerning the Gabčíkovo–Nagymaros Project (Hung. v. Slovk.), Judgment, 1997 I.C.J. 7, ¶ 83 (Sept. 25) (emphasis added).

19. Int'l L. Comm'n, *supra* note 7, at 129.

20. *Id.* at 130. For avoidance of all doubt, the Articles further explain: "Countermeasures may not be directed against States other than the responsible State." *Id.*

21. Brian J. Egan, *International Law and Stability in Cyberspace*, 35 Berkeley J. Int'l L. 169, 178 (2017).

22. Attorney General Jeremy Wright QC MP, United Kingdom, Address at Chatham House Royal Institute for International Affairs: Cyber and International Law in the 21st Century (May 23, 2018); *see also* Netherlands Letter, *supra* note 15, at 6 ("For a state to be held responsible under international law for a cyber operation and, by extension, for a target state to be able to take a countermeasure in response, it must be possible to attribute the operation to the state in question." [footnote omitted]).

23. Int'l L. Comm'n, *supra* note 7, at 130 ("A State taking countermeasures acts at its peril, if its view of the question of wrongfulness turns out not to be well founded and [it] may incur responsibility for its own wrongful conduct in the event of an incorrect assessment."); *see also Tallinn Manual 2.0 on the International Law Applicable to Cyber Operations* 82–83 (Michael N. Schmitt ed., 2d ed. 2017) [hereinafter *Tallinn Manual*

2.0] (explaining that "States taking countermeasures based on a decision that another State has breached an obligation owed to them do so at their own risk," and "[t]hus, while it might be reasonable to take a countermeasure . . . , for instance because significant evidence exists to support attribution to a State against which the cyber countermeasure is taken, if the conclusion as to attribution proves to be flawed, . . . the State itself will have committed an internationally wrongful act").

24. *See* Egan, *supra* note 21, at 178 (explaining that a state attempting to engage in countermeasures may be "held responsible for violating international law if it turns out that there wasn't actually an internationally wrongful act that triggered the right to take countermeasures, or if the responding State made an inaccurate attribution determination" and therefore that "countermeasures should not be engaged in lightly"); *see also* Deeks, *supra* note 8, at 6 (explaining that "States taking countermeasures in response to wrongful cyber activity bear the burden of attributing the wrongful activity to which they are responding to the proper actors—just as they do when responding to wrongful activity outside of cyberspace," and noting that "the elevated risk of misattribution in the cyber context suggests that states should have high levels of confidence before taking countermeasures in response to malicious cyber operations").

25. Int'l L. Comm'n, *supra* note 7, at 128; *see also* Egan, *supra* note 21, at 177 ("A State can always undertake unfriendly acts that are not inconsistent with any of its international obligations in order to influence the behavior of other States.").

26. *See, e.g.,* Int'l L. Comm'n, *supra* note 7, at 128 ("Acts of retorsion may include the prohibition of or limitations upon normal diplomatic relations or other contacts, embargoes of various kinds or withdrawal of voluntary aid programmes."); Egan, *supra* note 21, at 177 (citing examples of retorsion including "the imposition of sanctions or the declaration that a diplomat is *persona non grata*").

27. Netherlands Letter, *supra* note 15, at 7; *see also* Tallinn Manual 2.0, *supra* note 23, at 112 (Rule 20) cmt. 4 (suggesting that, as a type of retorsion, "a State may . . . employ an access control list to prevent communications from another State . . . so long as it violates no treaty obligation or applicable customary law norm").

28. In a recent article, Martha Finnemore & Duncan Hollis argue: "For a state to engage in either retorsion or counter-measures, however, requires some accusation articulating the requisite wrongful acts that form the basis for it to pursue the enforcement of its legal rights." Martha Finnemore & Duncan B. Hollis, *Beyond Naming and Shaming: Accusations and International Law in Cybersecurity*, 31 EUR. J. INT'L L. 969, 979 (2020). It is not clear whether they mean to argue that states are required to engage in cyberattack attribution before engaging in retorsion, because elsewhere in the same article they argue that what they term "accusations" "can occur without attribution (i.e. when accusers say, 'we do not know who did this, but it happened, and it was bad')." *Id.* at 976.

29. *See, e.g.,* GERMANY, POSITION PAPER, ON THE APPLICATION OF INTERNATIONAL LAW IN CYBERSPACE 12 (2021) (declaring that "there is no general obligation under international law as it currently stands to publicize a decision on attribution" and that "[a]ny such publication in a particular case is generally based on political considerations and does not create legal obligations for the State under international law");

Roy Schöndorf, *Israel's Perspective on Key Legal and Practical Issues Concerning the Application of International Law to Cyber Operations*, 97 Int'l L. Stud. 395, 405 (2021) ("[A]s a matter of international law, the choice whether or not to disclose the attribution information remains at the exclusive discretion of the State."); Wright, *supra* note 22 (recognizing that a state engaging in countermeasures "must be confident in its attribution of that act to a hostile state before it takes action in response" but also explaining that "there is no legal obligation requiring a state . . . to publicly attribute hostile cyber activity that it has suffered in all circumstances" and that the United Kingdom sometimes attributes "publicly" and "sometimes . . . do[es] so only to the country concerned").

30. *See* French Ministry of the Armies, International Law Applied to Operations in Cyberspace 10 (2019) (stating that "the identification of a State as being responsible for a cyberattack that is an internationally unlawful act does not in any way oblige the victim State to make a public attribution," and that "France reserves the right to attribute publicly, or not, a cyberattack against it and to bring that information to the attention of its population, other States or the international community"); *see also* Greg Miller et al., *Obama's Secret Struggle to Punish Russia for Putin's Election Assault*, Wash. Post (June 23, 2017) (reporting that President Obama privately warned Vladimir Putin in September 2016 to stop Russia's efforts to interfere in the election and that the first US public attribution to Russia occurred in October 2016).

31. I have elsewhere argued that recent public attributions bring transparency to state practice in cyberspace and can have an important influence on setting norms and customary international law to govern state behavior. *See* Eichensehr, *supra* note 2, at 556–58; *cf.* Germany, *supra* note 29, at 12 (noting that "States should provide information and reasoning" to support attributions and that doing so "may bolster the transparency, legitimacy and general acceptance of decisions on attribution and any response measures taken").

32. *See, e.g.*, Gary P. Corn, *Covert Deception, Strategic Fraud, and the Rule of Prohibited Intervention* 6–14 (Hoover Inst. Working Group on Nat'l Sec., Tech., and L., Aegis Series Paper No. 2005, 2020).

33. *See* US Dep't of Def., Summary: Department of Defense Cyber Strategy (2018); US Cyber Command, Achieve and Maintain Cyberspace Superiority: Command Vision for US Cyber Command (2018).

34. US Dep't of Def., *supra* note 33, at 1, 2.

35. US Cyber Command, *supra* note 33, at 6.

36. For an explanation of the relationship between "Defend Forward" and "Persistent Engagement," see Hon. Paul C. Ney Jr., General Counsel, Dep't of Def., DoD General Counsel Remarks at U.S. Cyber Command Legal Conference (March 2, 2020); *see also The Fiscal Year 2021 Budget Request for U.S. Cyber Command and Operations in Cyberspace: Hearing Before the H. Comm. on Armed Servs., Subcomm. on Intelligence and Emerging Threats and Capabilities*, 116th Cong. 44 (2020) (written statement of Gen. Paul M. Nakasone, commander, US Cyber Command) (describing Defend Forward as the "strategic direction" that "drives Cyber Command's doctrine called persistent engagement").

37. US CYBER COMMAND, *supra* note 33, at 6.

38. *See, e.g.,* Gary P. Corn & Robert Taylor, *Sovereignty in the Age of Cyber,* 111 AM. J. INT'L L. UNBOUND 208 (2017) (arguing that below the thresholds of use of force or intervention, "there is insufficient evidence of either state practice or *opinio juris* to support assertions that the principle of sovereignty operates as an independent rule of customary international law").

39. *See, e.g.,* Michael N. Schmitt & Liis Vihul, *Sovereignty in Cyberspace:* Lex Lata Vel Non?, 111 AM. J. INT'L L. UNBOUND 213 (2017) (defending the *Tallinn Manual* position that sovereignty is an independent rule of international law).

40. *Tallinn Manual 2.0, supra* note 23, at 17–27 (Rule 4).

41. Wright, *supra* note 22 (noting that although "some . . . argue for the existence of a cyber specific rule of a 'violation of territorial sovereignty' in relation to interference in the computer networks of another state without its consent," he was "not persuaded that we can currently extrapolate from that general principle a specific rule or additional prohibition for cyber activity beyond that of a prohibited intervention," and explaining that "[t]he UK Government's position is therefore that there is no such rule as a matter of current international law").

42. Ney, *supra* note 36.

43. *Id.*

44. French Ministry of the Armies, *supra* note 30, at 6. The extent to which this view represents the position of the entire French government as opposed to only the Ministry of the Armies is unclear. *See* Col. Gary Corn, *Punching on the Edges of the Grey Zone: Iranian Cyber Threats and State Cyber Responses,* JUST SEC. (Feb. 11, 2020) (noting that "the French document does not claim to be the official position of the French government," but rather may be more akin to the "DoD Law of War Manual which does not necessarily reflect the views of the U.S. Government as a whole").

45. Netherlands Letter, *supra* note 15, at 2.

46. *See* Przemysław Roguski, *The Importance of New Statements on Sovereignty in Cyberspace by Austria, the Czech Republic and United States,* JUST SEC. (May 11, 2020) (noting that in conjunction with the UN Open-Ended Working Group on developments in the field of information and telecommunications in the context of international security, Austria and the Czech Republic have both endorsed the sovereignty-as-a-rule position); Przemysław Roguski, *Iran Joins Discussions of Sovereignty and Non-Intervention in Cyberspace,* JUST SEC. (Sept. 3, 2020)(providing an overview of the statement on international law issued by the General Staff of the Iranian Armed Forces, including Iran's apparent endorsement of the sovereignty-as-a-rule position, but also noting caveats about the extent to which the statement itself and especially the available English translation reflect official Iranian policy).

47. Finnish Gov't, Min. for For. Aff., Press Release, Finland Published Its Positions on Public International Law in Cyberspace (Oct. 15, 2020) ("Finland sees sovereignty as a primary norm of public international law, a breach of which amounts to an internationally wrongful act and triggers State responsibility."); GERMANY, *supra* note 29, at 3 ("State sovereignty constitutes a legal norm in its own right and may apply directly as a general norm also in cases in which more specific rules applicable to

State behaviour, such as the prohibition of intervention or the use of force, are not applicable."); New Zealand For. Aff. & Trade, The Application of International Law to State Activity in Cyberspace (Dec. 1, 2020) ("New Zealand considers that the stand-alone rule of territorial sovereignty also applies in the cyber context but acknowledges that further state practice is required for the precise boundaries of its application to crystallise.").

48. *See, e.g.,* Netherlands Letter, *supra* note 15, at 2–3 (endorsing the sovereignty-as-a-rule position, while also noting that the "precise boundaries of what is and is not permissible have yet to fully crystallise"). For example, states that endorse the sovereignty-as-a-rule position might nonetheless include an exception for de minimis intrusions on sovereignty. *Cf.* Czech Republic, Statement by Mr. Richard Kadlčák, Special Envoy for Cyberspace, Director of Cybersecurity Department, 2nd Substantive Session of the Open-Ended Working Group on Developments in the Field of Info. & Telecomm. in the Context of Int'l Sec. of the First Comm. of the General Assembly of the United Nations Feb. 11, 2020 (explaining that "[t]he Czech Republic concurs with those considering the principle of sovereignty as an independent right," but listing examples of violations of sovereignty that appear to exclude those below certain thresholds); Germany, *supra* note 29, at 4 (explaining that "**negligible** physical effects and functional impairments below a certain impact threshold cannot—taken by themselves—be deemed to constitute a violation of territorial sovereignty"); New Zealand For. Affs. & Trade, *supra* note 47 (explaining New Zealand's view that although "sovereignty prohibits states from using cyber means to cause significant harmful effects manifesting on the territory of another state," there remains "a range of circumstances—in addition to pure espionage activity—in which an unauthorised cyber intrusion, including one causing effects on the territory of another state, would not be internationally wrongful").

49. Such operations are not hypothetical, though the details of the in-text hypothetical are. *See* Ellen Nakashima, *Cyber Command Has Sought to Disrupt the World's Largest Botnet, Hoping to Reduce Its Potential Impact on the Election,* WASH. POST (Oct. 9, 2020) (reporting that Cyber Command disrupted the TrickBot botnet, which was "run by Russian-speaking criminals" and for ransomware); David E. Sanger & Nicole Perlroth, *Microsoft Takes Down a Risk to the Election, and Finds the U.S. Doing the Same,* N.Y. TIMES (Oct. 12, 2020) (reporting on Microsoft and Cyber Command's operations to take down the TrickBot botnet).

50. For examples of the mechanics used in takedowns, see, for example, Robert Chesney, *Persistently Engaging TrickBot: USCYBERCOM Takes on a Notorious Botnet,* LAWFARE (Oct. 12, 2020); Brian Krebs, *U.S. Government Takes Down Coreflood Botnet,* KREBS ON SECURITY (Apr. 11, 2011).

51. *See* Int'l L. Comm'n, *supra* note 7, at 129 ("An injured State may only take countermeasures against a State which is responsible for an internationally wrongful act."); *see also Tallinn Manual 2.0, supra* note 23, at 113 (Rule 20) cmt. 7 ("Countermeasures are not available in response to a cyber operation conducted by a non-State actor unless the operation is attributable to a State."); Col. Gary Corn, *Tallinn Manual 2.0—Advancing the Conversation,* JUST SEC. (Feb. 15, 2017) (arguing

that the sovereignty-as-a-rule approach is problematic in part because "unlike self-defense, countermeasures cannot be invoked as a justification for actions taken against non-state actors" and thus a state seeking to take down a botnet operated by a non-state actor "can do so only with the consent of each State in whose territory the cyber action will occur, or based on a reasonable determination that those States are themselves in breach of an international obligation").

52. The analysis becomes even more complicated if the botnet command-and-control servers are located in third states. Although countermeasures may "incidentally affect the position of third States," if "a third State is owed an international obligation by the State taking countermeasures and that obligation is breached by the countermeasure, the wrongfulness of the measure is not precluded as against the third State." Int'l L. Comm'n, *supra* note 7, at 130. In other words, if the United States were to act against a command-and-control server in, for example, France, then at least according to the sovereignty-as-a-rule position, the United States could thereby breach a legal duty not to violate France's sovereignty. The US action might *not* constitute an unlawful violation of France's sovereignty if there is a de minimis exception to violations of sovereignty, *see supra* note 48, or if France had breached a duty of due diligence, which would itself violate international law and entitle the United States to take countermeasures. *See, e.g., Tallinn Manual 2.0, supra* note 23, at 30–50 (Rule 6) (discussing due diligence).

53. *Cf.* Egan, *supra* note 21, at 172 (recognizing that "states' relative silence could lead to unpredictability in the cyber realm, where States may be left guessing about each other's views on the applicable legal framework," and therefore that "in the context of a specific cyber incident, this uncertainty could give rise to misperceptions and miscalculations by States, potentially leading to escalation and, in the worst case, conflict").

54. Ney, *supra* note 36. He made a very similar point about non-intervention, explaining that "[b]ecause States take different views on this question [of the scope of the prohibition on intervention], DoD lawyers examining any proposed cyber operations must tread carefully, even if only a few States have taken the position publicly that the proposed activities would amount to a prohibited intervention." *Id.*

55. *Id.*

56. The ILC Draft Articles on State Responsibility set out a variety of procedural limitations on how countermeasures may be deployed, including that the injured state must call on the offending state to cease the internationally wrongful act and offer to negotiate before engaging in countermeasures. *See* Int'l L. Comm'n, *supra* note 7, at 134–37. Some states have challenged such provisions as not reflective of customary international law. *See, e.g.,* Ney, *supra* note 36 (noting "varying State views on whether notice would be necessary in all cases [of countermeasures] in the cyber context because of secrecy or urgency"); Wright, *supra* note 22 ("[W]here the UK is responding to covert cyber intrusion with countermeasures[,] . . . we would not agree that we are always legally obliged to give prior notification to the hostile state before taking countermeasures against it."); *see also* Sean D. Murphy, *U.S. Comments on ILC Draft Articles on State Responsibility*, 95 Am. J. Int'l L. 626, 626–28 (2001) (reporting US

government comments on the ILC Draft Articles that characterized provisions on countermeasures as not reflective of customary international law).

57. Nakashima, *supra* note 49; *see also* Chesney, *supra* note 50 (discussing the TrickBot operation as an example of Persistent Engagement).

58. Sanger & Perlroth, *supra* note 49.

59. For details on the executive's argument for presidential authority to use force, see, for example, Memorandum Opinion from Karl R. Thompson, Principal Deputy Assistant Att'y Gen., Office of Legal Couns., to the Couns. to the President, Authority to Order Targeted Airstrikes Against the Islamic State of Iraq and the Levant (Dec. 30, 2014); Memorandum Opinion from Caroline D. Krass, Principal Deputy Assistant Att'y Gen., Office of Legal Couns., to the Att'y Gen., Authority to Use Military Force in Libya (Apr. 1, 2011).

60. *See* Ney, *supra* note 36 ("The domestic legal authority for the DoD to conduct cyber operations is included in the broader authorities of the President and the Secretary of Defense to conduct military operations in defense of the nation."); *see also* Robert Chesney, *The Domestic Legal Framework for US Military Cyber Operations* 5 (Hoover Inst. Working Group on Nat'l Sec., Tech., and L., Aegis Series Paper No. 2003, 2020) (discussing the Office of Legal Counsel's high bar for when congressional authorization is required for military operations and suggesting that most cyber operations would not reach the level of "war" that the Office of Legal Counsel (OLC) believes is the triggering requirement for congressional authorization).

61. Youngstown Sheet & Tube Co. v. Sawyer, 343 U.S. 579, 635 (1952) (Jackson, J., concurring).

62. *See* Chesney, *supra* note 60, at 3–5 (discussing the AUMFs and Section 1642 of the 2019 NDAA as statutory authorizations available to US Cyber Command).

63. Pub. L. No. 115-232, 132 Stat. 1636 (codified at 10 U.S.C. § 394 note (2018)).

64. *Id.* § 1642(a)(1), 132 Stat. at 2132.

65. *See* Ney, *supra* note 36 (arguing that "in the context of cyber operations, the President does not need to rely solely on his Article II powers because Congress has provided for ample authorization," including in the 2019 NDAA and the 2001 AUMF).

66. Authorization for Use of Military Force, § 2(a), Pub. L. No. 107-40, 115 Stat. 224 (codified at 50 U.S.C. § 1541 note [2001]).

67. Authorization for Use of Military Force Against Iraq Resolution of 2002, § 3(a), Pub. L. No. 107-243, 116 Stat. 1498 (codified at 50 U.S.C. § 1541 note [2002]).

68. *See, e.g.*, Ney, *supra* note 36 ("Cyber operations against specific targets are logically encompassed within broad statutory authorizations to the President to use force, like the 2001 Authorization for Use of Military Force."). The Trump administration stretched the bounds of the 2002 AUMF beyond recognition when it argued that it authorized a drone strike on Iranian military commander Qassim Soleimani in Iraq in January 2020. *See generally* Jean Galbraith, *U.S. Drone Strike in Iraq Kills Iranian Military Leader Qasem Soleimani*, 114 AM. J. INT'L L. 313, 319 (2020) (citing a White House notice to Congress explaining that the president had authority for the strike under both his Article II Commander-in-Chief powers and the 2002 AUMF). Indeed, Congress itself rejected the administration's interpretation of the 2002 AUMF in a

joint resolution, which President Trump subsequently vetoed. S. J. Res. 68, sec. 1(3), 116th Cong. (2020). For additional criticism of the administration's interpretation, see Ryan Goodman, *White House '1264 Notice' and Novel Legal Claims for Military Action Against Iran*, JUST SEC. (Feb. 14, 2020); Ryan Goodman & Steve Vladeck, *Why the 2002 AUMF Does Not Apply to Iran*, JUST SEC. (Jan. 9, 2020).

69. *See supra* note 59 and accompanying text (discussing OLC opinions on executive authority to conduct military operations).

70. Chesney, *supra* note 60, at 4–5.

71. Pub. L. No. 115-232, § 1642(a)(1), 132 Stat. at 2132.

72. *Id.* § 1636, 132 Stat. at 2127.

73. Report of the Select Committee on Intelligence United States Senate on Russian Active Measures Campaigns and Interference in the 2016 U.S. Election, Vol. 1, at 55 (2019).

74. *See* Eichensehr, *supra* note 2, at 556–58; Finnemore & Hollis, *supra* note 28, at 981-84.

PART IV
COMPARATIVE PERSPECTIVES

12

Persistent Aggrandizement and Israel's Cyber Defense Architecture

Elena Chachko

Introduction

Defend Forward has emerged as a key pillar of current US cyber defense strategy. According to the 2018 Command Vision of the US Cyber Command (CYBERCOM), the concept means that the United States will "defend forward as close as possible to the origin of adversary activity, and persistently contest malicious cyberspace actors to generate continuous tactical, operational, and strategic advantage."[1] In other words, under Defend Forward, the United States will engage in cyber defense outside US networks and on foreign territory. It will take the initiative instead of waiting for threats to materialize at home.

A related yet distinct operational concept in CYBERCOM's strategic vision is Persistent Engagement. The vision states:

> Superiority through persistence seizes and maintains the initiative in cyberspace by continuously engaging and contesting adversaries and causing them uncertainty wherever they maneuver. It describes how we operate—maneuvering seamlessly between defense and offense across the interconnected battlespace. It describes where we operate—globally, as close as possible to adversaries and their operations. It describes when we operate—continuously, shaping the battlespace. It describes why we operate—to create operational advantage for us while denying the same to our adversaries.[2]

This chapter compares these core elements of the US cyber defense strategy with Israel's cyber defense architecture and recent reforms. Since 2011, the Israeli government has worked to centralize and streamline cybersecurity authorities and responsibilities. It has established a new civilian national security agency—the National Cyber Directorate—to oversee cybersecurity preparedness in both the government and the private sector, and to monitor and respond to cyber threats. The government has also drafted advanced, comprehensive cyber legislation in broad consultation with relevant stakeholders from within government, as well as private sector and civil society actors. Importantly, these reforms only extend to domestic cyber defense. Cyber action focusing on foreign targets outside Israeli territory has remained shielded from these reforms.

Substantively, Israel's cyber defense reforms echo the US concept of Persistent Engagement in recognizing the need for continuous monitoring of cyber vulnerabilities and threats. Like US decision makers, the Israeli government has highlighted the necessity of responding to such threats in an assertive and timely manner. A key difference, however, is that the Israeli approach to cyber defense envisions and invites government monitoring of and operations on *domestic* civilian networks. Moreover, it co-opts the private sector for that purpose.

Israel's cyber defense architecture and operational approach also share similarities with Defend Forward. While recent reforms have avoided regulation of cyber action on foreign territory, Israel has earned a reputation for being a major actor in the realm of international cyber action—both offensive and defensive.[3]

What follows compares the two national strategies. Before turning to the comparison, the chapter surveys the major components of the Israeli cyber architecture. The final section of the chapter briefly evaluates the Israeli reforms. It considers the trade-offs that the Israeli reforms make between the role of the government and that of the private sector, and between operational effectiveness and civil liberties. It argues that the trajectory of the Israeli reforms is best described as persistent aggrandizement on the government's part, at the expense of the private sector and privacy.

Israel's Cyber Defense Reform

Government Resolutions 3611 and 2444

Beginning in 2011, Israel's government adopted a series of resolutions to overhaul cyber defense authorities and create new national cybersecurity organs. These resolutions are executive directives issued by the government without parliamentary approval (I use the term "government" in this chapter to refer to the Israeli executive branch—government ministers and the administrative state—excluding parliament). Resolution 3611, adopted in August 2011, provided that the government would work toward advancing national cyber capabilities, strengthening protection of critical national infrastructure, and regulating powers and responsibilities in the cyber realm.[4]

In addition, the resolution approved the establishment of the National Cyber Bureau in the prime minister's office with wide-ranging cybersecurity responsibilities. The bureau was tasked with advising the government on cyber policy issues and coordinating policy across government, among other assignments. It was also responsible for facilitating cooperation among relevant stakeholders, including academia and the private sector, as well as government ministries and existing national security agencies: the Israel Defense Forces (IDF—the country's military); the Israeli Security Agency (ISA—the internal security service, colloquially known as Shabak); the Mossad intelligence agency; the police force; and the Director of Security of the Defense Establishment, a unit within the Defense Ministry.

Subsequently, in 2015, the government adopted Resolution 2444, which approved the establishment of another centralized cybersecurity organ—the National Cyber Defense Authority.[5] Resolution 2444 envisioned that the authority would operate side by side with the bureau in the prime minister's office. It shifted the focus of the bureau's responsibilities from operations to strategic planning and capacity building.

Resolution 2444 gave the cyber authority operational responsibility for preventing cyberattacks and addressing threats in real time in cooperation with other national security agencies. The resolution further provided that the authority would serve as a focal point for cyber-related intelligence and analysis, work to increase readiness to thwart cyberattacks across different sectors, issue guidelines, regulate cybersecurity services, and guide the work of cybersecurity units within government ministries.[6]

Furthermore, the authority was tasked with establishing a Cyber Emergency Response Team (CERT) that would service stakeholders across the economy. According to Resolution 2444, the national CERT would provide assistance in cyber defense, facilitate information sharing, and allow for coordination between security agencies and other actors.

Resolution 2444 defined the structure and powers of the authority in only general terms. It created many spaces of potential friction among the actors involved in cybersecurity policy and operations, and tasked different organs with seemingly overlapping responsibilities.

One example of these ambiguities was the resolution's treatment of the relationship between the authority and the ISA. While section 12 of Resolution 2444 stated that the resolution did not detract from the cyber-related statutory authorities of the ISA, section 9 invited the bureau to put forward a plan for the transfer of responsibility for cyber defense of critical computer infrastructure from the ISA to the authority through the amendment of the Regulation of Security in Public Bodies Law, 1998. As part of the implementation of Resolution 2444, in August 2016, the Israeli parliament (Knesset) passed a temporary amendment to the Regulation of Security in Public Bodies Law to facilitate the transfer of responsibility in this area from the ISA to the authority.[7]

This amendment addressed only one aspect of the authority's operations. At the time of its adoption, work was already under way at the Israeli Ministry of Justice and the bureau on comprehensive legislation that would regulate the authority's powers and responsibilities, as well as other cyber defense matters.[8]

The authority began operating in 2016, and the CERT was up and running by 2017. The CERT includes a National Incident Management Center, which works around the clock and handles reports on cyberattacks, vulnerabilities, and security breaches across the Israeli economy.[9] The center also facilitates information sharing on cyberattacks and threats. It operates under a set of "action principles" issued by the prime minister's office in coordination with Israel's attorney general.[10] In 2018, the authority and the CERT were merged with the bureau under a new National Cyber Directorate, due in part to overlapping authority and bureaucratic redundancies between the bureau and the authority under the original framework.[11]

The IDF also set cyber reforms in motion in parallel to the reforms on the civilian end. In June 2015, Lieutenant General Gadi Eisenkot, then chief of staff of the IDF, decided to create a unified cyber command that would take the lead on cyber readiness within the military.[12] Prior to that decision, the Telecommunications Directorate of the IDF was responsible for cyber defense within the military, while the Israeli equivalent to the NSA, the signals intelligence unit of the Directorate of Military Intelligence (DMI), was responsible for intelligence collection and foreign cyber operations.[13]

However, in early 2017, this ambitious plan was abandoned in favor of a more careful approach that largely preserved the previous organizational division of labor between the DMI and the Telecommunications Directorate.[14] The reason for the change of direction was reportedly fear that a unified cyber command might harm the intelligence collection and foreign cyber work of the DMI.[15]

Legislative Reform

In parallel to the continuous development of new executive cyber defense organs and authorities, the government has advanced comprehensive legislation to enshrine these reforms. In June 2018, the prime minister's office released a Cyber Defense and National Cyber Directorate Bill.[16] The proposed bill consisted of three main chapters: an organizational chapter, which outlined the responsibilities and authorities of the National Cyber Directorate as well as its structure; a cyber defense chapter, which addressed specific authorities related to detection and defense against cyber threats; and a regulatory chapter, which included provisions for improving the cybersecurity preparedness of the Israeli economy.

In February 2021, the government circulated a revised draft of the operational cyber defense portion of the bill to fast-track its enactment into law while continuing consultations on the bill's other components. The draft states that speedy adoption of new cyber defense legislation is necessary because threat levels have increased. A major contributing factor, the draft explains, is the COVID-19 pandemic and the resulting rise in the volume of online interactions.[17]

The legislative effort has not advanced beyond the draft stage because of Israel's prolonged political stalemate and the exigencies of the COVID-19 crisis. The combination of these factors caused major legislative efforts to grind to a halt while Prime Minister Benjamin Netanyahu was in office. Parliament has yet to take up both the 2018 bill and the more limited 2021 cyber defense draft under the new Bennett government. Still, the Israeli government is likely to continue to advance legislative cyber reform. Netanyahu had vowed to make Israel "one of the five global cyber superpowers," and cyber reform enjoys support across the political spectrum.[18] The draft legislation the government has put forward to date merits attention because it elaborates in detail the current Israeli cybersecurity strategy and its view of the public-private relationship in this area.

Guiding Principles

The 2018 comprehensive bill reflected the three key policy principles that have guided executive reform efforts to date: the need for a concerted national response, facilitating cooperation between government and the private sector, and preserving the cybersecurity authorities and responsibilities of the "old" national security establishment.

First, according to the explanatory remarks attached to the draft, underlying the bill was the assumption that addressing cyber threats requires a coordinated, national effort. The remarks pointed out that cyber threats can originate anywhere in the world, do not respect physical boundaries, allow attackers anonymity, and may cause significant harm to the national economy, critical infrastructure, and human lives.

Second, the bill underscored that cyberspace is a predominantly civilian space. Civilian organizations possess most of the relevant information for identifying threats to their networks. They also control key tools for addressing such threats. The bill therefore placed ultimate responsibility for network defense (excluding, of course, military and other security establishment networks) with civilian organizations and individuals. At the same time, the bill recognized that civilian organizations cannot defend themselves alone considering the scope of potential threats, the need for expertise to combat them, and the narrow perspective of individual organizations. Effective defense, it concluded, requires cooperation between the government and the private sector.

Finally, the bill stated that it "is not designed to change the purpose or authorities of additional bodies that operate in Israeli cyberspace under applicable legal frameworks, including the ISA."[19] This major exception alluded to the national security establishment. Given the broad, ill-defined authorities of Israel's existing national security agencies in the cyber realm (described in greater detail later in this chapter), vesting the operational responsibility to prevent and counter cyber threats at home in the new cyber directorate was bound to draw the ire of the security establishment, especially the ISA, and invite turf wars. Unlike the IDF and Mossad, whose operations are largely geared toward foreign threats, the ISA has certain domestic security responsibilities. Conflicts between the newly established civilian cybersecurity organs and the national security establishment have accordingly plagued the legislative effort.[20]

Disagreements over the scope and content of the legislation came to a head in 2017, with the publication of a letter from the leaders of the major

Israeli security agencies to the prime minister and his security cabinet. The security agencies expressed their strong objection to an early draft presented to them by the bureau. The letter stated that the draft legislation ignored the existing authorities of the security agencies and the government resolutions pertaining to cybersecurity that explicitly excluded the security establishment from their purview. The letter further stated that by granting the cyber authority expansive powers without clearly defining its purpose, the draft could severely harm the work of the security community in the cyber realm. The letter concluded with a call to scrap the draft and negotiate a new one that would take account of the position of the security agencies.[21]

The security establishment has subsequently been highly successful in defending its cyber equities in the framework of the new reform. The 2018 bill explicitly committed to leave those equities undisturbed, and the shorter 2021 cyber defense bill emphasizes that its provisions reflect understandings and arrangements with the national security establishment.[22] This means that the national security establishment will generally maintain whatever domestic cyber authorities it had and avoid new restrictions on its foreign operations under the proposed cyber reform.

The Cyber Defense Chapter

While there is much to consider with respect to other components of the 2018 bill, my discussion focuses on the element of the reform that tracks the US concept of Persistent Engagement: the cyber defense chapter of the 2018 draft and the 2021 cyber defense bill. Both drafts seek to regulate the operational aspects of preventing, identifying, and containing cyberattacks that impact civilian organizations, a category that includes both public entities and private sector actors. The 2021 draft builds on the corresponding chapter of the 2018 draft with slight modifications.

Defining "Cyberattack"

The definition of a cyberattack has evolved between the drafts. The 2018 version conceived of a cyberattack as an act falling within "the range of actions that constitute abuse of a computer or computerized information by computational means." Section 1 of the 2018 draft more specifically defined the term as "activity designed to impair use of a computer or computational material stored therein." It included a non-exhaustive list of more specific circumstances that meet this criterion.[23]

The 2021 draft adopts a modified version of that definition. It distinguishes between "ordinary" cyberattacks and "severe" cyberattacks. The former is a broad category covering any unauthorized infringement of computer infrastructure or networks. The latter is limited to abuses that could harm vital national interests or infrastructure. Notably, the 2021 bill also modified the definition of a vital interest. The list of recognized interests now appears to be exhaustive. The 2021 draft removed an open-ended provision that allowed the prime minister to determine that an interest is "vital" for the purposes of the bill.[24] Despite these revisions, however, the list of interests is still exceptionally broad—it includes pliable, all-encompassing interests such as "preventing severe harm to public well-being" and protecting the state's economy.

An anticipated or actual cyberattack is what triggers many of the directorate's prevention and response authorities. The breadth of the definition in both the 2018 and 2021 drafts means that the threshold for activating those authorities under the proposed legislative reform would be exceptionally low.

Prevention and Response Authorities

The operational authorities that would be granted to the Cyber Directorate by the proposed legislative reform can roughly be divided into two categories: (1) information collection, analysis, and dissemination, and (2) direction and intervention. The 2021 cyber defense bill focuses on the latter.

Information collection, analysis, and dissemination. The 2018 bill would empower the Cyber Directorate to collect and analyze incident information, as well as information about vulnerabilities, technologies, attack methods, and tools. The directorate would be allowed to require any organization—governmental or private—to provide relevant information under certain conditions.[25] Moreover, the 2018 bill would authorize the directorate to enter premises where cyber defense–related information is believed to be located and require the directorate to share information with all relevant stakeholders.[26] The 2021 version of this provision narrows down this proposed authority by requiring a court order for entering premises and seizing property.[27]

"Cyber defense–related information" is defined broadly in both the 2018 and 2021 drafts, although the 2021 draft appears to narrow the definition. The 2018 draft defines it as "information that could help detect, address or prevent a cyberattack." This includes information about vulnerabilities, malware, and attack methods, as well as information about response methods. The 2018 bill would restrict collection of information about identifiable individuals or organizations. It would also limit use of any information collected to cyber defense purposes—not law enforcement or general intelligence collection—and establish rules for handling information collected from civilian entities and preventing abuse. Finally, the 2018 bill would create both internal and semi-independent oversight and privacy protection mechanisms.

The 2021 cyber defense draft does not address all aspects of the directorate's information collection and dissemination authority, but it does narrow the definition of cyber defense–related information by restricting it to "technical" information.[28] This limiting principle would in theory confine the directorate's cyber defense information gathering authority to technical elements such as code, vulnerabilities, and internet protocol addresses while constraining the directorate's authority to demand other kinds of information that can be said to assist in preventing or containing a cyberattack. The 2021 draft also proposes certain privacy safeguards.[29] Nevertheless, the directorate's information gathering authority would remain extremely broad under the 2021 draft.[30]

In addition to these expansive information gathering powers, the 2018 draft contemplates the creation of a mechanism within the directorate that would allow it to continuously monitor network activity. Section 17 of the bill would empower the directorate to create a "Detection and Identification" apparatus to collect and process cybersecurity information from a non-exhaustive list of entities in real time. This provision implies constant directorate monitoring of the networks of the covered entities. Most of these entities are government ministries and public entities responsible for critical infrastructure, but Section 18(4) of the bill would also allow for the monitoring of telecommunications companies under certain conditions. Constant government monitoring of telecoms—the arteries of national communication—would invariably create a large opening for government abuse.

The 2021 cyber defense draft does not address the "Detection and Information" apparatus. It is unclear whether the absence of this authority from the 2021 draft is simply due to the draft's narrow focus on certain cyber defense authorities, or an indication that the government has abandoned the idea.

Direction and intervention. One of the legislative reform's main objectives is to augment the cyber directorate's power to oversee, direct, and even intervene in cyber defense across public and private civilian organizations.

The 2018 bill provided for two main methods of intervention: First, the bill would give the directorate authority to issue binding directives to entities that have been attacked or entities for which there is reason to believe that an attack is forthcoming.[31] Second, the bill would allow the directorate to operate directly on compromised networks—a more intrusive form of intervention that potentially gives the directorate direct access to the computer networks of private entities. To offset this invasive authority, the bill would require the directorate to obtain consent or a judicial warrant prior to operating on networks, although there was a twenty-four-hour emergency exception to this warrant requirement.[32]

The 2018 bill conditioned the activation of both these authorities on the identification of a potential cyberattack that threatened a vital national interest, broadly defined. It also imposed a requirement of proportionality between the benefits of direct directorate intervention and the harm to the attacked organization and privacy rights.[33] As previously mentioned, the "vital interest" threshold for directorate intervention in private-sector cybersecurity crises was thus alarmingly low and easily manipulable.

The 2021 cyber defense bill introduced a slightly modified version of these authorities that eliminated some of the most invasive elements. For instance, the draft removes the emergency exception to the requirement to obtain a judicial order prior to direct directorate operation on private networks. But the 2021 version would still allow the cyber directorate extensive latitude in directing private entities and even operating within their networks. As in the 2018 version, the authorities are triggered by the existence of a cyber threat to a vital interest or the targeted organization engaging in "vital operations." Many private entities and forms of cyber abuse could fall within these categories.[34]

It is important to emphasize that the powers granted to the directorate in both the 2018 and 2021 versions of the cyber defense portion of the bill are limited to identifying, containing, and analyzing cyberattacks at home (i.e., within Israel). The task of "handling the attacker" falls, according to the 2018 bill, to "the responsible actors." Presumably the IDF, Mossad, and the ISA would be the actors responsible for handling foreign attackers outside Israel's territory.[35] Likewise, the 2021 bill fully reserves the cyber defense authorities of the other security organs and exempts them from its provisions.[36]

Both drafts not only preserve the traditional cybersecurity division of labor between the directorate and the national security establishment but also augment the role of the latter. Section 71 of the 2018 bill allows the

ISA to assume the directorate's direction and intervention powers when a cybersecurity threat is related to counterterrorism or espionage. The 2021 version contains a similar provision.[37]

In other words, both versions of the bill would add to the ISA's existing authorities to operate on domestic networks by allowing the agency to step into the directorate's shoes. This would provide a significant boost to the domestic authority of a security organ primarily responsible for combating foreign threats. That authority has already been expanded greatly in Israel in the wake of COVID-19, as the ISA conducted intrusive domestic surveillance to enforce quarantine obligations and contact-trace infections. The prospect of a general security service having such access and powers over domestic private entities raises significant concerns from both an institutional and civil liberties standpoint.

Israel's Reform and US Strategy

The Israeli cyber defense architecture under these recent reforms echoes the US concepts of Defend Forward and Persistent Engagement. Nevertheless, there are key differences. For one, Israel's Defend Forward equivalent is far less constrained by domestic law than is its US parallel. Furthermore, the Israeli reforms create a substantial role for government in defending *domestic* networks—including private networks—*within* Israeli territory. The reforms also harness the private sector in ways that the current US strategy and statutory framework do not contemplate.

The Israeli Defend Forward Equivalent

Defend Forward's aim of operating "as close as possible to the origin of adversary activity" implies that it is mainly geared toward external action—action outside of US networks, outside US territory. It may involve offensive action designed to harm adversary networks and infrastructure as well as essentially defensive measures to neutralize or thwart ongoing or expected adversary operations.

The direct Israeli equivalent to this category of operations is the cyber-related work of the traditional national security establishment—mainly the IDF, Mossad, and the ISA. Although much is unknown about the nature and scope of their activities, these agencies reportedly carry out cyber operations against foreign adversaries outside Israeli networks and territory. Famous examples include Israel's role in the Stuxnet attack on Iran's nuclear facilities; a cyberattack attributed to Israel designed to disrupt the operations of an Iranian port in response to an Iranian attack on Israeli water infrastructure; and a cyberattack that caused a blackout at Iran's Natanz nuclear facility.[38] The roles and authorities of Israel's national security agencies in this area have remained untouched by the Israeli cyber defense reform described earlier in this chapter, which focuses on domestic cyber defense.

Section 5 of Resolution 3611 explicitly excluded national security agencies from the resolution's purview. The resolution noted only that national security agencies would be subject to special arrangements mutually agreed upon with the new cyber defense agency (now the National Cyber Directorate). Subsequent resolutions, including Resolution 2444, also excluded or otherwise exempted the national security establishment from their scope, reaffirming—with narrow exceptions—that the reform did not aim to detract from any of the establishment's existing cyber authorities and responsibilities. As we have seen, both the 2018 and 2021 cyber bills adopted this stance as well.

The exceptions for national security agencies in Israel's new domestic cyber defense regulatory scheme and in proposed cybersecurity legislation have created a bifurcated regime. Reform efforts have focused on domestic cyber defense regulation and established new institutions for that purpose, while the cyber work of the old national security establishment—domestic and foreign—has been allowed to continue largely under preexisting parameters. As a result, the virtually non-existent domestic legal regime that applies to these agencies, especially when they act against foreign targets, continues to govern their cybersecurity operations.

To appreciate just how rudimentary the domestic legal regime governing the operations of Israel's national security establishment is, consider Basic Law: The Military—which defines the authority of the vast and powerful IDF, subordinates it to civilian control of the government, and imposes mandatory service obligations. This fundamental constitutional norm consists of a grand total of six one-sentence paragraphs.[39] There is no statute that governs the work of the Mossad. The Knesset painstakingly passed an ISA Law in 2002, but even this law consists of broad and ambiguous language and says very little about the ISA's specific operational authorities.[40]

Generally, the foreign affairs and national security powers of the Israeli government are deemed residual powers, that is, discretionary executive powers that do not depend on explicit constitutional or statutory grants of authority. These are powers that the government may wield unless there is a conflicting statute, or the action in question violates constitutional rights.[41] Basic Law: The Government contains certain procedural and reporting requirements for initiating war or "significant military action" likely to lead to war, but it does not substantively constrain the government's war-making authority. The Basic Law exempts other military action necessary for national defense and security from its procedural requirements.[42]

On the sub-constitutional level, there are statutes that restrict unauthorized access by any actor to computer networks and impose civil and criminal penalties for violations. Other legislation governs data handling.[43] However, these statutes apply only to the domestic operations of the national security agencies (to the extent that they have authority to carry out domestic operations).[44] They do not cover external cyber action or foreign intelligence collection.

Consequently, very little is known about the domestic legal and policy frameworks that govern the cyber work of the IDF, Mossad, and the ISA outside Israeli territory and networks.[45] That framework consists of inscrutable classified internal orders, guidelines, and regulations.

The rudimentary legal framework that applies to the Israeli national security establishment's operations abroad is thus far less robust than the regime that applies to similar operations in the United States. Israel lacks a detailed constitutional framework to govern international use of force, much less action that falls below the use of force threshold—the type of action Defend Forward appears to contemplate. There is no parallel to the War Powers Resolution, nor is there a tradition of publishing detailed executive branch legal opinions about the legality of various uses of force abroad (flawed and permissive as they may be).

Furthermore, Israeli national security establishment cyber operations on foreign territory are not regulated by statute. By contrast, the US statutory scheme governing this area includes the general legal requirements of Titles 10 and 50 of the United States Code as well as cyber-specific reforms introduced in recent years through the National Defense Authorization Act. Robert Chesney's chapter offers a detailed overview of these legal authorities, which I will not repeat here. He observes: "The domestic legal framework for military cyber operations is surprisingly robust, considering its recent vintage. . . . Congress has responded to the maturation of USCYBERCOM by adopting relatively detailed rules of authorization, process, and transparency."[46]

In sum, Israel's cyber defense approach has operational elements similar to those that inform the US Defend Forward strategy. However, in contrast to the relatively robust legal regime that applies in the United States in this area, Israel's cyber activity abroad remains a legal black hole.

Israel's Persistent Engagement—At Home

The Israeli approach to cyber defense reflects the same threat perception and basic operational approach as does that of the United States. Its guiding principles are essentially similar to what Persistent Engagement calls for: continuous monitoring of global cyber threats to the homeland and determined and timely action. Like the US approach, the Israeli approach to Persistent Engagement also underscores the need for a whole-of-government response to cyber threats.[47]

However, the Israeli framework goes much further than does that of the United States in granting the government invasive cyber defense authorities *at home*. It also imposes a wide range of cybersecurity obligations on the private sector. For example, the new National Cyber Directorate is empowered to collect, synthesize, and disseminate cybersecurity information to and from private entities, including information about their vulnerabilities and other potentially sensitive or proprietary information. It also has authority to step in and direct the responses of private entities to actual or impending cyberattacks. Still more, under both proposed versions of a new cyber bill, the National Cyber Directorate will be allowed to operate directly on the networks of private actors to contain cyberattacks—even without their consent. The proposed "Detection and Identification" apparatus would involve mass data collection by the directorate on a regular basis and possibly even monitoring of domestic telecom networks.

The rough parallels to these authorities in the United States can be found in the Cybersecurity Information Sharing Act of 2015 (CISA 2015) and the Cybersecurity and Infrastructure Security Agency Act of 2018 (CISAA 2018).[48] CISA 2015 encourages companies to *voluntarily* share information about cyber threat indicators and related defensive measures by granting them certain protections for such disclosure. But it does not compel disclosure. CISAA 2018 reorganized the Department of Homeland Security by creating the Cybersecurity and Infrastructure Agency. The functions of this agency appear to be similar in some respects to those of the Israeli National Cyber Directorate. But the Cybersecurity and Infrastructure Agency's authority over the private sector is far more constrained than that of its Israeli counterpart.

For example, the Cybersecurity and Infrastructure Agency houses a national cybersecurity and communications integration center. The center's functions include facilitating information-sharing related to cyber threat indicators, defensive measures, cybersecurity risks, incidents, analysis, and warnings for federal and non-federal entities. The center is also tasked with coordinating preparedness and incident response both within and outside the federal government, integrating and analyzing cyber threats and defensive measures, and sharing that analysis with entities across the economy. None of these authorities authorize the center to issue binding directives to private actors in the event of a cyberattack or threat thereof. Nor do these authorities allow the Cybersecurity and Infrastructure Agency to step in and operate directly on the networks of affected private actors without their consent. The center can provide "timely technical assistance, risk management support, and incident response capabilities to Federal and non-Federal entities with respect to cyber threat indicators, defensive measures, cybersecurity risks, and incidents, which may include attribution, mitigation, and remediation." But it may only do so upon request.[49]

Furthermore, section 2202 of CISAA 2018 outlines the cybersecurity authorities of the secretary of Homeland Security. These authorities include authorization to coordinate various aspects of cyber policy with the private sector and to synthesize information originating in the private sector.[50] Similarly to the provisions that govern the operations of the cybersecurity and communications integration center, section 2202 allows the secretary only to invite voluntary private sector cooperation. Moreover, many of the secretary's section 2202 authorities are limited by the objective of detecting and responding to terrorist threats. The Israeli cyber bill as well as the 2021 revised draft of its cyber defense chapter lacks a similar subject-matter constraint. As previously mentioned, the bill's standard for the activation of the National Cyber Directorate's direction and intervention authorities, the "vital interest" or "vital activity" standard, is extremely broad and open to interpretation.

It may be that granting the government sweeping powers to direct and manage the containment of cyberattacks in the private sector is operationally necessary to defend against cyber threats effectively. That certainly appears to be the position of the Israeli government. We lack the tools to assess the operational necessity of these measures or their efficacy because relatively little is publicly known about the cyber threat landscape, how Israel has responded in practice in every instance, whether its responses achieved the desired outcomes, and whether coercion of private actors (as opposed to voluntary cooperation) was actually needed.

Since its inception, the new cyber directorate has advertised several instances of successful identification and containment of cyberattacks on civilian Israeli targets, but these examples probably reveal only a small part of the picture.[51] These reports provide little detail about directorate cooperation with the private sector, related conflicts and obstacles, and the extent to which the directorate had to compel private actors to cooperate.

I leave the operational analysis to others. Instead, the next section considers how the existing and proposed Israeli cyber defense architecture creates openings for government aggrandizement and potential abuse.

Collaboration or Aggrandizement?

At first glance, the government's statements to date and the explanatory remarks attached to the 2018 cyber bill espouse a collaborative model of responsibility for cyber defense and preparedness between government and the private sector. Israel's new cyber defense bureaucracy and related legal authorities are said to be predicated on the assumption that while the private sector has significant advantages in the area of cyber defense, and every organization should assume primary responsibility for its own security, the nature of the modern cyber threat environment is such that individual organizations cannot operate alone. An active governmental role is therefore essential.

Nevertheless, in practice, Israel's new cybersecurity architecture establishes the National Cyber Directorate as a highly centralized government component with wide-ranging authorities that the proposed legislation would expand even further. Israel's cybersecurity reform ultimately prioritizes the government and exudes government dominance, notwithstanding the rhetoric of private sector empowerment.

The proposed legislation would shift the balance of power between government and the private sector even more in favor of the government. It would undermine the collaborative prong of the regulatory model and create substantial risk of government overreach, politicization, and abuse. Naturally, the directorate's proposed far-reaching powers have drawn criticism from rights advocates and businesses—both local actors and global corporations like Google.[52] Critics have expressed concern over the prospect of government penetration into their networks, centralized synthesis and distribution of information about their vulnerabilities, and the sharing of other proprietary information.

Israel's cybersecurity architecture is particularly susceptible to politicization because the National Cyber Directorate effectively reports directly to the prime minister. The proposed legislation would enshrine the prime minister's broad discretion to expand the directorate's roles and authorities, from cybersecurity defined in the narrow sense of protecting critical computer infrastructure to sanctioning measures that involve extensive intervention in the operations of private entities to defend ill-defined "vital interests." While there is an argument to be made in favor of such authorities—for instance, to combat foreign disinformation campaigns for political aims on Israeli networks—the proposed bill would grant the Israeli executive what amounts to a blank check.

The expansive proposed powers of the National Cyber Directorate when it comes to domestic cyber defense would add to the relative freedom the government enjoys in the area of external cyber action. As we have seen, cyber action against foreign targets, conducted by the military and security agencies like the Mossad and ISA, remains a legal black hole. The operations of these bodies are lightly regulated in primary legislation. Other applicable legal instruments are classified and not subject to public scrutiny.

What is more, the national security establishment has been highly successful at protecting its turf and powers in the process of domestic cybersecurity reform, due in large part to the substantial influence it wields in internal decision making. While the precise division of labor between the National Cyber Directorate and Israel's national security establishment remains unclear, the government has gone to great lengths at every turn to emphasize that any new cybersecurity organs or authorities would not detract from the cybersecurity powers of the old national security establishment. The ISA in particular appears to have taken advantage of the Cyber Directorate's powers to augment and leverage its own.[53]

What emerges is a combination of broad, ill-defined, and intrusive government authorities in the domestic cybersecurity space, combined with even broader, less regulated government authority with respect to external cyber action and foreign threats. This outcome militates in favor of imposing meaningful restrictions and oversight—internal, parliamentary, and judicial—on the National Cyber Directorate's powers if the proposed legislation is to move forward. The 2021 draft shows some progress in that direction by modifying several of the operative definitions that trigger the directorate's authorities and tightening judicial oversight. Nevertheless, the 2021 draft still grants the executive ample latitude to inject politics into cybersecurity and commandeer private actors. As for external cyber operations, it is past time to consider whether granting the national security establishment free rein when it acts outside Israeli territory is consistent with the rule of law in a modern democracy.

Conclusion

Israel's cyber defense architecture shares much with that of the United States and has parallels with both Defend Forward and Persistent Engagement. There are, however, key differences: Israel's Defend Forward component is far less regulated than is its American counterpart. Its Persistent Engagement equivalent also goes much further than does the US approach in giving the government extensive authorities to direct and even take over cyber defense in the private sector.

Israel's cyber defense reform reflects awareness of the challenges involved in effective cyber defense and an understanding that successfully addressing these challenges requires an economy-wide effort. However, the regulatory balance in this area has shifted too much in favor of the government. This dynamic creates the potential for government aggrandizement, overreach, and abuse. More work is needed to refine the provisions of the proposed cyber legislation to eliminate vague and overly broad definitions and authorities and to put in place effective oversight mechanisms—internal, judicial, and parliamentary—to offset these concerns.

Notes

1. *See* US Cyber Command, Achieve and Maintain Cyberspace Superiority: Command Vision for US Cyber Command 4, (2018) [hereinafter US Cyber Command].

2. *Id.* at 6.
3. Ronen Bergman and David M. Halbfinger, *Israel Hack of Iran Port Is Latest Salvo in Exchange of Cyberattacks*, N.Y. TIMES (May 19, 2020); William J. Broad, John Markoff, and David E. Sanger, *Israeli Test on Worm Called Crucial in Iran Nuclear Delay*, N.Y. TIMES (Jan. 15, 2011)..
4. Government of Israel Resolution No.3611, Advancing National Capabilities in Cyberspace (Aug.7, 2011).
5. Government of Israel Resolution No. 2444, Advancing National Preparedness for Cyber Defense (Feb. 15, 2015).
6. *See* Government of Israel Resolution No. 2443, Advancing National Regulation and Government Leadership in Cyber Defense (Feb. 15, 2015) (adopted on the same day as Resolution 2444).
7. Temporary Amendment to the Law Regulating Security in Public Entities, 2016.
8. *See id.* at Part I.B.
9. *See* Israel National Cyber Directorate, *The Israeli Cyber Emergency Response Team (CERT)*, GOV.IL (Jun. 5, 2019).
10. National Cyber Directorate, *National Cyber Emergency Response Team Principles of Operation*, GOV.IL (retrieved Aug. 17, 2020).
11. Government of Israel Resolution No. 3270, Merging the Units of the National Cyber Directorate and Related Provisions (Dec. 17, 2017).
12. IDF to Establish New Cyber Arm, *Times of Israel*, n.d. (2015) (retrieved Aug. 17, 2020).
13. Meir Elran and Gabi Siboni, *Establishing an IDF Cyber Command*, INSS INSIGHT No. 719 (July 8, 2015).
14. Anna Ahronheim, *IDF Decides Not to Have a Cyber Command Department*, JERUSALEM POST (Jan. 1, 2017).
15. Gili Cohen, *Until a Cyber Arm Is Established: The IDF's Cyber Headquarters Will Be Subordinate to the Telecommunications Directorate*, HAARETZ (Jan. 2, 2017); Lilach Shoval, *IDF Chief Has Changed His Mind: A Cyber Command Will Not Be Established*, ISRAEL HA'YOM (Jan. 1, 2017).
16. The full text of the bill is available at Tazkirim.gov.il, https://www.tazkirim.gov.il/s/tzkirim?language=iw&tzkir=a093Y00001RFEcVQAX [hereinafter 2018 Bill].
17. *See* Draft Cyber Defense and National Cyber Directorate Bill (Temporary Provisions), 2021, https://www.law.co.il/media/computer-law/cyber-defense-bill-2021.pdf [hereinafter 2021 Bill].
18. Benjamin Netanyahu, *Israel—A Cyber Superpower*, GLOBES (Apr. 3, 2016)..
19. 2018 Bill, *supra* note 16, at § 2.
20. An August 2016 report by the Knesset Cyber Defense subcommittee described conflict and lack of cooperation between the new Cyber Authority (later the "Directorate") and the security establishment. It noted some improvement in cooperation after the signing of a Memorandum of Understanding between the ISA and the authority in June 2016. The report also predicted that there would be no avoiding at least some chipping away at ISA prerogatives with the entry of a new actor, the authority, into the cyber field, notwithstanding Resolution 2444's explicit guarantee that the power of the ISA would be preserved. The Knesset Foreign Affairs and National Security Committee, Report on the Evaluation of the Distribution of Responsibilities and Authorities with Respect to Cyber Defense in Israel (2016).

21. Jacob Magid, *Security Chiefs Slam Netanyahu over Planned Cyber Defense Body*, TIMES OF ISRAEL (Apr. 24, 2017).

22. *See* 2021 Bill, *supra* note 17, at § 3.

23. Such circumstances include, but are not limited to, obstruction of computational operations; deletion or modification of data; unauthorized network penetration or access to information; and obstruction of network communication.

24. See 2021 Bill, *supra* note 17, at § 1. Under the 2018 Bill, the list of vital interests included national security and public safety; human life; the national economy; functioning essential infrastructure; functioning of organizations providing services at a significant scale; preventing significant threats to the environment or public health; preventing significant infringement of privacy; and any other interest the prime minister determines. The new list in the 2021 draft includes a modified version of these interests excluding the prime minister's residual determination authority.

25. 2018 Bill, *supra* note 16, at § 20.

26. 2018 Bill, *supra* note 16, at § 22 (entering a residence generally requires a judicial order).

27. 2021 Bill, supra note 17, at § 6(b).

28. 2021 Bill, *supra* note 17, at § 1.

29. 2021 Bill, *supra* note 17, at § 7.

30. 2021 Bill, *supra* note 17, at § 1.

31. 2018 Bill, *supra* note 16, at § 26.

32. 2018 Bill, *supra* note 16, at §§ 27, 32; § 36.

33. 2018 Bill, *supra* note 16, at § 1.

34. 2021 Bill, *supra* note 17, at §§ 4-6.

35. 2018 Bill, *supra* note 16, at § 8, para. 5.

36. 2021 Bill, *supra* note 17, at §§ 11-12, 14.

37. 2021 Bill, *supra* note 17, at § 10. This version of the ISA authorization eliminates the link to espionage or terrorism but adds certain preconditions for the ISA to step in. Specifically, the ISA would be allowed to step in only to address a "severe" cyberattack. As I previously noted, however, the definition of "severe" cyberattack is so broad that it renders the requirement hollow.

38. Daniel Politi, *Israel Reportedly Behind Cyberattack That Caused Blackout at Iran Nuclear Facility*, SLATE (Apr. 11, 2021).

39. Knesset, Basic Law: The Military, 5736–1976, SH 1197 418 (Isr.).

40. General Security Service Law, 5762–2002, SH 1832 179 (Isr.).

41. *See* Knesset, Basic Law: The Government, 5761–2001, SH 1780 158 (Isr.), § 32.

42. *Id.* at § 40.

43. Amir Cahane and Yuval Shany, *Regulation of Online Surveillance in Israeli Law and Comparative Law*, ISRAEL DEMOCRACY INSTITUTE (2019). *See, e.g.*, The Criminal Procedure Law (Enforcement Authorities—Communications Data), 5768–2007, SH 2122 72 (Isr.); The Computers Law, 5755–1995, SH 1534 366 (Isr.); The Privacy Protection Law, 5741–1981, LSI 35 136 (1980–81), as amended (Isr.); Secret Monitoring Law, 5739–1979, SH 938 118 (Isr.), § 23A; The Criminal Procedure

Ordinance (Detention and Search) [New Version], 5729–1969, LSI 2 30 (Isr.). For an overview, *see* Library of Congress, *Online Privacy Law: Israel* (updated Dec. 30, 2020).

44. Save for the police and the ISA, which has certain domestic authorities, national security agencies do not operate domestically.

45. This chapter does not address international legal frameworks. However, it is noteworthy that Israel has recently outlined its view of the applicability of international law in cyberspace. In principle, "Israel considers that international law is applicable to cyberspace." Roy Schondorf, *Israel's Perspective on Key Legal and Practical Issues Concerning the Application of International Law to Cyber Operations*, EJIL:TALK! (Dec. 9, 2020). However, it maintains that international law rules and principles such as the law on use of force, sovereignty, non-intervention, and attribution were not designed for the challenges that cyberspace presents and therefore require careful and gradual translation before they could be applied effectively. To the extent that Israel accepts certain international law limitations on cyberoperations, those limitations would factor into its decisions about Defend-Forward type operations. *See id.*

46. *See infra* chpt. 13.

47. US CYBER COMMAND, supra note 1, at 4 ("Whole-of-government approaches for protecting, defending, and operating in cyberspace must keep pace with the dynamics of this domain.").

48. Pub. L. No. 114-113, 129 Stat. 2241, 2936 (2015) (codified at 6 U.S.C. §§ 1501–1510 [2018]); Pub. L. No. 115-278, 132 Stat. 4168 (2018) (codified at 6 U.S.C. §§ 651–674 [2018]).

49. 6 U.S.C. § 659 (2018).

50. For instance, the secretary is authorized to "access, receive, and analyze law enforcement information, intelligence information, and other information from federal government agencies, state, local, tribal, and territorial government agencies, including law enforcement agencies, and *private sector entities*, and to integrate that information" to counter terrorist threats. 6 U.S.C. § 652 (2018) (emphasis added). She is also authorized to "recommend measures necessary to protect the key resources and critical infrastructure of the United States in coordination with other federal government agencies, including sector-specific agencies, and in cooperation with state, local, tribal, and territorial government agencies and authorities, *the private sector*, and other entities" and to "consult with state, local, tribal, and territorial government agencies and *private sector* entities to ensure appropriate exchanges of information, including law enforcement-related information, relating to threats of terrorism against the United States." *Id.* (emphasis added).

51. Amir Buhbut and Tal Shalev, *Head of the National Cyber Directorate on the Attempted Attack on Water Infrastructure: "It Could Have Ended in Disaster,"* WALLANEWS (May 28, 2020); Udi Ezion and Naomi Zoref, *A Large-Scale Cyber Attack Paralyzed Numerous Israeli Websites: "Iranian Actors Hacked [the Sites],"* CALCALIST (May 21, 2020); Amitay Ziv, *The National Cyber Directorate Thwarted "A Large Scale Cyber Attack,"* The Attackers: Iranian Hackers, THEMARKER (Apr. 26, 2017).

52. *See, e.g.,* Comments by Google on the Draft Cyber Defense and National Cyber Directorate Bill (Aug. 28, 2018); Comments by the Israel Democracy Institute on the

Draft Cyber Defense and National Cyber Directorate Bill (July 11, 2018); Comments by the Israel Internet Union on the Draft Cyber Defense and National Cyber Directorate Bill (2018).

53. *See* Amitay Ziv, *In Lieu of Cyber Defense: The ISA's 200 Million "Marionette,"* THEMARKER (Aug. 28, 2018).

13

Adapting to the Cyber Domain: Comparing US and UK Institutional, Legal, and Policy Innovations

Robert M. Chesney

Prime Minister Boris Johnson made it official in a statement to Parliament on November 19, 2020. "I can announce that we have established a National Cyber Force, combining our intelligence agencies and service personnel," he proclaimed, adding that it "is already operating in cyberspace against terrorism, organised crime and hostile state activity."[1]

Public avowal of the National Cyber Force (NCF) came as no great surprise. Plans to take this institutional step had been discussed publicly before, after all.[2] Nonetheless, it was a significant moment in the ongoing process of tailoring UK institutions, policies, and legal frameworks to suit the evolving nature and scale of cyber domain threats and opportunities. The NCF embodies certain distinctive characteristics of the British system, including flexibility regarding institutional roles in general and the role of intelligence agencies in particular. As we shall see, these features are conducive to what the US government calls "defending forward": that is, conducting operations on a non-consensual basis in order to cause effects on foreign networks and other infrastructure in order to stop or preempt malicious cyber activity. Much the same can be said, moreover, for another recent British organizational innovation: creation of the National Cybersecurity Centre (the NCSC).

The American experience throughout this same period has been analogous in many respects, including the creation of new organizations with defensive and offensive missions. And the Defend Forward model is, after all, an American coinage. But a close comparison of the two systems reveals significant differences. As we shall see, institutional formalism is far more conspicuous in the American system, and so too are anxieties about the roles of intelligence agencies. Both of these qualities have implications for the implementation of the Defend Forward model. Whether those implications are bugs or features is, perhaps, in the eye of the beholder. The comparison between the UK and US models, at any rate, is instructive.

In the pages that follow, I explore the origins and evolution of both the defensive and offensive aspects of the UK and US models in order to place the pursuit of Defend Forward style operations by both countries into a fulsome institutional, policy, and legal context. The first part below focuses on *defensive* functions that all governments pursue, from protecting their own systems to helping with private-sector defense. Both the United Kingdom and the United States have engaged in a variety of institutional and policy innovations over time in an attempt to perform such functions, in both cases culminating recently in the establishment of new organizations that differ in intriguing ways. The second part below focuses on *offensive* functions: that is, government activities that entail overcoming rather than enhancing computer security. Both the US and UK governments have developed such capacities in service of familiar public policy priorities, ranging from the familiar (law enforcement, espionage, and armed conflict) to the exotic (adversarial statecraft below the level of war). Some of the resulting activities fall readily within the domains of well-established government institutions in both the United States and United Kingdom, but others present harder questions of institutional design and legal architecture.

Comparing US and UK Adaptation for Defensive Functions

All governments engage in a variety of activities to defend both themselves and their societies from unwelcome interventions by other states. From counterintelligence to military defense, these are familiar defensive functions for which governments have long-established institutions, along with legal and policy architectures that both enable and (in some countries more than others) constrain them.

There is nothing novel about the general idea that technological change can unsettle those institutional, policy, and legal arrangements. History is replete with—arguably even defined by—an endless succession of such developments. From steam power to nuclear power, from the rise of aircraft to the submerging of submarines, the practical possibilities relating to how states pursue their national interests in relation to one another are in constant flux. Incumbent structures—especially those involved in national defense and intelligence—have to adapt, sooner or later, both to exploit and to defend against the new possibilities that changes of this kind generate.

In some cases, technological change requires recognition of an entirely new domain of activity. So it was with the power of flight, with the resulting creation of air forces, international civil aviation arrangements, and (mostly unsuccessful) attempts to prevent the emergence of aerial bombing. So too with submarine technology and space-related technologies. And so too, obviously, with the proliferation of computers and networks that combine to constitute the cyber domain.

Predictably, the rapid growth of the cyber domain is having a significant disruptive impact on every nation's institutions and legal architectures. The features of the cyber domain that drive this disruption are well understood. They include the sharply reduced relevance of physical proximity as a constraint on the ability of one state to reach another; the relative difficulty (however often it is exaggerated) of reliably attributing a particular action in the cyber domain to a particular state; the speed with which operations are performed; the astonishing growth of data and systems that can be reached and thus put at risk of theft or even destruction; the relative affordability and practicality of establishing significant government capabilities to operate in this domain; the overlap with a globalized black market for increasingly capable hacking tools and services; the ability of private actors to have impacts akin to those previously thought the province of governments; and so forth.

Taken as a whole, these features result in a world in which more actors are more able to spy on one another, to steal from one another, to hold one another's valued assets at risk, and in extremis to harm one another. Our increasingly wired world is becoming more efficient but also more dangerous in this sense.

Both the United Kingdom and United States governments are in the midst of a protracted process of adapting to these rapidly evolving circumstances. They have pursued similar paths, but not identical ones. My aim in this first part is to describe their respective evolutions in terms of the *defensive* mission (i.e., protecting the confidentiality, integrity, and availability of information systems and associated data, particularly those systems and data associated with the government and with critical infrastructure).

Evolution of the US Defensive Model

In his book *Dark Territory*, Fred Kaplan opens with a vignette of President Ronald Reagan watching the hacker classic *War Games* at the White House in 1983. The film features Matthew Broderick as a teenage gamer who thinks he is hacking into a software company's game development system, when, in fact, it is a Pentagon system with its proverbial finger on the nuclear button. Reagan was alarmed by the film's depiction of poorly secured military code, and he pressed the Pentagon on whether anything of that sort could happen with real military systems. The answer, alas, was not reassuring.[3]

That was nearly four decades ago. Things have improved a vast amount since then. Perhaps not as much as one might expect, however. And what progress there has been has not been equally distributed across government national security systems, civilian government systems, and privately held critical infrastructure systems.

Not surprisingly, the path forward turned out to be smoothest with respect to enhancing the security of America's national security systems (NSS)—that is, those information systems associated with the US government's military and intelligence activities. Progress in this area has been facilitated by a combination of factors. Critically, the National Security Agency (NSA) was well-suited to adapt to this task. And though institutional changes were needed across the broader military establishment, the Department of Defense (DoD) by its nature has unusual capacity to reorganize itself (compared to other government entities). In contrast, there was no comparable incumbent institution arching across the numerous departments, agencies, and offices that constitute the rest of the executive branch. And the obstacles are still more difficult once one turns to the private sector and critical infrastructure.

Cybersecurity for National Security Systems

As long as there have been military communications worth intercepting and reading, there have been efforts by adversaries to acquire them and, if necessary, decrypt them. The military, accordingly, has a long history of pursuing communications security (COMSEC), particularly via cryptography but also through the screening of hardware—and eventually of software too. Since the early 1950s, these capabilities have been concentrated in the Defense Department's NSA, an agency far better known for its signals intelligence (SIGINT) espionage and analysis efforts.[4]

By the late 1970s, under the directorship of Admiral Bob Inman, NSA was beginning to expand its information security services more broadly throughout DoD. As Kaplan relates, NSA thus was in a good position to take on a still bigger role when Reagan's 1983 inquiry began to filter through the Pentagon.[5] At the same time, however, the idea of an expanded NSA role was anathema to others (especially to civil liberties advocates still flush with concerns rooted in domestic spying scandals that emerged in the 1970s). Ultimately, NSA's key role in setting security standards for "national security systems" was confirmed by statute, but Congress at the same time effectively blocked NSA from doing the same for the rest of the executive branch.[6] We will return to the topic of security for the rest of the executive branch shortly. For now, it is enough to say that what became NSA's Information Assurance Directorate (since folded into NSA's Cybersecurity Directorate) performs the full spectrum of security functions for national security systems (NSS)—that is, the systems handling classified information.

There is much more to the military's cybersecurity history than just NSA's role, however. Not every inch of attack surface related to military information technology (IT) is within the NSS domain, and NSA does not operationally defend all of it. Additional security-oriented structures were needed.

That need was documented, famously, by Cliff Stoll's book *The Cuckoo's Egg*, describing the seemingly endless and often comical futility of his efforts to alert government and military officials to a security breach involving military systems in the mid-1980s.[7] Of course, one might expect the situation to have improved a great deal over the decade that followed. Alas, the experience of 1997's Eligible Receiver exercise, during which an NSA red team quickly ran rampant through some of DoD's most crucial networks, suggested otherwise. As Kaplan relates, Deputy Defense Secretary John Hamre was stunned to discover in the aftermath of that exercise how poorly organized DoD was to address its cybersecurity failings.[8] And when that same lack of responsibility became still more glaring thanks to an actual hacking episode near that time, Hamre pressed for a solution.

He got one, or at least the beginning of one. Brigadier General John "Soup" Campbell of the Joint Chiefs of Staff J-39 bureau proposed formation of what came to be known as Joint Task Force-Computer Network Defense (JTF-CND). On paper, at least, JTF-CND consolidated a variety of defense-oriented operational functions. By late 1998 its skeleton was in place, building on the intrusion-detection and other network monitoring capabilities developed by the Air Force's Information Warfare Center in San Antonio.[9]

The first major change to JTF-CND involved an expansion of its remit to encompass, at least notionally, computer network *attack* in addition to its original defense mission, and a corresponding change to the JTF's name. It remained limited in practice, however, along critical dimensions including the number of expert personnel it could bring to bear, the technical infrastructure (from exploits to staging servers) it could access (let alone develop on its own), and the authorities it possessed to act. All that began to change, however, when Secretary of Defense Gates in 2009 transformed the JTF into US Cyber Command (USCYBERCOM) and intertwined it with NSA for incubation purposes.[10]

The incubation model was a bold stroke. Going forward, at least for a time, USCYBERCOM and NSA would share a single "dual-hatted" commander, ensuring (at least to some degree) an inherent understanding of and interest in the respective capabilities and missions of the two organizations where it would count most for purposes of cooperation on a day-to-day basis. Equally critical, USCYBERCOM would be co-located on site with NSA at Fort Meade and would share personnel and technical infrastructure. It is hard to imagine an approach that would more efficiently produce a rapid surge in USCYBERCOM's capabilities, for both its defensive and offensive missions, while also minimizing the deconfliction problems inherent to the overlapping interests of intelligence agencies and the military in cyberspace.

USCYBERCOM today is a full-fledged combatant command (rather than just a supporting command akin to a service branch) and has matured to the point of triggering a lively debate regarding whether to sever the dual-hat relationship and other elements of the incubation model. For now, however, what matters is that USCYBERCOM hosts a relatively well-developed institutional structure for the larger DoD defensive mission, apart from NSA's role. That mission is concentrated in a subordinate command called Joint Force Headquarters-DoD Information Networks (JFHQ-DoDIN).

JFHQ-DoDIN performs several critical defensive functions. First, it is a centralized mechanism for making DoD-wide determinations relating to cybersecurity risk management policies and practices. Second, it oversees compliance with those policies across the DoDIN. Third, it issues directives when necessary to compel or prohibit particular actions by a given DoD component. Fourth, it provides a degree of centralized operational defensive services for DoD. And fifth, it can deploy personnel (cyber protection teams) to provide further operational defensive services in specific settings if and when needed (that is, where the in-house operational capabilities of personnel defending a particular DoD organization are not sufficient to the task).

Cybersecurity for Federal Civilian Systems

Change has come far more slowly with respect to the vast array of federal government organizations that are not part of the military or the intelligence community and that sometimes are called, collectively, the Federal Civilian Executive Branch (FCEB).

The issue of FCEB cybersecurity began to get sustained attention in the mid-1990s. In 1996, Congress took an important preliminary step by creating a standard-setting function applicable to the FCEB as a whole. Going forward, the secretary of commerce would promulgate cybersecurity standards for all FCEB entities, drawing on the expertise of the National Institute of Standards and Technology (NIST) to do so. Unfortunately, Congress did not also empower Commerce (or any other entity) to audit and compel actual compliance with those standards.

Not long thereafter, Dick Clarke (famous for his efforts during the Clinton and George W. Bush administrations to draw attention to a variety of emerging threats, including cybersecurity and terrorism) proposed a bolder intervention: centralizing most, if not all, FCEB network infrastructure in order to facilitate monitoring of traffic at the network perimeter, possibly to be implemented by NSA. The proposal generated sharp pushback, however. Many still viewed cybersecurity as a prosaic aspect of IT management that should be left to the purview of the specific agencies, and the possible role of NSA added a privacy protection dimension to the opposition. The proposal crashed and burned.[11]

Congress came back to the drawing board in 2002, enacting the Federal Information Security Management Act (FISMA).[12] FISMA improved the existing standards-setting process in two promising ways. First, it shifted responsibility for promulgating NIST-based standards from Commerce (which had little purchase over other departments) to the White House Office of Management and Budget (OMB) (which had, at least in theory, a great deal of potential leverage). Second, FISMA gave OMB authority to monitor other agencies for actual compliance.

On a separate front, however, FISMA also innovated institutionally by mandating creation of what became US-CERT (Computer Emergency Readiness Team). US-CERT was not there to perform centralized security services à la the Clarke model, but it would be able to provide expert advice throughout the FCEB both ex ante (that is, pre-incident) and in specific response to an incident. This was a modest but significant step toward the possibility of centralized defensive services.

Other waves of innovation followed. By 2008, the Department of Homeland Security existed, and it included a component (known then as the National Protection and Programs Directorate [NPPD]) with at least nominal responsibilities relating to physical security and cybersecurity for both privately held critical infrastructure and the FCEB. President Bush decided to place US-CERT within NPPD and then added a fresh element of centralized defensive services: In a variant of Clarke's original plan, Bush directed NPPD to create a threat-detection capability for all FCEB network external access points. This resulted in the creation of a signature-based sensor system that monitors inbound and outbound traffic for indicators of compromise and the like, henceforth known as "Einstein."[13] Bush also called for NPPD to develop other defense-oriented services that other parts of the FCEB might choose to use. Then, in 2010, President Obama directed OMB to delegate to NPPD its compliance-checking function (overseeing FCEB compliance with the NIST standards), a move that Congress ratified in a 2014 update to FISMA.

With that 2014 FISMA update, Congress took an important additional step. Up until that point, NPPD lacked any enforcement authority. It could not impose direct costs on recalcitrant FCEB entities for failing to comply with NIST standards, and it certainly could not issue specific directives to other agencies making them take security measures. FISMA 2014 left the former gap in place, but it closed the latter one by authorizing NPPD to issue "binding operational directives" that compel FCEB entities to take particular actions in response to known or reasonably suspected vulnerabilities and other information security risks.[14]

NPPD's first use of this authority provides a good illustration of the need for it. NPPD had a program that scanned FCEB systems for known vulnerabilities, and each week would provide relevant departments and agencies with a customized report flagging critical vulnerabilities on their systems as well as describing the needed mitigation steps. Uptake on that information was not, however, anything like what it should have been. With the authority to issue binding operational directives, however, NPPD could now do more than make recommendations. Its first binding operational directive, in May 2015, gave agencies thirty days to act on critical vulnerability notifications impacting their internet-facing systems, or else provide a detailed account explaining the basis for any delay and the plan for eventually making the required changes. Congress supplemented the binding operational directive authority the very next year, moreover, adding a somewhat-overlapping capacity to issue "Emergency Directives" to compel action by the head of an FCEB agency in response to information security threats.

The next stage in this evolutionary process was of a different order: rebranding the anodyne-sounding NPPD as the Cybersecurity and Infrastructure Security Agency (CISA). This shift might seem inconsequential in formal terms, but perceptions matter, and branding can impact perception. The mission-specific clarity of the CISA brand helped spread understanding of the maturing organization's role both within the FCEB and, as we shall see, with the private sector as well. The timing in late 2018 was impeccable, moreover, given the degree to which the organization's authorities had matured by that stage and the fact that it enjoyed a particularly effective leader (in the person of Chris Krebs).

Over the next two years, CISA polished and expanded the defensive services it could offer to the FCEB (as well as to state and local government entities and to privately held critical infrastructure entities). The list encompasses everything from threat-hunting and incident response (remote or on-site) to continuous diagnostics and vulnerability scanning.[15] But two key constraints remained. First, CISA is not funded to the degree needed to provide such services on a comprehensive basis. Second, the entire system until very recently has been entirely voluntary, in the sense that CISA could provide its help to an FCEB entity only with that entity's consent. Threat hunting, for example, occurred only on request.

This is changing at the time of this writing. When Congress in December 2020 overrode President Trump's veto of the National Defense Authorization Act for Fiscal Year 2021, it enacted a raft of new cybersecurity provisions. Among the least noticed but most important of them was Section 1705, which gives CISA express authority to conduct threat-hunting operations on the information systems of FCEB agencies "with or without advance notice to or authorization from" them.[16] The federal government is not yet fully centralized when it comes to defensive services across the FCEB or even close to being so. But between CISA's authority to conduct threat hunting at will and to issue Binding Operational Directives and Emergency Directives, Congress has moved the government onto firmer ground in recent years. Given the furor surrounding the recent, high-profile breach at the company SolarWinds, which led to the penetration of numerous FCEB systems, this change appears to be arriving none too soon; at least some aspects of the harm from that breach might have been averted by more-effective network monitoring. All that authority will be for naught, of course, if it is not matched with the budgetary and personnel resources to execute effectively and at scale.

Cybersecurity for Private Critical Infrastructure

In the mid-1990s, the security of privately held critical infrastructure (CI) became a subject of increasing federal government interest as concerns about terrorism grew, particularly following the bombing of the Murrah Building in Oklahoma City in 1995. Soon after that attack, President Clinton ordered a committee to develop recommendations on this issue. The resulting "Critical Infrastructure Working Group," led by Deputy Attorney General Jamie Gorelick, included several participants who were well aware of the cybersecurity vulnerabilities of critical infrastructure, and CIWG became a vehicle for drawing attention to that risk and recommending interventions. This spurred a congressional committee hearing in the summer of 1996, one that identified a litany of obstacles to more effective cybersecurity in the CI area: the reluctance of private-sector entities to take steps that might erode competitive advantage over rivals; attribution uncertainty that confounded efforts to determine which federal agency should be in the lead in response to an attack (particularly in light of uncertainty as to whether an attack is coming from a domestic or foreign source); documented distrust of government involvement in this area; a private sector preference to seek help from private cybersecurity firms whose main charge was simply to disrupt or stop an attack but not to ensure identification and accountability for the attacker; lack of data to enable reliable threat estimates; lack of expertise and technical capacity among potentially responsible government agencies; and so forth.[17] It also spurred the Clinton administration to create a commission formally tasked with developing solutions.

The resulting "President's Commission on Critical Infrastructure Protection" (better known as the Marsh Commission, for its chair Robert Marsh) produced a 1997 report (the Marsh Report) that documented the threat in persuasive detail while offering an array of recommendations. The general thrust was to call for a public-private partnership to make progress on CI cybersecurity, centered around the voluntary exchange of information. The voluntary model, the report argued, would "be more effective and efficient than legislation or regulation."[18]

In 1998 these recommendations bore important fruit in the form of President Clinton's Presidential Decision Directive 63.[19] PDD-63 embraced both the importance of information sharing and the model of relying on voluntary partnerships (both public-private and private-private) to generate improvements to CI cybersecurity. On the organizational side, it called for creation of a National Infrastructure Protection Plan, establishment of a White House coordinator position within the NSC, identification of lead agencies for each CI sector, identification of specific officials to act as the lead liaison officer with private entities in each such sector, and identification of private-sector liaisons to be their counterparts. And this did lead to pockets of success, particularly the gradual accumulation of sector-specific Information Sharing and Analysis Centers (ISACs)—privately managed voluntary organizations facilitating enhanced sharing of threat indicators and other useful information. Consistent with the Marsh Report, however, there was no talk of regulatory or legislative intervention to impose cybersecurity-related rules on the private sector, let alone direct government access to private-sector systems for oversight or operational purposes.[20]

When President Bush promulgated the National Strategy to Secure Cyberspace in 2003, the overall approach remained focused on voluntary public-private partnerships, information sharing, and improved organizational structures to make all of this more efficient. From an organizational-innovation perspective, its most notable feature was to designate the newly created Department of Homeland Security as the notional "single point-of-contact for the federal government's interaction with industry and other partners."[21] As with the contemporaneous decision to insert DHS into the FCEB cybersecurity ecosystem, however, this charge was not yet paired with resources and compulsory authorities necessary to the scale of the task.

In the early years of the Obama administration, the federal approach to cybersecurity for private sector critical infrastructure stayed relatively constant. That changed to some extent in early 2013, however, with the simultaneous promulgation of Executive Order (EO) 13636 and Presidential Policy Directive 21 (PPD-21).[22] Together, these directives sought to boost CI cybersecurity by further encouraging voluntary sharing of information, by directing NIST to develop a risk-management framework (to be known as the cybersecurity framework), and by helping CI owner/operators to understand industry best practices with respect to "standards, methodologies, procedures, and processes."[23] Notably, Section 9 of the order called on DHS to identify especially sensitive CI entities (ones where a cybersecurity failure "could reasonably result in catastrophic regional or national effects"), and Section 10 in turn directed relevant regulatory agencies to bear these designations in mind in the course of determining whether new cybersecurity-relevant regulations might be needed.[24]

In the final analysis, however, nothing in EO 13636 or PPD-21 attempted to compel private sector CI owner/operators to take any particular actions. The president could not simply order the private sector around in that way, after all; that would require legislation.

Toward that end, the Obama administration explored the possibility of including some form of mandatory cybersecurity standards for key private sector entities, in connection with the legislative process that ultimately culminated in the Cybersecurity Information Sharing Act of 2015.[25] The proposal went nowhere, however. In the end, even the information-sharing provision in the 2015 statute was wholly voluntary from the private-sector perspective, and nothing in it spoke to the question of minimum security standards.

Not long after the act's passage, the administration in 2016 announced a further enhancement of its efforts to promote cybersecurity across several dimensions, including with respect to CI.[26] Among other things, this meant creation of a mechanism whereby CI owners/operators could simulate attacks on their systems and an expansion of DHS personnel charged with assisting private-sector cybersecurity efforts with on-site assessments and support for improvements. These measures contributed to the ongoing maturation of DHS, a trend that continued to accelerate with the transformation of NPPD into CISA (as noted above). Today, CISA is able to offer to the private sector owners of CI most of the same cybersecurity assessment and support services that it can provide to FCEB agencies (though significant resource constraints limit the practical impact of this capability).

Not surprisingly, no one has yet has made a serious effort to confer on CISA (let alone NSA) the ability to provide such services to the private sector involuntarily. Nor, for the most part, is there serious momentum toward a more heavy-handed approach to regulation in this area. The last notable gesture in that direction occurred in 2017 when the Trump administration issued Executive Order 13800.[27] Among other things, EO 13800 directed a review of existing regulatory authorities relevant to cybersecurity for the CI entities deemed most important under the Section 9 framework mentioned above, with a specific charge to identify existing regulatory authority that might be useful to improve security for such entities. It is not clear what effect this review may have had, however.

There is one exception to this general state of affairs, involving the Defense Industrial Base (DIB). In 2020, the Department of Defense employed the leverage inherent in its contracting in order to introduce significant new incentives for DIB companies to improve their own cybersecurity and to in turn force their supply chains to do the same. The DIB acquisitions rules already had nominal requirements of this kind, but with little teeth in terms of a likelihood of auditing for compliance. Now, under the Cybersecurity Maturity Model Certification (CMMC) system, firms would not be able to obtain contracts with DoD in the first place without meeting cybersecurity requirements appropriate to the scale and sophistication of their operations and obtaining a certification of compliance from an outside auditor. The actual rollout of CMMC will, inevitably, be a rocky one. If successful over time, however, it is not hard to imagine that it becomes a model toward which the US government might turn if and when some shock to the system creates the political will to intervene aggressively to improve CI cybersecurity in general.

Evolution of the UK Defensive Model

In some respects, the UK defensive model closely tracks that of the United States. Like America's NSA, the UK's Government Communications Headquarters (GCHQ) is both a world-class SIGINT collection organization and an equally capable information-assurance organization. And like NSA, GCHQ therefore has always played the leading role in protecting the British equivalent to what the United States calls "national security systems." But whereas the United States rather sharply confines NSA's role, most notably by excluding it from operational involvement in the protection of "civilian" government systems and private-sector systems, the British take a far more flexible approach with GCHQ.

This appears to stem from certain fundamental differences between the United States and United Kingdom. First, public anxieties about the role of NSA in the United States are considerably sharper than corresponding fears about the role of GCHQ in the United Kingdom. As a consequence, it is simply more toxic, politically, to permit a broad role to NSA, no matter how capable NSA may be. Second, the American legal framework is considerably more formalistic than the UK framework when it comes to the affirmative "authorities" allocated to particular agencies. In the American system, agencies typically conceive of their functional lanes as affirmatively defined and hence bounded (and, more to the point, agencies perceive one another as operating within such boundaries and will act to protect their own turf accordingly). The British system, in contrast, operates against a background assumption that general authority to act is there, subject, of course, to whatever constraints law may impose. In combination, these conditions go far to explain why the role of GCHQ over time has broadened considerably beyond that of NSA, occupying functions that in the US system ultimately required the creation of separate institutions.

The pages that follow trace this evolution and the many nuances and complexities that have arisen along the way. In contrast to the section above on the US defensive model, defined by its distinct subsections on national security systems, civilian government systems, and private critical infrastructure, here I follow a single, blended chronology—as befits a model that in many ways eschews such distinctions.

Critical National Infrastructure Concerns in the 1990s

In his history of GCHQ, Richard Aldrich describes the arrival in the 1990s of the "new age of ubiquitous computing" and the complicated impact this had on GCHQ.[28] Computing itself had long been central to GCHQ's work, of course, going back to the legendary wartime work of Alan Turing and others at Bletchley Park. As Aldrich points out, however, the driving force behind GCHQ's computing during the Cold War had been the imperative of breaking the encryption used by the Soviets and others (and, by extension, protecting the United Kingdom's own information system from similar efforts by hostile intelligence agencies). The possibility that significant national interests—let alone strategic ones—might become intertwined with the security of run-of-the-mill computer systems and networks, and that GCHQ might play a key role in supporting such security, was not self-evident early on.[29] A gradual shift in priorities was bound to occur, though, thanks to the massive shift toward computer-based communications, commerce, and control of machinery and other tangible systems.

As noted earlier, critical-infrastructure vulnerability drove such a shift in perspective in the United States in the 1990s. So too, contemporaneously, in the United Kingdom (which uses the phrase "critical national infrastructure," or CNI). Aldrich relates a particularly telling incident that unfolded in 1995, in which a number of financial institutions in the City of London were blackmailed by hackers who made a convincing case that they had access to the banks' systems and were in a position to destroy data. The Bank of England and the Department of Trade and Industry were the regulatory leads for this CNI sector. They lacked the expertise to contribute effectively to the cybersecurity aspects of the situation, however. GCHQ, accordingly, was brought in to investigate the situation. This was an early demonstration of the flexibility of the British model in terms of taking advantage of the forensic expertise of the intelligence community in a context involving the private sector. And soon, GCHQ was "under pressure to defend the whole underlying electronic system upon which banking, commerce and indeed all the public services that supported national life now depended."[30] Indeed, GCHQ soon found itself in the awkward position of supporting the use by private entities of advanced forms of encryption, notwithstanding a long tradition (stemming from its SIGINT collection mission) of resisting the spread of high-grade cryptography.[31]

In the United Kingdom, growing appreciation in the late 1990s for the threat to CNI associated with cybersecurity had the same effect as it was having at that moment in the United States: It led officials to ponder how best to increase the sharing of threat information, and also how to spread awareness of risk-management best practices. As noted earlier, the main US response at that time was to encourage formation of private-sector ISACs. The United Kingdom did this too, in the form of "information exchanges,"[32] but it also went a step further by forming a new government entity charged with supporting these information-sharing missions (something the United States would not do until DHS took on aspects of this mission in the post-9/11 period, and which would take years thereafter to come into its own). Specifically, in 1999, the government formed an interdepartmental organization called the National Infrastructure Security Co-ordination Centre (NISCC). NISCC had no operational role but rather focused on providing "regularly updated advice and warnings" helping entities engage in "effective risk management and assurance of their systems."[33] NISCC drew on capabilities across the government, most notably including the component of GCHQ that initially focused on information assurance for the UK's "defence and security assets" and, later, for other government entities: the Communications-Electronics Security Group, or CESG.[34]

In this way too, then, the emerging UK model proved open to direct involvement from GCHQ in a way that contrasted sharply with the American model. NSA, after all, plays no direct role in the mechanisms the United States eventually adopted to perform comparable information-sharing and risk-management advice functions for critical infrastructure owners and operators.

In 2007, NISCC was folded into a new entity focused on CNI protection, the Centre for the Protection of National Infrastructure ("CPNI"). At that point, it became housed at MI5, the UK's domestic security intelligence organization. As before, however, it had no operational role, but rather focused on sharing advice and other defense-relevant information.[35]

Reorganizing with the 2009 and 2011 Strategies

By 2007, some senior officials were convinced that more ambitious and organized efforts were needed and that a larger national-strategy framework would be necessary to drive such changes. The government had engaged in a modicum of national strategic planning relating to cybersecurity previously, via the Cabinet Office's periodic publication of National Information Assurance Strategies (once in 2003, and again that very year). These documents made general promises about enhanced government efforts to treat information assurance as a priority, and they broadly encouraged the private sector to have clearer and more effective risk management policies. But labels aside, that is a far cry from having an actual national strategy in the sense of setting strategic priorities and matching them with funded initiatives.

In 2007, Prime Minister Gordon Brown commissioned an effort to close that gap. The result that emerged two years later was the United Kingdom's first true cybersecurity strategy document (the 2009 strategy).[36] It endorsed several distinct interventions. Some focused on budgetary commitments. For example, it called for a substantial increase in government funding for development of cybersecurity-related technologies and likewise for a resource surge intended to expand the pool of people with cybersecurity-relevant training. But it also proposed two important organizational reforms.

First, the 2009 strategy called for creation of an interdepartmental Cyber Security Operations Centre, to be hosted by GCHQ's CESG. The Operations Centre was charged with several missions. One was an intelligence-coordination function (improving the government's collective understanding of the cyber threat environment). Another involved the sharing of threat intelligence and advice for the benefit of the general public (thus expanding on the information-sharing work already performed for CNI owner/operators by CPNI [the former NISCC]). The Operations Centre also would have an operational role—helping to coordinate incident response in at least some scenarios. This was something GCHQ already had been doing to some extent, notably, tracing back at least to the 1995 extortion attempts targeting financial institutions in the City of London. And it was another illustration of the way that the British model all along has operated without the same formalistic constraints that define the American model.[37]

A second organizational reform dictated by the 2009 strategy concerned the Cabinet Office itself. Heretofore, attention to cybersecurity matters at that level had been an ad hoc affair, with no sustained commitment and no formal touchpoints of responsibility. In such circumstances, interdepartmental coordination was more difficult than it might otherwise be. The 2009 strategy sought to change that, identifying seventeen separate "workstreams" relating to the broad goals set forth in the document and calling for the creation in the Cabinet Office of a new Office of Cyber Security (renamed soon thereafter the Office of Cyber Security and Information Assurance [OCSIA]), charged with monitoring progress across all relevant agencies with respect to the execution of those workstreams.[38]

With Prime Minister Gordon Brown replaced by David Cameron in 2010 and with growing national attention to cybersecurity challenges, it perhaps is not surprising that the 2009 strategy was superseded in 2011 by a new document: the UK Cyber Security Strategy: Protecting and Promoting the UK in a Digital World (the 2011 strategy).[39] The 2011 strategy was largely consistent with its predecessor, albeit with still more emphatic rhetoric concerning the nature of the threat and the imperative need to address it effectively. Critically, it also came with a commitment to spend approximately £860 million over a five-year period culminating in 2016: the National Cyber Security Programme.

Sailing before these winds, information-sharing efforts evolved further. In 2013, GCHQ teamed with MI5 and the National Crime Agency to create a single government entity to participate in what would be called the Cyber Security Information Sharing Partnership (CiSP). CiSP expanded on the less-centralized ISAC models already in existence. It is a public-private partnership for the real-time exchange of cyber threat intelligence, overarching across sectors rather than being specific to a particular one. By 2015, nearly 800 private-sector organizations and more than 2,000 individuals were participating in its digital collaboration environment, and it has grown significantly more since then.[40]

Separately, this period also saw the government beginning to play a more proactive role pushing private sector entities to adopt specific defensive measures. Specifically, GCHQ began to work directly with UK telecommunication companies to urge them—and to help them—to adopt systems for automated detection of known indicators-of-compromise (IOCs).[41] However commonplace such in-network threat-hunting methods may be today, they were comparatively novel then in some circles and stood in contrast to more passive approaches to defense. Perhaps for that reason, the phrase "active defense" eventually became common in UK cybersecurity policy circles as shorthand for more active forms of in-network defensive capabilities.[42]

Other institutional innovation followed in that same period. The most visible of these was the establishment of the Computer Emergency Response Team-UK (CERT-UK).[43] The creation of a national-level CERT—something the United States had done long ago and that had caught on as a useful model adopted by many others—was a long time coming for the United Kingdom and had been a key plank in the 2011 strategy. It addressed a question spawned by the proliferation of cybersecurity entities in recent years: Who should be the main point of contact and lead coordinator in the event of a major cyber incident? Given that role for CERT-UK, moreover, it made sense to fold CiSP into that organization. Meanwhile, in 2013, the United Kingdom established a fusion center for all source analysis of cyber threats and incidents. The new Center for Cyber Assessment (CCA) was modeled on a similar all-source center MI5 had established for counterterrorism purposes. Though personnel from a variety of agencies staffed the CCA, it was housed, not surprisingly, within GCHQ.[44]

The National Cyber Security Centre

By 2015, much progress thus had been made, particularly on the information-sharing front. Yet the collective impact of malicious cyber activity was continuing to grow and was increasingly occupying the attention of senior policymakers. The head of the OCSIA (the Cabinet Office body established by the 2009 strategy), Matthew Gould, pondered what other steps might help. Gould previously had served as the British ambassador to Israel and had seen firsthand how effectively the Israelis had organized for cybersecurity both within government and in terms of the public-private interface. Notwithstanding the achievements of CERT-UK and CiSP, perhaps more could be done on that front.[45] Relatedly, perhaps the time had come for the government to play a more direct role in improving private sector

defenses. With limited exceptions such as GCHQ's push for telecommunication companies to adopt automated threat detection, the government's
efforts to improve private-sector defenses to this point had focused heavily
on information sharing and on voluntary actions more generally. This relatively hands-off approach left it to the private sector, by and large, to determine the nature and scale of its investments in security, and it was becoming
apparent that this was not resulting in improvements quickly enough. As
then-Director of GCHQ Robert Hannigan would later explain:

> Any new technology tends not to be developed with safety or security at
> the front of mind. A combination of government regulation, insurance and
> self-regulation through market forces tends to put this right over time, the
> automotive industry in the 20th Century being the obvious example. In
> cyber security, too much of the burden fell on consumers, whether compa-
> nies or individuals.[46]

Simply put, there was a market failure of sorts at work. Companies did not
internalize the full set of costs inflicted on society due to cybersecurity lapses
and hence did not have strong economic incentives to invest in reducing
such harms ex ante.[47]

The options for ameliorating such failures are well understood. We see
them on display in the context of the auto industry, in fact. One can modify
rules of legal liability (substantive or procedural) so as to force companies
to internalize more of those societal costs. One can empower a regulator to
mandate, directly, that certain interventions be used or procedures followed.
Or one can do all of the above. None of these tools is easy to bring to bear,
however, given the complicated politics they entail. Relatedly, both risk sti-
fling much-needed innovation if not handled deftly enough. As a result, if
a promising alternative approach can be found, one that might provide real
systematic improvements without incurring such costs, it can prove highly
attractive.

This perhaps explains why the Cameron administration ultimately sought
to address the problem of systematically insufficient cybersecurity through
another round of institutional innovation, rather than through a major intervention in the form of liability or regulations. Yes, many institutional
innovations already had occurred, as we have seen. But an upshot of all this
was organizational multiplicity and complexity, and thus uncertainty and
coordination challenges. To remedy this, one might consolidate an array of

government cybersecurity institutions and functions under the rubric of a single, highly visible, and public-facing entity, one capable of ensuring alignment across these functions and of building a brand to which trust could attach. One might also give such an entity a mandate to take on a more active role in driving specific defensive improvements in the private sector, and resources to take on coordination and operational functions to boot. Thus was born the National Cyber Security Centre (NCSC), with GCHQ's Ciaran Martin as its founding Chief Executive.[48]

NCSC consolidates many of the organizations we have discussed, including CERT-UK (and, by extension, the CiSP information-sharing system), CCA (the fusion-center for cyber intelligence analysis), and the cybersecurity-specific aspects of CPNI.[49] But where to place NCSC itself?

One option was for it to stand alone as an independent government agency (in the way that the American CIA stands apart from any larger department). Another option would be to have NCSC exist only as a thin layer of bureaucracy for interdepartmental coordination, superimposed above the incumbent agencies but leaving those agencies where they had been located previously in the organizational chart (akin to America's Office of the Director of National Intelligence). Or it could be embedded within a larger, existing organization (the path the United States followed with what became CISA, within DHS). In the end, that last approach prevailed; NCSC would be a component of GCHQ.

In his speech formally announcing the launch of NCSC (delivered at GHCQ, naturally), Chancellor George Osborne reviewed the accomplishments of the most-recent five-year plan for cybersecurity and spelled out key elements of the next one. The new plan would include a resource surge directed at cyber crime investigations and at the defense of government systems. But most notably, it also would feature the consolidation of a variety of existing defensive functions (and some new ones as well) in the form of the new NCSC. By placing it at GCHQ, Osborne noted, NCSC would be able to "draw on the necessarily secret world-class expertise within this organization," even as it also developed a public-facing aspect.[50] This hybridization was the not-so-secret sauce driving the NCSC model. As former Foreign Secretary William Hague later summed up the point:

> The most crucial decision in creating a strong cyber security centre was to place responsibility for it with the appropriate intelligence agency, GCHQ, but simultaneously to make part of its work open and accessible to the

population we need to protect. This is an innovative way to develop intelligence work in an age of cyber, which other nations might well wish to
follow.[51]

Plainly, this is a significant difference between the NCSC model and the
CISA model, as if CISA was not part of DHS but rather NSA. But though
the American political and policy environment has no trouble incubating
a military organization like USCYBERCOM with NSA, such an approach
was never a serious consideration for what became CISA. Wide swaths of
the American private sector most certainly would have balked at voluntary participation in programs associated with an NSA-hosted CISA. In the
final analysis, there is no better marker of the distinct reception of NSA and
GCHQ in their respective societies than the ease with which the new NCSC
was placed squarely within the GCHQ organizational fold. Given the long-
standing centrality of GCHQ to all of these functions, described above, no
one should have been surprised by this.

GCHQ's director later would observe that British businesses, if anything,
turned out to appreciate rather than mind that NCSC was ensconced within
the most expert of the cyber-relevant parts of government. Ironically, more
friction may have arisen from within GCHQ itself, as some found the prospect of interactions with the public jarring and perhaps also a distraction
from more traditional missions. But, in the end, the affirmative arguments
for placing NCSC within GCHQ were numerous and cumulatively compelling. GCHQ is, after all, the best source of cybersecurity expertise across the
UK government. And it typically was the first part of government to detect
the most significant attacks. Critically, placement at GCHQ also created optimal conditions for persuading foreign intelligence partners (particularly
but not only Five Eyes partners) that they can share information with NCSC
without undue risk. Placement of NCSC at GCHQ also signaled seriousness
of purpose while averting potential limitations on GCHQ's support to NCSC
that might have arisen had NCSC been placed elsewhere.[52]

Under the leadership of its founding chief executive officer, Ciaran Martin,
NCSC quickly became the undisputed focal point for the government's defensive cybersecurity efforts. In many respects, in fact, Martin's founding
tenure at NCSC tracked that of his contemporary Chris Krebs at CISA in
the United States. Both are personable leaders who took the reins of organizations that had substantial preexisting roots yet needed a new collective
identity, and over a period of years both earned positive reputations for their

agencies (often running against the grain of the reputations of the larger governments of which they were part).

And the organizations themselves have many parallels. Both have obligations encompassing government systems as well as private critical infrastructure, including the promulgation of defense-relevant advice and threat information. Both also provide an array of security-supporting services, including vulnerability assessments, testing, exercises, and entity-specific technical advising. And both are creative in seeking to identify active technical measures that could be adopted to make the public as a whole (and critical infrastructure in particular) safer (something NCSC does in particular through its "active cyber defence" initiative, which aspires among other things to reduce the impact of "high-volume commodity attacks by stopping them before they reach end users").[53]

The organizations are by no means identical as a functional matter, however. NCSC's role in relation to coordinating responses to major cyber incidents is far more robust than that of CISA (particularly now that the Biden administration has reestablished a National Security Council post charged with such responsibility, not to mention the passage of legislation creating a new office of National Cyber Director as part of the larger White House bureaucracy). And though the details of NCSC's *operational* defensive functions are less than clear from the public record, they nonetheless must be much broader than those of CISA given CISA's limited authority in that space.[54] In both these senses, we see that the British approach has evolved to a point that is more unified, and better connected to the expertise of its largest and most capable institution (GCHQ), than the American model.

That is, of course, exactly what one might expect given the greater flexibility inherent in the British model of government organization, combined with the British political system's relative comfort with its intelligence services. As Chancellor Osborne stated in his 2015 speech announcing the plan to create NCSC:

> I am clear that the answer to the question 'who does cyber?' for the British government is—to a very large degree—'GCHQ'. . . . GCHQ has a unique role. It is the point of deep expertise for the UK government. It has an unmatched understanding of the internet and of how to keep information safe. It is a centre of capability that we cannot duplicate, which must sit at the heart of our cyber security.[55]

That is a set of claims which would be equally true if uttered by an American president with respect to NSA. Yet even in the aftermath of fiascos such as SolarWinds there remains little if any talk—let alone serious policy and political momentum—about a change in American policy in the direction of the British model.

Before turning to the comparison of American and British approaches to offensive aspects of cybersecurity, a final note is in order. Like the American model, the British model has a long tradition of "light touch" regulation of the private sector, even in the context of critical national infrastructure. More to the point, only a few critical national infrastructure sectors had regulators with relatively strong regulatory authority relevant for cybersecurity. Beyond the nuclear power and financial services sectors, the notional authority of these entities was limited.[56] The beginnings of a shift appeared to emerge in May 2018, though, as the United Kingdom moved to implement the European Union's Network and Information Systems Directive. The implementing rules—known as the NIS Regulations—in theory will "drive change in behaviour and alertness among the operators" who "provide essential services, with an emphasis on ensuring continuity of service."[57] The resulting regulatory interventions may or may not prove significant. Meanwhile, however, a clearly significant shift is on the way for the telecommunications sector thanks to the Telecommunications (Security) Bill. This bill, which is still pending at the time of this writing, will impose a variety of specific security requirements and empower regulators to conduct compliance investigations and impose substantial fines.[58]

Adaptation for Offensive Functions

From a government perspective, the increasing centrality of the cyber domain constitutes more than just a source of massive risks resulting in the array of defensive functions described above. By the same token, it also gives rise to stunning opportunities for pursuing other public policy goals (from law enforcement and espionage to armed conflict and covert action). As a result, violating computer security, rather than defending it, at times may become a government policy preference. That, in turn, raises critical questions of institutional and legal design, particularly where the pursuit of such offensive goals comes into direct tension with pursuit of defensive ones. The following comparison of the US and UK "offensive models"—this time conducted side by side with reference to a series of particular offensive functions—illustrates the resulting complexity.

Espionage

The espionage function—that is, stealing secrets to inform planning and decision making—is an area in which the emergence of the cyber domain was not particularly disruptive for the United States or the United Kingdom. Each country possessed world-class intelligence agencies focused on capturing intelligence through electronic means long before the blossoming of the digital age, and both countries' agencies paid close attention to key advances in computing and encryption (and, indeed, generated many of the most important of those advances). Whatever frictions may have attended the process of reallocating resources, capabilities, and personnel toward the new digital communication and storage systems that emerged over the years, there was never any doubt that NSA and GCHQ would be their countries' respective lead agencies when it came to hacking for espionage purposes, nor any surprise that they would become world-class practitioners of the art.[59]

For the United States, the emergence of hacking as a vector for espionage has not prompted legislative changes. To be sure, the legal architecture for US espionage has evolved considerably over the past two decades, particularly when it comes to SIGINT. But the changes have not been specific to hacking. Several rounds of changes to the Foreign Intelligence Surveillance Act (FISA) have occurred, for example, with the most notable changes involving the creation and tailoring of the "Section 702" system (which enables the US government to compel companies subject to US jurisdiction to cooperate in efforts to locate and access the communications of specific non-US persons located outside the United States for foreign-intelligence purposes). Neither Section 702 nor any other statute attempts to regulate the ability of NSA to conduct hacking outside the United States for espionage purposes.

GCHQ's situation is somewhat different in that hacking is addressed specifically (if euphemistically) in a somewhat analogous framework. Under pressure from the European Court of Human Rights in the early 1990s, the United Kingdom passed the Intelligence Services Act of 1994 in order to establish that all of its secret intelligence services, GCHQ included, operated with express parliamentary approval.[60] Notably, the Intelligence Services Act of 1994's description of GCHQ's activities included "interfere[nce] with . . . equipment" associated with electronic communications.[61] The "equipment interference" (EI) category is widely understood today to encompass hacking,[62] and since 2016 EI has been subject to the Investigatory Powers Act (IPA). Under the IPA, the secretary of state is empowered to issue warrants for GCHQ to carry out EI activities in various ways, subject to oversight from an independent judicial commissioner.[63] The warrant process is obligatory if "there is a British Islands connection."[64] If there is not, the secretary still may opt to employ the warrant procedure (which might be useful, should the cooperation of a third party such as a telecommunications company be needed), though this is not obligatory.[65]

The more interesting changes for espionage-related hacking, for both the United States and United Kingdom, involve a particular type of institutional innovation. Thanks to the distinctive attributes of hacking as a form of espionage, it eventually became necessary in both countries to develop a novel mechanism for managing a question that almost never otherwise arises in the espionage setting: Should the government undermine its own ability to use certain tools for espionage purposes in order to protect the broader public from others exploiting the vulnerabilities on which those tools depend?

The traditional tools of SIGINT—such as advanced antennae technology—rarely if ever raised such questions. When NSA and GCHQ placed antennae in places that could intercept Soviet military communications, their success usually did not depend on preserving the secrecy of latent vulnerabilities in the systems that enabled such communications. The trick, rather, was to get close enough to effectuate the interception as a matter of physics, and then to overcome whatever encryption might have been used. Even where the collection depended on exploitation of some otherwise undiscovered vulnerability in the underlying system, moreover, it was not likely that that system was one also used by the US and UK governments, let alone their general publics.

All of that is reversed in the case of hacking. Or at least hacking raises the critical question: Might the greater national interest sometimes lie in making sure that vendors become aware of (and hopefully try to patch) vulnerabilities, rather than keeping quiet about the vulnerabilities in order to exploit them for espionage purposes? Over time, both the US and UK governments have determined that this question demands an institutionalized response. The result, in both countries, was the creation of an interagency "vulnerability equities process," or VEP, in which the interests of intelligence collection are weighed, systematically, against competing considerations in a bureaucratic process that includes input from entities outside the intelligence community.[66] For both the United States and United Kingdom, further evolution in this space is very likely.

Of course, intelligence agencies are not the only government entities with a stake in preserving the viability of a vulnerability. The ability to hack is increasingly important for other government purposes.

Armed Conflict

There was a time, not long ago, when it was thought newsworthy when a government avowed that its military had hacking capabilities. Yet there was never any real doubt that militaries would establish such capabilities. Electronic warfare has been a staple of armed conflict ever since militaries began making use of electricity-based technologies. In today's world, computers have become essential for a range of military functions, with everything from command and control across military formations to supply chains to the operation of weapons systems depending on them. Every military must mind the cybersecurity aspects of these systems, just as every military must aspire to overcome an enemy's cyber defenses by hacking them in order to understand, disrupt, manipulate, or even destroy adversary capabilities during armed conflict.

Like other modern militaries, both the United States and the United Kingdom accordingly have developed their offensive military cyber capabilities in addition to their defensive ones. But they have not done so in precisely the same way, as an institutional matter.

For every military, the need to have offensive cyber capabilities in the event of armed conflict presents an interesting institutional design challenge. There are at least two reasons for this. First, the capabilities that make for a talented hacker are different in kind from those traditionally prized in the context of run-of-the-mill military recruitment and training, more so than with other domains of military operations. This suggests the utility of developing distinct institutional processes for recruitment, training, and career development of cyber-capable soldiers. Second, sophisticated hacking operations at least sometimes call for expensive or scarce computing infrastructure that militaries normally would not develop and sustain. This too suggests the need for something distinctive, just as is the case for sea, air, and (now) space operations.

In both the United States and United Kingdom, it did not escape notice that world-class capabilities of the sort that militaries could use, in terms of personnel and supporting infrastructure, already existed at NSA and GCHQ, respectively. In both contexts, military officials accordingly were drawn to the possibility of somehow drafting off of those capabilities rather than attempting to generate them from scratch. And that is exactly what happened, though the two countries went about things in distinct ways.

As described earlier in the section on defense, the United States chose an incubation model. As related by Michael Warner, the US established USCYBERCOM as a distinct military organization, yes, but embedded it in every practical sense of the word alongside NSA at Fort Meade.[67] With shared personnel and infrastructure, and even a dual-hatted leader, USCYBERCOM to this day is formally a purely military organization that, functionally, shares substantial DNA with the intelligence community. And though the original expectation of the incubation model was for USCYBERCOM eventually to emerge from NSA's shadow, the moment of separation seems to continually recede.[68]

This is not just because Congress has enacted legislation precluding formal separation until the secretary of defense certifies that USCYBERCOM has reached certain sustainability benchmarks (though these benchmarks in fact have not been reached as of the time of this writing).[69] There are many who feel that the United States has created, however unintentionally, an attractive hybrid model providing an optimal degree of capability and efficiency, one that ensures USCYBERCOM can punch above its weight. Defenders also contend that this model inherently ensures thoughtful consideration of competing equities when the benefits that might flow from disrupting an adversary's system threaten to undermine those that come from instead simply collecting intelligence from within that system.

Others disagree. Critics have argued that separation is needed if ever USCYBERCOM is to reach its full potential, much as training wheels must come off a bicycle. And critics also have inverted the equities-deconfliction point, arguing that the current arrangement unduly empowers NSA to protect its intelligence-collection equities (which typically will favor monitoring rather than disruption of adversary systems) at the expense of the military operational equities that USCYBERCOM might otherwise prioritize.

This line of argument came to a head, publicly, amid the war against the Islamic State. ISIS was making use of the online environment for both command and control and external recruitment and fundraising efforts. Then-Secretary of Defense Ash Carter became concerned that USCYBERCOM was not acting aggressively enough to disrupt ISIS systems, perhaps because intelligence-collection equities were receiving too much consideration. Ultimately, USCYBERCOM did begin conducting disruption operations with greater frequency, under the rubric of Operation Glowing Symphony. The results disappointed some observers (ISIS was able to reconstitute at least some functionality relatively quickly). Supporters of the status quo saw this as evidence that intelligence-collection equities should indeed often prevail (and thus that the current arrangement should be preserved). Critics concluded that, on the contrary, this was evidence of the need to break the mold so that USCYBERCOM might develop more robust capabilities and have an easier time making use of them.

Notably, certain aspects of Operation Glowing Symphony drew attention to critical and hotly contested questions at the intersection of international law, international relations, and the interagency tensions inherent in a model that maintains formal separation between military and intelligence-agency authorities. Servers used by ISIS for its communications (particularly their public-facing recruitment efforts) were not always (or even often) located inside the zone of active hostilities in Syria and Iraq. As a result, some counter-ISIS cyber operations required accessing systems that were physically located in third-party countries, including Germany. The State Department, CIA, and FBI were concerned that such operations, if conducted without the consent of the country in question, might result in backlash impacting bilateral cooperation on other fronts. Objections also may have been raised on international law grounds on the basis of a claim that operating on those servers without consent from the country involved might violate that country's sovereignty.

On the domestic legal front, moreover, it might also be argued that USCYBERCOM, unlike the CIA, lacks authority to conduct such third-country operations when they violate international law.[70] The Pentagon countered such claims by asserting that the planned operations would have no significant collateral effects and, in any event, that its existing authorities sufficed to cover non-consensual operations such as these. It appears likely that the Pentagon may also have disputed that there is a general international law rule of sovereignty as such (as distinct from the clearly established rules concerning the "use of force" and coercive interventions in international affairs).[71]

A significant period of time elapsed as the interagency debate played out. In the end, it seems a compromise emerged. The United States gave advance notice to as many as fifteen countries that it might seek to execute such operations. But it did not actually make consent from these countries a condition for conducting those operations. Ultimately, USCYBERCOM appears to have conducted operations in five or six of them, including Germany, without host-state consent.[72]

Given this breakthrough for USCYBERCOM, the United States may at some point conclude that its current hybrid model is, in fact, an attractive end-state rather than just a transitional framework. Whatever its fate, though, it was never the only institutional pathway for enabling armed forces to get the benefit of intelligence agency capabilities. The UK experience illustrates how this same general goal can be pursued in a more direct and integrated, though smaller-scale, way.

Unlike NSA's relationship to the Department of Defense, GCHQ is not a component of the Ministry of Defence (MoD). But like NSA, GCHQ nonetheless has always played a critical role in support of combat operations (as its famous World War II exploits remind us). Traditionally, this centered on SIGINT collection and protection of military communications. This had implications for the United Kingdom as it became clear over time that cyberspace was becoming an important domain for actual operations during armed conflict and not just a medium for SIGINT. Like the United States, the United Kingdom faced an institutional design choice. It could seek to build up an independent capability within the military to conduct offensive cyber operations, either from scratch or by following the American incubation model described above. Or it could just allocate this function to GCHQ, matching the new mission with existing expertise and capacity.

As former GCHQ Director Hannigan has explained, practical considerations compelled selection of the GCHQ option. "In governance and structural terms," Hannigan writes, "we made an early decision not to imitate the US model of a separate Cyber Command alongside the NSA. Given the scale of the UK system, duplication was not viable or affordable, and an integrated military-civilian model seemed preferable."[73] Even if resource constraints had been otherwise, moreover, the case for the GCHQ model was strong. "The skills and access necessary to do this resided almost exclusively in GCHQ," Hannigan writes.[74] And since "support for military operations has always been a key part of GCHQ's mission," GCHQ already employed "a large number of military officers as part of the workforce," a consideration that smoothed the way for further integration.[75] Nor did GCHQ require any new legal authorization to take on this offensive role. Unlike NSA, GCHQ "had always had the legal authority to mount offensive cyber operations," and in fact it already had crossed this particular Rubicon "under ministerial authorization in limited cases."[76]

This combination of efficiency, efficacy, and authority ultimately led to the formalization, in 2014, of the National Offensive Cyber Programme (NOCP). It had been clear since the year before that something was afoot, as then-Defence Secretary Philip Hammond in 2013 had avowed the United Kingdom's development of "a full spectrum military cyber capability, including a strike capability."[77] What had not been clear was the institutional arrangement that would make this possible. And so it was significant when Chancellor Osborne in his 2015 speech at GCHQ explained that NOCP "is a partnership between the Ministry of Defence and GCHQ, harnessing the skills and talents of both organisations to deliver the tools, techniques and tradecraft required for the UK to establish a world class capability."[78]

It was not long before that capacity was put into practice. Just as USCYBERCOM eventually went into action against Islamic State assets via Operation Glowing Symphony, so too did GCHQ, in partnership with MoD. Years later, UK officials would avow that the organizations began conducting disruption operations against the Islamic State in 2016. GCHQ's then-director, Jeremey Fleming, disclosed in his first public speech that they conducted operations that included, apparently, both disruption and manipulation of ISIS online communications, degrading both operations and propaganda. This work made it "almost impossible [for ISIS] to spread their hate online, to use their normal channels to spread their rhetoric, or trust their publications."[79] The impacts were not just functional, either. Fleming disclosed that some of the operations "destroyed equipment and networks."[80] Later disclosures elaborated that these operations disrupted ISIS control over their drones and at times shut down or altered cellphone and laptop communications for ISIS fighters in the field (including sending false orders that would lead the fighters into an ambush).[81]

NOCP was not an interagency end state, however. Word began to circulate that the GCHQ-MoD partnership would take on a more formal institutional structure, with a greater emphasis on "jointness." One early account described plans for a 2,000 member task force combining GCHQ and MoD personnel, and another described ongoing debates about whether the new entity would be directed by a GCHQ figure, a military officer, or perhaps even both in rotation.[82]

By 2019, it was reported that the new strategic partnership between GCHQ and MoD was to be known as the National Cyber Force, or NCF,[83] and Defence Secretary Ben Wallace confirmed this in a speech that year.[84] And then came the announcement from Prime Minister Johnson quoted at the opening of this chapter: NCF was now in operation, and indeed had been since April 2020. Though its dedicated personnel at that time apparently numbered around 300, plans called for it to expand to 3,000 over the following ten years.[85] Along with GCHQ and MoD, moreover, MI6 (i.e., the Secret Intelligence Service, which from a US perspective is analogous to CIA) is a participating organization as well. A longtime GCHQ official is at the helm, at least for now.[86]

In the final analysis, NCF is a manifestation of the same hybridization trends that led to the incubation model for USCYBERCOM in the United States. It is far more thoroughly integrated than its US cousin, however, more of a true hybrid. As Rory Cormac recently observed, NCF illustrates how "the United Kingdom takes a whole-of-government approach, without the distinctions made in the United States between covert action and special military operations."[87] The resulting "fuzziness," Cormac notes, "allows a more flexible and nimble response to fast-moving threats, free from too many bureaucratic constraints."[88] We see this with NCF even at the level of ministerial accountability, moreover, as (in contrast to NCSC) both the Defence and Foreign Secretaries have purview over NCF's affairs (though the particulars as to when the approval of both or either might be required for certain types of operations is not clear from the public record).[89]

As we shall see in the final section below, this has implications for the frictions these entities encounter with respect to a growing segment of their respective missions.

Disrupting Malicious Cyber Activity Apart from Armed Conflict

Neither the United States nor the United Kingdom went down these complex institutional paths strictly to establish and enhance cyber capabilities to be used in combat. In both cases, there is a separate motivating force in play.

From information operations to ransomware, the strategic significance of harmful cyber activities occurring outside the context of armed conflict is on the rise (including not just activities that inflict harm in the cyber domain itself but also those that depend on the cyber domain as a vector for inflicting non-cyber harms). This has spurred attempts to elevate defenses, as well as efforts to impose costs on attackers via prosecution, sanctions, and the like. Too often defensive improvements seem not to keep pace, however, and the perpetrators cannot be reached effectively with punitive tools. And so some governments—including the United States and the United Kingdom—have turned their attention to the possibility of using cyber means to disrupt these harmful activities at their source.

The stories of USCYBERCOM and the NCF cannot be fully understood apart from this. Independent of their combat missions, both entities have missions that call for what the Americans describe as "defending forward" and the British describe as "offensive" operations—that is, operations designed to cause disruptive effects in adversary networks in order to halt or forestall malicious activity. Those missions raise critical questions of institutional design and legal architecture.

For the United Kingdom, it is proving relatively easy to address the institutional issues this mission set raises, thanks to the fully hybridized nature of first NOCP and now NCF. After all, neither was ever intended to be limited to combat-related operations. On the contrary, descriptions of their functions have routinely emphasized non-combat scenarios. When discussing the need for NCF, for example, General Sir Patrick Sanders of Strategic Command noted that foreign governments have been tearing at "the fabric of society" through disinformation operations leveraging social media. "[O]ffensive cyber," he concluded, "is unquestionably one of the tools" governments need to respond to such attacks on "the cohesion of society and . . . our democratic processes."[90]

An earlier report in the *Times* similarly anticipated that NCF would respond to foreign disinformation campaigns by hacking foreign systems to "remove fake news."[91] Nor would NCF's role be limited to responding to the malicious activities of state actors. As part of the formal NCF rollout in late 2020, Foreign Secretary Dominic Raab emphasized that NCF would operate not only against hostile foreign states and terrorists but also against certain crime challenges like "online child abuse."[92] Prime Minister Johnson has underscored the point as well, stating that NCF's objectives will include operations against "criminal gangs," while former NCSC Chief Executive Ciaran

Martin notes that the UK's offensive capabilities have "always included an emphasis on disrupting organized cyber crime."[93] NCF's remit, in short, is comparatively broad in this respect, encompassing both state-sponsored and non-state threats that might effectively be mitigated through disruptive operations conducted in the cyber domain.[94]

These examples of activity NCF might respond to do not readily all fall into a single traditional threat category such as "intelligence" or "crime." Rather, they share in common a functional characteristic: they emanate from activity that is sourced overseas in physical locations that have proven resistant to traditional means of response (such as diplomatic efforts to persuade host states to intervene effectively to stop the harms), but which depend on online systems and hence are vulnerable to disruption in that domain. NCF as a practical matter is well-suited to take advantage of that vulnerability, both in terms of its technical capabilities and its hybrid nature. Since the UK model does not stand on categorical formalities in the same way as does the US model, moreover, NCF is unlikely to face objections on grounds of exceeding the scope of its institutional role.

It does not follow that NCF's role in such missions raises no concerns, of course. Conrad Prince, for example, has pointed out that the uncertain scope of NCF's "offensive" mission makes it more difficult to have an effective discussion of the ethical and legal boundaries that may govern NCF's operations in such unconventional settings.[95] The legal and ethical issues are complex enough with respect to cyber operations in the context of armed conflict, after all. Once one moves beyond that context, they grow murkier. Without a firm grasp of what the UK government considers out-of-scope for NCF in the first place, it is hard to have a serious conversation about such matters.

This problem may be less significant than first appears, however. Much depends on the connotations of the terms "offense" and "offensive." Taken for all they are worth, those terms imply that NCF might even act as an aggressor, initiating malicious online activity rather than using online means to disrupt malicious activity initiated by an adversary. It seems unlikely, however, that NCF's mission actually extends that far. The examples of NCF missions that ministers and others have cited all appear to involve "offense" only in the much narrower, tactical sense in which any act of hacking might be described as offensive (i.e., because it involves breaching a system's security).

There is a world of difference between hacking a system in order to cause harm in the first instance and, instead, doing it to stop someone else from causing ongoing harm. The latter is, in the sense that counts most, a *defensive* use of hacking.[96] All the examples given for NCF are defensive ones in that sense, fortunately. It is worth noting, too, that former GCHQ Director Hannigan has expressly cautioned against the United Kingdom engaging in what would instead be genuinely offensive non-combat cyber operations, pointing out that the United Kingdom is asymmetrically vulnerable in the cyber domain and that such activities might be unlawful and inconsistent with the United Kingdom's values.[97]

Those who follow US cyber strategy should recognize in all of this a close parallel to the often-confusing debates associated with the Defend Forward model adopted by USCYBERCOM in recent years. This is no coincidence. The US model faces the same category-blurring threats as does the British one, and likewise sees the attraction of conducting disruption operations inside adversary networks (given the poor track record of more traditional modes of response). When USCYBERCOM speaks of defending forward, this encompasses an array of operational circumstances including operating by consent within the networks of allies in a wholly defensive capacity. But it also encompasses "red space" operations to disrupt malicious activity at its (overseas) source in some circumstances.

The analogy to NCF's circumstance is by no means complete, though. As an initial matter, USCYBERCOM also has conventional defensive responsibilities concerning the US military's own system whereas NCF has no comparable role. More interesting for our purposes, however, is the comparative degree of hybridization between the two approaches. Questions of institutional scope, as we have seen, are far more consequential in the US model, and USCYBERCOM is not institutionally hybridized to the same degree as NCF. USCYBERCOM, as a result, already has faced considerable friction and likely will experience more of the same in the years ahead.

As described in my separate chapter in this book (Chapter 4), on the domestic legal architecture of US military cyber operations, USCYBERCOM initially faced objections that neither it nor the Defense Department in general had affirmative authority to conduct cyber operations abroad outside the context of armed conflict.[98] Relatedly, some objected that the operations it sought to conduct might have to be categorized as "covert action" for purposes of the complicated statutory oversight frameworks usually associated with the CIA, meaning either that USCYBERCOM should not conduct them at all or else that it would have to submit to the covert-action oversight system (including the requirement of written presidential authorizations) if it did so.

Ultimately, Congress over a period of years took note of and largely eliminated each of these objections through a series of statutory amendments. As a result, USCYBERCOM today enjoys relatively clear affirmative authority to engage in out-of-network operations in at least some circumstances. This authority is clearest in circumstances involving Russia, China, Iran, and North Korea, for Congress has enacted an express authorization for cyber operations to disrupt malicious campaigns attributable to those states in particular (subject to certain conditions).[99] Where attribution does not run to one of those states, the picture necessarily is more complicated given the absence of an on-point statutory authorization. In such cases, authority to act still may exist (indeed, it plainly would exist given a sufficient threat to the United States) but it must be inferred from a combination of the inherent national self-defense authorities the Constitution confers on the president and other, more general statutes. This, in turn, suggests that it likely is more difficult (perhaps far more difficult) for USCYBERCOM than for NCF to engage in disruption operations involving, say, non-state actors engaged in crime (though recent reports of a USCYBERCOM operation targeting the TrickBot network illustrates that here, too, the US and UK models may be converging in practice).

A final comparison concerns the international legal frameworks that govern such "offensive" operations outside the context of armed conflict. Here we find another possible point of departure between the US and UK models.

Both the United States and United Kingdom accept, naturally, that international law as a default rule prohibits the "use of force" in international affairs as well as coercive "interventions" into the *domaine réservé* of other states. Hard questions abound regarding just which activities would implicate those rules, but the existence of the rules themselves is settled. It is different, however, with respect to the proposition that there also is a rule of international law forbidding interference with the "sovereignty" of other states below the threshold of coercive intervention. The US and UK governments currently seem to adhere to a similar understanding on this issue, but there is reason to wonder if that might change.

The position of the United Kingdom on the sovereignty question is clear. In a 2018 address at Chatham House, Attorney General Jeremy Wright raised the question of whether sovereignty should be recognized as a rule of international law entailing prohibitions beyond those already associated with the well-recognized rules involving the use of force and coercive intervention.

He recognized that some advocates "have sought to argue for the existence of a cyber specific rule of a 'violation of territorial sovereignty' in relation to interference in the computer networks of another state without its consent."[100] Wright responded by acknowledging that the *principle* of sovereignty "is of course fundamental to the international rules-based system."[101] It was not itself a stand-alone rule of international law, however. "I am not persuaded," he explained, "that we cannot currently extrapolate from that general principle a specific rule or additional prohibition for cyber activity beyond that of a prohibited intervention."[102] Accordingly, the "UK Government's position is therefore that there is no such rule as a matter of current international law."[103] Combined with the integration of GCHQ, MoD, and MI6 elements into NCF, this clarity on the international legal framework paves the way for NCF to operate on a non-consensual basis if and when it takes action on systems that happen to be physically located in other countries.

Matters are not quite as clear with the United States, though for the time being it appears that the US approach does track that of the United Kingdom.

The US government has never quite offered an unambiguous position on the sovereignty question as such, at least not on par with Attorney General Wright's speech. In 2016, State Department Legal Advisor Brian Egan stated that "cyber operations involving computers or other networked devices located on another State's territory do not constitute a *per se* violation of international law," and that "[p]recisely when a non-consensual cyber operation violates the sovereignty of another State is a question lawyers within the US government continue to study carefully, and it is one that ultimately will be resolved through the practice and opinio juris of States."[104] This left open the possibility that the United States might recognize, at some point, at least some form of sovereignty rule extending beyond the concept of coercive intervention, with some non-consensual cyber operations perhaps crossing that line even if not all did. Then, in early 2020, Defense Department General Counsel Paul Ney gave a speech at USCYBERCOM's annual legal conference in which he took up this issue. Ney first restated Egan's position, arguing that "there is not sufficiently widespread and consistent State practice resulting from a sense of legal obligation to conclude that customary international law generally prohibits such non-consensual cyber operations in another State's territory."[105] Ney then went a step further, arguing that USCYBERCOM's Defend Forward model, in particular, "comports with our obligations under international law and our commitment to the rules-based international order."[106] It was not quite the same thing as denying that there exists any rule of sovereignty as such, and Ney conspicuously emphasized that his office's position "shares similarities with the view expressed by the U.K. Government in 2018" rather than simply asserting full agreement with that view. Nor was it a position for the US government as a whole, meaning that other agencies (such as the State Department) might not agree with all he had said. But it was at least an assertion that, as far as DoD lawyers were concerned, there was no international law constraint that would be violated by the particular range of activities contemplated by the Defend Forward model.

Perhaps over time the United States will move closer to the clarity of the UK position. Then again, it is possible either might move in the opposite direction. As described by Jack Goldsmith and Alex Loomis in Chapter 7, there are those who take the position that there is indeed a distinct international law rule of sovereignty, and among them are some who contend that this rule would indeed be violated by at least some non-consensual cyber operations that might take place outside the context of armed conflict.[107] This is, for example, the position taken by the scholars who produced the *Tallinn Manual 2.0* on the International Law Applicable to Cyber Operations.[108] Goldsmith and Loomis offer a sharp critique of that position, but the fact remains that a number of states have endorsed a similar view.[109]

Were the United States to make such a shift, it might have complicated institutional implications. USCYBERCOM's operations are not subject to the US domestic legal framework for "covert action."[110] In some respects that may be liberating, but in one notable respect it is otherwise. Federal law provides that covert action must comply with the Constitution and statutes of the United States, but not necessarily with international law.[111] When the CIA conducts a cyber operation under color of its Title 50 covert action authorities, consequently, it would not necessarily matter (from a US domestic law perspective, at least) if it violated a supposed international law rule of sovereignty. USCYBERCOM's operations ordinarily would not constitute covert action, however, thanks to a series of interventions by Congress in recent years. Between that consideration and the general DoD policy of international law compliance, then, a US shift in favor of a rule of sovereignty might well result in genuine constraints on USCYBERCOM's freedom of action.

A similar shift in legal policy by the United Kingdom might have a still-broader impact. Whereas the American model contemplates (however quietly) the prospect of activities that might violate international law (so long as they are conducted under the formal covert action rubric), it is far from obvious that the same is true in the British system. When British officials speak about the relevance of international law to cyber operations, as did then-Attorney General Wright in his 2018 address, the emphasis is on the obligation to states to ensure that their cyber operations are "carried out in accordance with international law."[112] Of course, American officials say similar things, but as noted above, the American statutory framework for covert action paves the way for circumvention in that limited context. There is no comparable British domestic law pathway, however. This perhaps helps us understand why the British have been at greater pains than the Americans to state their views on just where the international law boundaries run—not to mention why Wright so clearly rejected the idea that sovereignty should be recognized as a rule rather than just a principle of international law. As Ashley Deeks has written,

> [A]ssertions that its intelligence activities comply with UK international legal obligations (including the ECHR) appear to compel the UK to take aggressive legal interpretations of international law itself, so as to cabin its scope in a way that is compatible with the imperatives of its IC.[113]

A change of policy on the sovereignty question would have government-wide implications for the United Kingdom, then, not just for MoD.

Conclusion

As in so many other respects, there is more that unites the United States and United Kingdom than separates them when it comes to questions of cyber policies, laws, and institutions. The gradual processes through which both have adapted to the growing strategic significance of the cyber domain in terms of defensive liabilities and offensive opportunities bear this out. With comparable legal systems, rule of law commitments, and legacy institutional structures, as well as generations of close collaboration in military and intelligence matters, this should come as no surprise.

Yet the pathways followed by London and Washington have not been identical. It is not just that the United States brings disproportionate resources to bear when developing and supporting its security-related institutions (a proposition that rings true with USCYBERCOM much more so than for CISA, it should be noted). There are, too, notable differences in their respective societies, including ones that manifest in their respective approaches to structuring government institutions. The United Kingdom does not share the US predilection for compartmentalized lines of formal authority. And GCHQ involvement in matters beyond traditional overseas intelligence collection does not appear to set off quite the same antibodies in the body politic of the United Kingdom as would NSA or USCYBERCOM in the United States.[114]

The upshot of it all is that we see a strong degree of convergence between the United States and United Kingdom, especially from the purely defensive perspective. But we also see important elements of variation, above all in terms of the degree to which the two governments integrate their most capable operators—NSA and GCHQ—into their non-intelligence activities. Time may demonstrate that one model or the other is superior in practice as a general rule. More likely, though, it will instead teach that there are moments and contexts that favor both, with no one set of institutional solutions always ideal.

Notes

1. Hon. Boris Johnson MP, U.K. Prime Minister, Statement to the House on the Integrated Review (Nov. 19, 2020).
2. Hon. Ben Wallace MP, U.K. Def. Sec'y, Ministry of Def., Address at the NATO Parliamentary Assembly (Oct. 14, 2019) ("The UK will soon solidify plans for a National Cyber Force to ensure a stronger presence in the new contested frontier.").
3. FRED M. KAPLAN, DARK TERRITORY: THE SECRET HISTORY OF CYBER WAR 1-2 (2016).
4. See THOMAS L. BURNS, CTR. FOR CRYPTOLOGIC HISTORY, NAT'L SEC. AGENCY, THE QUEST FOR CRYPTOGRAPHIC CENTRALIZATION AND THE ESTABLISHMENT OF NSA: 1940-1952, at 2 (2005).
5. Kaplan, *supra* note 3, at 18–19.
6. *Id.* at 20, 35; *see also* THE OFFICE OF THE WHITE HOUSE, NATIONAL SECURITY DIRECTIVE 42: NATIONAL POLICY FOR THE SECURITY OF NATIONAL SECURITY TELECOMMUNICATIONS AND INFORMATION SYSTEM (1990); NATIONAL SECURITY DECISION DIRECTIVE 145: NATIONAL POLICY ON TELECOMMUNICATION AND AUTOMATED INFORMATION SYSTEMS SECURITY (1984).
7. CLIFFORD STOLL, THE CUCKOO'S EGG (1989).
8. KAPLAN, *supra* note 3, at 71.
9. *Id.* at 81–84.
10. Michael Warner, US Cyber Command's First Decade 4–5 (Hoover Inst., Aegis Paper Series No. 2008, 2020).

11. KAPLAN, *supra* note 3, at 100–101.

12. Federal Information Security Management Act of 2002, Pub. L. No. 107-347, 116 Stat. 2899 (codified as amended at 44 U.S.C § § 3551 to 3559 (2018)).

13. For a discussion of EINSTEIN's origins and subsequent evolution, see Steven M. Bellovin, Scott O. Bradner, Whitfield Diffie, Susan Landau, and Jennifer Rexford, *Can It Really Work? Problems with Extending EINSTEIN 3 to Critical Infrastructure,* 3 HARVARD NATIONAL SECURITY JOURNAL 1 (2011).

14. 44 U.S.C § 3553 (2018).

15. *See* CYBERSECURITY AND INFRASTRUCTURE SECURITY AGENCY, SERVICES CATALOG (2020).

16. National Defense Authorization Act of 2021, Pub. L. No. 116-283, § 1705, 134 Stat 3388 (2021).

17. *Security in Cyberspace: Hearing Before the Permanent Subcomm. on Investigations,* 104th Cong. 43 (1996) (statement of the minority staff).

18. PRESIDENT'S COMMISSION ON CRITICAL INFRASTRUCTURE PROTECTION, CRITICAL FOUNDATIONS: PROTECTING AMERICAN'S INFRASTRUCTURE 23 (1997).

19. THE WHITE HOUSE OFFICE, PRESIDENTIAL DECISION DIRECTIVE 63–CRITICAL INFRASTRUCTURE PROTECTION (1998).

20. Kaplan observes that PPD-63's lead author, Richard Clarke, believed that sufficient progress would not be made without imposing regulatory mandates on CI owners. "Clinton's economic advisers strenuously opposed the idea," however, "arguing that regulations would distort the free market and impede innovation." KAPLAN, *supra* note 3, at 100.

21. THE WHITE HOUSE OFFICE, THE NATIONAL SECURITY STRATEGY TO SECURE CYBERSPACE 22 (2003).

22. Exec. Order No. 13636, 78 Fed. Reg. 11739 (2013); THE WHITE HOUSE OFFICE, PRESIDENTIAL POLICY DIRECTIVE 21– CRITICAL INFRASTRUCTURE SECURITY AND RESILIENCE (2013).

23. Exec. Order No. 13636, 78 Fed. Reg. 11739 (2013).

24. *Id.*

25. Pub. L. No. 114-113, §§ 101–407, 129 Stat. 2242, 2936–2985 (codified as amended 6 U.S.C §§ 1501 to 1533 (2018)).

26. Press Release, White House Office of the Press Secr'y, FACT SHEET: Cybersecurity National Action Plan (Feb. 9. 2016).

27. Exec. Order No. 13800, 82 Fed. Reg. 22391 (2017).

28. RICHARD J. ALDRICH, GCHQ: THE UNCENSORED STORY OF BRITAIN'S MOST SECRET INTELLIGENCE AGENCY 486–508 (2010).

29. *Id.* at 488.

30. *Id.*

31. *Id.* at 488–89.

32. *See* Tony Proctor, *The Development of Warning, Advice, and Reporting Points (WARPs) in UK National Infrastructure, in* CRITICAL INFORMATION INFRASTRUCTURE SECURITY 164, 167 (Bologna, Hämmerli, Gritzalis, Wolthusen eds. 2011).

33. *See* 661 Parl Deb HL (5th ser.) (2004) col. WA 20 (UK); *see also, e.g.*, Eric Byers, John Karsch, & Joel Carter, *Good Practice Guide: Firewall Deployment for SCADA and Process Control Networks*, CENTRE FOR THE PROTECTION OF NATIONAL INFRASTRUCTURE (Feb. 15 2005) (updating a good practice guide previously published by the National Infrastructure Security Co-ordination Centre).

34. Ciaran Martin, Cyber as Intelligence Contest: The Example of the United Kingdom (manuscript on file with author), at 2, n.2. Robert Hannigan, who served as GCHQ's director from 2014 to 2017, notes that CESG historically was seen as "secondary and unglamorous in comparison to signals intelligence gathering," and that "[o]utside a core group of dedicated experts, many GCHQ staff regarded a posting to the CESG as a step backwards or downwards" during that earlier period. Robert Hannigan, *Organising a Government for Cyber: The Creation of the UK's National Cyber Security Centre*, ROYAL UNITED SERVS. INST. FOR DEF. AND SECURITY STUD. 4–5 (Feb. 2019).

35. *Id.* at 4.

36. CABINET OFFICE, CYBER SECURITY STRATEGY OF THE UNITED KINGDOM: SAFETY, SECURITY, AND RESILIENCE IN CYBER SPACE, 2009, Cm. 7642 (UK).

37. *See id.* at 4–5, 17.

38. *See id.*; Hannigan, *supra* note 34, at 4.

39. CABINET OFFICE, THE UK CYBER SECURITY STRATEGY: PROTECTING AND PROMOTING THE UK IN A DIGITAL WORLD, 2011 (UK).

40. *See* Stuart Murdoch & Nick Leaver, *Anonymity vs. Trust in Cyber-Security Collaboration, in* WISCS '15: PROCEEDINGS OF THE 2ND ACM WORKSHOP ON INFO. SHARING AND COLLABORATIVE SEC. 27, 28 (OCT. 2015); Hannigan, *supra* note 34, at 10.

41. Hon. George Osborne, Chancellor, HM Treasury, Chancellor's Speech to GCHQ on Cyber Security (Nov. 17, 2015); Hannigan, supra note 34, at 8.

42. Unfortunately, that same phrase for many observers (particularly in the United States) has a distinct connotation associated with the scenario in which a hacking victim retaliates with an out-of-network operation against the attacker; that is not the British usage. *See* Martin, *supra* note 34, at 8 (observing this distinction); John Strand, *Active Defense, Offensive Countermeasures and Hacking Back*, BLACKHAT (Aug., 2018), https://www.blackhat.com/us-18/training/active-defense-offensive-countermeasures-and-hacking-back.html (offering a course on "active defense" at Blackhat 2018).

43. Press Release, Cabinet Off. & Hon. Lord Maude of Horsham, UK, Launches First National CERT (Mar. 31, 2014).

44. Hannigan, *supra* note 34, at 10. CERT-UK, notably, was housed in the Cabinet Office rather than GCHQ or any other specific agency. *See* Martin, *supra* note 34, at 4.

45. *Id.* at 13. Hannigan also cites the leadership of Chancellor George Osborne, who at that time headed the cabinet committee responsible for cyber matters.

46. *Id.*

47. Ciaran Martin, Chief Executive, National Cyber Security Centre, Speech in Belfast (Oct. 20, 2017).

48. Hannigan, *supra* note 34, at 13–14. In addition to Hannigan's speech, those interested in the origins of the NCSC should read the excellent account forthcoming from Ciaran Martin. *See* Marin, *supra* note 34.

49. *Id.* at 14.

50. Osborne, *supra* note 41.

51. William Hague, *Foreword,* to Hannigan, *supra* note 34, at vii.

52. Hannigan, *supra* note 34, at 14–15.

53. JOINT COMMITTEE ON NATIONAL SECURITY STRATEGY, CYBER SECURITY OF THE UK's CRITICAL NATIONAL INFRASTRUCTURE, 2017-19, HL 222 & HC 1708, at 20 [hereinafter JOINT COMMITTEE REPORT]. Ciaran Martin has noted that the creators of NCSC wanted the organization to be more than just a reorganization of existing entities, and in particular to have fresh operationally relevant capacities such as this. *See* Ciaran Martin, Director-General, Cyber at Government Communications Headquarters, and Chief Executive, National Cyber Security Centre, Speech at the Billington Cyber Security Summit: A New Approach for Cyber Security in the UK (Sep. 13, 2016). Toward the latter end, Ian Levy developed a task list involving a dozen technical advances to be pursued under the general brand of "active cyber defence," including pursuing changes to the implementation of Border Gateway Protocol, requiring Domain-Based Message Authentication, Reporting and Conformance (DMARC) for government, working with private-sector partners to take down malicious domains, promoting DNS filtering, offering web-vulnerability scanning services to government entities. *See* Ian Levy, *Active Cyber Defence—Tackling Cyber Attacks on the UK*, NATIONAL CYBER SECURITY CENTRE (Nov. 1, 2016); Hannigan, *supra* note 34, Appendix II at 40–42; *see also* HM GOVERNMENT, PROSPECTUS INTRODUCING THE NATIONAL CYBER SECURITY CENTRE (2016).

54. Hannigan, *supra* note 34, at 16, 21–23, 34.

55. Osborne, *supra* note 41.

56. JOINT COMMITTEE REPORT, *supra* note 53, at 26.

57. *Id.* at 23–24.

58. Explanatory materials are available at https://www.gov.uk/government/collections/telecommunications-security-bill.

59. That is not to say they are the only agencies that perform intelligence collection with cyber means for their respective governments. The public record yields little, however, about how the CIA and MI6 operate in the cyber domain.

60. *See* ALDRICH, *supra* note 28, at 484.

61. *See* Intelligence Services Act 1994, c. 13, § 3(1)(A) (Eng.).

62. THE HOME OFFICE, INVESTIGATORY POWERS BILL FACTSHEET: TARGETED EQUIPMENT INTERFERENCE, 2015, at 1 (UK) ("Equipment Interference (EI), sometimes referred to as computer network exploitation, is the power to obtain a variety of data from equipment. This includes traditional computers or computer-like devices. . . . EI can be carried out either remotely or by physically interacting with equipment.").

63. *See* Investigatory Powers Act 2016, c. 25, §§ 13, 99–135, 176–198 (Eng.).

64. *See id.* at § 13.

65. *Id.*
66. *See* Ian Levy, *Equities Process*, NATIONAL CYBER SECURITY CENTRE (Nov. 29, 2018) (providing a frank account of NCSC's equities process). For a comparable overview of the US model, *see* Press Release, White House Office, FACT SHEET: Vulnerabilities Equities Process (Nov. 2017).
67. Warner, *supra* note 10.
68. There was a half-baked attempt to rush through a formal separation of NSA and USCYBERCOM during the waning days of the Trump administration. But that bid collapsed in the face of congressional objections and the fact that a federal statute forbids separation unless and until such time as the secretary of defense certifies in writing that such a move would not undermine USCYBERCOM's operational capabilities and that an adequate equities-deconfliction process has been put in place. Thus, as of the time of this writing, the incubator-based hybrid model employed by the US remains as it was.
69. *See* National Defense Authorization Act for FY 2017, Pub. L. No. 114-328, §1642, 130 Stat. 2000, 2601 (2016).
70. Under the relevant aspects of Title 50 of the US Code, activities constituting "covert action" must comply with the US Constitution and federal statutes, but not international law as such. That subtle but significant provision does not extend to military operations (unless they qualify as "covert action" in a statutory sense), and the Pentagon at any rate has a policy of conducting all operations in accordance with international law. *See* Robert Chesney, *Title 10 and Title 50 Issues When Computer Network Operations Impact Third Countries*, LAWFARE (Apr. 12, 2018).
71. *See* Hon. Paul C. Ney, Speech at U.S. Cyber Command Legal Conference (Mar. 2, 2020).
72. Ellen Nakashima, *U.S. Military Cyber Operation to Attack ISIS Last Year Sparked Heated Debate over Alerting Allies*, WASH. POST (May 9, 2017); *see also* Dustin Volz, *How a Military Cyber Operation to Disrupt Islamic State Spurred a Debate*, WALL STREET J. (Jan. 21, 2020); Chris Bing, *Command and Control: A Fight for the Future of Government Hacking*, CYBERSCOOP (Apr. 11, 2018).
73. Hannigan, *supra* note 34, at 32.
74. *Id.* at 31.
75. *Id.*
76. *Id.*
77. Conrad Prince, *On the Offensive: The UK's New Cyber Force*, ROYAL UNITED SERVS. INST. (Nov. 23, 2020) (quoting then-Def. Sec'y Philip Hammond).
78. Osborne, *supra* note 41.
79. *UK Launched Cyber-Attack on Islamic State*, BBC NEWS (Apr. 12, 2018).
80. *Id.*
81. Deborah Haynes, *Into the Grey Zone: The 'Offensive Cyber' Used to Confuse Islamic State Militants and Prevent Drone Attacks*, SKY NEWS (Feb. 8, 2021).
82. *See, e.g., Britain Steps Cyber Offensive: New £250m Unit Take Russian Terrorists*, TELEGRAPH (Sep. 21, 2018); Deborah Haynes, *Britain to Create 2,000-strong Cyber Force to Tackle Russian Threat*, SKY NEWS (21 Sep., 2018).

83. *See, e.g.*, Richard Kerbaj, *Female Spy to Net Terrorists as Head of 'Cyber-SAS'*, THE TIMES (Sep. 8, 2019).

84. Wallace, *supra* note 2.

85. *See, e.g.*, Dan Sabbagh, *UK Unveils National Cyber Force of Hackers to Target Foes Digitally*, THE GUARDIAN (Nov. 19, 2020).

86. *See Britain Puts a New Offensive Cyber Force at the Heart of Its Defence*, THE ECONOMIST (Dec. 1, 2020).

87. Rory Cormac, *The United Kingdom Doubles Down on Covert Operations*, THE MOD. WAR INST. AT WEST POINT (Apr. 2, 2021).

88. *Id.*

89. *Cf.* Gordon Corera, *UK's National Cyber Force Comes Out of the Shadows*, BBC NEWS (Nov. 20, 2020) ("It has been agreed that the foreign secretary and defence secretary will have a role in signing off different types of operations.").

90. Haynes, *supra* note 81.

91. Kerbaj, *supra* note 83.

92. Press Release, Government Communication Headquarters, National Cyber Force Transforms Country's Cyber Capabilities to Protect the UK (Nov. 19, 2020).

93. Tom Houghton, *Boris Johnson Confirms New National Cyber Force Will Be Set Up in North West*, BUSINESS LIVE (Mar. 16, 2021); Martin, *supra* note 34, at 15.

94. It should be noted that GCHQ has express statutory authority to carry out its functions not only in support of defense and foreign policy goals but also, among other things, directly and explicitly "in support of the prevention or detection of serious crime." *See* Intelligence Services Act 1994, *supra* note 61, § 3(2)(c). NSA and USCYBERCOM do not have such a charge, though there are ample pathways for those entities to share with criminal investigators crime-relevant information that they encounter in the course of their missions, as well as pathways for criminal investigative authorities to seek technical assistance. *See supra* chpt. 6.

95. Prince, *supra* note 77.

96. Reports of an operation to take down Russian-sponsored anti-vaccine disinformation, in late 2020, may illustrate this model in action. Lucy Fisher & Chris Smyth, *GCHQ in Cyberwar on Anti-Vaccine Propaganda*, THE TIMES (Nov. 9, 2020).

97. Hannigan, *supra* note 34, at 30.

98. *See supra* chpt. 4.

99. 10 U.S.C. § 394 note (2018) (Active Defense Against the Russian Federation, People's Republic of China, Democratic People's Republic of Korea, and Islamic Republic of Iran Attacks in Cyberspace).

100. Hon. Jeremy Wright, Att'y Gen., U.K. Att'y Gen. Off., Speech at Chatham House Royal Institute for International Affairs: Cyber and International Law in the 21st Century (May 23, 2018).

101. *Id.*

102. *Id.*

103. *Id.*

104. Brian Egan, Legal Advisor, U.S. Dep't of State, Remarks at Berkeley Law School: International Law and Stability in Cyberspace (Nov. 10, 2016) (emphasis added).

105. Robert Chesney, *The Pentagon's General Counsel on the Law of Military Operations in Cyberspace*, LAWFARE (Mar. 9, 2020).

106. Ney, *supra* note 71.

107. *See supra* chpt. 7.

108. *See* TALLINN MANUAL 2.0 ON THE INTERNATIONAL LAW APPLICABLE TO CYBER OPERATIONS 17 (Michael N. Schmitt & Liis Vihul eds., 2017) ("A State must not conduct cyber operations that violate the sovereignty of another State.").

109. The list includes France, Austria, the Czech Republic, Finland, Germany, the Netherlands, New Zealand, and others. *See, e.g.,* Jack Kenny, *France, Cyber Operations and Sovereignty: The 'Purist' Approach to Sovereignty and Contradictory State Practice*, LAWFARE (Mar. 12, 2021).

110. For a full account, *see supra* chpt. 4.

111. *See supra* note 70 and accompanying text.

112. Wright, *supra* note 100.

113. Ashley Deeks, *Intelligence Communities and International Law: A Comparative Approach*, *in* COMPARATIVE INTERNATIONAL LAW 259 (Anthea Roberts, Paul B. Stephan, Pierre-Hugues Verdier, and Mila Versteeg eds., Oxford Univ. Press 2018).

114. *See* Martin, *supra* note 34, at 9 (observing that concerns unleashed in the UK by the disclosures of former NSA employee Edward Snowden "did not provide the ideal backdrop" for announcing that NCSC would be placed within GCHQ, but also noting that the UK public's reaction to those disclosures "was far more muted than it was in the United States").

Index

For the benefit of digital users, indexed terms that span two pages (e.g., 52–53) may, on occasion, appear on only one of those pages.